IN THE NAME OF

ALLAH

THE ALL-COMPASSIONATE, ALL-MERCIFUL

The Ideal Muslimah

- Title: The Ideal Muslimah
- Author: Dr. Muhammad ‘Ali al-Hashimi
- English Edition 5 (2005)
- Translator: Nasiruddin al-Khattab
- Layout: IIPH, Riyadh, Saudi Arabia
- Filming & Cover Designing: Samo Press Group

The Ideal Muslimah

The True Islamic Personality of the Muslim Woman as Defined in the Qur'an and Sunnah

شخصية المرأة المسلمة

Dr. Muhammad 'Ali al-Hashimi

Translated by

Nasiruddin al-Khattab

الدار العالمية للكتاب الإسلامي

INTERNATIONAL ISLAMIC PUBLISHING HOUSE

King Fahd National Library Cataloging-in-Publication Data

Al-Hashimi, Muhammad Ali

The Ideal Muslimah: The true Islamic personality of the Muslim woman as defined in the Qur'an and Sunnah / Muhammad Ali al-Hashimi; translated by Nasiruddin al-Khattab - 5th ed.,- Riyadh, 2005

...p ; 22 cm

1- Woman in Islam I- Nasiruddin al-Khattab (trans.)
II- Title

219.1 dc 1424/3701
1424/3703

ISBN Hard Cover: **9960-850-39-0** Legal Deposit no. **1424/3701**
ISBN Soft Cover: **9960-850-40-4** Legal Deposit no. **1424/3703**

International Islamic Publishing House (IIPH)
P.O.Box 55195 Riyadh 11534, Saudi Arabia
Tel: 966 1 4650818 – 4647213 – Fax: 4633489
E-Mail: iiph@iiph.com.sa – iiphsa@gmail.com
www.iiph.com.sa

Contents

Publisher's Note

All praise and thanks belong to Allah (ﷻ) 'the Exalted', the Lord of the universe. May the choicest blessings and peace of Allah be upon the last of the messengers and prophets, Muhammad, his family, Companions and all those who follow his footsteps till the end of this universe.

Faith is not the matter of claims or wishful thinking; rather it is both belief and the practical application of that belief in daily life. It is impossible for a Muslim woman to lead a happy and contended life without the pristine faith and its correct application in her day-to-day life.

Woman plays an essential role in the formation of society. The saying goes that a woman is the first school for her children. If she is able to bring them up aright, then the nation will emerge prosperous and contented.

IIPH was eager to produce a book dealing with the characteristics which a Muslim woman should adopt and follow in order to become a true role model and example to be emulated in both Muslim and non-Muslim societies. Through her behaviour and conduct, she should strive to correct the erroneous — or, rather, malicious — stereotypes of Muslim women propagated by the media on the basis of the un-Islamic practices of a few. Thus, we will become able to revive the great, enlightened era of the Muslim woman through the rejuvenation of the Muslim society by propagating the true teachings of Islam.

With this idea in mind, IIPH selected this book by Dr. Hashimi to be rendered into a number of languages. It is a matter of great satisfaction that Dr. Hashimi's sincere effort has attracted a large readership in all the languages into which it has been translated so far.

This is the third revised edition, produced in line with the 4th Arabic edition of this book, with a new layout. Every effort has been made to correct printing or other discripancies that had crept into previous editions.

May Allah, the Exalted, bless with acceptance the sincere efforts of the author, translator and all those associated with the publication of this work.

Muhammad ibn 'Abdul-Muḥsin Al Tuwaijri

General Manager
International Islamic Publishing House,
Riyadh, K. S. A.

Translator's Foreword

Praise be to Allah (ﷻ), Lord of the Worlds, and may the blessings and peace of Allah be upon our beloved Prophet Muhammad (ﷺ) and his family and the Companions.

The Ideal Muslimah: the true Islamic personality of the Muslim woman as defined by the Qur'an and Sunnah offers the reader a comprehensive overview of the woman's place in the Islamic scheme of things. The many roles which a woman may play throughout her life — daughter, wife, mother, friend — are explored in detail. Extensive quotations from Hadith and historical accounts of the lives of the early Muslim women provide a vivid picture of how the Muslim woman at the time of the Prophet (ﷺ) went about putting Islam into practice; this is an example which Muslim women of all places and eras may follow in their own lives.

An important point is the fact that the first chapter addressed the Muslim woman's relationship with Allah (ﷻ). Dr. Muhammad 'Ali al-Hashimi rightly puts first things first, and reminds readers that they must pay attention to this most important aspect of our lives. If our *'aqeedah* (belief) and worship is sound and sincere, then other things will begin to fall into place, *in-shā' Allah* (If Allah wills).

From there, the author takes us by stages from a woman's care of her own self — body, mind and soul — to her relationships and dealings with her family, friends, neighbours and society as a whole. Far from being the passive, oppressed victim of popular stereotype, the Muslim woman is seen to be a whole person with a valid contribution to make at every level of community life.

This is, above all, an immensely practical book. Dr. Al-Hashimi addresses real issues that face Muslim women throughout the world, and supports every point made with extensive quotations from the Qur'an and hadith.

At a time when Muslim women are being increasingly attracted by "feminist theories" and "women's studies," this book serves as a timely reminder that the unique and authentic sources of Islam have always spoken of the rights of women and recognized them as full partners in the human venture of history. The translation of this book into English will render this valuable information more readily accessible to Muslims whose mother-tongue is not Arabic.

Husbands, fathers, brothers and sons will also benefit from reading this book. Studied in conjunction with the author's *Ideal Muslim:* the Islamic personality as defined by the Qur'an and Sunnah, it will enable both men and women to have a deeper insight into the complementary roles of men and women and the harmony between the genders envisaged by Islam.

The interpretations of Qur'anic quotations have been taken from the well-known translation by Abdullah Yusuf 'Ali. The archaic style of this translation has been amended and modernized, so that "thou" becomes "you," "goeth" becomes "goes," etc.

Many Islamic concepts are difficult to express in English, where "religious" words carry much cultural baggage that gives connotations that do not exist in Arabic. For this reason, many Arabic religious terms have been retained, with explanations given either in the text or in the Glossary that may be found at the end of the book.

May Allah reward the author for his efforts to educate the Muslims, men and women alike, about their religion; may He cause this book to be a source of beneficial instruction to all readers; and may He (ﷻ) guide us and keep us on the Straight Path.

Naṣiruddin al-Khaṭṭab

Preface to the Third Edition

Praise be to Allah, the Exalted, Almighty, All-Glorious, as befits His glory and the greatness of His power. I offer the praise of a humble, repentant slave who is in need of His guidance and help. I thank Him for the blessings which He has bestowed upon me, and for honouring me with His aid to write this book, which has been so well-received by its readers and has been more popular than I ever expected. The first and second editions (of the Arabic original) sold out within a few months of publication, and there was a great demand for the book, so I promptly prepared a third edition, with some important revisions and additions, most notably a new chapter, entitled *The Muslim Woman and Her Sons and Daughters-in-Law.*

The circulation of this book was not confined only to Arab readers; it has also reached a Turkish audience. It has been translated by more than one publishing house in Turkey, and tens of thousands of copies have been printed. I have received copies of two of these Turkish editions. All this, if it indicates anything, shows that there is a great thirst among non-Arab Muslim peoples for knowledge from the pure sources of Islam. There is a deep longing for serious, useful Islamic books from the Arab world, especially on the topic of the Muslim woman. Publishers are racing to translate this book into their own languages, so that they could present it to those people who have woken up to the authentic, pure guidance of Islam, which offers nourishment to their minds and souls. This is the best provision for the Muslim peoples at this time of re-awakening.

I have received offers from a number of publishers to translate this book into English and French, which should be done soon, *insha Allah*.

All praise, glory and thanks are due to Allah Alone, the Lord of the Worlds.

Dr. Muhammad 'Ali al-Hashimi

Preface to the First Edition

All praise and blessings be to Allah, as befits His glory and the greatness of His power. Peace and blessings be upon our Prophet Muhammad (ﷺ), the most noble of the Prophets and Messengers, whom Allah (سبحانه وتعالى) sent to bring life to the Arabs and mercy to the worlds.

For a long time, I have been desiring to write a book on the Muslim woman, but I was not able to find the means to fulfil this wish, as life kept me too busy with other things. But I was still very keen to write a book that would explain the character of the righteous Muslim woman who is guided by the teachings of her religion, understands its wisdom, follows its commandments and adheres to its limits.

Years passed by, when I was preoccupied with other matters, but my interest in this issue grew deeper. My desire to produce a book on this topic increased, because I felt that it was of great importance: it would cast light on the life of the Muslim woman and explain how her character should be, in accordance with the will of Allah and her understanding of the high status to which Allah (سبحانه وتعالى) has raised her. For years, I was determined to write such a book, until Allah blessed me and enabled me to write it in 1410 AH/1994 CE.

The reason for my interest in presenting the character of the Muslim woman stems from the inconsistencies I had noticed in the lives of contemporary women, whereby they exaggerate some aspects of Islam and neglect others.

For example, you might see a Muslim woman who is pious and righteous, observing all the rites of her religion, but she neglects oral and bodily hygiene and does not care about the offensive smell emanating from her mouth and body; or she may pay attention to her health and hygiene, but is failing to observe all the rites and acts of worship prescribed by her religion; or she may be performing all the acts of worship required, but she does not have a proper understanding of the holistic Islamic view of life and humanity; or she may be religious, but she does not control her tongue in gatherings and refrain from gossip and slander; or she may be religious and knowledgeable, but she does not treat her neighbours and friends properly; or she may treat (female) strangers well, but she is failing to give her parents the love and respect that they deserve; or she may be treating her parents properly, but neglecting her husband's rights and failing to be a good wife to him, making herself look beautiful at women's gatherings but neglecting her appearance in front of her husband; or she may be taking good care of her husband, but not taking care of his parents or encouraging him to be righteous, to fear Allah (ﷻ) and to do good works; or she may respect the rights of her husband, but she is neglecting her children and failing to bring them up properly, teach them, direct their spiritual, physical and mental development, and monitor the pernicious influences of their environment; or she may be paying attention to all that, but failing to uphold the ties of kinship; or she may uphold the ties of kinship, but fail to uphold social ties, focusing only on her private affairs with no concern for Muslim men and women in general; or she may be concerned with both her own and society's affairs, but she is not taking care of her own intellectual growth by continually reading and seeking to increase her knowledge; or she may be totally absorbed in reading and studying, but she ignores her house, her children and her husband.

What is strange indeed is to see these contradictions, or some of them, among those who consider themselves to be educated Muslim women who have benefitted from an extensive Islamic education. It may be a matter of negligence or carelessness, or it may be a failure to fully understand the idea of balance on which Islam bases its holistic view of man, life and the universe, a view which gives everything the place it deserves in life, without neglecting any one aspect at the expense of another.

The true sources of Islam, the Qur'an and Sunnah, explain the ideal behaviour which the Muslim woman should adopt in her relationship with her Lord, in her personal development, in her relationships with others, whether they are related to her or not, and in her social dealings in general. Whoever takes the time to research these texts will be amazed at their abundance and comprehensiveness: they deal with all major and minor aspects of a woman's life, setting out the guidelines for a balanced, upright, virtuous life which guarantees happiness and success in this world, and an immense victory and reward in the Hereafter.

I was astounded when I realized how far the so-called modern Muslim woman falls short of the noble level which Allah (ﷻ) wants for her. Nothing stands between her and the attainment of that level but the need to devote herself to seeking knowledge of the true Islamic character described in the Qur'an and Sunnah, which will make her a refined, noble woman who is distinguished by her feelings, thoughts, behaviour, conduct and dealings, and will make her adhere with determination to her religion.

It is of the utmost importance that a woman does reach that refined level, because of the great influence she has in bringing up the next generation, instilling in them virtues and values, filling their lives with love, compassion and beauty, and creating an atmosphere of security, tranquillity and stability in the home.

The Muslim woman is the only woman who has the potential to achieve this in a world where modern women are exhausted and tired of materialistic philosophies and the wave of ignorance (*jaahiliyah*) that has overwhelmed those societies that have gone astray from the guidance of Allah. She may achieve this through knowing who she is, following the pure intellectual sources (the Qur'an and Sunnah) and forming the genuine character which Allah (ﷻ) wants her to have, by which she will be distinguished from all other women in the world.

So I began to collect texts from the Qur'an and authentic *aḥaadeeth* (Prophet's Sayings) which spoke about the character of the Muslim woman, and I sorted them according to their subject-matter. This enabled me to draw up an intergrated plan for researching personal and general woman's issues, as follows:

1. The Muslim woman and her Lord
2. The Muslim woman and her own self
3. The Muslim woman and her parents
4. The Muslim woman and her husband
5. The Muslim woman and her children
6. The Muslim woman and her sons and daughters-in-law
7. The Muslim woman and her relatives
8. The Muslim woman and her neighbours
9. The Muslim woman and her Muslim sisters and friends
10. The Muslim woman and her community/society

Whilst I was examining these texts, an important fact became apparent to me, one which we frequently overlook. That is, that the mercy of Allah to the Muslim woman is great indeed. Islam has rescued her from the abyss of humiliation, (being regarded as valueless) and total subordination to men, and has raised her to the highest level of honourable and respected femininity, free from the exhausting burden of having to fend for herself and earn a living; even if she is rich, she does not have to provide for herself. Islam has made her independent, entitled to dispose her own wealth — if she is wealthy — as she wishes, and equal with man in human worth and in general religious duties. She has rights and duties, just as a man has rights and duties. Women and men are equal in the sight of Allah and may be rewarded or punished equally.

The blessings of Islam did not stop at raising women from humiliation and backwardness to a level of progress, honour, security and protection. Islam is also concerned with the formation and development of every aspect of her personality, whether it affects her alone or her relationship with her family and society, so that she may become refined and highly developed, worthy of her role as Allah's vicegerent (*khaleefah*) on earth.

How does Islam form her personality? How may her development reach such a high level that had never been attained before in the history of womankind, except in this religion of Islam?

This is the question to which the reader will find the answer in the following pages. I ask Allah (سبحانه وتعالى) to accept my work and make it purely for His sake. May He benefit others through it, make it a source of reward for me in this life and the next, and make it a help for me on the Day of Reckoning. May He guide me through it to what is right, and protect me from errors of thinking, bad intentions, slips of the pen, weakness of arguments and excessive verbiage.

Dr. Muhammad 'Ali al-Hashimi

CHAPTER ONE

The Muslim Woman and Her Lord

The believing woman is alert

One of the most prominent distinguishing features of the Muslim woman is her deep faith in Allah (ﷻ) (the Exalted) and her sincere conviction that whatever happens in this universe, and whatever fate befalls human beings, only happens through the will and decree of Allah; whatever befalls a person could not have been avoided, and whatever does not happen to a person could not have been made to happen. A person has no choice in this life but to strive towards the right path and to do good deeds — acts of worship and other acts — by whatever means one can, putting all his trust in Allah (ﷻ), submitting to His will, and believing that he is always in need of Allah's help and support.

The story of Haajar (Prophet Ibraheem's wife) offers the Muslim woman the most marvellous example of deep faith in Allah and sincere trust in Him. The Prophet Ibraheem (Abraham) (عليه السلام) (may peace be upon him) left her at the Ka'bah in Makkah, above the well of *Zamzam*, at a time when there were no people and no water in the place. Haajar had no one with her except her infant son Isma'eel (Ishmael). She asked Ibraheem, calmly and with no trace of panic: "Has Allah commanded you to do this, O' Ibraheem?" Prophet Ibraheem (عليه السلام) said, "Yes." Her response reflected her acceptance and optimism: "Then He is not going to abandon us." Reported by Bukhari in *Kitaab al-Anbiya.*[1]

---

[1] *Baab Yaziffoon*. See Ibn Ḥaajar, *Fatḥ al-Baari Sharḥ Ṣaḥeeḥ al-Bukhari*, published by Daar al-Ma'rifah, vol. 6, p. 396.

Here was an extremely difficult situation: a man left his wife and infant son in a barren land, where there were no plants, no water, and no people, and went back to the distant land of Palestine. He left nothing with her but a sack of dates and a skin filled with water. Were it not for the deep faith and trust in Allah that filled Haajar's heart, she would not have been able to cope with such a difficult situation; she would have collapsed straight away, and would not have become the woman whose name is forever remembered day and night by those who perform Ḥajj and 'Umrah at the house of Allah, every time they drink the pure water of Zamzam, and run between the mounts of Safa and Marwah, as Haajar did on that most tiring day.

This deep faith and awareness had an amazing effect on the lives of Muslim men and women: it awoke their conscience and reminded them that Allah (سبحانه وتعالى) witnesses and knows every secret, and that He is with a person wherever he may be. Nothing gives a clearer idea of that consciousness and fear of Allah at all times than the story of the young Muslim girl related in *Ṣifat aṣ-Ṣafwah* and *Wafiyat al-A'yaan*, and cited by Ibn al-Jawzi in *Aḥkaam an-Nisaa'* (pp. 441, 442):

"Narrated 'Abdullah ibn Zayd ibn Aslam, from his father, from his grandfather, who said: 'When I was accompanying 'Umar ibn al-Khaṭṭab (رضي الله عنه) (may Allah be pleased with him) on his patrol of Madeenah at night, he felt tired, so he leant against a wall. It was the middle of the night, and (we heard) a woman say to her daughter, 'O' my daughter, get up and mix that milk with some water.' The girl said, 'O' Mother, did you not hear the decree of *Ameer al-Mu'mineen* (chief of the believers — the caliph) today?' The mother said, 'What was that?' The girl said, 'He ordered someone to announce in a loud voice that milk should not be mixed with water.' The mother said, 'Get up and mix the milk with water; you are in a place where 'Umar cannot see you.' The girl told her mother, 'I cannot obey him in public and disobey him in private.' 'Umar heard this, and told me: 'O' Aslam, go to that place and see who that girl is, and to whom she was speaking, and whether she has a husband.' So I went to that place, and I saw that she was unmarried, the other woman was her mother, and neither of them had a husband. I came to 'Umar and told him what I had found out. He called his sons together, and said to them: 'Do any of you need a wife, so I can arrange the marriage for you? If I had the desire to get married, I would have been the first one to marry this young woman.' 'Abdullah said: 'I have a wife.' 'Abdur-Raḥmaan said: 'I have a wife.' 'Aṣim said: 'I do not have a wife, so let me marry her.' So 'Umar arranged for her to be married to 'Aṣim. She gave him a daughter, who grew up to be the mother of 'Umar ibn 'Abdul-'Aziz.''''

This is the deep sense of awareness that Islam had implanted in the heart of this young woman. She was righteous and upright in all her deeds, both in public and in private, because she believed that Allah (سبحانه وتعالى) was with her at all times and saw and heard everything. This is true faith, and these are the effects of that faith, which raised her to the level of *iḥsaan* (excellence). One of the immediate rewards with which Allah honoured her was this blessed marriage, one of whose descendants was the fifth rightly-guided *khaleefah*, 'Umar ibn 'Abdul-'Aziz (رضي الله عنه).

The *'Aqeedah* (faith) of the true Muslim woman is pure and clear, uncontaminated by any stain of ignorance, illusion or superstition. This *'Aqeedah* is based on faith in Allah, the One, the Most High, the Eternal, Who is able to do all things, Who is in control of the entire universe, and to Whom all things must return:

> *"Say: 'Who is it in Whose hands is the governance of all things — Who protects [all], but is not protected [by any]? [Say] if you know.' They will say, '[It belongs] to Allah,' Say: 'Then how are you deluded?'"*
>
> *(Qur'an 23: 88-89)*

This is the pure, deep faith which increases the character of the Muslim woman in strength, understanding and maturity, so that she sees life as it really is, which is a place of testing whose results will be seen on the Day which will undoubtedly come:

> "*Say: 'It is Allah Who gives you life, then gives you death; then He will gather you together for the Day of Judgement about which there is no doubt': but most men do not understand.*" *(Qur'an 45: 26)*

> "*Did you then think that We had created you in jest, and that you would not be brought back to Us [for account]?*" *(Qur'an 23: 115)*

> "*Blessed is He in Whose hands is Dominion; and He over all things has Power — He Who created Death and Life, that He may try which of you is best in deed; and He is the Exalted in Might, Oft-Forgiving.*" *(Qur'an 67: 1-2)*

On that Day, man will be brought to account for his deeds. If they are good, it will be good for him, and if they are bad, it will be bad for him. There will not be the slightest injustice:

> "*That Day will every soul be requited for what it earned; no injustice will there be that Day, for Allah is Swift in taking account.*" *(Qur'an 40: 17)*

The Balance (in which man's deeds will be weighed) will measure everything with the utmost precision, either in a person's favour or against him:

> "*Then shall anyone who has done an atom's weight of good, see it! And anyone who has done an atom's weight of evil, shall see it.*" *(Qur'an 99: 7-8)*

Nothing could be hidden from the Lord of Glory on that Day, not even if it were as insignificant as a grain of mustard seed:

> "*We shall set up scales of justice for the day of Judgement, so that not a soul will be dealt with unjustly in the least. And if there be [no more than] the weight of a mustard seed, We will bring it [to account]: and enough are We to take account.*" *(Qur'an 21: 47)*

No doubt that the true Muslim woman, when she ponders the meaning of these verses, would think about that crucial Day and would turn to her Lord (Allah) in obedience, repentance and gratitude, seeking to do as many righteous deeds as she is able, in preparation for the Hereafter.

She worships Allah (ﷻ)

It is no surprise that the true Muslim woman enthusiastically worships her Lord, because she knows that she is obliged to observe all the commandments that Allah (ﷻ) has enjoined upon every Muslim, male or female. So she carries out her Islamic duties properly, without making excuses or compromises, or being negligent.

She regularly prays five times a day

She offers each of the five daily prayers at its appointed time, and does not let domestic chores or her duties as a wife and mother prevent her from doing so. Prayer is the pillar of the religion — whoever establishes prayer establishes faith, and whoever neglects prayer destroys the faith.[2] Prayer is the best and most noble of deeds, as the Prophet (ﷺ) explained in the hadith narrated by 'Abdullah ibn Mas'ood (رضي الله عنه): "I asked the Messenger of Allah (ﷺ): 'What deed is

[2] Ghazaali: *Iḥya' 'Uloom ad-Deen*, 1/147.

most beloved by Allah?' He said,

> 'To offer each prayer as soon as it is due.' I asked him, 'Then what?' He said, 'Treating one's parents with mercy and respect.' I asked him, 'Then what?' He said, 'Jihad (struggling / fighting) for the sake of Allah.'"[3]

Prayer is the link between the slave and his Lord. It is the rich source from which a person derives strength, steadfastness, mercy and contentment, and it is a means of cleansing the stain of his or her sins. Abu Hurayrah (رضي الله عنه), the Companion of the Prophet narrated: "I heard the Messenger of Allah (ﷺ) say:

> 'What would you think if there were a river running by the door of any of you, and he bathed in it five times every day, would any trace of dirt be left on him?' The people said: 'There would be no trace of dirt on him.' He said: 'This is like the five daily prayers, through which Allah erases sins.'"[4]

Jaabir (رضي الله عنه), an another Companion, said: "The Messenger of Allah (ﷺ) said:

> 'The five daily prayers are like a deep river flowing by the door of any of you, in which he bathes five times every day.'"[5]

Prayer is a mercy, which Allah (تعالى) has bestowed upon His slaves; they seek its shade five times a day and praise their Lord, glorifying Him, asking for His help and seeking His mercy, guidance and

---

3 Imam al-Baghawi, *Sharḥ as-Sunnah*, 2/176 (*Kitaab aṣ-Ṣalaah, baab faḍl aṣ-ṣalawaat al-khams*); published by Al-Maktab al-Islami.

4 *Sharḥ as-Sunnah*, 2/175, *Kitaab aṣ-Ṣalaah, baab faḍl aṣ-ṣalawaat al-khams.*

5 *Ṣaḥeeḥ Muslim bi Sharḥ an-Nawawi, Kitaab al-Masaajid, baab faḍl aṣ-ṣalaah al-maktoobah fi jama'ah*, 5/170, published by the Head Office of Academic Research, Ifta and Da'wah, Saudi Arabia.

forgiveness. Thus prayer becomes a means of purification for those who pray, men and women alike, cleansing them from their sins. 'Uthmaan ibn 'Affaan (ﷺ) said: "I heard the Messenger of Allah (ﷺ) say:

> 'There is no Muslim person who, when the time for prayer comes, performs *wuḍoo'* properly, concentrates on his prayer and bows correctly, but the prayer will be an expiation for the sins committed prior to it, so long as no major sin has been committed. This is the case until the end of time.'"[6]

There are very many Hadiths which speak of the importance of *ṣalaah* and the blessings it brings to the men and women who pray, and the rich harvest of benefits that they may reap thereby, every time they stand before Allah in an attitude of humility and repentance.

She may attend the Jama'ah (Congregational prayer) in the Mosque

Islam has excused women from the obligation to attend the *jama'ah* prayer in the mosque, but at the same time, they are permitted to go out of the house to attend *jama'ah* on condition that they dress up well enough not to cause any temptation. Indeed, the first Muslim women did go out and pray in the mosque behind the Prophet (ﷺ). 'Aa'ishah (ﷺ) (may Allah be pleased with her) said:

> "The Messenger of Allah (ﷺ) used to pray *fajr*, and the believing women would pray with him, wrapped up in their outer garments; then they would go back to their homes, and nobody would recognize them."[7]

---

[6] Muslim, 3/112, *Kitaab aṭ-Ṭahaarah, baab faḍl al-wuḍoo' waṣ-ṣalaah 'aqaabahu.*

[7] *Fatḥ al-Baari*, 1/482, *baab fi kam tuṣalli al-mar'ah fith-thiyab.*

And:

> "The believing women used to attend *fajr* prayer with the Messenger of Allah (ﷺ), wrapped up in their outer garments. Then they would go back to their homes after they had finished praying, and no one would recognize them because of the darkness."[8]

The Prophet (ﷺ) used to shorten his prayer if he heard a child crying, because he understood the concern the child's mother would be feeling. In a hadith whose authenticity is agreed upon, he (ﷺ) said:

> "I begin the prayer, intending to make it lengthy, but then I hear a child crying, so I shorten my prayer because I know the stress facing the mother because of his crying."[9]

Allah (سبحانه وتعالى) showed great mercy to women by sparing them the obligation to offer the five compulsory prayers in congregation in the mosque. If He had made this obligatory, it would have placed an intolerable burden on women, and they would not have been able to fulfil it, just as we see many men failing to pray regularly in the mosque and finding themselves with no other choice but to pray wherever they are, in the workplace or at home. The woman's heavy burden of household chores and attending to the needs of her husband and children do not permit her to leave the house five times a day; it would be impossible for her to do so. Thus, the wisdom behind the limiting of compulsory attendance at the mosque to men only becomes quite clear. Her prayer at home is described as being better for her than her prayer in the mosque, but Allah, the Exalted, All-High, gives her the

---

[8] (Bukhari and Muslim) See *Sharḥ as-Sunnah*, 2/195, *Kitaab as-Ṣalaah, baab ta'jeel ṣalaat al-fajr*.

[9] (Bukhari and Muslim) See *Sharḥ as-Sunnah*, 3/410, *Kitaab aṣ-Ṣalaah, baab takhfeef fi amrin yaḥdath*.

freedom of choice: she may pray at home if she wishes, or she may go out to pray in the mosque. If she asks her husband for permission to go out to the mosque, he is not allowed to stop her, as the Prophet (ﷺ) stated in a number of hadiths, for example:

> "Do not stop your women from going to the mosque, although their houses are better for them."[10]

> "If the wife of any of you asks permission to go to the mosque, do not stop her."[11]

The men heeded the command of the Prophet (ﷺ), and allowed their women to go to the mosque even if this was against their own wishes. There is no clearer indication of this than the hadith of 'Abdullah ibn 'Umar, in which he said:

> "One of 'Umar's wives used to pray *fajr* and *'isha'* in congregation in the mosque. She was asked, 'Why do you go out (to the mosque) when you know that 'Umar dislikes this and is a jealous man?' She said, 'What is stopping him from forbidding me (to do so)?' He said, 'The words of the Messenger of Allah (ﷺ): 'Do not prevent the female slaves of Allah from attending the mosques of Allah.'"'[12]

In accordance with the Prophet's teaching which allowed women to attend the mosque, and forbade men to stop them from doing so, the mosques were full of women coming and going, both at the time of

---

[10] Abu Dawood, 1/221, *Kitaab aṣ-Ṣalaah, baab ma ja'a fi khurooj an-nisa' ila al-masjid*; Aḥmad, 2/76; it is *ḥasan li ghayrihi.*

[11] *Fatḥ al-Baari*, 2/351, *Kitaab al-Adhaan, baab isti'dhan al-mar'ah zawjaha bil-khurooj ila al-masjid*; *Ṣaḥeeḥ Muslim*, 4/161, *Kitaab aṣ-Ṣalaah, baab khurooj an-nisa' ila al-masaajid.*

[12] *Fatḥ al-Baari*, 2/382, *Kitaab al-Jumu'ah, baab al-idhn lin-nisa' bil-khurooj ila al-masaajid.*

the Prophet (ﷺ), and whenever it was possible in the following periods. Women would come to pray, attend lectures and classes, and take part in the public life of the Muslims. This was the case from the time congregational prayer was prescribed for the Muslims. The Muslims used to pray in the direction of *Bayt al-Maqdis* (Jerusalem), before the *qiblah* was changed to the Holy Ka'bah. When the command of Allah to take the Ka'bah as their *qiblah* was revealed, the men and women who were praying were facing towards Palestine, so they turned to face the direction of the Ka'bah, which meant that the men and women had to change places.[13]

The mosque was, and still is, the centre of light and guidance for Muslim men and women; in its pure environment, acts of worship are performed, and from its *minbar* (pulpit), messages of truth and guidance are transmitted. From the dawn of Islam, the Muslim woman has had her role to play in the mosque.

There are many *ṣaḥeeḥ* (authentic) reports, which confirm the woman's presence and role in the mosque. They describe how women attended *ṣalaat al-jumu'ah* (Friday prayer), the eclipse prayer, and the Eid prayers, responding to the call of the *muadh-dhin* to join the prayer.

A report in *Ṣaḥeeḥ Muslim* tells us that Umm Hisham bint Harithah ibn an-Nu'maan said:

> "I never learned *'Qaaf. Wal-Qur'an al-Majeed...'*, except from the Prophet (ﷺ) himself. He used to recite it from the *minbar* every Friday, when he addressed the people."[14]

---

[13] *Fatḥ al-Baari*, commentary on *Ṣaḥeeḥ Bukhari*, 1/506, *Kitaab aṣ-Ṣalaah, baab ma ja'a fil-qiblah*; *Ṣaḥeeḥ Muslim*, 5/10, *Kitaab aṣ-Ṣalaah, baab taḥweel al-qiblah min al-quds ila al-ka'bah.*

[14] *Ṣaḥeeḥ Muslim*, 6/162, *Kitab al-Jumu'ah, baab taḥiyyah al-masjid wal-Imam yakhṭub.*

Imam Muslim also narrates that the sister of 'Amrah bint 'Abdur-Raḥmaan said:

> "I learned '*Qaaf. Wal-Qur'an al-Majeed...*' from the Messenger of Allah himself on Fridays, when he used to recite it from the *minbar* every Friday."[15]

The Prophet (ﷺ) taught the Muslims to prepare themselves and present a neat and clean appearance at *jumu'ah* prayers by encouraging both men and women to take a shower (*ghusl*):

> "Whoever comes to *jumu'ah*, man or woman, should take a shower first."[16]

Hadith reports also tell us that Asma' bint Abi Bakr (رضي الله عنها) attended the eclipse prayer (*ṣalaat al-kusoof*) with the Prophet (ﷺ). She could not hear the Prophet's words clearly, so she asked a man who was nearby what he was saying. This hadith is reported by Bukhari from Asma' herself:

> "The Messenger of Allah stood up to address us (after the eclipse prayer), and spoke about the testing — torments — that a person will undergo in the grave. When he mentioned that, there was an outbreak of cries because of the panic among the Muslims, and this prevented me from hearing the latter part of the Prophet's speech. When the hubbub died down, I asked a man who was nearby, 'May Allah bless you, what did the Messenger of Allah say at the end of his speech?' He said, 'It has been revealed to me that you will be tested

---

[15] *Ṣaḥeeḥ Muslim*, 6/160, *Kitaab al-Jumu'ah, baab khuṭbah al-ḥaajah.*

[16] This hadith, narrated by 'Abdullah ibn 'Umar, is recorded by Abu 'Awanah, Ibn Khazaymah and Ibn Ḥibban in their *Ṣaḥeehs*; see also *Fatḥ al-Baari*, 2/357, *Kitaab al-Jumu'ah, baab faḍl al-ghusl yawm al-jumu'ah.*

in the grave with something similar in severity to the test (*fitnah*) of the Dajjal...'"[17]

Bukhari and Muslim also narrate another report from Asma', in which she says:

> "There was a solar eclipse at the time of the Prophet... I finished what I was doing, then I came to the mosque. I saw the Messenger of Allah standing (in prayer), so I joined him. He stood for so long that I felt I needed to sit down, but I noticed a woman who looked weak and tired and said to myself: 'This woman is weaker than I, so I must continue to stand.' Then he bowed, and remained in that position for a long time; then he raised his head and stood for such a long time that anyone who came in at this point would think that he had not yet bowed in *rukoo'*. He completed the prayer when the eclipse was over, then he addressed the people, praising and glorifying Allah, and saying *'Amma ba'd.*'"[18]

During that golden era, the time of the Prophet (ﷺ), the Muslim woman knew about her religion and was keen to understand the events and affairs that concerned the Muslims in this world and the next. When she heard the call to prayer, she would rush to the mosque to hear the words of the Prophet (ﷺ) from the *minbar*, guiding and teaching the people. Faṭimah bint Qays, one of the earliest migrant women (*muhajiraat*), said:

> "The people were called to prayer, so I rushed with the others to the mosque, and prayed with the Messenger of

[17] *Fatḥ al-Baari*, 3/236, 237, *Kitaab al-Jana'iz, baab ma jaa' fi 'adhaab al-qabar.*

[18] (Bukhari and Muslim) *Fatḥ al-Baari*, 2/529, *Kitaab al-Kusoof, baab aṣ-ṣadaqah fil-kusoof*; *Ṣaheeḥ Muslim*, 6/212, *Kitaab al-Kusoof, baab ma 'araḍa 'ala an-Nabi fi ṣalaat al-kusoof min al-jannah wan-naar.*

> Allah. I was in the first row of women, which was just behind the last row of men."[19]

It is clear, from the *ṣaḥeeḥ* reports quoted above, that Muslim women attended the mosque on various occasions and that this attendance was an approved custom at the time of the Prophet (ﷺ). Once, a woman was attacked on her way to the mosque, but this incident did not make the Prophet (ﷺ) have any reservations about allowing women to go out to the mosque. He still allowed them to do so, and forbade men to prevent them, because there was so much benefit — spiritual, mental and otherwise — for them in attending the mosque from time to time.

> Waa'il al-Kindi reported that a woman was assaulted by a man in the darkness of the early morning, whilst she was on her way to the mosque. She shouted to a passer-by for help, then a large group of people came by, and she called to them for help. They seized the man to whom she had first called for help, and her attacker ran away. They brought the (innocent) man to her, and he said, "I am the one who answered your call for help; the other man got away." They brought him to the Messenger of Allah and told him that this man had assaulted the woman, and they had seized him whilst he was running away. The man said, "I was the one who answered her call for help against her attacker, but these people seized me and brought me here." The woman said, "He is lying; he is the one who attacked me." The Messenger of Allah said: "Take him away and stone him." Then a man stood up and said, "Do not stone him, stone me, for I am the one who did it." Now the

---

[19] Muslim, 18/84, *Kitaab al-Fitan wa Ashraaṭ as-Saa'ah, baab qaḍiyat al-jasaasah.*

> Messenger of Allah had three people before him: the one who had assaulted the woman, the one who had answered her cries for help and the woman herself. He told the attacker, "As for you, Allah has forgiven you," and he spoke kind words to the one who had helped the woman. 'Umar said, "Stone the one who has admitted to the crime of adultery." The Messenger of Allah said: "No, for he has repented to Allah" — I think he said, "with an act of repentance so great that if the people of Madeenah were to repent in this way, it would be accepted from them."[20]

The Prophet (ﷺ) appreciated the circumstances of the women who attended the congregational prayers, so he used to be kind to them and would shorten the prayer if he heard a child crying, so that the mother would not become distressed — as we have seen in the hadith quoted above (see foot note 9). Once he delayed the *'isha'* prayer, and 'Umar (رضي الله عنه) called him saying, "The woman and children have gone to sleep." The Prophet (ﷺ) came out and said,

> "No-one on earth is waiting for this prayer except you."[21]

Many *ṣaḥeeḥ* (authentic) reports describe how the Prophet (ﷺ) used to organize women's attendance at congregational prayers, for example, the hadith reported by Muslim:

> "The best rows for men are those at the front, and the worst are those at the back; the best rows for women are those at the back, and the worst are those at the front."[22]

---

[20] Aḥmad, see *Silsilat al-aḥaadeeth aṣ-ṣaḥeeḥah*, 2/601, hadith no. 900.

[21] *Fatḥ al-Baari*, 2/347, *Kitaab al-Adhaan, baab khurooj an-nisa' ila al-masaajid*; Muslim, 5/137, *Kitaab al-Masaajid, baab waqt al-'isha' wa taakhiriha.*

[22] Muslim, 4/159, *Kitaab aṣ-Ṣalaah, baab taswiyat aṣ-ṣufoof wa iqaamatiha.*

Another hadith, reported by Bukhari, deals with giving the women room to leave the mosque before the men, after the prayer is over.

> Hind bint al-Ḥaarith said that Umm Salaamah, the wife of the Prophet told her that at the time of the Prophet when the obligatory prayer was over, the women would get up to leave, and the Messenger of Allah and the men who were with him would wait as long as Allah willed. When the Messenger of Allah got up to leave, then the men would get up.[23]

Bukhari and Muslim also report a hadith concerning how women should draw the Imam's attention to something during the prayer. It was by clapping. Sahl ibn Sa'd al-Saa'idi said: "The Messenger of Allah (ﷺ) said,

> 'Why do I see you clapping so much? Whoever notices any error in my prayer should say *Subḥaan Allah*, for by doing so he will alert me to the error. Clapping is only for women.'"[24]

The number of women who attended the mosque increased daily until — at the time of the Abbasids — they filled the courtyard of the mosque, and men would have no choice but to pray behind them. This was the verdict (*fatwa*) of Imam Maalik, as recorded in *Al-Mudawwanah al-Kubra*: Ibn al-Qasim said, "I asked Maalik about people who come to the mosque and find the courtyard (of the mosque) filled with women, and the mosque itself filled with men: may those men pray with the Imam behind the women?" Maalik said:

---

[23] *Fatḥ al-Baari*, 2/349, *Kitaab al-Adhaan, baab intiẓaar an-naas qiyaam al-Imam al-'aalim.*

[24] Bukhari and Muslim. See *Sharḥ as-Sunnah*, 3/273, *Kitaab aṣ-Ṣalaah, baab at-tasbeeḥ idha nabaha shay' fiṣ-ṣalaah.*

"Their prayer is valid; they do not have to repeat it."[25]

But women's going out to the mosque should not be a cause of *fitnah* (ordeal/trial), and women should behave in accordance with Islamic teachings of purity of thought and behaviour. If, for any reason, there is the fear of *fitnah* associated with women's going out to the mosque, then it is better for women to pray at home, and they should do so. This is what is indicated by the hadith of Ibn 'Umar, quoted above, in which the Prophet (ﷺ) said:

> "Do not stop your women from going to the mosque, although their houses are better for them."

It appears that some men feared the possibility of *fitnah*, and took this as an excuse to forbid their women to go to the mosque. This is why the Prophet (ﷺ) forbade men to prevent women from attending the mosque from time to time. This is what is indicated in the first part of the hadith quoted above. Other hadiths confirm the Prophet's keenness for women to attend gatherings in the mosque, for example, the report of Mujaahid ibn 'Umar: "The Prophet (ﷺ) said:

> 'Do not prevent the women from going to the mosque at night.' One of the sons of 'Abdullah ibn 'Umar said, 'We will not let them go out because it will give rise to deviation and suspicion.' Ibn 'Umar rebuked him and said, 'I tell you that the Messenger of Allah said such-and-such and you say, 'No, we will not let them!'"[26]

Bilal ibn 'Abdullah ibn 'Umar reported from his father that the Prophet (ﷺ) said:

> "Do not deny the women their share of the mosque, if

---

[25] *Al-Mudawwanah*, 1/106.

[26] Muslim, 4/161, 162, *Kitaab aṣ-Ṣalaah, baab khurooj an-nisa' ila al-masaajid.*

> they ask your permission." Bilal said, "By Allah, we will most certainly prevent them (from going to the mosque)!" 'Abdullah (his father) said to him: "I tell you that the Messenger of Allah said such-and-such, and you say 'We will most certainly prevent them!'"[27]

The Prophet (ﷺ) said:

> "Do not prevent your women from attending the mosque if they seek your permission to do so."[28]

> "Do not prevent the female slaves of Allah from attending the mosques of Allah."[29]

> "If your womenfolk seek your permission to go to the mosque, then let them do so."[30]

It is permissible for Muslim women to attend the gatherings of the Muslims in the mosque, and there is much to be gained from them doing so, but certain conditions apply to this permission, the most important of which is that the woman who goes to the mosque should not wear perfume or make-up. Zaynab ath-Thaqafiyah reported that the Messenger of Allah (ﷺ) said:

> "If any of you (women) wishes to attend *'isha'* prayer, she should not wear perfume that night (before going for *'isha'* prayer)."[31]

Numerous other hadiths also forbid women to wear perfume when

---

[27] Ibid., 4/162, 163.

[28] Ibid., 4/161.

[29] *Fatḥ al-Baari*, 2/382, *Kitaab al-Jumu'ah, baab al-idhn lin-nisa' bil-khurooj ila al-masaajid*; Muslim, 4/161, *Kitaab aṣ-Ṣalaah, baab khurooj an-nisa' ila al-masaajid.*

[30] Muslim, 4/161, *Kitaab aṣ-Ṣalaah, baab khurooj an-nisa' ila al-masaajid.*

[31] Ibid., 4/163.

they go to the mosque, for example:

> "If any of you (women) goes to the mosque, she should not wear perfume."[32]
>
> "Any women who has perfumed herself with incense should not attend *'isha'* prayers with us."[33]

She attends 'Eid prayers

Islam has honoured woman and made her equal with man as regards obligatory acts of worship. Women are also encouraged to attend public gatherings on *'Eid al-Fiṭr* (Feast of Breaking the Ramadan Feast) and *'Eid al-Aḍha* (Feast of Immolation), so that they may take part in these blessed occasions. This is demonstrated in a number of hadiths reported by Bukhari and Muslim, in which we see that the Prophet (ﷺ) commanded that all women should come out on these occasions, including adolescent and prepubescent girls, those who usually remained in seclusion, and virgins; he even commanded that menstruating women should come out, to take part in the joyous occasion, but they were to keep away from the prayer-place itself. His concern that all women should attend the prayer on the two 'Eids was so great that he ordered the one who had more than one *jilbaab* (outer garment) to give one to her sister who had none. In this way, he encouraged both the attendance of all women at 'Eid prayers and mutual support and help to do good and righteous deeds. Umm 'Aṭiyah said:

> "The Messenger of Allah commanded us to bring out to the 'Eid prayers the adolescent and prepubescent girls, those who usually remained in seclusion, and virgins,

---

32 Ibid.

33 Ibid.

and he ordered those who were menstruating to keep away from the prayer-place."[34]

"We (women) used to be commanded to go out on the two 'Eids, including those who usually stayed in seclusion, and virgins. The menstruating women went out too, and stayed behind the people, joining in the *takbiraat* (Pl. of takbir, i.e., "saying Allahu Akbar")."[35]

"The Messenger of Allah commanded us to take them out on *'Eid al-Fiṭr* and *'Eid al-Aḍḥa*, the adolescent and prepubescent girls, the menstruating women, and those who usually remained in seclusion, so that they could share in the festive occasions of the Muslims, but the menstruating women were not to pray. I said, 'O' Messenger of Allah, one of us does not have a *jilbaab*.' He said, 'Let her sister dress her in one of her own *jilbaabs*.'"[36]

Bukhari reports on the authority of Muhammad ibn Sallam, who told us that 'Abdul-Wahhab reported from Ayyoob from Ḥafṣah bint Sireen, who said: "We used to prevent our prepubescent girls from going out on the two 'Eids,"

A woman came and stayed at the castle of Banu Khalaf, and reported something from her sister. Her sister's husband had taken part in twelve military campaigns with the Prophet (ﷺ), and her sister herself had accompanied him on six of them. She said: "We used to take care of the sick and wounded." Her sister asked the Prophet (ﷺ): "Is there anything wrong if one of us does not have a *jilbaab*

---

[34] Ibid., 6/178, 179, *Kitaab Ṣalaat al-'Eidayn, baab ibaaḥah khurooj an-nisa' fil-'eidayn ila al-muṣalla.*

[35] Ibid., 6/179.

[36] Ibid., 6/180.

and never goes out for that reason?" He said:

> "Let her friend give her one of her *jilbaabs*, so that she can come out and join the righteous gatherings of the Muslims."

Ḥafṣah said: "When Umm 'Atiyah arrived, I went to her and asked her, 'Did you hear the Prophet (ﷺ) say that?' She said, 'May my father be sacrificed for him, yes I did.' (She never mentioned him without saying 'may my father be sacrificed for him') I heard him say,

> 'Let the young girls who usually stay in seclusion, or the young girls and those who usually stay in seclusion, and the menstruating women, go out and attend the righteous gathering of the believers, but let the menstruating women keep away from the prayer-place itself.' Ḥafṣah said: 'I asked her, 'Even the menstruating women?' She said, 'Yes, are menstruating women not present at 'Arafah and on other occasions?'"[37]

Bukhari also narrates another report from Umm 'Atiyah, in which she says:

> "We used to be commanded to go out on the day of Eid, and we even brought the virgins out of their seclusion, and the menstruating women, who would stay behind the people, joining in their *takbiraat* and *du'aa's* (invocations), hoping for the blessing and purity of that day."[38]

These *ṣaḥeeḥ* hadiths give a clear indication of the Prophet's concern

---

[37] *Fatḥ al-Baari*, 2/469, *Kitaab al-'Eidayn, baab idha lam yukun laha jilbaab fil-'eid.*

[38] Ibid, 2/461, *Kitaab al-'Eidayn, baab at-takbeer ayyaam al-muna.*

for the intellectual and spiritual benefit of women. He ordered all the women to go out to the 'Eid prayers, including those who were menstruating, even though menstruating women are excused from praying and are not allowed to enter the prayer-place itself. But his call was addressed to all women, because of his concern that they should take part in these two blessed events and attend the righteous gathering of the Muslims, joining in the *takbiraat* and *du'aa's*, and being a part of the public life of Islam which is discussed in the *khuṭbah* (sermon) following the 'Eid prayer.

The Prophet (ﷺ) was concerned with the teaching and guidance of women, and wanted them to play a part in building the Muslim society, so he devoted part of his *khuṭbah* to women. He would come to the place where the women were gathered, and exhort and remind them, and he made doing this a duty of the Imam. We find this in a hadith narrated by Bukhari and Muslim from Ibn Jurayj (may Allah be pleased with him), who said:

" 'Aṭaa' told me: 'I heard Jaabir ibn 'Abdullah say:

> 'The Prophet stood up on the occasion of '*Eid al-Fiṭr* and led the people in prayer. He began the prayer before the *khuṭbah* (sermon). Then he addressed the people. When the Prophet of Allah had finished his *khuṭbah*, he came to the women and spoke to them, whilst leaning on Bilal's arm, and Bilal spread out his cloak for the women to put their *sadaqah* (charity) in it.' I (Ibn Jurayj) said to 'Aṭaa', 'Was it *zakaat al-fiṭr?*' He said, 'No, it was the *sadaqah* that they gave at that time; one woman threw her ring into it, then others followed her lead.' I said to 'Aṭaa', 'Is it a duty nowadays for the Imam to come to the women and address them when he has finished his *khuṭbah*?' He said, 'It most certainly is.

> This is a duty on them (Imams); what is wrong with them that they do not do that nowadays?'"[39]

According to this hadith, the Prophet (ﷺ) exhorted and reminded the women, and accepted the *sadaqah* that they themselves willingly gave. Another hadith, also narrated by Bukhari and Muslim from Ibn 'Abbaas (رضي الله عنه) via Ibn Ṭaawoos, adds that the Prophet (ﷺ) also reminded the women of their *bay'ah* (oath of allegiance) and reconfirmed their adherence to it. Ibn 'Abbaas said:

> "I attended 'Eid prayers with the Prophet and (after his death) with Abu Bakr, 'Umar and 'Uthmaan. All of them used to perform the prayer before the *khuṭbah*. The Prophet came down (from the *minbar*) — and it is as if I can see him now, gesturing to them to sit down — then he would come through the crowd, until he reached the women. Bilal was with him, and he recited:
>
> "*O' Prophet! When believing women come to you to take the oath of fealty to you, that they will not associate anything whatever with Allah...*" *(Qur'an 60: 12)*,
>
> — until the end of the *aayah*. Then he said, 'Are you adhering to that?' Only one woman answered, 'Yes, O' Prophet of Allah,' and he did not know at that time who she was.[40] He said, 'Then give *sadaqah*,' and Bilal spread out his cloak. The Prophet said, 'Come on, may my father and my mother be sacrificed for you!' So they

---

[39] *Fatḥ al-Baari*, 2/466, *Kitaab al-'Eidayn, baab maw'idhat al-Imam an-nisa' yawm al-'eid*; Muslim, 6/171, *Kitaab Ṣalaat al-'Eidayn.*

[40] Ibn Ḥajar mentioned in *Fatḥ al-Baari*, 2/468, that she was Asma' bint Yazeed ibn as-Sakan, who was known as the spokeswoman for the women, and was a very confident woman.

began to throw their rings and jewellery onto Bilal's cloak."[41]

There is no doubt that the Prophet (ﷺ) addressed the women in the 'Eid prayer-place, reminding them about their religion, and that he took charity from them, reconfirmed their adherence to their oath of allegiance, enjoined them to remember the teachings of Islam, and motivated them to do good deeds. All of this was achieved by calling them to attend the congregational prayer on both 'Eids. This is indicative of the importance of congregational prayer in the life of the Muslim individual and the Islamic society.

Although Islam does not oblige women to attend congregational prayers in the mosque, but whenever women gather together, they are encouraged to offer the *fard* prayers in congregation. In this case, the one who is leading them in prayer should stand in the middle of the (first) row, not in front, and they do not have to recite the *adhaan* or *iqaamah*. This is what Umm Salaamah, the wife of the Prophet (ﷺ), used to do when she led other women in prayer.[42]

She prays Sunnah and Nafl prayers

The Muslim women does not limit herself to the five daily obligatory prayers; she also prays those sunnah prayers which the Prophet (ﷺ) used to perform regularly (*ar-rawaatib*), and prays as many of the *nafl* (supererogatory) prayers as her time and energy allow. These prayers include *salaat aḍ-ḍuḥa*, sunnah prayers following *maghrib*, and prayers offered at night. *Nafl* prayers bring a person closer to Allah (ﷻ), earn him or her the love and pleasure of Allah, and make him or her one of the victorious, obedient and righteous ones. There

[41] *Fatḥ al-Baari*, 2/466, *Kitaab al-'Eidayn, baab maw'izat al-Imam an-nisa' yawm al-'eid*; Muslim, 6/171, *Kitaab Ṣalaat al-'Eidayn.*

[42] Ibn al-Jawzi, *Aḥkaam an-nisa'*, 186, 204 (Beirut edition); Ibn Qudaamah, *Al-Mughni*, 2/202 (Riyadh edition).

is no clearer indication of the great status attained by the believer who draws closer to Allah by performing *nafl* deeds than the hadith *qudsi*:

> "My slave continues to draw near to Me with supererogatory deeds so that I will love him. When I love him, I am his hearing with which he hears, his seeing with which he sees, his hand with which he strikes, and his foot with which he walks. Were he to ask (something) of Me, I would surely give it to him; and were he to ask Me for refuge, I would surely grant it to him."[43]

Because of Allah's love for His servant, that person will be loved by the inhabitants of heaven and earth, as is described in a report narrated by Abu Hurayrah (ﷺ) in which the Prophet (ﷺ) said:

> "When Allah loves one of His servants, He calls *Jibreel* (Gabriel) and tells him: 'I love so-and-so, so love him.' Then *Jibreel* will love him, and will proclaim to the inhabitants of heaven: 'Allah loves so-and-so, so love him.' So the inhabitants of heaven will love him too, and he will be well accepted by the inhabitants of the earth. If Allah hates one of His servants, He calls *Jibreel* and tells him: 'I hate so-and-so, so hate him.' Then *Jibreel* will hate him and will proclaim to the inhabitants of heaven: 'Allah hates so-and-so, so hate him.' Then the inhabitants of heaven will hate him and he will also be detested by the inhabitants of earth."[44]

The Prophet (ﷺ) used to pray so much at night that his feet would become swollen. 'Aa'ishah (ﷺ) asked him:

---

43 *Fatḥ al-Baari*, 11/341, *Kitaab ar-Riqaaq, baab at-tawaaḍu'.*

44 Muslim, 16/184, *Kitaab al-Birr wal-Aadaab waṣ-Ṣilah, baab idha aḥabba Allahu 'abdan.*

> "Why do you do this, O' Messenger of Allah, when Allah has forgiven all your past and future sins?" He answered, "Should I not be a grateful slave?"[45]

> The Prophet's wife Zaynab used to perform *nafl* prayers, and make them lengthy. She put up a rope between two columns (in the mosque), so that when she felt tired and exhausted she could lean against it and restore her energy. The Messenger of Allah entered the mosque, saw the rope, and asked, "What is this?" The people told him, "It belongs to Zaynab: she prays, and when she feels tired, she leans against it." He said, "Untie it; let any of you pray as long as he has the energy to do so, and if he feels tired, he can sit down (or let him sit down)."[46]

A woman of Banu Asad, whose name was Al-Ḥawlaa' bint Tuwayt, used to pray all night, and never sleep. One day she called on 'Aa'ishah when the Prophet (ﷺ) was present. 'Aa'ishah told him, "This is Al-Ḥawlaa' bint Tuwayt. They say that she never sleeps at night." The Messenger of Allah (ﷺ) said:

> "She never sleeps at night! Do only as much as you can, for by Allah, Allah never gets tired, although you do."[47]

The Prophet (ﷺ) encouraged Muslim men and women to do more *nafl* deeds, but at the same time he told them to be balanced in their approach to worship, and disliked exaggeration therein. He wanted the Muslims to have a balanced personality, so that their worship

---

45 Bukhari and Muslim. See *Sharḥ as-Sunnah* 4/45, *Kitaab aṣ-Ṣalaat, baab al-ijtihaad fi qiyaam al-layl.*

46 Muslim, 6/72, 73, *Kitaab Ṣalaat al-Musaafireen, baab faḍeelat al-'amal ad-daa'im.*

47 Ibid., 6/73.

would be enthusiastic, but consistent, and would not be so burdensome that people would not be able to persist in it. He also taught that the most beloved deed in the sight of Allah is that which is done continuously, even if it is a little, as is stated in the hadith in which 'Aa'ishah (رضي الله عنها) said: "The Messenger of Allah (ﷺ) said:

> 'The most beloved deed to Allah is that which is continuous, even if it is little.' If 'Aa'ishah started to do something, she would adhere to it."[48]

This attitude of keeping up the habit of doing righteous deeds was not confined to 'Aa'ishah alone; it was the attitude of all members of the Prophet's household, and of those who were nearest and dearest to him. We see this in the hadith reported by Muslim from 'Aa'ishah (رضي الله عنها):

> "The Messenger of Allah had a mat which he used for making a compartment at night in which he would pray, and the people began to pray with him; he used to spread the mat during the day time. The people crowded around him one night. He then said, 'O' people, perform only such acts as you are capable of doing, for Allah does not grow weary but you will get tired. The acts most pleasing to Allah are those which are done continuously, even if they are small.' And it was the habit of the family of Muhammad that whenever they did any deed they did it continuously."[49]

She performs her prayers properly

The true Muslim woman tries hard to perform her prayers properly,

---

[48] Ibid., 6/72.

[49] Muslim, 6/70-72, *Kitaab Ṣalaat al-Musaafireen, baab faḍeelat al-'amal ad-daa'im.*

with deep concentration and precision of physical movements. She thinks about the meaning of the *ayat* (verses) she is reciting, and the words of praise and glorification that she is uttering. Her soul is flooded with fear of Allah, and with gratitude to Him and sincere worship of Him. If the *Shayṭaan* (Satan) happens to whisper some idea to her during the prayer, to distract her from concentrating properly, to keep him away she focuses on the words that she is reciting from the Qur'an, and the words of praise that she is uttering.

The Muslim woman does not rush back to her housework and chores when she has finished her prayer. Rather, as the Prophet (ﷺ) used to do, she asks Allah's forgiveness by saying "*Astaghfirullah*" three times, and repeats the *du'aa'*:

> "*Allahumma antas-salaam wa minka as-salaam, tabaarakta yaa dha'l-jalaali wal-ikraam* (O' Allah, You are Peace and from You comes peace, Blessed are You, O' Lord of majesty and honour.)"[50]

Then she repeats the *adhkaar* and *du'aa'* that the Prophet (ﷺ) is known to have recited after completing his prayer. There are many such *adhkaar*,[51] one of the most important of which is to repeat "*Subḥaan Allah*" thirty-three times, "*Laa ilaha ill-Allah*" thirty-three times, "*Allahu Akbar*" thirty-three times, then to complete one hundred with "*Laa illaha ill-Allah waḥdahu laa shareeka lah, lahul-mulk wa lahul-ḥamd, wa huwa 'ala kulli shayin qadeer.*"

According to a *ṣaḥeeḥ* hadith, the Prophet (ﷺ) said:

> "Whoever glorifies Allah (says, *Subḥaan Allah*) after

---

[50] Op.cit, 5/89, 90, *Kitaab al-Masaajid, baab istiḥbaab adh-dhikr ba'd aṣ-ṣalaah.*

[51] Imam an-Nawawi, *Riyaḍ uṣ-Ṣaaliḥeen*, p. 621, *Kitaab al-Adhkaar, baab faḍl adh-dhikr wal-ḥathth 'alayhi*; Muslim, 5/83-95, *Kitaab al-Masaajid, baab adh-dhikr ba'd aṣ-ṣalaah.*

every prayer thirty three times, praises Allah (says, *Al-Ḥamdu lillah*) thirty three times, and magnifies Allah (says, *Allahu Akbar*) thirty-three times, which adds up to ninety-nine, then completes one hundred by saying *Laa illaha ill-Allah waḥdahu laa shareeka lah, lahul-mulk wa lahul-ḥamd, wa huwa 'ala kulli shayin qadeer*, his sins will be forgiven, even if they were like the foam of the sea."[52]

Then she turns to Allah humbly asking Him to correct all her affairs, in this world and the next, and to bless her abundantly and guide her in everything.

Thus the Muslim woman finishes her prayers, purified in heart and mind and reinvigorated with a dose of spiritual energy, which will help her to cope with the burdens of everyday life, knowing that she is under the protection of Allah. She will not panic if anything bad befalls her, nor will she become miserly if she enjoys good fortune. This is the attitude of those righteous women who pray and fear Allah:

> "*Truly man was created very impatient; Fretful when evil touches him; and niggardly when good reaches him. Not so those devoted to prayer. Those who remain steadfast to their prayer; And those in whose wealth is a recognized right for the [needy] who asks and him who is prevented [for some reason from asking].*"
>
> *(Qur'an 70: 19-25)*

She pays zakah on her wealth

The Muslim women pay zakah on her wealth, if she is wealthy enough to be liable for zakah. Every year at a specified time, she calculates how much she owns and pays what she has to, because

---

[52] Muslim, 5/95, *Kitaab al-Masaajid, baab adh-dhikr ba'd aṣ-ṣalaah.*

zakah is a pillar of Islam, and there can be no compromise or excuse when it comes to paying it every year, even if the amount comes to thousands or millions. It would never occur to the true Muslim woman to try to avoid paying some of the zakah that she is obliged to pay.

Zakah is a clearly-defined financial obligation and act of worship which Allah (ﷻ) has enjoined upon every Muslim, man or woman, who owns the minimum prescribed amount (*nisaab*) or more. Withholding zakah, or denying that it is obligatory, is tantamount to apostasy (*riddah*) and *kufr*, for which a person may be fought and even killed, until or unless he pays in full as required by Islam. The words of Abu Bakr (رضي الله عنه), the first Caliph, concerning the apostates who withheld their zakah echo down the centuries to us: "By Allah I will fight whoever separates *ṣalaah* from zakah."[53]

These immortal words demonstrate the greatness of this religion, which made the connection between "religious" and "secular" affairs, and reveal Abu Bakr's deep understanding of the nature of this integrated, holistic way of life, which combines abstract beliefs with the practical application of their principles. Many *ayat* (verses) of the Qur'an confirm the interdependence of *ṣalaah* and zakah in the structure of faith:

> "*...Those who establish regular prayer and regular charity...*" *(Qur'an 5: 55)*

> "*And be steadfast in prayer: practise regular charity.*" *(Qur'an 2: 43)*

> "*...[those who]...establish prayers and regular charity...*" *(Qur'an 2: 277)*

---

[53] Muslim, 1/207, *Kitaab al-Eemaan, baab wujoob qitaal taarik aḥad arkaan al-Islam.*

It is clear to the true Muslim woman that Islam — although it has given her the right to financial independence, and has not obliged her to support herself or others, which is, rather, the duty of men — has indeed enjoined zakah on her, and has made zakah a right to which the poor are entitled. So the Muslim woman would not hesitate to pay it in the ways prescribed by shari'ah. She cannot claim to be excused because she is a woman and no woman is obliged to spend on others. Any woman who makes such a claim has a poor understanding of Islam, her faith is weak and there is some fault in her personality. Or else, she is a woman who appears to be religious, but she is ignorant and negligent, or is stingy and loves money, and it would never occur to her to pay zakah even though she fasts, prays and performs Ḥajj, and occasionally gives a small charitable donation from her great wealth. These types of women — ignorant or stingy — are nothing like the true Muslim woman as envisaged by Islam.

She fasts during the day and prays at night in Ramaḍaan

The true Muslim woman fasts the month of Ramaḍaan, and her soul is filled with faith that:

> "Whoever fasts Ramaḍaan out of faith and hope of reward, all his/her previous sins will be forgiven."[54]

She has the attitude of one who truly fasts, whose faculties keep away from all kinds of sins that may invalidate the fast or diminish its reward. If she finds herself exposed to the trials of hostility or argument, she follows the Prophet's advice to men and women who fast:

> "When any of you is fasting, he should not utter foul words or raise his voice in anger. If then anyone

[54] Bukhari and Muslim, See *Sharḥ as-Sunnah*, 6/217, *Kitaab aṣ-Ṣiyaam, baab thawaab man ṣaama Ramaḍaan.*

provokes or fights him, he should say, 'I am observing a fast.'"[55]

"Whoever does not give up false speech and evil actions, Allah has no need of his giving up his food and drink."[56]

During Ramaḍaan, the true Muslim woman feels that she is immersed in the atmosphere of a month unlike any other, when good deeds should be multiplied and the gates of goodness should be opened wide. She knows that her fasting during this month should be only for Allah, and that He will give the reward for it, for the reward of Allah, the Bountiful and Munificent, is greater and vaster than anyone could even imagine:

"The reward for every good deed of the children of Adam will be multiplied anywhere between ten and seven hundred times. Allah said: 'Except for fasting, because it is for Me and I Myself will give recompense for it. He gives up his food and his passion for Me.' For the one who fasts, there are two times of rejoicing, one when he breaks the fast, and one when he meets his Lord. Verily the smell that comes from the mouth of one who is fasting is more pleasing to Allah than the scent of musk."[57]

Therefore, the wise Muslim woman must strike a balance, during this all-too-short blessed month, between her domestic duties and the opportunity this month brings, to draw closer to Allah through

---

[55] Bukhari and Muslim, See *Riyaḍ uṣ-Ṣaaliḥeen*, p. 570, *Kitaab al-Faḍaa'il, baab fi 'amr aṣ-ṣaa'im bi ḥifẓ lisaanihi wa jawaariḥihi 'an al-mukhaalifaat.*

[56] *Fatḥ al-Baari*, 4/116, *Kitaab aṣ-Ṣawm, baab man lam yada' qawl az-zoor wal-'amal bihi fiṣ-ṣawm.*

[57] Bukhari and Muslim, See *Sharḥ as-Sunnah*, 6/221, *Kitaab aṣ-Ṣawm, baab faḍl aṣ-ṣiyaam.*

worship and good deeds. She should not let her household chores distract her from performing the obligatory prayers at the appointed times, or from reading the Qur'an or praying *nafl* prayers. Nor should she let traditional late-night family gatherings keep her from praying *qiyaam al-layl* and *tahujjud*, and making *du'aa'*. She knows the great reward and abundant forgiveness that Allah (ﷻ) has prepared for those who stay up to pray during the night in Ramaḍaan:

> "Whoever spends the night in prayer during Ramaḍaan out of faith and hope of reward, all his previous sins will be forgiven."[58]

The Prophet (ﷺ) used to strive to do more good deeds during Ramaḍaan than at other times, especially during the last ten days of it. 'Aa'ishah (رضي الله عنها) said:

> "The Messenger of Allah used to strive during Ramaḍaan, and especially the last ten days of it, more than he used to at other times."[59]

'Aa'ishah (رضي الله عنها) also said:

> "When the last ten days of Ramaḍaan began, the Messenger of Allah would stay up for the whole night, wake his family up, strive extra hard, and abstain from marital relations."[60]

The Prophet (ﷺ) used to command the Muslims to seek *laylat al-qadr*, and encouraged them to spend that night in prayer:

---

[58] Bukhari and Muslim, See *Sharḥ as-Sunnah*, 4/116, *Abwaab an-Nawaafil, baab qiyaam shahr Ramaḍaan wa faḍluhu.*

[59] Muslim, 8/70, *Kitaab aṣ-Ṣawm, baab al-ijtihaad fil-'ashar al-awaakhir min shahr Ramaḍaan.*

[60] Bukhari and Muslim, See *Sharḥ as-Sunnah*, 6/389, *Kitaab aṣ-Ṣiyaam, baab al-ijtihaad fil-'ashar al-awaakhir.*

> "Seek *laylat al-qadr* during the last ten days of Ramaḍaan."[61]

> "Whoever spends the night of *laylat al-qadr* in prayer and worship out of faith and hope of reward, all his previous sins will be forgiven."[62]

This blessed month is a time that is purely for worship. The serious-minded Muslim woman has no time to spend on chatting and idle pursuits throughout the night. She should not be among those who while away the night until dawn approaches, whereupon she offers her family something to eat and they fall into a deep sleep, and may even miss the *fajr* prayer!

The true Muslim woman and her family should live an Islamic life during Ramaḍaan, striving to organize themselves in such a way that when they all come back from *taraaweeḥ* prayers, they do not stay up for too long, because in a few short hours' time, they will get up to pray *qiyaam al-layl* and then eat *saḥoor*, for the Prophet (ﷺ) commanded us to eat *saḥoor*, as there is much benefit in it:

> "Eat *saḥoor*, for in *saḥoor* there is blessing."[63]

The true Muslim woman helps all the members of her family to get up for *saḥoor*, in obedience to the command of the Prophet (ﷺ) and in the hope of obtaining the blessings of *saḥoor*, such as the reminder to pray *qiyaam al-layl*, and encouragement to go out to the mosque to pray *fajr* in congregation, as well as the physical benefits of strengthening the body for the day's fast. This is what the Prophet

---

[61] Bukhari and Muslim, See *Sharḥ as-Sunnah*, 6/380, *Kitaab aṣ-Ṣiyaam, baab ma jaa' fi laylat al-qadr.*

[62] Bukhari and Muslim, See *Sharḥ as-Sunnah*, 6/379, *Kitaab aṣ-Ṣiyaam, baab ma jaa' fi laylat al-qadr.*

[63] Bukhari and Muslim, See *Sharḥ as-Sunnah*, 6/251, *Kitaab aṣ-Ṣiyaam, baab faḍl as-saḥoor.*

(ﷺ) used to do and trained his Companions to do likewise. Zayd ibn Thabit (رضي الله عنه) said:

> "We ate *saḥoor* with the Messenger of Allah, then we got up to pray." Someone asked, "How much time was there between the two?" He said: "Fifty *ayat* (i.e. the time it would take to recite fifty *ayat*)."[64]

There is no doubt that Allah (سبحانه وتعالى) will increase the reward of the Muslim woman who is the means of bringing these blessings to her family during Ramaḍaan:

> "*As to those who believe and work righteousness, verily We shall not suffer to perish the reward of any who do a [single] righteous deed.*" *(Qur'an 18: 30)*

She observes nafl fasts

The true Muslim woman also observes *nafl* (supereragatory) fasts at times other than Ramaḍaan, if it is not too difficult for her to do so. So she fasts the day of *'Arafaah*, and *'Aashoora'*, and the ninth day of *Muḥarram*, because fasting on these days and others is one of the righteous deeds that may expiate sins, as the Prophet (ﷺ) told us, Abu Qataadah (رضي الله عنه) said:

> "The Messenger of Allah was asked about fasting on the day of *'Arafaah*, and he said: 'It is an expiation for the sins of the previous year and the current year.'"[65]

> Ibn 'Abbaas said that the Messenger of Allah fasted the day of *'Aashoora'*, and commanded others to fast on this day too.[66]

---

64 Ibid, 6/253.

65 Muslim, 8/51, *Kitaab aṣ-Ṣiyaam, baab istiḥbaab ṣiyaam yawm 'Arafaah.*

66 Muslim, 8/12, *Kitaab aṣ-Ṣiyaam, baab ṣawm yawm 'aashoora'.*

Abu Qataadah (ﷺ) said that the Messenger of Allah (ﷺ) was asked about fasting on the day of *'Aashoora'*, and he said:

> "It is an expiation for the sins of the previous year."[67]

Ibn 'Abbaas said that the Messenger of Allah (ﷺ) said:

> "If I am still alive next year, I will fast on the ninth day (of *Muḥarram*)."[68]

Fasting six days of *Shawwaal* is also encouraged, as the Prophet (ﷺ) said:

> "Whoever fasted Ramaḍaan then followed it with six days of *Shawwaal*, it will be as if he fasted for a lifetime."[69]

It is also recommended to fast for three days of each month, concerning which Abu Hurayrah (ﷺ) said:

> "My dearest friend (i.e., the Prophet) advised me to do three things: to fast for three days of each month, to pray two *rak'ahs* of *ḍuḥa* prayer, and never to sleep until I pray *witr*."[70]

Abu ad-Darda' (ﷺ) said:

> "My beloved friend (i.e., the Prophet) advised me to do three things that I shall never give up as long as I live: to fast three days of each month, to pray *ḍuḥa*, and not to sleep until I have prayed *witr*."[71]

---

[67] Muslim, 8/51, *Kitaab aṣ-Ṣiyaam, baab istiḥbaab ṣiyaam yawm 'aashoora'.*

[68] Muslim, 8/13, *Kitaab aṣ-Ṣiyaam, baab ṣawm yawm 'aashoora'.*

[69] Muslim, 8/56, *Kitaab aṣ-Ṣiyaam: baab istaḥbaab ṣiyaam sittat ayyaam min shawwaal.*

[70] *Fatḥ al-Baari*, 4/226, *Kitaab aṣ-Ṣawm, baab ṣiyaam al-ayyaam al-beeḍ*; Muslim, 5/234, *Kitaab Ṣalaat al-Musafireen, baab istiḥbaab ṣalaat aḍ-ḍuḥa.*

[71] Muslim, 5/235, *Kitaab Ṣalaat al-musaafireen, baab istiḥbaab ṣalaat aḍ-ḍuḥa.*

'Abdullah ibn 'Amr ibn al-'Aaṣ (عليه) said that the Messenger of
Allah (ﷺ) said:

> "Fasting for three days of each month is like fasting for
> an entire lifetime."[72]

Some reports describe these three days as being the thirteenth,
fourteenth and fifteenth of each month, which are called *al-ayyaam
al-beeḍ* (the white days); other reports state that the Prophet (ﷺ) used
to fast on three unspecified days of each month.

Mu'adhah al-'Adawiyah said:

> "I asked 'Aa'ishah, 'Did the Messenger of Allah used to
> fast three days in each month?' She said, 'Yes.' I asked
> her, 'In which part of the month did he used to fast?'
> She said, 'He did not mind in which part of the month
> he would fast.'"[73]

She goes on Ḥajj to the sacred House of Allah

The true Muslim woman intends to go on Ḥajj to the House of Allah
when she is able to do so and it is easy for her to travel. Before she
sets out on her journey, she takes the time to study the rules (*aḥkaam*)
of Ḥajj in depth, so that when she begins to perform the rituals of
Ḥajj, her actions will be based on true understanding and her Ḥajj
will be complete according to the conditions laid down by the
shari'ah. It will also be the equivalent of jihad for men, as the Prophet
(ﷺ) described it in a hadith narrated by 'Aa'ishah (عنها):

> "I ('Aa'ishah) said: 'O' Messenger of Allah, can we

---

[72] Bukhari and Muslim, See *Sharḥ as-Sunnah*, 6/362, *Kitaab aṣ-Ṣiyaam, baab
ṣawm ad-dahr.*

[73] Muslim, 8/48, *Kitaab aṣ-Ṣiyaam, baab istiḥbaab ṣiyaam thalathat ayyaam
min kulli shahr.*

(women) not go out on military expeditions and fight in jihad with you (men)?' He said, 'You (women) have the best of jihad, and the best of it is Ḥajj, a blessed Ḥajj.' 'Aa'ishah said, 'I should never stop going for Ḥajj after I heard this from the Messenger of Allah.'"[74]

She goes for 'Umrah

Just as Ḥajj is obligatory for the Muslim woman, so also is *'Umrah*, if she is able to go — especially *'Umrah* during Ramaḍaan, the reward for which is equivalent to that of performing Ḥajj with the Prophet (ﷺ). This is seen in the hadith narrated by Imam Bukhari from Ibn 'Abbaas (رضي الله عنه) who said:

> "When the Prophet came back from Ḥajj, he said to Umm Sinan al-Anṣaariyah, 'What stopped you from going to Ḥajj?' She said, 'Abu so-and-so — meaning her husband — has two camels; he took one to go to Ḥajj, and we need the other to irrigate our land.' He said, 'When Ramaḍaan comes, go for *'Umrah*, for *'Umrah* in Ramaḍaan is like Ḥajj.'"

According to another report also narrated by Ibn 'Abbaas, the Prophet (ﷺ) said:

> "For (performing) *'Umrah* in Ramaḍaan is equivalent to (performing) Ḥajj with me."[75]

She is obedient to the commands of Allah

The true Muslim woman does not forget that she is duty bound to perform all the religious duties that Allah (سبحانه وتعالى) has commanded her to do. In this regard her situation is the same as that of a man, and there

---

[74] *Fatḥ al-Baari*, 4/72, *Kitaab Jaza' aṣ-Ṣayd, baab ḥajj an-nisa'*.

[75] Ibid.

is no difference between them except in a few regulations which apply exclusively to either men or women. Other than that, women and men are equally responsible before Allah. Allah (ﷻ) says:

> "*For Muslim men and women, for believing men and women, for devout men and women, for true men and women, for men and women who are patient and constant, for men and women who humble themselves, for men and women who give in charity, for men and women who fast [and deny themselves], for men and women who guard their chastity, and for men and women who engage much in Allah's praise — for them has Allah prepared forgiveness and great reward.*"
>
> *(Qur'an 33: 35)*

> "*Whoever works righteousness, man or woman, and has Faith, verily, to him will We give a new Life, and life that is good and pure, and We will bestow on such their reward according to the best of their actions.*"
>
> *(Qur'an 16: 97)*

> "*And their Lord has accepted of them, and answered them: 'Never will I suffer to be lost the work of any of you, be he male or female: you are members, one of another; those who have left their homes and were driven out therefrom, and suffered harm in My Cause, and fought and were slain — verily, I will blot out from them their iniquities, and admit them into Gardens with rivers flowing beneath — a reward from the Presence of Allah, and from His Presence is the best of rewards.*"
>
> *(Qur'an 3: 195)*

Whenever the phrase "*ya ayyuhan-naas* (O' people or O' mankind)" appears in the Qur'an or hadith, it includes both men and women. Evidence of this may be found in the hadith narrated by Imam

Muslim from the Prophet's wife Umm Salaamah (﵄), who said:

> "I used to hear the people talking about *al-hawḍ* (the cistern), and I had never heard about it from the Messenger of Allah. One day, whilst a young girl was combing my hair, I heard the Messenger of Allah saying 'O' people!' I said to the young girl, 'Leave me alone now.' She said, 'That call is for men only; he is not calling the women.' I said, 'I am one of the people.' The Messenger of Allah said: 'I am the one who will be at the cistern (in the Hereafter) before you. So be careful, lest one of you should come to me and be driven away like a stray camel. I will ask the reason why, and I will be told, 'You do not know what innovations they wrought after your death,' and I will say, 'Away with them!'"

According to another report also narrated by Muslim, he (ﷺ) said:

> "...and I will say, 'Away, away with the one who changed (the religion) after my death!'"[76]

Men and women are equal before Allah (ﷻ), and both must pay heed to His commands and prohibitions. So the Muslim woman does what Allah has commanded and keeps away from what He has forbidden, believing that she will be questioned about what she did in this life: if they are good, it will be good for her, and if they are bad, then will be bad for her. She does not transgress the limits laid down by Allah, and does not do anything that is *ḥaraam* (prohibited). She always seeks the ruling of Allah and His Messenger, and accepts it no matter what happens to her in her life.

Islamic history is filled with the stories of great women who kept the

---

[76] Muslim, 15/56, 54, *Kitaab al-Faḍaa'il, baab ḥawḍ nabiyyina wa ṣifatuhu.*

rule of Allah in mind at all times, and did not deviate from it or look for alternatives. Among these stories is that of Khawlah bint Tha'labah and her husband Aws ibn aṣ-Ṣaamit, narrated by Imam Aḥmad and Abu Dawood, and quoted by Ibn Katheer in his *tafseer* of the beginning of *Soorat al-Mujaadilah* (the 58th chapter of the Qur'an). Khawlah said:

> "By Allah, concerning me and Aws ibn aṣ-Ṣaamit, Allah revealed the beginning of *Soorah al-Mujaadilah*. I was married to him, and he was an old man who was bad-tempered. One day, he came in and I raised a particular issue with him again; he became angry and said, 'You are to me as the back of my mother.' Then he went out and sat for a while in the meeting-place of his people. Then he came back, and wanted to resume marital relations with me. I said, 'No way! By the hand of the One in Whose hand is the soul of Khuwaylah (i.e., Khawlah), you will never get what you want from me after saying what you said, until Allah and His Messenger decide between us.' He tried to force himself on me, but I was able to resist because I was a young woman and he was a weak old man. I pushed him away, then I went to one of my (female) neighbours and borrowed a cloak from her and went to the Messenger of Allah. I sat before him, told him what (my husband) had done to me, and began to complain to him about my sufferings because of my husband's bad temper. The Messenger of Allah said, 'O' Khuwaylah, your cousin is an old man, so fear Allah with regard to him.' I did not leave him until the Qur'an was revealed concerning me: he was overcome as he usually was when the Qur'an was revealed to him, and when it was over, he said: 'O' Khuwaylah, Allah has revealed the Qur'an concerning you and

your husband.' Then he recited to me:

'*Allah has indeed heard [and accepted] the statement of the woman who pleads with you concerning her husband and carries her complaint [in prayer] to Allah: and Allah [always] hears the arguments between both sides among you: for Allah hears and sees [all things]'. If any men among you divorce their wives by ẓihaar* [77] *[calling them mothers], they cannot be their mothers: none can be their mothers except those who gave them birth. And in fact they use words [both] iniquitous and false: but truly Allah is One that blots out [sins], and forgives [again and again]. But those who divorce their wives by ẓihaar, then wish to go back on the words they uttered — [it is ordained that such a one] should free a slave before they touch each other: this are you admonished to perform: and Allah is well-acquainted with [all] that you do. And if any has not [the wherewithal], he should fast for two months consecutively before they touch each other. But if any is unable to do so, he should feed sixty indigent ones. This, that you may show your faith in Allah and His Messenger, those are limits [set by] Allah. For those who reject [Him], there is a grievous Penalty.*'

(Qur'an 58: 1-4)

---

[77] A *jaahili* (pre-Islamic) form of divorce where the husband would say to his wife "You are to me like the back of my mother." According to pre-Islamic Arabian custom, this freed the husband from marital duties, but effectively imprisoned the woman as she was not free to leave her husband's home or enter into another marriage; the husband was also not obliged to provide for the children of the marriage. The Qur'an clearly abolished this cruel and oppressive practice. See 'Abdullah Yusuf Ali's Note Number 5330. (Translator)

> He told me, 'Let him release a slave.' I said, 'O' Messenger of Allah, he does not have the means to do that.' He said, 'Then let him fast for two consecutive months.' I said, 'By Allah, he is an old man, he is not able to do that.' He said, 'Then let him feed sixty poor people with a *wasq* [78] of dates.' I said, 'O' Messenger of Allah, he does not have that much.' He said, 'Then we will help him with a *faraq* [79] of dates.' I said, 'And I will help him with another *faraq*, O' Messenger of Allah.' He said, 'You have done right and done well. Go and give it in charity on his behalf, then take care of your cousin properly.' And I did so."[80]

Khawlah bint Tha'labah could not bear to stay for one moment with her husband after he had spoken the words of *dhihaar* to her, which was a form of divorce at the time of *jaahiliyah*, until she had referred the matter to the Prophet (ﷺ), so that she might know how Allah would judge between her and her husband. She did not even have a suitable garment with which to go out and appear before the Prophet (ﷺ), so she borrowed a robe from one of her neighbours, and rushed to where the Prophet (ﷺ) was sitting, so that she could hear Allah's ruling concerning her, and follow it.

It comes as no surprise that this great woman enjoyed such high standing among the *Ṣahaabah* (Companions of the Prophet) who were her contemporaries and knew her virtues, above all was 'Umar ibn al-Khaṭṭab (رضي الله عنه). She met him one day outside the mosque, when Al-Jaarood al-'Abdi was with him. 'Umar, who was the *khaleefah*

---

[78] *Wasq*: The amount of fruit a date-palm would bear in one season. (Author)

[79] *Faraq*: A measurement of weight approximately equivalent to 60 kilograms. (Author)

[80] See *Mukhtaṣar Tafseer Ibn Katheer*, 3/459, *Soorah al-Mujaadalah* 58: 1-4 (published by Daar al-Qur'an al-Kareem, Beirut).

(Caliph) at that time, greeted her, and she said to him, “O’ ‘Umar, I remember you when you were called ‘Umayr in the marketplace of ‘Ukaaẓ, taking care of the sheep with your stick. So fear Allah (ﷻ) in your role as *a khaleefah* taking care of the people, and know that the one who fears the threat of punishment in the Hereafter realises that it is not far away, and the one who fears death fears missing some opportunity in this life.” Al-Jaarood said, “You have spoken too harshly to *Ameer al-Mu’mineen*, woman!” ‘Umar said, “Let her be. Do you not know that this is Khawlah, to whose words Allah listened from above the seven heavens? By Allah, ‘Umar should by rights listen to her.”

Ibn Katheer mentions in his *Tafseer* that a man said to ‘Umar, when he saw him welcoming her warmly and listening to her, “You left a man of Quraysh to come to this old woman?” ‘Umar said, “Woe to you! Do you not know who this is?” The man said, “No.” ‘Umar said, “This is a woman whose complaint Allah listened to from above the seven heavens: this is Khawlah bint Tha‘labah. By Allah, if she did not leave me until night fell, I would not tell her to leave until she had got what she came for, unless the time for prayer came, in which case I would pray, and then come back to her until she had got what she came for.”

The true Muslim woman always bears in mind the words of Allah:

> “*It is not fitting for a Believer, man or woman, when a matter has been decided by Allah and His Messenger, to have any option about their decision: if anyone disobeys Allah and His Messenger, he is indeed on a clearly wrong Path.*” *(Qur’an 33: 36)*

Obedience to Allah and His Messenger is much more important than one’s own whims and desires; it comes before pleasure and individual choice. Zaynab bint Jaḥsh (رضي الله عنها) set the best example of obedience to the command of Allah and His Messenger when he asked her to agree to marry his freed slave and adopted son Zayd ibn Ḥarithah. This marriage achieved two legislative (*tashri'i*) aims:

1. To achieve total equality among people:

The beautiful woman of Quraysh, the noblewoman of the sons of 'Abd Shams, and the cousin of the Prophet, married a freed slave. Freed slaves were of a lower class than the nobility; indeed, the differences between the classes were so great and so deep that nothing could abolish them except a decisive, public act on the part of the Prophet (ﷺ), that the Muslim community would have to take as an example, so that these barriers might be torn down and people would not be viewed as superior except in terms of their level of *taqwa* (piety).

2. To abolish the custom of adoption which was widely spread at the time of *jaahiliyah*:

Hence, the Prophet (ﷺ) married Zaynab, after she had been divorced by his adopted son Zayd, to demonstrate in practical terms that if Zayd had been his real son, Allah would not have commanded him in the Qur'an to marry Zaynab.

The choice fell to Zaynab, the cousin of the Prophet, to achieve these two legislative aims within the environment of the Prophet's household, so that the people could accept them in obedience to the command of Allah and His Messenger. When he chose her to be the wife of Zayd ibn Ḥarithah, she disliked the idea, and said, "O' Messenger of Allah, I will never marry him, for I am the noblewoman of the tribe of 'Abd Shams." The Prophet (ﷺ) replied, calmly but firmly, "You have to marry him." Whilst they were discussing the matter, Allah revealed to His Messenger:

> "*It is not fitting for a Believer, man or woman, when a matter has been decided by Allah and His Messenger, to have any option about their decision: if anyone*

> *disobeys Allah and His Messenger, he is indeed on a clearly wrong Path."* *(Qur'an 33: 36)*

Then Zaynab accepted the command of Allah and His Messenger, and said: "I will not disobey Allah and His Messenger, and I will give myself in marriage to him."

Subsequently, the differences between Zaynab and Zayd led to their divorce. When Zaynab had completed her *'iddah* (a period after which a widow or a divorced woman may marry another man), Allah (ﷻ) revealed the following *aayah* (verse):

> "*Behold! You did say to one who had received the grace of Allah and your favour: 'Retain [in wedlock] your wife, and fear Allah.' But you did hide in your heart that which Allah was about to make manifest: you did fear the people, but it is more fitting that you should fear Allah. Then when Zayd had dissolved [his marriage] with her, with the necessary [formality], We joined her in marriage to you: in order that [in future] there may be no difficulty to the Believers in [the matter of] marriage with the wives of their adopted sons, when the latter have dissolved with the necessary [formality] [their marriage] with them. And Allah's command must be fulfilled.*" *(Qur'an 33: 37)*

The Prophet (ﷺ) recited this *aayah*, smiling, then he said, "Who will go to Zaynab and tell her the good news that Allah has arranged my marriage to her from heaven?"

It was as if Allah (ﷻ) was rewarding Zaynab for her absolute obedience to Allah and His Messenger. She had accepted their decision that she should marry Zayd, then she became the wife of the Prophet by the command of Allah, in *ayat* which the Muslims will recite when they worship Allah by reciting the Qur'an, until the end of time. This honour was bestowed only on Zaynab, who was unique among the wives of the Prophet. She was proud of the favour of Allah to her, and used to boast to the other wives of the Prophet:

> "Your families arranged your marriages, but Allah arranged my marriage from above the seven heavens."[81]

She does not sit alone with a "stranger"

Obedience to Allah (ﷻ) and His Messenger (ﷺ) can only be achieved by following their commands and keeping away from that which they have prohibited. One way in which the Muslim woman obeys Allah and His Messenger is by not sitting alone with a "stranger" (*ajnabi*) i.e., a man to whom she is not closely related (i.e., non-*maḥram* — marriagable person), because doing so is *ḥaraam* according to the consensus of the scholars, on the basis of the hadith:

> "A man should not sit alone with a woman unless a *maḥram* is with her, and a woman should not travel without a *maḥram*. A man stood up and said: 'O' Messenger of Allah, my wife has set out for Ḥajj, and I have enlisted for such-and-such military expedition.' He said, 'Go and perform Ḥajj with your wife.'"[82]

The *maḥram* is a man to whom marriage is forever forbidden for a woman, such as the father, brother, paternal uncle, maternal uncle, etc.

The *ajnabi* or "stranger" is a man to whom marriage is allowed in principle, even if he is a relative, especially the husband's brother and other similarly close relatives. It is forbidden for a woman to sit alone with all of these, because the Prophet (ﷺ) said:

---

[81] *Fatḥ al-Baari*, 13/402, *Kitaab at-Tawḥeed, baab wa kaana 'arshuhu 'ala'l-maa'*.

[82] Bukhari and Muslim, See *Sharḥ as-Sunnah*, 7/18, *Kitaab al-Ḥajj, baab al-mar'ah la takhruj illa ma'a maḥram.*

"Beware of visiting women." A man of the Anṣaar asked, 'O' Messenger of Allah, what about the brother-in-law?' He said, 'The brother-in-law is death.'"[83]

The brother-in-law is the husband's brother or other similarly close relatives by marriage. The Prophet's words, "The brother-in-law is death" mean that evil is more likely to occur from these quarters than from elsewhere, because of the ease with which he enters his brother's house. The word "death" is used for emphasis and as a sharp warning, as if sitting alone with the brother-in-law may lead to immorality and calamitous consequences that would be akin to the calamity of death.

The true Muslim woman does not fall into such errors as are committed by so many careless people nowadays.

She wears correct ḥijaab

The Muslim woman wears correct *ḥijaab* when she goes out of her house. *Ḥijaab* is the distinctive Islamic dress whose features have been clearly defined by the Qur'an and Sunnah. She does not go out of the house, or appear before non-*maḥram* men, wearing perfume, make-up or other fineries, because she knows that this is *ḥaraam* according to the Qur'an:

> "*And say to the believing women that they should lower their gaze and guard their modesty; that they should not display their beauty and ornaments except what [must ordinarily] appear thereof; that they should draw their veils over their bosoms* [84] *and not display their beauty except to their husbands, their fathers, their husbands'*

---

[83] Bukhari and Muslim, See *Sharḥ as-Sunnah*, 9/26, *Kitaab an-Nikaah, baab al-nahy 'an an yakhlu ar-rajul bil-mar'ah al-ajnabiyah.*

[84] *Juyoobihinna* includes the face and neck as well as the bosom. (Translator)

fathers, their sons, their husbands' sons, their brothers or their brothers' sons, or their sisters' sons, or their women, or the slaves whom their right hands possess, or male servants free of physical needs, or small children who have no sense of the shame of sex; and that they should not strike their feet in order to draw attention to their hidden ornaments. And O' you Believers! Turn all together towards Allah, that you may attain Bliss." *(Qur'an 24: 31)*

The Muslim woman, therefore, is not one of those dressed-but-naked women who abound in societies which have deviated from the guidance of Allah. She would tremble with fear at the terrifying picture which the Prophet (ﷺ) draw of those painted and adorned temptresses who have gone astray:

> "There are two types of the people of Hell that I have not seen: people with whips like the tails of oxen, with which they beat the people, and women who are dressed yet appear naked, who are inclined to evil and make their husbands incline towards it also. Their heads are like the humps of camels, leaning to one side. They will not enter Paradise, or even smell its scent, although its scent can be discerned from such-and-such a distance."[85]

The Muslim woman who has been truly guided by her faith and has received a sound Islamic education does not wear *ḥijaab* just because it is a custom or tradition inherited from her mother or grandmother, as some (foolish) men and women try to describe it with no evidence or logic whatsoever. The Muslim woman wears *ḥijaab* on the basis of her belief that it is a command from Allah, revealed to protect the Muslim woman, to make her character distinct, and to keep her away

---

85 Muslim, 14/109, *Kitaab al-Libaas waz-zeenah, baab an-nisa' al-kaasiyaat al-'aariyaat.*

from the slippery slope of immorality and error. So she accepts it willingly and with strong conviction, as the women of the *Muhaajireen* (emigrants) and Anṣaar (helpers — the Madeenites) accepted it on the day when Allah (ﷻ) revealed His clear and wise command. According to a report narrated by Bukhari, 'Aa'ishah (رضي الله عنها) said:

> "May Allah have mercy on the *Muhaajir* women. When Allah revealed:
> '*...that they should draw their veils over their bosoms...*" *(Qur'an 24: 31)*,
> — they tore their wrappers and covered their heads and faces with them."

According to another report given by Bukhari, 'Aa'ishah said:

> "They took their wrappers and tore them at the edges, then covered their heads and faces with them."[86]

Ṣafiyah bint Shaybah said:

> "When we were with 'Aa'ishah, we mentioned the women of Quraysh and their virtues. 'Aa'ishah said, 'The women of Quraysh are good, but by Allah I have never seen any better or more strict in their adherence to the Book of Allah than the women of the Anṣaar. When *Soorah an-Noor* (24th chapter of the Qur'an) was revealed — "*...that they should draw their veils over their bosoms...*" — their menfolk went to them and recited to them the words that Allah had revealed. Each man recited it to his wife, his daughter, his sister and other female relatives. Every woman among them got

---

[86] *Fatḥ al-Baari*, 8/489, *Kitaab at-Tafseer, baab wal yadribna bi khumoorihinna 'ala juyoobihinna.*

> up, took her decorated wrapper, and wrapped herself up in it out of faith and belief in what Allah had revealed. They appeared behind the Messenger of Allah, wrapped up, as if there were crows on their heads.'"[87]

May Allah have mercy on the women of the *Muhaajireen* and the Anṣaar: how strong their faith was, and how sincere their Islam! How beautiful was their obedience to the truth when it was revealed! Every woman who truly believes in Allah and His Messenger cannot but follow the example of these virtuous women, so she herself must wear the distinctive Islamic dress with no regard to the nakedness and wanton display that surrounds her. I remember a young university student who wore *ḥijaab*, whose attitude was no less admirable than that of the women of the *Muhaajireen* and Anṣaar, may Allah be pleased with them: when a journalist who was visiting the University of Damascus asked her about her *ḥijaab* and whether it was not too hot for her in the extreme heat of summer, she responded by quoting:

> "*Say: The fire of Hell is fiercer in heat.*" *(Qur'an 9: 81).*

It is Muslim girls such as this who will build Muslim homes and families, and raise a virtuous generation which will fill society with constructive and noble elements. Today there are many such young women, *Al-ḥamdu lillah* (Praise and thanks be to Allah).

Proper dress for women was not something novel introduced by Islam; it existed in all the laws of Allah revealed before Islam. This can be seen in what remains of those laws in the altered books (i.e. the Bible). We also see it in the modest dress of the Christian nuns who live in the Islamic world and also in the West, and in the fact that the women of the people of the Book cover their heads when they enter their churches. The modern rejection of the idea that women should be covered and modest goes against all divine laws, from the

---

[87] Ibid, 8/489, 490.

time of the Prophets Ibraheem (Abraham), Moosa (Moses) and 'Eesa (Jesus) (۩), until the *ḥaneefi* way brought by Islam. This attitude is an attempt to escape the decree of Allah, which Allah has sent to mankind throughout the ages, brought time after time by His Messengers to guide mankind to truth and righteousness, so that they would become one nation, worshipping and obeying one Lord:

> *"Mankind was but one nation, but differed [later]. Had it not been for a Word that went forth before from your Lord, their differences would have been settled between them."*   *(Qur'an 10: 19)*

> *"O' messengers! Enjoy [all] things good and pure, and work righteousness; for I am well-acquainted with [all] that you do. And verily this Brotherhood of yours is a single Brotherhood. And I am your Lord and Cherisher: therefore fear Me [and no other]."* *(Qur'an 23: 51-52)*

> *"And [remember] her who guarded her chastity: We breathed into her of Our Spirit, and We made her and her son a Sign for all peoples. Verily, this Brotherhood of yours is a single Brotherhood, and I am your Lord and Cherisher: therefore serve [worship] Me [and no other]."*   *(Qur'an 21: 91-92)*

The determination of many modern societies that women should be uncovered, living naked and immoral lives, is an indication of how far they have deviated from the guidance of Allah, not only in the Muslim lands, but in all countries of the world. The Westerners may not care about this, and may go ahead and invent more means of immorality without finding any deterrent in their corrupted books. But the Muslims who worship Allah by reciting His perfectly preserved Book, night and day, will never accept such deviance, no matter how negligent and weak they are in their practice of Islam, because they constantly hear the definitive words of the Qur'an and

Sunnah, warning those who disobey Allah and His Messenger, of the test in this life, and the severe punishment to come in the Hereafter:

> "*...Let those beware who withstand the Messenger's order, lest some trial befall them, or a grievous Penalty be inflicted on them.*" *(Qur'an 24: 63)*

So those men and women who have sold out to the West and called for women to uncover themselves and take off *ḥijaab*, have failed miserably in the face of the determination of the men and women of the Islamic revival, which is taking place throughout the world. Rightly-guided, educated Muslim women have gone back to their distinctive Islamic dress and correct, decent *ḥijaab*, in many Muslim countries which had previously witnessed the call for Westernization and the abolishing of *ḥijaab* and decency. For example, the followers of Ataturk in Turkey, Reza Pahlevi in Iran, Muhammad Amanullah Khan in Afghanistan, Aḥmed Zogo and Enver Hoxha in Albania, Marcus Fahmi, Qasim Ameen and Hoda Sha'rawi in Egypt. Some of those who supported women's "liberation" from *ḥijaab* and modesty, have now renounced their former opinions about women's showing off and mixing freely with men.

Dr. Nawaal as-Sa'daawi, who for a long time attacked *ḥijaab* and those who wear it, vehemently calling women to take off *ḥijaab*, now condemns the vulgarity and scandalous nakedness of women in the West. She says:

> "In the streets of London ... I see women who are nearly naked, showing off their bodies like merchandise. Clothing has a function, which is to protect the body from the natural environment and not to transmit messages of temptation. If a woman saw herself as a human being, and not as merchandise, she would not need to show her nakedness."[88]

---

[88] *Al-Mujtama'* magazine, Kuwait, issue no. 932.

It became clear to Nawaal as-Sa'daawi after a while, that the veil should be removed from the mind, not the body, especially in the case of those men and women who are educated. Those women of lesser education, but with intelligence and openness of mind, who wear *ḥijaab*, are worth tens of those foolish educated women who make a wanton display of themselves, uncovering their faces, heads and bodies whilst veiling their minds and instincts! This is why she describes her future plans as "lifting the veil from the minds of educated men and women."[89] She adds:

> "I know many female professors, doctors and engineers who are politically, socially and culturally illiterate."[90]

The famous novelist Iḥsaan 'Abdul-Quddoos, who flooded the literary market with his stories that called women to go out of the house and mingle with men, dancing with them at parties and night-clubs, said in an interview with the Kuwaiti newspaper *Al-Anba'* (18 January 1989):

> "I think that the basic responsibility of any woman is her house and children. This applies to me above all. If it were not for my wife, I would not have been able to enjoy success, stability and family life. All this is because she is devoted to the house and children..."

In the same interview, he said:

> "I never in all my life envisaged marrying a woman who works, and I am well-known for this, because I knew from the beginning that the house is a heavy burden or responsibility for women."

---

89 *Al-Mujtama'* magazine, Kuwait, issue no. 931.

90 Ibid.

She avoids mixing freely with men

The true Muslim woman avoids mixing with men as much as possible; she does not pursue it or encourage it. Thus, she follows the example of Faṭimah, the daughter of the Prophet (ﷺ), the Prophet's wives, the women of the *salaf* (the *Ṣaḥaabah* and *Tabi'een*), and those who followed their way sincerely.

The harm that may be done to both sexes as a result of free mixing, that is obvious to the Muslim woman, is now becoming clear to Westerners who have practised free mixing on the widest scale. They have seen that it leads to a fall in standards of education, so they have now begun to segregate male and female students in some universities and institutes of education. A number of the greatest Muslim educators, who have visited Europe, America and Russia, have witnessed this segregation. For example, Professor Aḥmad Maẓhar al-'Aẓmah, who was sent by the Syrian Ministry of Education to Belgium, visited a number of schools there. On a visit to a girls' elementary school, he asked the Principal, "Why do you not let boys and girls mix at this level of education?" She replied, "We noticed the harm that mixing can do to children even at the elementary level."

There was news that Russia had reached a similar conclusion, and had established separate, segregated branches of universities, where male and female students did not mix.

In America, there are more than 170 university branches in which male and female students do not mix. They were set up because the educators and supervisors noticed the harm that was caused by mixing, even in a society that is used to mixing in every area of social life.

The evidence of the harm caused by mixing is too vast to be enumerated. All of it points to the wisdom of Islam in putting an end to mixing, and protecting the Muslim societies which adhere to

Islamic guidance from its destructive, harmful effects.

She does not shake hands with a non-maḥram man

It is natural that a Muslim woman who does not mix with men would not wish to shake hands with anyone who is not her *maḥram*, in accordance with the teaching and example of the Prophet (ﷺ). Bukhari reports that 'Aa'ishah (رضي الله عنها) said: "When the believing women made *hijrah* (migration from the land of disbelief to the land of Islam) to the Prophet, he would examine and test them, in accordance with the *aayah*:

> "*O' you who believe! When there come to you believing women refugees, examine [and test] them...*"
> *(Qur'an 60: 10)*

Whoever accepted these conditions required of the believing women, has thereby accepted their *bay'ah* (allegiance). When the Messenger of Allah (ﷺ) accepted their words, he told them (the women),

> "You may go now, for I have accepted your *bay'ah*.' By Allah, the Prophet's hand never touched the hand of a woman; he accepted their *bay'ah* by words only. By Allah, he never put any conditions on women other than those that Allah commanded him, and when he had confirmed the *bay'ah* he would say 'I have accepted your *bay'ah* by your words.'"[91]

She does not travel except with a maḥram

One of the rulings of Islam concerning women is that a woman should not travel without a *maḥram*, because travel is full of dangers

[91] *Fatḥ al-Baari*, 9/420, *Kitaab aṭ-Ṭalaaq, baab idha aslamat al-mushrikah aw an-nasraaniyah taḥt adh-dhimmi aw al-ḥarbi.*

and hardships and it is not right for a woman to face all this alone, without a *maḥram* to protect her and take care of her. So the Prophet (ﷺ) forbade women to travel alone without a *maḥram*; this is recorded in numerous hadiths, but it will suffice to quote just two of them here:

> "A woman should not travel for three days except with a *maḥram*."[92]

> "It is not permitted for a woman who believes in Allah and the Last Day to travel the walking-distance of three days without a *maḥram*."[93]

All the hadiths on this topic state that the presence of a *maḥram* is the condition for women's travel, except in cases of utter necessity as defined by the scholars, whose points of view differ somewhat.[94]

In this way, the Muslim woman is truly obedient to Allah (ﷻ), following His commands, heeding His prohibitions, and accepting His rulings. She adheres to the teachings of Islam and bears with patience any difficulties that may be involved in obeying Allah, even if this goes against many of the prevalent social ideas. She is filled with hope that she will ultimately be successful and victorious, as the Qur'an states:

> "*By [the Token of] Time [through the Ages], Verily Man is in loss, Except such as have Faith, and do righteous deeds, and [join together] in the mutual teaching of Truth, and of Patience and Constancy.*"
>
> *(Qur'an 103: 1-3)*

---

[92] Bukhari: *Fatḥ al-Baari*, 2/566, *Kitaab Taqṣeer aṣ-Ṣalaat, baab fi kam yaqṣur aṣ-ṣalaat.*

[93] Muslim, 9/103, *Kitaab al-Ḥajj, baab safar al-mar'ah ma'a maḥram.*

[94] Ibid, 9/102-109.

She accepts the will and decree of Allah

The Muslim woman who is obedient to the command of her Lord naturally accepts His will and decree, because this is one of the greatest signs of faith, obedience, *taqwa* and righteousness in a person. So the Muslim woman who is guided by the teachings of Islam always accepts whatever befalls her in life, whether it is good or bad, because this attitude of acceptance is good for her in all cases, as the Prophet (ﷺ) explained:

> "How amazing is the affair of the Muslim! His affairs are all good. If he experiences ease, he is grateful, and that is good for him. If he experiences hardship, he faces it with patience and perseverance, and that is also good for him."[95]

The Muslim woman is convinced that whatever befalls her in life could not have been avoided, and whatever does not befall her could not have been made to happen. Everything happens according to the will and decree of Allah, so her affairs are all good. If something good happens to her, she voices her praise to Allah, the Munificent Bestower, and she becomes one of those who are grateful, obedient and successful; if something bad happens to her, she faces it with patience and fortitude, so she becomes of those who are patient, redeemed and victorious.

With this deep faith, the Muslim woman faces the upheavals and calamities of life with a calm soul that accepts the will and decree of Allah. She seeks His help with patience, prayer and hope for reward from Him. She voices her praise to Allah (ﷻ) for what He has willed and decreed, as Al-Khansa' did on the day when she heard the news about her four sons and said:

---

[95] Muslim, 18/25, *Kitaab az-Zuhd, baab fi aḥaadeeth mutafarriqah,*

> "Praise be to Allah Who has honoured me by their martyrdom; I hope that Allah will gather me with them under His Mercy."[96]

She goes to the places where she usually prays, and seeks Allah's help with prayer and patience, as Asma' bint 'Umays used to do when disasters and tragedies stuck one after the other. She lost her first husband, Ja'far ibn Abi Ṭaalib (رضي الله عنه), then she was stricken by the death of her second husband, Abu Bakr aṣ-Ṣiddeeq (رضي الله عنه), and of her son, Muhammad ibn Abi Bakr (رضي الله عنه).

There are many other examples in history of Muslim women who had faith, hoping for reward from Allah and facing difficulties with patience and fortitude. Allah (سبحانه وتعالى) will reward them greatly:

> "*Those who patiently persevere will truly receive a reward without measure!*" *(Qur'an 39: 10)*

She turns to Allah in repentance often

The Muslim woman may find herself becoming neglectful and slipping from the Straight Path, so she may fall short in her practice of Islam in a way that does not befit the believing woman. But she will soon notice her error, seek forgiveness for her mistakes or shortcomings, and return to the protection of Allah (سبحانه وتعالى):

> "*Those who fear Allah, when a thought of evil from Satan assaults them, bring Allah to remembrance, when lo! They see [aright]!*" *(Qur'an 7: 201)*

The heart that is filled with love and fear of Allah will not be overcome by negligence. It is those who ignore Allah's commands and guidance who will be led astray. The heart of the sincere Muslim woman is ever eager to repent and seek forgiveness, and rejoices in obedience, guidance and the pleasure of Allah.

---

[96] *Al-Iṣaabah*, 8/66,67.

She feels a sense of responsibility for the members of her family

The responsibility of the Muslim woman for the members of her family is no less, in the sight of Allah, than that of the man. Her responsibility is in fact even greater than a man's, because of what she knows of the secret life of her children who live with her most of the time: they may tell her things that they do not tell their father. The Muslim woman feels this responsibility every time she hears the words of the Prophet (ﷺ):

> "Each of you is a shepherd and each of you is responsible for his flock. The leader is a shepherd and is responsible for his flock; a man is the shepherd of his family and is responsible for his flock; a woman is the shepherd in the house of her husband and is responsible for her flock; the servant is the shepherd of his master's wealth and is responsible for it. Each of you is a shepherd and is responsible for his flock."[97]

This sense of responsibility constantly motivates her to put right any faults or shortcomings she finds in her family's behaviour. A woman does not keep quiet about any deviance, weakness or negligence in her family or home, unless she is lacking in religion, her character is weak and her understanding is incomplete.

Her main concern is the pleasure of Allah

The true Muslim woman always seeks to earn the pleasure of Allah in everything she does. So she measures everything against this precise standard, and will retain or discard any practice accordingly.

Whenever there is a conflict between what pleases Allah, and what

---

[97] Bukhari and Muslim, See *Sharḥ as-Sunnah*, 10/61, *Kitaab al-Imaarah wal-qaḍa', baab ar-ra'ee mas'ool 'an ra'iyatihi.*

pleases other people, she chooses what pleases Allah (ﷻ), with no hesitation or argument, even if it will anger other people. She does this because she knows, with her deep understanding of Islam and her own common sense, that pleasing the people is a goal that can never be achieved, and it will only bring about the wrath of Allah. The Prophet (ﷺ) said:

> "Whoever seeks the pleasure of Allah at the risk of displeasing the people, Allah will take care of him and protect him from them. But whoever seeks the pleasure of the people at the risk of displeasing Allah, Allah will abandon him to the care of the people."[98]

By weighing up her deeds in this precise fashion, the Straight Path will be clearly signposted for the Muslim woman. She will know what she is allowed to do and what she should avoid; her unfailing standard is the pleasure of Allah. Thus the life of the Muslim women will be free from ridiculous contradiction which have ensnared so many of those who have deviated from the guidance of Allah.

There are women whom one sees praying perfectly, but in many instances they follow their own desires and deviate from the right path. In social gatherings, they involve themselves in gossip and backbiting, criticising people, plotting against anybody they dislike, and putting words in their mouths so as to discredit them. These people are suffering from weakness of faith and failure to understand the true reality of this holistic religion which Allah (ﷻ) revealed to guide mankind in all aspects of life, both public and private, so that people might seek the pleasure of Allah by obeying His commands and emulating the behaviour of the Prophet (ﷺ).

There are also women who obey Allah in some matters, but disobey Him in others, acting according to their own whims and desires. Such

---

[98] Tirmidhi, 4/34, at the end of the section on *Zuhd*; it is a *ḥasan* hadith.

people are, as it were, half-Muslims, and the split personality of those who have deviated from the guidance of Islam is one of the most dangerous psychological and spiritual disorders facing modern man.

She understands the true meaning of being a servant of Allah

The true Muslim woman has the firm belief that she has been created to serve an important purpose in life, which Allah (ﷻ) has defined in the Qur'an:

> "*I have only created jinns and men, that they should worship Me Alone.*" *(Qur'an 51: 56)*

Life, for the true Muslim woman, is not to be spent solely on daily chores or enjoyment of the good things of this world; life is an important mission, in which every believer must take on the responsibility of living in such a way that he or she will be a true and sincere worshipper of Allah. This can only be achieved by checking one's intention, in all one's deeds, to ensure that they are done for the sake of Allah and to please Him. According to Islam, all deeds are tied to the intentions behind them, as the Prophet (ﷺ) said:

> "Actions are but by intention, and every man shall have but that which he intended. Thus he whose migration was for Allah and His Messenger, his migration was for Allah and His Messenger; and he whose migration was to achieve some worldly benefit or to take some woman in marriage, his migration was for that which he intended."[99]

Hence, the Muslim woman may be in a continuous state of worship,

---

[99] Bukhari and Muslim, See *Sharḥ as-Sunnah*, 1/401, *Kitaab aṭ-Ṭahaarah, baab an-niyyah fil-wuḍoo' wa ghayrihi min al-'ibaadaat.*

which may encompass all of her deeds, so long as she checks her intentions and ensures that she is carrying out her mission in life, as Allah (ﷻ) wants her to do. So, she may be in a state of worship when she treats her parents with kindness and respect, when she is a good wife to her husband, when she takes care of her children's upbringing and education, when she goes about her domestic chores, when she upholds the ties of kinship, etc., so long as she does all this in obedience to the commands of Allah, and with the intention of serving and worshipping Him.

She works to support the religion of Allah

The most important act of worship that the Muslim woman can do is to strive to establish the rule of Allah on earth, and to follow the way of life that He has prescribed, so that Islam will govern the life of the individual, the family, the community and the nation.

The sincere Muslim woman will feel that her worship is lacking if she does not strive to achieve the purpose for which Allah created jinn and men, namely promoting the supremacy of the authority of Allah on earth, which is the only way in which mankind can truly worship Allah (ﷻ):

> *"I have only created jinns and men, that they may worship Me."* (Qur'an 51: 56)

This is the only way in which the true meaning of the words "*Laa ilaha ill-Allah, Muhammadun Rasoolullah* (There is no god except Allah, Muhammad is the Messenger of Allah)" will be realized in our own lives.

The first Muslim women had a sound grasp of this meaning, which penetrated deep into their souls. They were no less enthusiastic than the men, when it came to sacrifice and courage for the sake of Allah. Some of the women of the early generations of this ummah excelled many of the men in this regard.

Asma' bint 'Umays, the wife of Ja'far ibn Abi Ṭalib, hastened to embrace Islam along with her husband in the earliest days of Islam, the days of hardship and suffering. She migrated with him to Abyssinia, in spite of the risks and hardships involved, for the sake of Allah and to support His religion. When 'Umar ibn al-Khaṭṭab joked with her and said, "O' Ḥabashiyah (Abyssinian woman)! We beat you to Madeenah," she said, "You have most certainly spoken the truth. You were with the Messenger of Allah, feeding the hungry and teaching the ignorant, whilst we were far away in exile. By Allah, I shall go to the Messenger of Allah and tell him that." She came to the Prophet (ﷺ) and said, "O' Messenger of Allah, some men are criticizing us and claiming that we were not among the early *muḥaajireen*." The Messenger of Allah (ﷺ) said,

> "But you have two *ḥijrahs*; you migrated to the land of Abyssinia, whilst we were detained in Makkah, then you migrated to me afterwards."[100]

Asma' bint 'Umays was successful in establishing the virtue of those who had migrated to Abyssinia in the early days of Islam, and she understood from the Prophet (ﷺ) that this distinguished group would have the reward of two *ḥijrahs*. This was a great honour which was theirs, because they had not hesitated to support the Prophet, even though it meant leaving behind their families and homeland for the sake of Allah.

Muslim women were also present at the Treaty of 'Aqabah, which took place in secret, under cover of darkness, and which played such an important role in supporting the Prophet (ﷺ). Among the delegation of Anṣaar were two women of status and virtue: Naseebah bint Ka'b al-Maaziniyah, and Umm Manee' Asma' bint 'Amr al-Sulamiyah, the mother of Mu'aadh ibn Jabal (رضي الله عنه); the latter was

---

[100] *Ṭabaqaat Ibn Sa'd*, 8/280 (Beirut edition).

present with the Prophet (ﷺ) at Khaybar, where she performed extremely well.

When the Prophet (ﷺ) began his Mission, calling for pure *Tawḥeed* (belief in the Unity of Allah) and the abandonment of idol-worship, the *mushrikoon* (pagans) were very angry with him, and plotted to break into his house at night and kill him. The conspirators kept quiet and vowed to let their plot to kill the Prophet remain a secret amongst themselves. Nobody even sensed that there was a plot, apart from one Muslim woman, who was over one hundred years old. Her name was Ruqayqah bint Ṣayfi, and she did not let the weakness of old age stop her from hastening to save the Prophet's life. She made her way to him, and told him what the people were planning to do. He embarked upon his *ḥijrah* straight away, leaving the land that was the most beloved to him on earth, and leaving his cousin 'Ali (رضي الله عنه) sleeping in his bed, so that the conspirators surrounding his house would think that he was there, and this would keep them from following him and killing him on the road.[101]

What a tremendous service this great woman did for Islam and the Muslims! How great was her jihad to save the life of the Messenger of Allah (ﷺ) at the most dangerous time he ever faced.

When the Prophet (ﷺ) and his Companion (Abu Bakr aṣ-Ṣiddeeq) left Makkah, and stayed out of sight in the cave of Hira' at the top of Mount Thawr, it was a young girl who brought them food and water, and news of the people who were lying in wait for them. Her name was Asma' bint Abi Bakr aṣ-Ṣiddeeq (رضي الله عنها).

This brave young girl used to cover the great distance between Makkah and Mount Thawr at night; the difficulty and isolation of this journey, and the presence of watchful enemies, did not deter her. She knew that by saving the life of the Prophet (ﷺ) and his Companion,

---

101 *Ṭabaqaat Ibn Sa'd*, 7/35 and *Al-Iṣaabah*, 8/83.

helping them to reach their goal of going to Madeenah, she was supporting the religion of Allah, and working towards making His word supreme on earth. So, she undertook her difficult mission every day, ever alert and striving to conceal herself as she walked and climbed up the mountain, until she had brought whatever supplies and news she was carrying to the Prophet (ﷺ) and his Companion. Then she would go back down to Makkah under cover of darkness.[102]

This mission, which even the strongest of men could have failed to achieve, is not all that Asma' did to support the Prophet (ﷺ) and Islam. She was tested severely, and proved to be as solid as a rock, on the day when the *mushrikeen* surrounded her and asked about her father. She denied knowing anything, and they placed severe pressure on her, so much so that Abu Jahl struck her a blow that sent her earring flying from her ear. But this did not weaken her resolve or her determination to keep her secret hidden. She kept up her mission of taking food and news to the Prophet (ﷺ) and his Companion, until the time came for them to leave the cave and head for Madeenah. She had already brought them provisions for the journey, but when she checked the cloth in which they were wrapped, she found that she had nothing with which to tie it apart from her own girdle. She told her father, who told her to tear it in two and use one piece to tie the water skins and the other to tie the cloth holding the food. Hence Asma' became known as *Dhat an-Niṭaqayn* (she of the two girdles).[103]

It was the attitude of the early Muslim women to support the religion of Allah and join the forces of *da'wah*, because their hearts were

---

[102] *Seerat Ibn Hishaam: Al-Ḥijrah ila al-Madeenah.*

[103] *Fatḥ al-Baari Sharḥ Ṣaḥeeḥ al-Bukhari*, 7/233, 240, *Kitaab Manaaqib al-Anṣaar, baab ḥijrat an-Nabi wa aṣḥaabihi ila al-Madeenah*, and 6/129, *Kitaab al-Jihaad, baab ḥaml az-zaad fil-ghazw.*

filled with strong, vibrant faith. They could not bear to stay in the land of *kufr*, (disbelief) far from the centre of Islam, so they migrated — with their husbands, if they were married — and their *ḥijrah*, like that of the men, was in obedience to Allah and in support of His religion. Their faith was like that of the men, and they made sacrifices just as the men did.

This deep faith is what motivated Umm Kalthoom bint 'Uqbah ibn Abi Mu'ayṭ to migrate to Madeenah alone, at the time of the Treaty of Ḥudaybiyah, where the Prophet (ﷺ) had promised to return to the *mushrikeen* anyone who came to him to embrace Islam. The Prophet (ﷺ) had already kept his promise and sent two men back. When Umm Kalthoom reached Madeenah, she said to the Prophet (ﷺ): "I have fled to you with my religion, so protect me and do not send me back to them, for they will punish me and torture me, and I do not have the patience and fortitude to endure that. I am a mere woman, and you know the weakness of women. I see that you have already sent two men back." The Prophet (ﷺ) said:

> "Allah has cancelled this treaty with regard to women."[104]

Allah (ﷻ) knew the faith of Umm Kalthoom bint 'Uqbah ibn Abi Mu'ayṭ, and other *muḥaajir* women who had migrated solely out of love for Allah and His Messenger and Islam.

He revealed the Qur'an concerning them, abolishing the treaty between the Prophet and the *mushrikeen* in the case of women only, and forbidding their being sent back to the *mushrikeen* once the Prophet (ﷺ) had tested them and ensured that they had not migrated for the sake of a husband or wealth or some other worldly purpose, and that they had indeed migrated for the sake of Allah and His Messenger:

---

104 Ibn al-Jawzi, *Aḥkaam an-Nisa'*, 43420.

> *"O' you who believe! When there come to you believing women refugees, examine [and test] them: Allah knows best as to their Faith: if you ascertain that they are Believers, then send them not back to the Unbelievers. They are not lawful [wives] for the Unbelievers, nor are the [Unbelievers] lawful [husbands] for them."*
>
> *(Qur'an 60: 10)*

One of those virtuous women who were among the first people to support Islam and the Prophet was Umm al-Faḍl bint al-Ḥaarith, Lubabah, the full-sister of the Prophet's wife Maymoonah. She was the second woman to embrace Islam: she became Muslim after Khadeejah (رضي الله عنها). She was a source of great support and consolation for the Prophet (ﷺ).

Lubabah was the wife of the Prophet's paternal uncle 'Abbaas ibn 'Abdul-Muṭṭalib, and was diametrically opposed to Umm Jameel bint Ḥarb, the wife of his other paternal uncle Abu Lahab, whom the Qur'an described as the carrier of firewood who would have a twisted rope of palm-leaf fibre around her neck (Qur'an 111: 4-5), because of her determination to harm the Prophet (ﷺ), whilst Lubabah was the first to come to his support and to make sacrifices to support his religion during the most testing days that the early Muslims faced.

Lubabah, her husband 'Abbaas and their sons used to conceal their Islam, in obedience to the Prophet's command and in accordance with a well-thought-out plan.

Thus, they were able to learn the secrets of the *mushrikeen* and pass them on to the Messenger of Allah (ﷺ). When the battle of Badr was waged between the Muslims and the *mushrikeen*, and news came of the defeat of Quraysh, Umm al-Faḍl urged her sons and her freed slave Abu Raafi' to conceal their joy at this defeat, because she feared that the *mushrikeen*, especially Abu Lahab who was filled with hatred towards Muhammad (ﷺ), his Companions and his message, might do them some harm.

But her freed slave Abu Raafi‘ was not safe from the wrath of Abu Lahab. When he expressed his joy at the Muslims’ victory, Abu Lahab was enraged and vented his fury on the poor man, beating him in the presence of Umm al-Faḍl. At this point, Umm al-Faḍl became like a fierce lioness, and attacked him shouting, “You pick on him when his master is absent!” She struck him with one of the (wooden) pillars of the house and dealt him a fatal blow to the head. Abu Lahab did not live more than seven days after that.

Umm al-Faḍl bore her separation from her husband ‘Abbaas with patience, for the sake of Allah and in support of His religion, when the Prophet (ﷺ) issued a command that ‘Abbaas should stay in Makkah, and she should migrate to Madeenah. Their separation was a lengthy and difficult one, but Umm al-Faḍl bore it patiently, hoping for reward and seeking help from Allah through prayer and fasting, waiting for her beloved husband to finish what he had to do in Makkah and come to Madeenah. As it turned out, he was one of the last to migrate to Madeenah. The only thing that helped to ease the pain of this separation was seeing her eldest son ‘Abdullah, accompanying the Prophet (ﷺ) daily and drinking deeply from the pure wellspring of Islam. It never occurred to her that history was preparing her to enter its widest gate, for she was to be the great mother of the great authority on Islamic teaching and the interpretation of the Qur’an: ‘Abdullah ibn ‘Abbaas (may Allah be pleased with them both).

Another one of the early Muslim women, who thought little of the sufferings and torture they endured for the sake of Islam, was Sumayyah, the mother of ‘Ammar ibn Yaasir. When the mid-day heat was at its most intense, and the desert sands were boiling, Banu Makhzoom would drag her and her son and husband out to an exposed area, where they would pour burning sand over them, place heated shields on them, and throw heavy rocks at them, until her son and husband sought to protect themselves from this appalling torture by saying some words to agree with the *mushrikeen* (pagans), although they hated to do so. Concerning them and others in similar situations, Allah (ﷻ) revealed the *aayah*:

> "*Anyone who, after accepting faith in Allah, utters Unbelief, except under compulsion, his heart remaining firm in faith...*" *(Qur'an 16: 106)*

But Sumayyah remained steadfast and patient, and refused to say what the *mushrikeen* wanted to hear. The despicable Abu Jahl stabbed her with a spear, killing her, and thus she had the honour of being recorded as the first martyr in Islam.

The history of Islam is filled with other women who endured even worse torture for the sake of Islam. This suffering did not weaken their resolve or exhaust their patience; rather they willingly accepted whatever befell them, hoping for reward from Allah. They never said anything that would undermine their religion, and they never humiliated themselves by begging for mercy. Historians record that many of the men who were oppressed — apart from Bilaal (رضي الله عنه) — were forced to say something that would please their oppressors, in order to save their lives, but not one of the women who were similarly oppressed was reported to have given in.

These brilliant Muslim women welcomed the oppression they suffered for the sake of Allah and for making His word supreme on earth. They never stopped preaching the word of Islam, no matter what trials and suffering came on their way.

In the story of Umm Shareek al-Qarashiyah al-'Aamiriyah, Ibn 'Abbaas gives an eye-witness account of the depth of the women's faith, and how they rushed to devote themselves to Allah's cause, patiently enduring whatever trials this entailed. Ibn 'Abbaas said:

> "Umm Shareek began to think about Islam whilst she was in Makkah. She embraced Islam, then began to mix with the women of Quraysh in secret, calling them to Islam, until this became known to the people of Makkah. They seized her and said, 'If it were not for your people, we would have done what we wanted to you, but we will send you back to them.' She said, 'So they seated me on a camel with no saddle or cushion beneath me, and left me for three days without giving me anything to eat or drink. After three days I began to lose consciousness. Whenever they stopped, they would leave me out in the sun whilst they sought shade, and keep food and drink away from me until they resumed their journey...'"

This was not all that Muslim women did in support of Islam; they also went out on military expeditions with the Prophet (ﷺ) and his Companions, where, when the forces of *Eemaan* and the forces of *kufr* met in armed combat, they performed the important duty of preparing the waterskins and bringing water to the fighters, and tending the wounded, and carrying the dead away from the battlefield.

At the most critical moments, they never shrank from taking up weapons and entering the fray alongside the Prophet (ﷺ) and his Companions.

Bukhari and Muslim narrate many hadiths which illustrate the brilliance of the Muslim women during that golden age, when hearts were filled with vibrant faith, deep love for Allah and His Messenger, and the desire to make Islam victorious.

One of these reports is the account given by Imam Muslim of Umm 'Aṭiyah al-Anṣaariyah, who said:

> "I went out on seven military campaigns with the Messenger of Allah. I stayed behind in the camp,

> making food for them and tending to the sick and wounded."[105]

Anas ibn Maalik said:

> "The Messenger of Allah used to go out on military campaigns accompanied by Umm Sulaym and some of the Anṣaar women; they would bring water and tend the wounded."[106]

Imam Bukhari reported that Al-Rubayyi' bint Mu'awwidh said:

> "We were with the Prophet, bringing water, tending the wounded, and bringing the dead back to Madeenah."[107]

Bukhari and Muslim report that Anas (رضي الله عنه) said:

> "On the day of Uḥud, when some of the people ran away from the Prophet, Abu Ṭalḥah stood before the Prophet, defending him with a shield. Abu Ṭalḥah was a highly-skilled archer, and on that day he broke two or three bows. Whenever a man passed by who had a quiver full of arrows, he would say, 'Give it to Abu Ṭalḥah.' Whenever the Prophet of Allah raised his head to see what was happening, Abu Ṭalḥah told him, 'O' Prophet of Allah, may my father and mother be sacrificed for you! Do not raise your head, lest an arrow strike you. May it hit my chest rather than yours.' He (Anas) said: I saw 'Aa'ishah bint Abi Bakr and Umm Sulaym, both of whom had tucked up their garments so

---

[105] Muslim, 12/14204, *Kitaab al-Jihaad was-Siyar, baab an-nisa' al-ghaaziyaat.*

[106] Muslim, 12/188, *Kitaab al-Jihaad was-Siyar, baab ghazwat an-nisa'.*

[107] *Fatḥ al-Baari*, 6/80, *Kitaab al-Jihaad, baab mudawaat an-nisa' al-jarḥa fil-ghazw.*

> that their anklets were not visible. They were carrying waterskins on their backs and were pouring water into the mouths of the people. They would go back and fill the waterskins again, then come and pour water into the mouths of the people again. Abu Ṭalḥah's sword fell from his hands two or three times because of exhaustion."[108]

What a noble deed these two great women did in quenching the thirst of the *mujaahideen* (Fighters for Allah's sake) in the midst of a raging battle and in the intense heat of the Ḥijaaz climate. They were moving about the battlefield, not caring about the falling arrows and clashing swords that surrounded them.

For this reason, the Rightly-Guided *khaleefah* 'Umar ibn al-Khaṭṭab (رضي الله عنه) preferred Umm Saleeṭ to his own wife Umm Kalthoom bint 'Ali, when he was sharing out some garments among the women of Madeenah, because she had sewn waterskins on the day of Uḥud, and this had played an important role in helping the *mujaahideen* and renewing their energy. Bukhari reports from Tha'labah ibn Abi Maalik:

> "Umar ibn al-Khaṭṭab shared out some garments among the women of Madeenah. There was one good garment left, and some of the people with him said, 'O' *Ameer al-Mu'mineen*, give this to your wife, the grand-daughter of the Messenger of Allah,' meaning Umm Kalthoom bint 'Ali. 'Umar said, 'Umm Saleeṭ has more right to it.' Umm Saleeṭ was one of the Anṣaari women who had pledged their allegiance to the Prophet. 'Umar

---

[108] *Fatḥ al-Baari*, 7/361, *Kitaab al-Maghaazi, baab idh hammat ṭaa'ifatan minkum an tufshila*; Muslim, 12/18420, *Kitaab al-Jihaad was-Siyar, baab ghazwat an-nisa' ma'a ar-rijaal.*

said, 'She carried the water-skins to us on the day of Uḥud.'"[109]

At Uḥud, the Prophet's cheek and upper lip were wounded and his tooth was broken. His daughter Faṭimah (رضي الله عنها) washed his wounds, whilst 'Ali poured the water. When Faṭimah saw that the water only made the bleeding worse, she took a piece of matting, burned it, and applied it to the wound to stop the bleeding.[110]

Among the women who stood firm at the most intense moments of the battle of Uḥud was Ṣafiyah bint 'Abdul-Muṭṭalib (رضي الله عنها), the (paternal) aunt of the Prophet (ﷺ). She stood with a spear in her hand, striking the faces of the people and saying, "Are you running away from the Messenger of Allah?!" When the Prophet (ﷺ) saw her, he gestured to her son Az-Zubayr ibn al-'Awwaam that he should bring her back so that she would not see what had happened to her brother Ḥamzah (رضي الله عنه). She said, "Why? I have heard that my brother has been mutilated, but that is nothing for the sake of Allah. We accept what has happened, and I shall hope for reward and be patient, *in-shā' Allah* (If God Wills)."

Ṣafiyah was also present at the battle of Al-Khandaq (the trench). When the Prophet (ﷺ) set out from Madeenah to fight his enemies, he put his wives and womenfolk in the fortress of the poet Ḥassaan ibn Thaabit, which was the most secure fortress in Madeenah. A Jewish man came by, and began to walk around the fortress. Ṣafiyah said, "O' Ḥassaan, this Jew is walking around the fortress, and by Allah I fear that he will go and tell the other Jews out there where we are. The Messenger of Allah (ﷺ) and his Companions are too busy to come and help us, so go down and kill him." Ḥassaan said, "May Allah forgive you, O' daughter of 'Abdul-Muṭṭalib. By Allah, you know that

---

[109] *Fatḥ al-Baari*, 6/7420, *Kitaab al-Jihaad, baab ḥaml an-nisa' al-qurab ilan-naas fil-ghazw* and 7/366, *Kitaab al-Maghaazi, baab dhikr Umm Saleeṭ.*

[110] *Fatḥ al-Baari*, 7/372, *Kitaab al-Maghaazi, baab ma aṣaba an-Nabi* (ﷺ) *min al-jiraaḥ yawma Uḥud.*

I am not like that." When Ṣafiyah heard this, she stood up, took hold of a wooden post, and went down from the fortress herself. She struck the Jew with the wooden post and killed him, then went back to the fortress and said, "O' Ḥassaan, go down and strip him of his arms and armour; the only thing that is preventing me from doing so is that he is a man." Ḥassaan said, "I have no need of this booty, O' daughter of 'Abdul-Muṭṭalib." Ṣafiyah was also present at the battle of Khaybar.

One of the most distinguished women who took part in the battle of Uḥud, if not the most distinguished of them, was Naseebah bint Ka'b al-Maaziniyah, Umm 'Umaarah (رضي الله عنها). At the beginning of the battle, she was bringing water and tending the wounded, as the other women were doing. When the battle was going in the favour of the Muslims, the archers disobeyed the command of the Prophet (ﷺ), and this turned the victory into defeat, as the Qur'an described it:

> "*Behold! You were climbing up the high ground, without even casting a side glance at anyone, and the Messenger in your rear was calling you back...*"
>
> *(Qur'an 3: 153)*

At this point Naseebah went forward with her sword unsheathed and her bow in her hand, to join the small group who were standing firm with the Prophet (ﷺ), acting as a human shield to protect him from the arrows of the *mushrikeen*. Every time danger approached the Prophet (ﷺ), she hastened to protect him. The Messenger of Allah (ﷺ) noticed this, and later said, "Wherever I turned, to the left or the right, I saw her fighting for me."

Her son 'Umaarah also described what happened on that tremendous day:

> "On that day, I was wounded in my left hand. A man who seemed to be as tall as a palm-tree struck me, then went away without pursuing to finish me off. The blood began to flow copiously, so the Messenger of Allah told

me, 'Bind up your wound.' My mother came to me, and she was wearing a waist-wrapper, which she had brought, for the purpose of wrapping wounds. She dressed my wound, whilst the Prophet was looking on. Then she told me, 'Get up, my son, and fight the people.' The Prophet said, 'Who could bear what you are putting up with, O' Umm 'Umaarah?' She said: 'The man who had struck my son came by, and the Messenger of Allah said, 'This is the one who struck your son.' I intercepted him and hit him in the thigh, and he collapsed. I saw the Messenger of Allah smiling so broadly that I could see his back teeth. He said, 'You have taken your revenge, O' Umm 'Umaarah!' Then we struck him with our weapons until we killed him, and the Prophet said: 'Praise be to Allah, who granted you victory over him, gave you the satisfaction of taking revenge on your enemy, and let you see the vengeance for yourself.'"

On this day, Naseebah herself received many wounds whilst she was fighting the people and striking their chests. The Prophet (ﷺ) saw her, and called to her son,

"Your mother! Your mother! See to her wounds, may Allah bless you and your household! Your mother has fought better than so-and-so." When his mother heard what the Prophet said, she said, "Pray to Allah that we may accompany you in Paradise." He said, "O' Allah, make them my companions in Paradise." She said, "I do not care what befalls me in this world."[111]

---

[111] See the reports on the Battle of Uḥud in the *Seerah* of Ibn Hisham, and in *Insaan al-'Uyun wal-Athaar al-Muḥammadiyah, the Ṭabaqaat of Ibn Sa'd, Al-Iṣaabah*, and *Asad al-Ghaabah.*

Umm ‘Umaarah’s jihad was not confined to the battle of Uḥud. She was also present on a number of other occasions, namely the treaty of ‘Aqabah, Al-Ḥudaybiyah, Khaybar and Ḥunayn. Her heroic conduct at Ḥunayn was no less marvellous than her heroic conduct at Uḥud. At the time of Abu Bakr’s *khilaafah*, she was present at Al-Yamamah, where she fought brilliantly, received eleven wounds and lost her hand.

It is no surprise that the Prophet (ﷺ) gave her the good news that she would enter Paradise, and that she was later held in high esteem by the *khaleefah* Abu Bakr aṣ-Ṣiddeeq (رضي الله عنه) and his commander Khalid ibn al-Waleed (رضي الله عنه), and subsequently by ‘Umar ibn al-Khaṭṭab (رضي الله عنه).[112]

During this golden age of the Muslim woman’s history, there was another woman who was no less great than Naseebah bint Ka‘b: Umm Sulaym bint Milḥaan. Like Umm ‘Umaarah, ‘Aa’ishah, Faṭimah and the other women, she also brought water and tended the wounded, but here we will tell another story. When the Muslims were preparing to go out with the Prophet (ﷺ) to conquer Makkah, her husband Abu Ṭalḥah was among them. Umm Sulaym was in the later stages of pregnancy, but this did not stop her from wanting to accompany her husband Abu Ṭalḥah and to earn alongside him the reward for jihad for the sake of Allah. She did not care about the hardships and difficulties that lay ahead on the journey. Her husband felt sorry for her and did not want to expose her to all that, but he had no choice but to ask the Prophet’s permission. The Prophet (ﷺ) gave his permission, and Umm Sulaym was delighted to accompany her beloved husband and witness the conquest of Makkah with him, on that great day when the hills of Makkah echoed with the cries of the believers and *mujaahideen*: “There is no god but Allah alone. He has kept His promise, granted victory to His servant, and alone has

---

112 *Siyar a‘laam al-nubala’*, 2/281.

defeated the confederates. There is nothing before Him or after Him. There is no god but Allah, and we worship Him alone, adhering faithfully to His religion, although the disbelievers may hate this." This was the day when the bastions of idolatry and *shirk* (polytheism) in the Arabian Peninsula were forever destroyed, and the idols were thrown down by the Prophet (ﷺ), as he declared,

> "*Truth has [now] arrived, and Falsehood perished: for Falsehood is [by its nature] bound to perish.*"
>
> *(Qur'an 17: 81)*

These events filled Umm Sulaym's soul with faith, and increased her courage and her desire to strive for the sake of Allah. Only a few days later, came the battle of Ḥunayn, which was such a severe test for the Muslims. Some of the people ran away from the battle, not caring about anything. The Prophet (ﷺ) stood to the right and said, "Where are you going, O' people? Come to me! I am the Messenger of Allah, I am Muhammad ibn Abdullah." Nobody stayed with him except for a group of *Muhaajireen* and Anṣaar, and members of his household, and Umm Sulaym and her husband Abu Ṭalḥah were among this group. The Messenger of Allah saw Umm Sulaym wrapping a garment around her waist; she was pregnant with 'Abdullah ibn Abi Ṭalḥah, and she was trying to control Abu Ṭalḥah's camel, which she was afraid would get away from her, so she pulled its head down towards her and took hold of its nose-ring. The Messenger of Allah called her, "O' Umm Sulaym!" and she replied, "Yes, may my father and mother be sacrificed for you, O' Messenger of Allah."

A report in *Ṣaḥeeḥ Muslim* states:

> "On the day of Ḥunayn, Umm Sulaym took hold of a dagger and kept it with her. Abu Ṭalḥah saw her, and said, 'O' Messenger of Allah, Umm Sulaym has a dagger.' The Messenger of Allah asked her, 'What is this dagger?' She said, 'I took it so that if any one of the

> *mushrikeen* comes near me, I will rip his belly open with it.' The Messenger of Allah began to laugh. She said, 'O' Messenger of Allah, kill all of the *tulaqa*[113] who have run away and left you.' The Messenger of Allah said, 'Allah is sufficient for us and He has taken care of us.'"[114]

Umm Sulaym stood firm with the Prophet (ﷺ) when the battle intensified and even the bravest of men were put to the test. She could not bear even to see those who had run away and left the Prophet, so she told him, "Kill those who ran away and left you..." It comes as no surprise that the Messenger of Allah (ﷺ) gave her the glad tidings that she would enter Paradise. In a hadith reported by Bukhari, Muslim and others from Jaabir ibn 'Abdullah (رضي الله عنه), he (ﷺ) told her:

> "I saw myself in Paradise, and suddenly I saw Al-Rumaysa'[115] bint Milḥaan, the wife of Abu Ṭalḥah..."[116]

The Messenger of Allah (ﷺ) used to visit Umm Sulaym, and her sister Umm Ḥaraam bint Milḥaan. Just as he gave glad tidings to Umm Sulaym that she would enter Paradise, so he also gave good news to Umm Ḥaraam that she would ride the waves of the sea with those who went out to fight for the sake of Allah.

Bukhari reports that Anas ibn Maalik (رضي الله عنه) said:

> "The Messenger of Allah visited the daughter of Milḥaan, and rested there for a while. Then he smiled,

---

[113] Those who entered Islam on the day of the Conquest of Makkah. (Author)

[114] Muslim, 12/187, 188, *Kitaab al-Jihaad was-Siyar, baab ghazwat an-nisa' ma'a ar-rijaal.*

[115] Al-Rumaysa': A nickname of Umm Sulaym, on account of a *ramas* (white secretion) in her eye. (Author)

[116] Bukhari and Muslim, See *Sharḥ as-Sunnah*, 14/86, *Kitaab Faḍaa'il aṣ-ṣaḥaabah, baab faḍaa'il 'Umar ibn al-Khaṭṭab.*

> and she asked him, 'Why are you smiling, O' Messenger of Allah?' He said, 'Some people of my *ummah* (nation) will cross the green sea for the sake of Allah, and they will look like kings on thrones.' She said, 'O' Messenger of Allah, pray to Allah that I will be one of them.' He said, 'O' Allah, make her one of them.' Then he smiled again, and she asked him again why he was smiling. He gave a similar answer, and she said, 'Pray to Allah that I will be one of them.' He said, 'You will be one of the first ones, not one of the last ones.'"

The Prophet's words came true, as Anas (رضي الله عنه) reported: "She married 'Ubaadah ibn aṣ-Ṣaamit, and went out for jihad with him, and she travelled across the sea with the daughter of Qaraẓah.[117] When she came back, her riding animal threw her, and she fell and died."[118]

Her grave in Cyprus remains to this day as a memorial to a Muslim woman who fought in jihad for the sake of Allah. When people visit the grave they say, "This is the grave of a righteous woman, may Allah have mercy on her."[119]

Another of the women who took part in military campaigns and jihad with the Prophet (ﷺ), helping to defend Islam, was Umm Ayman, the nurse of the Prophet (ﷺ). She was present at Uḥud, Khaybar, Mu'tah and Ḥunayn, where she worked hard, tending the wounded and bringing water to the thirsty.[120]

There was also Kabshah bint Rafi' al-Anṣaariyah, the mother of Sa'd ibn Mu'adh (رضي الله عنه). During the campaign of Uḥud, she came running

---

[117] i.e., the wife of Mu'aawiyah. (Author)

[118] *Fatḥ al-Baari*, 6/76, *Kitaab al-Jihaad, baab ghazw al-mar'ah fil-baḥr.*

[119] *Al-Hilyah*, 2/62; *Ṣifat aṣ-Ṣafwah*, 2/70.

[120] *Al-Maghaazi*, 1/278; *Anṣaab al-Ashraaf*, 1/326; Al-Bayhaqi, *Dalaa'il an-Nubuwwah*, 3/311.

towards the Prophet (ﷺ), who was on his horse, and Sa'd ibn Mu'adh (رضي الله عنه) was holding onto its reins. Sa'd said, "O' Messenger of Allah, this is my mother." The Messenger of Allah (ﷺ) said, "She is most welcome." He stopped for her, and she came closer; he offered his condolences for the death of her son 'Amr ibn Mu'aadh, told her and her family the glad tidings of the martyrs in Paradise, and prayed for them.[121]

Among these great women are Al-Furay'ah bint Maalik, and Umm Hisham bint Ḥaarithah ibn an-Nu'maan (رضي الله عنه). They were among those who gave their oath of allegiance to the Prophet (ﷺ) under the tree at Ḥudaybiyah. This was *Bay'at ar-Riḍwaan*, which the Prophet (ﷺ) called for when the *mushrikeen* prevented the believers from entering Makkah; the Prophet (ﷺ) had sent 'Uthmaan ibn 'Affaan to Quraysh, and they detained him for so long that the Muslims thought Quraysh had betrayed their trust and killed him. Allah honoured His Messenger and those who were present on this blessed occasion, and He bestowed upon them His pleasure which many die before they can attain it, and beside which all other hopes and aspirations pale into insignificance. Allah (سبحانه وتعالى) revealed *ayat* of the Qur'an on this occasion, which will be recited until heaven and earth pass away:

> "*Allah's Good Pleasure was on the Believers when they swore Fealty to you under the Tree: He knew what was in their hearts, and He sent down Tranquillity to them; and He rewarded them with speedy Victory.*"
>
> *(Qur'an 48: 18)*

Umm al-Mundhir Salma bint Qays was present at *Bay'at ar-Riḍwaan*, and had previously been present at *Bay'at al-Mu'minaat*, hence she was known as *Mubaya'at al-Bay'atayn* (the one who gave two oaths of allegiance). When the Prophet (ﷺ) and his

---

121 *Al-Maghaazi*, 2/301, 310, 316; Adh-Dhahabi, *Taarikh al-Islam*, 2/201; *As-Seerat al-Ḥalabiyah*, 2/545, 546.

Companions went out to besiege Banu Qurayẓah, this great *Ṣaḥaabiyah* (female Companion) went with them, and earned the reward for jihad for the sake of Allah.

Asma' bint Yazeed ibn as-Sakan al-Anṣaariyah took part in the battle of Al-Khandaq with the Prophet (ﷺ). She was also present at Al-Ḥudaybiyah and *Bay'at ar-Riḍwaan* and at the battle of Khaybar. She continued her worthy efforts for the sake of Islam until the Prophet's death, and he died pleased with her. After his death, she never stopped working in support of Islam. In 13 AH, she travelled to Shaam (i.e., Syria, Jordan and Palestine) and was present at the battle of Yarmuk, when she brought water to the thirsty, tended the wounded and encouraged the fighters to stand firm. Yarmuk is one of the most famous battles in which the Muslim women took part alongside the fighting men. The Muslim army was sorely tested, and some of them retreated. The *mujaahid* women were fighting a rear-guard action, rushing towards those who were running away with pieces of wood and stones, urging them to go back and stand firm. Ibn Katheer has recorded the courage of the Muslim women and the important role they played in this battle:

> "The Muslim women fought on this day, and killed a large number of Romans. They struck whoever among the Muslims ran away, and said, 'Where are you going, to leave us at the mercy of these infidels?!' When they told them off in this manner, they had no choice but to return to the fight."[122]

The Muslim women's stance and encouragement played a major role in making the *mujahideen* stand firm until Allah decreed that they would be victorious over the Romans.

---

[122] *Al-Bidayah wan-Nihayah*, 7/13; Ṭabari, *At-Taareekh*, 2/335 and after, (published by Daar al-Kutub al-'Ilmiyah).

On this tremendous day, Asma' bint Yazeed did extremely well, and demonstrated a type of courage that was unknown among many of the men. She went forth into the battle lines, and struck down a number of the *mushrikeen*. Ibn Ḥajar also recorded her bravery:

> "Umm Salaamah al-Anṣaariyah, i.e., Asma' bint Yazeed ibn as-Sakan, was present at Al-Yarmuk. On that day she killed nine Romans with her tent-pole. She lived for a while after that."[123]

It seems that this great heroine spent the rest of her life in Shaam (i.e., Syria, Jordan and Palestine), where the battle of Yarmuk took place, as she went with those of the *Ṣaḥaabah* who went there. She lived until the time of Yazeed ibn Mu'awiyah, and when she passed away, she was buried in the cemetery of *Al-Baab aṣ-Ṣagheer*. Her grave is still there, bearing proud testimony to the jihad of Muslim women for the sake of Allah.[124]

These golden pages of Muslim women's history were written by those virtuous women themselves, through the depth of their faith and the completeness of their understanding of the Muslim woman's mission in life and her duty towards her Lord and her religion. What I have cited represents only a small part of a vast and noble record of rare sacrifice, proud determination, unique talents and deep faith. Undoubtedly, Muslim women today may find in these accounts an example worthy of following, as they seek to form their own modern Islamic character and identity.

---

123 *Al-Iṣaabah*, 4/229; see also *Majma' az-Zawaa'id* by Al-Haythami, who quotes this story, stating that it was narrated by Ṭabaraani and that the men of its isnad are *thiqaat*. See also *Siyar a'laam an-nubala'*, 2/297.

124 *Siyar a'laam an-nubala'*, 2/297.

She is distinguished by her Islamic character and true religion

No doubt, the true Muslim woman is distinguished by her Islamic character, and she is proud of the high status which Islam gave her at a very early stage, before women in other nations attained anything like it. Fifteen centuries ago, Islam proclaimed the full rights of women for the first time in history, and Muslim women enjoyed human rights, centuries before the world had ever heard of human rights organizations, or witnessed any "Declaration of Human Rights."

At that early stage, Islam declared that women were the twin halves of men, as stated in the hadith narrated by Abu Dawood, Tirmidhi, Ad-Darimi and Aḥmad. At a time when the Christian world doubted the humanity of woman and the nature of her soul, the Qur'an declared:

> "*And their Lord has accepted of them, and answered them: 'Never will I suffer to be lost the work of any of you, be he male or female: you are members, one of another.*'" *(Qur'an 3: 195)*

The Prophet (ﷺ) accepted women's oath of Islam and obedience, just as he accepted that of men. The women's *bay'ah* was independent of and separate from that of their menfolk, and was not done as an act of blind obedience. This is a confirmation of the independence of the Muslim woman's identity, and of her competence to bear the responsibility of giving the oath of allegiance and making the commitment to obey Allah and be loyal to Him and His Messenger. All of this happened centuries before the modern world recognized woman's right to freedom of expression and the right to vote independently. This is in addition to other important rights, such as her independent right to own wealth and her freedom from the responsibility to spend on others, even if she is rich, and her equality with men in human worth, education, and general religious and legal duties. A full discussion of the rights which Islam has given to women, and the respect which it has bestowed upon them, is not possible here.

The level of respect, rights and competence attained by the Muslim woman is astonishing for Western women. I remember the comment of an American woman at a lecture given in the United States by the Syrian scholar Shaykh Bahjat al-Bayṭaar on the rights of women in Islam. This lady was amazed at the rights which the Muslim woman had gained fifteen hundred years ago; she stood up and asked, "Is what you say about the Muslim woman and her rights true or is it just propaganda? If it is true then take me to live with you for a while, then let me die!" Many other Western women have also expressed their astonishment at the status and respect given to women in Islam.

The modern Muslim woman, if she understands all this, is also filled with admiration for her true religion; her faith deepens and her conviction of the greatness and perfection of this divine programme for human happiness, the well-being of men and women alike — grows ever stronger. It is sufficient for her to know that, fifteen hundred years ago, Islam achieved more for women in one blow than any other nation has achieved in the twentieth century.

It is sufficient to know that the French Revolution of the late eighteenth century produced a human-rights document entitled "Declaration of the Rights of Men and Citizens." The first clause of this document states: "Men are born free and equal under the laws." There was an attempt to add the words "and women," but this was rejected, and the statement remained confined to men only: "Man is born free, and he should not be enslaved." A century later, the great French scholar Gustave le Bon, in the late nineteenth century and early twentieth century, stated in his book *The Psychology of Peoples* that woman had never been equal to man except in periods of decline; this comment came in his refutation of demands that women should be made equal with men by giving them the same right to vote.

This is how the situation remained until the advent of the League of Nations, following the First World War, and the United Nations Organization following the Second World War. Women's-rights advocates succeeded in stating the equality of women with men only after a great deal of hard work, because they were faced with the obstacle of quasi-religious traditions and customs; they did not have access to any text of national or international law that treated women with any measure of justice, which they could have used to overturn these obstacles and free women from the oppressive legacy of the past. Meanwhile, fifteen hundred years ago, Islam had definitively shown, in the Qur'an and Sunnah, that men and women were equal in terms of reward, punishment, responsibility, worship, human worth and human rights.

When Islam made men and women equal in terms of human rights, it also made them equal in terms of human duties, as they were both charged with the role of *khaleefah* (vicegerent) on earth and were commanded to populate and cultivate it, and to worship Allah therein. Islam gave each of them his or her unique role to play in establishing a righteous human society. These roles are complementary, not opposite, and they apply to every man and woman. Each sex must play the role for which it is better suited and qualified, in order to build solid individuals, families and societies and achieve solidarity, mutual assistance and co-operation between the two sexes, without preventing anyone from doing any permitted deed which he or she wishes to do. Men and women are equally governed by whatever is in the interest of humanity, and both will be rewarded in accordance with their deeds in this life, as Allah (سُبْحَانَهُ وَتَعَالَى) says:

> "*Whoever works righteousness, man or woman, and has Faith, verily, to him will We give a new Life, and life*

> *that is good and pure, and We will bestow on such their reward according to the best of their actions."*
>
> *(Qur'an 16: 97)*

Both men and women are regarded as "shepherds" who are responsible for their "flocks," as is stated in the well-known hadith of the Prophet.

The Muslim woman, who understands the high status which Islam gave her fifteen centuries ago, knows fully well that the position of women in every nation governed by ancient laws was appalling, especially in India and Rome, in the Middle Ages in Europe, and in Arabia prior to the advent of Islam. So, her pride in her Islamic identity, true religion and high human status increases.

The position of women under ancient laws may be summed up in the comment of the Indian leader Jawaharlal Nehru in his book *The Discovery of India*:

> "The legal position of women, according to Manu[125], was undoubtedly very bad. They were always dependent on either a father or a husband or a son."

It is known that inheritance in India always passed from male to male, and excluded females completely.

Nehru commented on this:

> "In any case, the position of women in ancient India was better than that in ancient Greece or Rome, or during the early Christian period."

The position of woman in ancient Roman law was based on a complete denial of her civic rights, and on requiring her to be constantly under the tutelage of a guardian, whether she was a minor or had reached the age of majority, simply because she was female.

---

125 Hindu Mythology: the progenitor and law giver of the human race.

So she was always under her father's or husband's tutelage, and had no freedom whatsoever to do as she wished. In general, she could be inherited, but she had no rights of inheritance.

Under Roman law, a woman was simply one of the possessions of her husband, deprived of her own identity and freedom of conduct. The effects of this law are still visible in the twentieth century, in most of the modern states whose laws are still influenced by Roman law.

As a result of the influences of Roman law, women's position during the early Christian period was as appalling as Nehru suggests. Some religious councils shed doubts on the humanity of woman and the nature of her soul; conferences were held in Rome to debate these matters, and to discuss whether woman possessed souls like men, or were their souls like those of animals such as snakes and dogs? One of these gatherings in Rome even decided that women did not possess a soul at all, and that they would never be resurrected in the afterlife.

In the Arabian Peninsula, most tribes, prior to the advent of Islam, regarded women as something to be despised and abhorred. They were seen as a source of shame, which many would try to avoid by burying infant girls alive as soon as they were born.

Islam condemned this appalling situation of women in more than one place in the Qur'an. Referring to the low esteem in which women were held at the time of *jaahiliyah*, Allah (ﷻ) said:

> "*When news is brought to one of them, of [the birth of] a female [child], his face darkens, and he is filled with inward grief! With shame does he hide himself from his people, because of the bad news he has had! Shall he retain it on [sufferance and] contempt, or bury it in the dust? Ah! What an evil [choice] they decide on!*"
>
> *(Qur'an 16: 58-59)*

Explaining the enormity of the crime of burying alive an innocent infant who has never committed any sin, Allah (ﷻ) says:

> "*When the female [infant], buried alive, is questioned — For what crime she was killed...*" *(Qur'an 81: 8-9)*

Women were in the most appalling and humiliating situations, in which their very humanity was in doubt — especially in the Arab world before the advent of Islam, and in most of the civilized world at that time, in Rome, and during the early Christian period. Most of the modern nation-states are still influenced by Roman law, as is well-known to scholars of law.[126]

The Muslim woman understands the great blessing, which Allah (ﷻ) bestowed upon her the day when the brilliant light of Islam shone upon the Arab world:

> "*This day have I perfected your religion for you, completed My favour upon you, and have chosen for you Islam as your religion.*" *(Qur'an 5: 3)*

The Muslim woman's soul is filled with happiness, contentment and pride, and her status and position are raised by the fact that Islam gives the mother a higher status than the father. A man came to the Prophet (ﷺ) and asked him:

> "O' Messenger of Allah, who among people is most deserving of my good company?" He said, "Your mother." The man asked, "Then who?" The Prophet said, "Your mother." The man asked, "Then who?" The Prophet said, "Your mother." The man asked, "Then who?" The Prophet said, "Then your father."[127]

---

126 Dr. Ma'roof ad-Duwaalibi, *Al-Mar'ah fil-Islam*, p. 23.

127 Bukhari and Muslim, See *Sharḥ as-Sunnah*, 13/4, *Kitaab al-Isti'dhaan, baab birr al-waalidayn.*

Because of the way she is created, the woman is unique in her ability to bear a child, then breast-feed and nurture him, a role that is difficult and involves much hard work, as the Qur'an noted:

> *"And We have enjoined on man [to be good] to his parents: in travail upon travail did his mother bear him, and in years twain was his weaning: [hear the command], 'Show gratitude to Me and to your parents: to Me is [your final] Goal.'"* *(Qur'an 31: 14)*

Just as this heavy burden is placed on women's shoulders, men are given the role of maintaining and protecting the family *qawwamoon* (guardians); they have the duty of earning money and spending on the family. However, many men still do not understand the status of the mother in Islam, as is reflected in the hadith quoted above, in which a man asked the Prophet (ﷺ) who was most deserving of his good company.

Islam raised the status of women by placing the status of the mother above that of the father, and it has also given women the right to keep their own family names after marriage. The Muslim woman keeps her own surname and identity after marriage, and does not take her husband's name, as happens in the West, where the married woman is known by her husband's name as "Mrs. So-and-so," and her maiden name is cancelled from civic records. Thus, Islam preserves the woman's identity after marriage: although the Muslim woman is strongly urged to be a good wife, obeying and respecting her husband, her identity is not to be swallowed up in his.

If we add to this the fact that Islam has given women the right to complete freedom in how they dispose of their own wealth, and that they are not expected to spend on anyone else's upkeep, the high status to which Islam has raised women becomes crystal-clear. Hence, we can understand how much Islam wants women to be free, proud, respected, and able to fulfil their tremendous mission in life.

Her loyalty is to Allah alone

One of the results of the Muslim woman's pride in her Islamic identity is that she will never be loyal to anything or anyone other than Allah, not even her husband or her father, who are among the closest people to her. We see the epitome of this loyalty (*wala'*) in the life of the Prophet's wife Umm Ḥabeebah (ﷺ), Ramlah bint Abi Sufyan, the chief of Makkah and leader of the *mushrikeen*. She was married to the Prophet's cousin (son of his paternal aunt) 'Ubaydullah ibn Jaḥsh al-Asadi, the brother of the Prophet's wife Zaynab. Her husband 'Ubaydullah embraced Islam, and she entered Islam with him, whilst her father Abu Sufyan was still a *kaafir* (disbeliever). She and her husband migrated to Abyssinia with the first Muslims who went there, and left her father in Makkah, boiling with rage because his daughter had embraced Islam and there was no way he could get at her.

But the life of this patient Muslim woman was not free from problems. Sadly, her husband 'Ubaydullah left Islam and became a Christian, joining the religion of the Abyssinians. He tried to make her join him in his apostasy, but she refused and remained steadfast in her faith. She had given birth to her daughter Ḥabeebah, and was now known as Umm Ḥabeebah (may Allah be pleased with her). She withdrew from people, and felt as if she would die of grief and sorrow, because of all the disasters that had befallen her. She and her daughter were alone in a strange land, and all the ties between her and her father and husband had been cut. The father of her small daughter was now a Christian, and the child's grandfather at that time was a *mushrik* and an enemy of Islam who had declared all-out war on the Prophet (ﷺ), in whom she believed, and the religion that she followed.

Nothing could save her from this distress and grief except the care of the Prophet (ﷺ), who was losing sleep over the believers who had migrated, concerned for their welfare and checking on them. He sent word to the Negus to request him to arrange his marriage to Umm Ḥabeebah, the daughter of Abu Sufyan, one of the immigrants to his country, as is explained in the books of *Seerah* (biography) and history. Thus, Umm Ḥabeebah, the daughter of Abu Sufyan, became one of the "Mothers of the Believers."

Time passed, and as the conquest of Makkah drew closer, the threat to Quraysh, who had broken the treaty of Al-Ḥudaybiyah, became ever more apparent. Their leaders met and realized that Muhammad (ﷺ) would never keep quiet about their betrayal or accept the humiliation they had inflicted on him. So they agreed to send an envoy to Madeenah, to negotiate a renewal and extension of the treaty with Muhammad (ﷺ). The man chosen for this task was Abu Sufyan ibn Ḥarb.

Abu Sufyan came to Madeenah, and was nervous about meeting Muhammad (ﷺ). Then he remembered that he had a daughter in the Prophet's household, so he sneaked into her house and asked her to help him achieve what he had come for.

Umm Ḥabeebah (رضي الله عنها) was surprised to see him in her house, as she had not seen him since she had left for Abyssinia. She stood up, filled with confusion, not knowing what to do or say.

Abu Sufyan realised that his daughter was overwhelmed with the shock of his sudden arrival, so he asked for her permission to sit down, and went over to sit on the bed. He was stunned when his daughter Ramlah rushed to grab the mattress and roll it up. He said, "O' my daughter, I do not understand. Is this mattress not good enough for me or am I not good enough for it?" She said, "It belongs to the Messenger of Allah, and you are a *mushrik*, so I do not want you to sit on it."

Ramlah bint Abi Sufyan affirmed her loyalty (*wala'*) to Allah (سبحانه وتعالى). She had no regrets about her worthless husband, who had sold his religion for this world. She remained steadfast in her faith, bearing the pain of grief and loneliness in a strange land, where she was most in need of a husband to protect her and take care of her daughter. Allah, the Munificent Bestower, compensated her with the best that any woman could have hoped for at that time, and made her the wife of the Prophet, and so her status was raised to that of one of the "Mothers of the Believers."

The shock of seeing her father so suddenly after many years did not make her forget her loyalty to Allah and His Messenger. She pulled the Prophet's mattress away from her father because he was a *kaafir*, and she did not want to let him contaminate it by sitting on it. This is the attitude of a Muslim woman who is proud of her religion. Her soul is filled with faith and there is no room for tribalism or loyalty to any other than Allah and His religion.

Throughout history, Muslim women's pride in their Islamic identity gave them the strength and determination to resist temptations and threats, and protected them from being overwhelmed by the forces of *kufr* and falsehood, no matter how powerful these were. The Muslim women's souls were filled with the unquenchable fire of faith, as we see in the steadfastness of Pharaoh's wife, who challenged the entire Pharaonic world with all its temptations and pleasures, caring little about the punishments heaped upon her by her husband because of her faith, and repeating her prayer:

> *"O' my Lord! Build for me, in nearness to You, a mansion in the Garden, and save me from Pharaoh and his doings, and save me from those that do wrong."*
> *(Qur'an 66: 11)*

Seeking the pleasure of Allah and striving to make His word supreme on earth come above any other goals or ambitions. The true Muslim woman never forgets this truth, and as time passes, her pride in her Islamic identity, her devotion to this unique divinely-ordained way of life and her loyalty to Allah go from strength to strength.

She enjoins what is good and forbids what is evil

The Muslim woman who understands her religion reads the *aayah* (verse):

> *"The Believers, men and women, are protectors, one of another: they enjoin what is just, and forbid what is evil: they observe regular prayers, practise regular charity, and obey Allah and His Messenger. On them will Allah pour His Mercy: for Allah is Exalted in Power, Wise."* *(Qur'an 9: 71)*

— which Allah revealed fifteen hundred years ago, and she finds herself on the highest level of intellectual and social status that any woman of any nation or race has ever known. Islam has stated that women are fully human, and are legally competent and independent. There is no difference between women and men when it comes to owning property, buying or selling, or arranging a marriage. This is something which had never previously been the case in any nation, where women were seen as possessions of men, under their tutelage and command. This *aayah*, "*The Believers, men and women, are protectors, one of another...*" raises women to the level of loyalty and friendship with men, and makes them partners in the work of enjoining what is good and forbidding what is evil. Women are responsible for fulfilling this duty on equal terms with men, as both are charged with the duty of populating and cultivating the earth, and worshipping Allah (ﷻ) therein.

Thus, Islam rescued women from their position of being mere chattels of men, which in most cases had given men control over life and death., and raised them to the level of equality and human dignity.

When Islam gave women the duty of enjoining what is good and forbidding what is evil, it gave her the status of a human being who, for the first time in history, was giving orders whereas under other systems she was the one to whom orders were always given.

Islam declared that in the sight of Allah, both sexes were equally qualified to worship Him, and were equally deserving of His mercy. There is a great deal of proof of this in the Qur'an and Sunnah.

Our history is filled with women whose words and deeds reflect their noble Islamic character. They spoke the truth, and felt that they had a responsibility before Allah to do so, and were never afraid to do it.

One example of the strength and maturity of Muslim women's character, and the freedom that they had to express their opinions, is the criticism voiced by a woman who was listening to the *khaleefah* 'Umar ibn al-Khaṭṭab forbidding excessive dowries and advocating that they should be limited to a certain amount. This woman stood up and said, "You have no right to do that, O' 'Umar!" He asked, "Why not?" She said, "Because Allah (ﷻ) says:

> '*But if you decide to take one wife in place of another, even if you had given the latter a whole treasure for dower, take not the least bit of it back; would you take it by slander and a manifest wrong?' (Qur'an 4: 20)*"

'Umar said, "The woman is right, and the man is mistaken."[128]

The *khaleefah* 'Umar listened to this woman, and when it became apparent that she was right, he admitted that she was right, and he was mistaken. Thus a Muslim woman set the earliest historic precedent of criticizing the head of state, and what a head of state! This was the rightly-guided *khaleefah*, the greatest ruler of his age, a man who was feared, the conqueror of Persia and Byzantium. This woman could not have criticized and opposed him if it were not for

---

128 *Fatḥ al-Baari, Kitaab an-Nikaah*; also Shaykh 'Ali aṭ-Ṭanṭaawi, *Akhbaar 'Umar*, p. 393.

her deep understanding of the religion that had given her the right to freedom of expression, and commanded her to enjoin that which was good and forbid that which was evil.

She reads the Qur'an often

In order to reach this high level of obedience, righteousness and *taqwa*, the Muslim woman has no choice but to seek guidance in the blessed Book of Allah, sheltering herself in its shade every day. She should read the Qur'an regularly, reciting it carefully and thinking about the meaning of the *ayat*. Then its meaning may penetrate her mind and emotions, and her heart and soul will be filled with the light of its pure guidance.

It is enough for the Muslim woman to know the status of the one who reads the Qur'an in the sight of Allah, as the Prophet (ﷺ) described it in a number of hadiths. So she should read the Qur'an whenever she has the opportunity, and her days and nights should be filled with recitation of its *ayat* and reflection upon its meaning.

The noble Prophet (ﷺ) said:

> "The likeness of a believer who reads the Qur'an is like a citron, whose smell is pleasant and whose taste is pleasant; the likeness of a believer who does not read the Qur'an is like a date, which has no smell, but its taste is sweet; the likeness of the hypocrite who reads the Qur'an is like a fragrant flower which has a pleasant smell but whose taste is bitter; and the likeness of a hypocrite who does not read the Qur'an is like a colocynth (bitter-apple), which has no smell and its taste is bitter."[129]

---

[129] Bukhari and Muslim, See *Sharḥ as-Sunnah* 4/431, *Kitaab Faḍaa'il al-Qur'an*: *baab faḍl tilaawat al-Qur'an.*

> "Read the Qur'an, for it will come forward on the Day of Resurrection to intercede for its readers."[130]

> "The one who reads the Qur'an fluently is with the honourable pious scribes,[131] and the one who reads the Qur'an and struggles to read it even though it is difficult for him, will receive a double reward."[132]

Knowing this, how can any Muslim woman fail to read the Qur'an, no matter how busy she is with household duties and the role of wife and mother? Can she neglect the Qur'an and deprive herself of its great blessing and the reward which Allah has prepared for those who read it?

In conclusion, this is the attitude of the true Muslim woman towards her Lord: she has deep faith in Allah (ﷻ) and willingly submits to His will and decree; she worships Him sincerely, obeying all His commands and heeding all His prohibitions; she understands what it means to be a true servant of Allah; she constantly strives to support His religion and to make His word supreme on earth; she is proud of her Muslim identity, which draws its strength from her understanding of the purpose of human existence in this life, as defined by Allah (ﷻ) in the Qur'an:

> *"I have only created jinns and men, that they should worship Me Alone."* *(Qur'an 51: 56)*

---

[130] Muslim, 6/90, *Kitaab Ṣalaat al-Musafireen, baab faḍl qira'at al-Qur'an.*

[131] i.e., the angels who record the deeds of man. The meaning is that one who is well-versed in Qur'an will enjoy such a high status in the Hereafter that he will be in the exalted company of these pious scribes. (Translator)

[132] Bukhari and Muslim, See *Sharḥ as-Sunnah*, 4/429, 430, *Kitaab Faḍaa'il al-Qur'an, baab faḍl tilaawat al-Qur'an.*

CHAPTER TWO

The Muslim Woman and Her Own Self

Introduction

Islam encourages the Muslims to stand out among people, readily distinguishable by their dress, appearance and behaviour, so that they will be a good example, worthy of the great message that they bring to humanity. According to the hadith narrated by the great *Ṣaḥaabi* Ibn al-Ḥanẓaliyah (ﷺ), the Prophet (ﷺ) told his Companions (may Allah be pleased with them all), when they were travelling to meet some brothers in faith:

> "You are going to visit your brothers, so repair your saddles and make sure that you are dressed well, so that you will stand out among people like an adornment, for Allah does not love ugliness."[1]

The Prophet (ﷺ) considered an unkempt and careless appearance, and scruffy clothes and furnishings, to be forms of ugliness, which is hated and forbidden by Islam.

Islam encourages Muslims in general to stand out among the people; the Muslim woman, in particular, is encouraged to be distinct from other people in her appearance, because this reflects well on her, and on her husband, family and children.

The Muslim woman does not neglect her appearance, no matter how busy she is with her domestic chores and the duties of motherhood.

---

[1] Abu Dawood, 4/83, *Kitaab al-Libaas, baab ma jaa' fi isbaal al-izaar*; its isnad is *ṣaḥeeḥ*.

She is keen to look good, without going to extremes, because a good appearance is an indication of how well she understands herself, her Islamic identity, and her mission in life. The outward appearance of a woman cannot be separated from her inner nature: a neat, tidy and clean exterior reflects a noble and decent inner character, both of which go to make up the character of the true Muslim woman.

The smart Muslim woman is one who strikes a balance between her external appearance and internal nature. She understands that she is composed of a body, a mind and a soul, and gives each the attention it deserves, without exaggerating in one aspect to the detriment of others. In seeking to strike the right balance, she is following the wise guidance of Islam which encourages her to do so.

How can the Muslim woman achieve this balance between her body, mind and soul?

Her Body

Moderation in food and drink

The Muslim woman takes good care of her body, promoting its good health and strength. She is active, not flabby or overweight. So, she does not eat to excess; she eats just enough to maintain her health and energy. This is in accordance with the guidance of Allah (ﷻ) in the Qur'an:

> "*...Eat and drink: but waste not by excess, for Allah loves not the wasters.*" *(Qur'an 7: 31)*

The Prophet (Blessings and Peace be upon him) also advised moderation in food and drink:

> "There is no worse vessel for the son of Adam to fill than his stomach, but if he must fill it, then let him allow

> one-third for food, one-third for drink, and one-third for air."[2]

'Umar (رضي الله عنه), the Caliph, said:

> "Beware of filling your stomachs with food and drink, for it is harmful to the body and causes sickness and laziness in performing prayers. Be moderate in both food and drink, for that is healthier for your bodies and furthest removed from extravagance. Allah will hate the fat man (one who revels in a life of luxury), and a man will not be condemned until he favours his desires over his religion."[3]

The Muslim woman also steers clear of drugs and stimulants, especially those which are clearly known to be *ḥaraam*. She avoids the bad habits that many women have fallen into in societies that have deviated from the guidance of Allah and His Messenger, such as staying up late at night to waste time in idle pursuits. She goes to sleep early and gets up early to start the day's activities with energy and enthusiasm. She does not weaken her energy with late nights and bad habits; she is always active and efficient, so that her household chores do not exhaust her and she can meet her targets.

She understands that a strong believer is more loved by Allah (سبحانه وتعالى) than a weak believer, as the Prophet (صلى الله عليه وسلم) taught, so she always seeks to strengthen her body by means of a healthy lifestyle.

---

[2] A *ṣaḥeeḥ ḥasan* hadith narrated by Aḥmad, 4/132, and Tirmidhi, 4/18, in *Kitaab az-Zuhd, baab ma jaa' fi karaahiyat katheerat al-akl.*

[3] *Kanz al-'Ummaal*, 15/433. See also the valuable article on the harmful effects of over-filling the stomach on a person's body, mind and soul, by Muhammad Naaẓim Naseemi MD in *Ḥaḍaarat al-Islam*, Nos. 5, 6, from the Sunnah: 15.

She exercises regularly

The Muslim woman does not forget to maintain her physical fitness and energy by following the healthy practices recommended by Islam. But she is not content only with the natural, healthy diet referred to above: she also follows an organized exercise programme, appropriate to her physical condition, weight, age and social status. These exercises give her body agility, beauty, good health, strength and immunity to disease. This will make her more able to carry out her duties, and more fit to fulfil her role in life, whether it be as a wife or mother, young girl or old woman.

Her body and clothes are clean

The Muslim woman who truly follows the teachings of Islam keeps her body and clothes very clean. She bathes frequently, in accordance with the teachings of the Prophet (ﷺ), who advised Muslims to take baths, especially on Fridays.

> "Have a bath on Fridays and wash your heads, even if you are not in a state of *janaabah* (impurity, e.g. following marital relations), and wear perfume."[4]

> "Whoever attends Friday prayer, man or woman, should take a bath (*ghusl*)."[5]

The Prophet (ﷺ) placed such a great emphasis on cleanliness and bathing that some of the Imams considered performing *ghusl* before Friday prayer to be obligatory (*waajib*).

---

[4] *Fatḥ al-Baari*, 2/370, *Kitaab al-Jumu'ah, baab ad-dahn lil-jumu'ah*. Note: The command to wear perfume applies to men only; it is forbidden for women to wear perfume when they go out. (Translator)

[5] A hadith narrated by 'Abdullah ibn 'Umar and recorded as *ṣaḥeeḥ* by Abu 'Awaanah, Ibn Khuzaymah and Ibn Ḥibbaan. See also *Fatḥ al-Baari*, 2/356, *Kitaab al-Jumu'ah, baab faḍl al-ghusl yawm al-jumu'ah.*

Abu Hurayrah (رضي) reported that the Prophet (صلى) said:

> "It is the duty of every Muslim to take a bath (at least)
> once every seven days, and to wash his head and
> body."[6]

Cleanliness is one of the most essential requirements of people, especially women, and one of the clearest indicators of a sound and likeable character. Cleanliness makes a woman more likeable not only to her husband, but also to other women and her relatives.

Imam Ahmad and An-Nasaa'i report that Jaabir (رضي) said:

> "The Messenger of Allah came to visit us, and saw a
> man who was wearing dirty clothes. He said, 'Could
> this person not find anything with which to wash his
> clothes?'"

The Prophet (صلى) hated to see people come out in public wearing dirty clothes when they were able to clean them; he drew attention to the fact that the Muslim should always be clean, smart and pleasing to look at.

This teaching which is directed at men, is directed even more so at women, who are usually thought of as being more clean, the source of joy and tranquillity in the home. There is no doubt that the woman's deep sense of cleanliness reflects on her home, her husband and her children, because it is by virtue of her concern for cleanliness that they will be clean and tidy.

No researcher, of whatever era or country, can fail to notice that this teaching which encourages cleanliness and bathing, came fifteen hundred years ago, at a time when the world knew next to nothing of such hygienic habits. A thousand years later, the non-Muslim world

---

6 *Sharh as-Sunnah*, 2/166, *Kitaab al-Hayd, baab ghusl al-jumu'ah.*

had still not reached the level of cleanliness that the Muslims had reached.

In her book *Min ar-Riqq ila as-Siyaadah* (from Slavery to Sovereignty), Saamiḥah A. Wirdi says:

> "There is no need for us to go back to the time of the Crusades, in order to know the level of civilization in Europe at that time. We need go back no further than a few hundred years, to the days of the Ottoman Empire, and compare between the Ottomans and the Europeans to see what level the Ottoman civilization had reached.
>
> In 1624, Prince Brandeboug wrote the following on the invitations to a banquet that he sent to other princes and nobles:
>
> 'Guests are requested not to plunge their hands up to the elbow in the dishes; not to throw food behind them; not to lick their fingers; not to spit on their plates; and not to blow their noses on the edges of the tablecloths.' The author adds:
>
> 'These words clearly indicate the level of civilization, culture, knowledge and manners among the Europeans. At the same time, in another part of Europe, the situation was not much different. In the palace of the King of England (George I), the ugly smell emanating from the persons of the King and his family overpowered the grandeur of their fine, lace-edged French clothes. This is what was happening in Europe. Meanwhile in Istanbul, the seat of the *khilaafah* (Caliphate), it is well-known that the European ambassadors who were authorized by the Ottoman state would be thrown into baths before they could approach the sultan. Sometime around 1730, during the reign of Sultan Aḥmad III, when the Ottoman state entered its political and military decline, the wife of the English ambassador in Istanbul, Lady Montague, wrote many letters which were later published, in which she described the level of cleanliness, good manners and high standards among

the Muslims. In one of her memoirs, she wrote that the Ottoman princess Ḥafeeẓah had given her a gift of a towel that had been hand-embroidered; she liked it so much that she could not even bear to wipe her mouth with it. The Europeans were particularly astounded by the fact that the Muslims used to wash their hands before and after every meal. It is enough to read the words of the famous English nurse Florence Nightingale, describing English hospitals in the mid-nineteenth century, where she describes how these hospitals were full of squalor, negligence and moral decay, and the wings of these hospitals were full of sick people who could not help answering the call of nature on their beds...'"[7]

What a great contrast there is between the refined civilization of Islam and other human civilizations!

She takes care of her mouth and teeth

The intelligent Muslim woman takes care of her mouth, for no-one should ever have to smell an unpleasant odour coming from it. She does this by cleaning her teeth with a *siwaak*, toothbrush, toothpaste and mouthwash after every meal. She checks her teeth and visits the dentist at least once a year, even if she does not feel any pain, in order to keep her teeth healthy and strong. She consults otolaryngologists (ear, nose and throat doctors) if necessary, so that her breath will remain clean and fresh. This is undoubtedly more befitting for a woman.

'Aa'ishah (رضي الله عنها) used to be very diligent in taking care of her teeth: she never neglected to clean them with a *siwaak*, as Bukhari and Muslim reported from a number of the *Ṣaḥaabah*. Bukhari reported from 'Urwah (رضي الله عنه) via 'Aṭaa':

---

[7] Saamiḥah A. Wirdi, *Min ar-Riqq ila as-Sayaadah*, Damla Yayinevi No. 89, p. 28ff.

> "We heard 'Aa'ishah the Mother of the Believers cleaning her teeth in the room..."[8]

Muslim also reports from 'Urwah (ﷺ) via 'Aṭaa':

> "We heard her using the siwaak..."[9]

'Aa'ishah (ﷺ) said:

> "The Messenger of Allah never woke from sleeping at any time of day or night without cleaning his teeth with a *siwaak* before performing *wuḍoo'*."[10]

The Prophet's concern for oral hygiene was so great that he said:

> "If it were not for the fact that I did not want to overburden my ummah, I would have ordered them to use the *siwaak* before every prayer."[11]

'Aa'ishah (ﷺ) was asked what the Prophet (ﷺ) used to do first when he came home. She said,

> "Use *siwaak*."[12]

It is very strange to see that some Muslim women neglect these matters, which are among the most important elements of a woman's character, besides being at the very heart of Islam.

They are among the most important elements of a woman's gentle nature, and they reveal her feminine elegance and beauty. They are

---

8 *Fatḥ al-Baari*, 3/599, *Kitaab al-'Umrah, baab kam a'tamara an-Nabi* (ﷺ).

9 Muslim, 8/236, *Kitaab al-Ḥajj, baab 'adad 'amar an-Nabi* (ﷺ) *wa zamaanihinna.*

10 A *ḥasan* hadith, narrated by Aḥmad, 6/160, and Abu Dawood, 1/46, in *Kitaab aṭ-Ṭahaarah, baab as-siwaak.*

11 *Fatḥ al-Baari*, 2/374, *Kitaab al-Jumu'ah, baab as-siwaak yawm al-jumu'ah*; Muslim, 3/143, *Kitaab aṭ-Ṭahaarah, baab as-siwaak.*

12 Muslim, 3/143, *Kitaab aṭ-Ṭahaarah, baab as-siwaak.*

also at the heart of Islam, because the Prophet (ﷺ) urged cleanliness on many occasions, and he detested unpleasant odours and ugly appearances. He said:

> "Whoever eats onions, garlic or leeks should not approach our mosque, because whatever offends the sons of Adam may offend the angels."[13]

The Prophet (ﷺ) banned those who had eaten these pungent vegetables from coming anywhere near the mosque, lest the people and the angels be offended by their bad breath, but these smells pale into insignificance beside the stench of dirty clothes, filthy socks, unwashed bodies and unclean mouths that emanates from some careless and unkempt individuals who offend others in gatherings.

She takes care of her hair

The Prophet (ﷺ) also taught Muslims to take care of their hair, and to make it look attractive and beautiful, within the limits of Islamic rulings.

This is reported in the hadith quoted by Abu Dawood from Abu Hurayrah (رضي الله عنه), who said: "The Messenger of Allah (ﷺ) said:

> 'Whoever has hair, let him look after it properly.'"[14]

Looking after one's hair, according to Islamic teaching, involves keeping it clean, combing it, perfuming it, and styling it nicely.

The Prophet (ﷺ) did not like people to leave their hair uncombed and unkempt, so that they looked like wild monsters; he likened such ugliness to the appearance of the *Shayṭaan* (Satan). In *Al-Muwaṭṭa'*, Imam Maalik reports a hadith with a *mursal* isnad from 'Aṭaa' ibn

---

13 Muslim, 5/50, *Kitaab al-Masaajid, baab nahi akil ath-thom wal-baṣal 'an ḥuḍoor al-masjid.*

14 Abu Dawood, 4/108, in *Kitaab at-Tarajjul, baab fi iṣlaaḥ ash-sha'r.*

Yassaar, who said:

> "The Messenger of Allah was in the mosque, when a man with unkempt hair and an untidy beard came in. The Prophet pointed to him, as if indicating to him that he should tidy up his hair and beard. The man went and did so, then returned. The Prophet said, 'Is this not better than that any one of you should come with unkempt hair, looking like the *Shayṭaan*?'"[15]

The Prophet's likening a man with untidy hair to the *Shayṭaan* clearly shows how concerned Islam is with a neat and pleasant appearance, and how opposed it is to scruffiness and ugliness.

The Prophet (ﷺ) always took note of people's appearance, and he never saw a scruffily-dressed man with untidy hair but he criticized him for his self-neglect. Imam Aḥmad and An-Nasaa'i report that Jaabir (رضي الله عنه) said:

> "The Messenger of Allah came to visit us, and he saw an unkempt man whose hair was going in all directions, so he said, 'Could he not find anything with which to calm his head?'"[16]

If this is how the Prophet (ﷺ) taught men to take care of themselves, then how much more applicable are his teachings to women, for whom beauty and elegance are more befitting, as they are the ones to whom men draw close and seek comfort, tranquillity and happiness in their company! It is obvious to the sensitive Muslim woman that the hair is one of the most important features of a woman's beauty and attractiveness.

---

15 *Al-Muwaṭṭa'*, 2/949, *Kitaab ash-Sha'r, baab iṣlaaḥ ash-sha'r.*

16 A *ṣaḥeeḥ* hadith reported by Aḥmad, 3/357; An-Nasaa'i, 8/183, in *Kitaab az-Zeenah, baab taskeen ash-sha'r.*

Good appearance

It is no surprise that the Muslim woman is concerned with her clothes and appearance, without going to extremes or making a wanton display of herself. She presents a pleasing appearance to her husband, children, *maḥram* relatives and other Muslim women, and people feel comfortable with her. She does not put them off with an ugly or untidy appearance. She always checks herself and takes care of herself, in accordance with the teachings of Islam, which asks its followers to look good in ways that are permitted.

In his commentary on the *aayah*:

> "*Say: Who has forbidden the beautiful [gifts] of Allah, which He has produced for His servants, and the things, clean and pure, [which He has provided] for sustenance?...*" *(Qur'an 7: 32)*

Al-Qurṭubi said: "Makḥool reported from 'Aa'ishah (رضي الله عنها):

> 'A group of the Companions of the Prophet were waiting at the door for him, so he prepared to go out to meet them. There was a vessel of water in the house, and he peered into it, smoothing his beard and his hair. ('Aa'ishah said) I asked him, 'O' Messenger of Allah, even you do this?' He said, 'Yes, when a man goes out to meet his brothers, let him prepare himself properly, for Allah is beautiful and loves beauty.'''[17]

The Muslim does all of this in accordance with the Islamic ideal of moderation, avoiding the extremes of either exaggeration or negligence:

---

17 *Tafseer al-Qurṭubi*, 7/197 (7: 32).

> *"Those who, when they spend, are not extravagant and not niggardly, but hold a just [balance] between those [extremes]."* *(Qur'an 25: 67)*

Islam wants its followers, and especially its advocates and missionaries (*da'is*), to stand out in gatherings in an attractive fashion, not to appear unsightly or unbearable. Neglecting one's appearance, to the extent of being offensive to one's companions in the name of asceticism and humility, is not part of Islam. The Prophet (ﷺ), who was the epitome of asceticism and humility, used to dress in decent clothes and present a pleasant appearance to his family and Companions. He regarded dressing well and looking good to be a demonstration of the Blessings of Allah (ﷻ):

> "Allah loves to see the signs of His gifts on His slave."[18]

Ibn Sa'd reports in *Aṭ-Ṭabaqaat* (4/346) that Jundub ibn Makeeth (رضي الله عنه) said:

> "Whenever a delegation came to meet the Messenger of Allah, he would wear his best clothes and order his leading Companions to do likewise. I saw the Prophet on the day that the delegation of Kindah came to meet him; he was wearing a Yemeni garment, and Abu Bakr and 'Umar were dressed similarly."

Ibn al-Mubarak, Ṭabaraani, Al-Ḥaakim, Al-Bayhaqi and others report that 'Umar (رضي الله عنه) said:

> "I saw the Messenger of Allah ask for a new garment. He put it on, and when it reached his knees he said, 'Praise be to Allah, Who has given me clothes with

---

[18] A *ḥasan* hadith narrated by Tirmidhi, 4/206, in *Kitaab al-Isti'dhan, baab athar an-ni'mah 'ala al-'abd.*

which to cover myself and make myself look beautiful in this life.'"[19]

So long as this taking care of one's outward appearance does not go to extremes, then it is part of the beauty that Allah has allowed for His servants and encouraged them to adopt:

> "*O' Children of Adam! Wear your beautiful apparel at every time and place of prayer: eat and drink: but waste not by excess, for Allah loves not the wasters. Say, Who has forbidden the beautiful [gifts] of Allah, which He has produced for His servants, and the things, clean and pure, [which He has provided] for sustenance? Say: They are, in the life of this world, for those who believe, [and] purely for them on the Day of Judgement. Thus do We explain the Signs in detail for those who understand.*" *(Qur'an 7: 31-32)*

Muslim reports from Ibn Mas'ood (رضي الله عنه) that the Prophet (ﷺ) said:

> "No-one who has even an atom's-weight of pride in his heart will enter Paradise." A man asked him, "What if a man likes his clothes and shoes to look good?" (Meaning, is this counted as pride?) The Prophet said: "Allah is beautiful and loves beauty. Pride means denying the truth and looking down on other people."[20]

This is the understanding adopted by the *Ṣaḥaabah* and those who followed them sincerely. Therefore, Imam Abu Ḥaneefah always took care to dress well and to ensure that he smelled clean and fresh, and urged others to do likewise. One day he met a man who used to attend his circle, who was dressed in scruffy clothes. He took him to one side and offered him a thousand *dirhams* with which to smarten

---

[19] *At-Targheeb wat-Tarheeb*, 3/93, *Kitaab al-Libaas waz-Zeenah.*

[20] Muslim, 2/89, *Kitaab al-Eemaan, baab taḥreem al-kibr.*

himself up. The man told him, "I have money; I do not need this." Abu Ḥaneefah admonished him: "Have you not heard the hadith, 'Allah loves to see the signs of His gifts on His servant'? So you have to change yourself, and not appear offensive to your friend."

Naturally, those who call people to Allah (ﷻ) should be better and smarter in appearance than others, so that they will be better able to attract people and make their message reach their hearts.

Indeed, they, unlike others, are required to be like this, even if they do not go out and meet people, because those who proclaim the word of Allah should take care of their appearance and pay attention to the cleanliness of their bodies, clothes, nails and hair. They should do this even if they are in a state of isolation or retreat, in response to the call of the natural inclination of man (*fiṭrah*) which the Prophet (ﷺ) told us about and outlined its requirements:

> "Five things are part of the *fiṭrah*: circumcision, removing the pubic hair, plucking hair from the armpits, cutting the nails, and trimming the moustache."[21]

Taking care of oneself in accordance with this *fiṭrah* is something encouraged by Islam and supported by every person of common sense and good taste.

She does not go to extremes of beautification or make a wanton display of herself

Paying attention to one's appearance should not make a Muslim woman fall into the trap of wanton display (*tabarruj*) and showing her beauty to anyone other than her husband and *maḥram* relatives. She should not upset the balance which is the basis of all Islamic teachings, for the Muslim woman always aims at moderation in all

---

[21] *Fatḥ al-Baari*, 10/334, *Kitaab al-Libaas, baab qaṣṣ ash-shaarib*; Muslim, 3/146, *Kitaab aṭ-Ṭahaarah, baab khiṣaal al-fiṭrah.*

things, and is on the alert to prevent any one aspect of her life from taking over at the expense of another.

She never forgets that Islam, which encourages her to look attractive within the permitted limits, is also the religion that warns her against going to such extremes that she becomes a slave to her appearance, as the hadith says:

> "Wretched is the slave of the *dinaar, dirham* and fancy clothes of velvet and silk! If he is given, he is pleased, and if he is not given, he is displeased."[22]

Our women today, many of whom have been influenced by the international fashion houses to such an extent that a rich woman will not wear an outfit more than once, have fallen into that slavery of which the Prophet (ﷺ) warned and, as a result, they are trapped in the misery of that senseless enslavement to excessively luxurious clothing and accessories. Such women have deviated from the purpose for which mankind was created in this world.

One of the worst excesses that many modern Muslim women have fallen into is the habit of showing off expensive outfits at wedding parties, which have become fashion shows where competition is rife and is taken to extremes far beyond the realms of common sense and moderation. This phenomenon becomes clearest when the bride herself wears all her outfits, which may number as many as ten, one after the other: each time she changes, she comes out and shows it off to the other women present, exactly like the fashion models in the West. It does not even occur to the women among whom this habit is common, that there may be women present who are financially unable to buy such outfits, and who may be feeling depressed and jealous, or even hostile towards the bride and her family, and other rich people. Nothing of this sort would happen if brides were more moderate, and just wore one or two outfits at their wedding parties.

---

22 *Fatḥ al-Baari*, 6/81, *Kitaab al-Jihaad, baab al-ḥiraasah fil-ghazw fi sabeel-Allah.*

This is better than that extravagant showing-off which is contradictory to the balanced, moderate spirit of Islam.

No doubt the Muslim woman who has surrounded herself with the teachings of this great religion is spared and protected from such foolish errors, because she has adopted its principles of moderation.

Her Mind

She takes care of her mind by persuing knowledge

The sensitive Muslim woman takes care of her mind just as she takes care of her body, because the former is no less important than the latter. Long ago, the poet Zuhayr ibn Abi Sulma said: "A man's tongue is half of him, and the other half is his heart; What is left is nothing more than the image of flesh and blood."[23]

This means that a person is essentially composed of his heart and his tongue, in other words what he thinks and what he says. Hence the importance of taking care of one's mind and supplying it with all kinds of beneficial knowledge is quite clear.

The Muslim woman is responsible just as a man is, so she is also required to seek knowledge, whether it is "religious" or "secular", that will be of benefit to her. When she recites the *aayah*:

> "*...But say, O' my Lord! Advance me in knowledge.*"
> *(Qur'an 20: 114)*

And hears the hadith,

> "Seeking knowledge is a duty on every Muslim,"[24]

---

[23] Hashimi (ed.), *Jamharat Ash'aar al-'Arab*, 1/300, published by Daar al-Qalam, 1406 AH.

[24] A *ḥasan* hadith narrated by Ibn Maajah, 1/81, in *Al-Muqaddimah, baab faḍl al-'ulama' wal-hath 'ala ṭalab al-'ilm.*

— she knows that the teachings of the Qur'an and Sunnah are directed at men and women equally, and that she is also obliged to seek the kinds of knowledge that have been made obligatory for individuals and communities (*farḍ 'ayn* and *farḍ kifaayah*) to pursue them from the time that this obligation was made known to the Muslim society.

The Muslim woman understands the high value that has been placed on knowledge since the earliest days of Islam. The women of the Anṣaar asked the Prophet (ﷺ):

> "Appoint a special day for us when we can learn from you, for the men have taken all your time and left nothing for us." He told them, "Your time is in the house of so-and-so (one of the women)." So he came to them at that place and taught them there.[25]

The Muslim women had a keen desire for knowledge, and they never felt too shy to ask questions about the teachings (*aḥkaam*) of Islam, because they were asking about the truth, and,

> "*Allah is not ashamed [to tell you] the truth*"
> *(Qur'an 33: 53).*

Many reports illustrate the confidence and maturity with which the early Muslim women posed questions to the Prophet (ﷺ), this great teacher, seeking to understand their religion more fully.

'Aa'ishah (رضي الله عنها) reported that Asma' bint Yazeed ibn as-Sakan al-Anṣaariyah asked the Prophet (ﷺ) about performing *ghusl* after menstrual period. He said,

> "Let one of you (who has finished her period) take her water and purify herself properly, then pour water over herself, then take a piece of cloth that has been

[25] *Fatḥ al-Baari*, 1/195, *Kitaab al-'Ilm, baab hal yuj'al lin-nisaa' yawm 'ala ḥidah fil-'ilm.*

> perfumed with musk, and clean herself with it." Asma' asked, "How should she clean herself?" The Prophet said, "*Subhaan Allah!* You clean yourself with it!" 'Aa'ishah told her in a whisper, "Wipe away the traces of blood."

Asma' (ﷺ) also asked him about performing *ghusl* when one is in a state of *janaabah*. He said,

> "You should take your water and purify yourself with it properly, and clean yourself all over, then pour water on your head and rub it so that the water reaches the roots of the hair, then pour water all over yourself."[26] 'Aa'ishah said, "How good are the women of the Anṣaar! Shyness did not prevent them from understanding their religion properly."[27]

Umm Sulaym bint Milḥaan, the mother of Anas ibn Maalik, came to the Prophet (ﷺ) and said, "O' Messenger of Allah, Allah is not ashamed (to tell) the truth, so tell me, does a woman have to perform *ghusl* if she has an erotic dream?" The Messenger of Allah (ﷺ) said,

> 'Yes, if she sees water (i.e., a discharge).' Umm Salamah covered her face out of shyness, and said, 'O' Messenger of Allah, could a woman have such a dream?' He said, 'Yes, may your right hand be covered with dust, otherwise how could her child resemble her?'[28]

---

[26] *Fatḥ al-Baari*, 1/414, *Kitaab al-Ḥayḍ, baab dalk al-mar'ah nafsaha idha taṭahharat min al-maḥeeḍ*; Muslim, 4/15, 16, *Kitaab al-Ḥayḍ, baab istiḥbaab isti'maal al-mughtasilah min al-ḥayḍ al-misk.*

[27] *Fatḥ al-Baari*, 1/228, *Kitaab al-'Ilm, baab al-ḥaya' fil-'ilm*; Muslim, 4/16, *Kitaab al-Ḥayḍ, baab ghusl al-mustaḥaaḍah wa ṣalaatiha.*

[28] *Fatḥ al-Baari*, 1/228, *Kitaab al-'Ilm, baab al-ḥaya' fil-'ilm*; Muslim, 3/223, 224, *Kitaab al-Ḥayḍ, baab wujoob al-ghusl 'ala al-mar'ah bi khurooj al-manee minha.*

Muslim reports that Umm Sulaym came to the Prophet (ﷺ), when 'Aa'ishah (رضي الله عنها) was with him, and when Umm Sulaym asked this question, 'Aa'ishah said, "O' Umm Sulaym, you have exposed women's secret, may your right hand be rubbed with dust!" The Prophet (ﷺ) said to 'Aa'ishah,

> "Rather your hand should be rubbed with dust; O' Umm Sulaym, let a woman perform *ghusl* if she saw such a dream."[29]

The women of that unique generation never hesitated to strive to understand their religion; they would put questions directly to the Prophet (ﷺ) about whatever happened to them. If they doubted a person's opinion (*fatwa*), or were not convinced of it, they would enquire further until they were sure that they understood the matter properly. This is the attitude of the wise and intelligent woman. This was the attitude of Subay'ah bint al-Ḥaarith al-Aslamiyah, the wife of Sa'd ibn Khawlah, who was from Banu 'Amir ibn Lu'ayy and had been present at Badr. He died during the Farewell Pilgrimage; she was pregnant, and gave birth shortly after his death. When her *nifaas* (a period of impurity upon delivery) ended, she prepared herself to receive offers of marriage. Abu as-Sanaabil ibn Ba'kak (a man from Banu 'Abd ad-Daar) came to her and said, "Why do I see you preparing to receive offers of marriage? By Allah, you will never get married until four months and ten days have passed."

Subay'ah (later) narrated:

> "When he said this to me, I got dressed and went to see the Messenger of Allah in the evening. I asked him about it, and he told me that my *'iddah* had ended when

[29] Muslim, 3/220, *Kitaab al-Ḥayḍ, baab wujoob al-ghusl 'ala al-mar'ah bi khurooj al-manee minha.*

> I gave birth to my child, and said that I could get married if I wished."[30]

Subay'ah's efforts to understand the *shar'i* (Islamic) ruling precisely represent a blessing and benefit not only for Subay'ah herself, but for all Muslim women until the Day of Judgement. Her hadith was accepted by the majority of earlier and later scholars, above all the four Imams, who said that the *'iddah* (waiting period) of a widowed woman, if she is pregnant, lasts until she gives birth, even if she were to give birth so soon after her husband's death that his body had not yet been washed and prepared for burial, and it becomes permissible for her to re-marry.[31]

What a great service Subay'ah did to the scholars of the Muslim ummah by seeking to understand the *shar'i* rulings precisely and to reach a level of certainty about this issue.

Islam has made the pursuit of knowledge obligatory on women and men alike, as the Prophet (ﷺ) said:

> "Seeking knowledge is a duty on every Muslim."[32]

In other words, it is a duty on every person, man or woman, who utters the words of the *shahaadah* (testimony), so it comes as no surprise to see Muslim women thirsting for knowledge, devoting themselves to its pursuit. Muslim women of all times and places have understood the importance of seeking beneficial knowledge, and the positive effects this has on their own characters and on their children,

---

30 *Fatḥ al-Baari*, 7/310, *Kitaab al-Maghaazi, baab istifta' Subay'ah bint al-Ḥaarith al-Aslamiyah*; Muslim, 10/110, *Kitaab aṭ-Ṭalaaq, baab inqiḍa' 'iddat al-mutawaffa 'anha zawjuha wa ghayruha.*

31 *Sharḥ an-Nawawi li Ṣaḥeeḥ Muslim*, 10/109, *Kitaab aṭ-Ṭalaaq, baab inqiḍa' 'iddat al-mutawaffa 'anha zawjuha bi waḍ' al-ḥaml.*

32 A *ḥasan* hadith, narrated by Ibn Maajah, 1/81, in *Al-Muqaddimah, baab faḍl al-'ulama' wal-haththa 'ala ṭalab al-'ilm.*

families and societies. So they seek knowledge enthusiastically, hoping to learn whatever will benefit them in this world and the next.

What the Muslim woman needs to know

The first thing that the Muslim woman needs to know is how to read the Qur'an properly with *tajweed*, and to understand its meaning. Then she should learn something of the sciences of hadith, the *Seerah* (Biography) of the Prophet (ﷺ), and the history of the women of the *Ṣaḥaabah* (Prophet's companions) and *Taabi'een* (The generation of Muslims following the Ṣaḥabah), who are prominent figures in Islam. She should acquire as much knowledge of *fiqh* (Islamic jurisprudence) as she needs, to ensure that her worship and daily dealings are correct, and she should ensure that she has a sound grasp of the basic principles of her religion.

Then she should direct her attention to her primary specialty in life, which is, to take proper care of her house, husband, family and children, for she is the one whom Allah (ﷻ) has created specially to be a mother and to give tranquillity and happiness to the home. She is the one to whom Islam has given the immense responsibility of raising intelligent and courageous children. Hence, there are many proverbs and sayings nowadays which reflect the woman's influence on the success of her husband and children in their working lives, such as, "Look for the woman," "Behind every great man is a woman," and "The one who rocks the cradle with her right hand rocks the world with her left," etc. No woman can do all of that unless she is open-minded and intelligent, strong of personality and pure of heart. So she is more in need of education, correction and guidance in forming her distinct Islamic personality.

It is unwise for women's education to be precisely the same as that of men. There are some matters that concern women only, that men cannot deal with; and there are matters that concern men only, that women cannot deal with. There are things for which women were created, and others for which men were created, and each person should do that for which he or she was created, as the Prophet (ﷺ) taught. When the Muslim woman seeks to learn and specialize in some field, she should bear in mind the Islamic teachings regarding her intellectual, psychological and social make-up, so that she will prepare herself to fulfil the basic purpose for which she was created, and will become a productive and constructive member of her family, society and ummah, not an imitation of men, competing with them for work and taking up a position among men, as we see in those societies which do not differentiate between males and females in their educational curricula and employment laws.

Whatever a woman's academic specialty is, she tries to understand it thoroughly and do her work perfectly, in accordance with the teachings of the Prophet (ﷺ):

> "Allah loves for any of you, when he does something, to do it well."[33]

Muslim women's achievements in the field of knowledge

The gates of knowledge are open to the Muslim woman, and she may enter whichever of them she chooses, so long as this does not go against her feminine nature, but develops her mind and enhances her emotional growth and maturity. We find that history is full of prominent examples of remarkable women who sought knowledge and became highly proficient.

Foremost among them is the Mother of the Believers 'Aa'ishah (رضي الله عنها), who was the primary source of hadith and knowledge of the sunnah,

---

[33] A *ḥasan* hadith by Al-Bayhaqi in *Shu'ab al-Eemaan*, 4/334, from 'Aa'ishah.

and was the first *faqeehah* (female jurist) in Islam, when she was still a young woman no more than nineteen years of age. Imam az-Zuhri said:

> "If the knowledge of 'Aa'ishah were to be gathered up and compared to the knowledge of all the other wives of the Prophet (ﷺ) and all other women, 'Aa'ishah's knowledge would be greater."[34]

How often did the greatest of the *Ṣaḥaabah* refer to her, to hear the final word on matters of the fundamentals of Islam and precise meanings of the Qur'an!

Her knowledge and deep understanding were not restricted only to matters of religion; she was equally distinguished in poetry, literature, history and medicine, and other branches of knowledge that were known at that time. The *faqeeh* of the Muslims, 'Urwah ibn az-Zubayr, was quoted by his son Hishaam as saying:

> "I have never seen anybody more knowledgeable in *fiqh* or medicine or poetry than 'Aa'ishah."[35]

Imam Muslim reports that she heard her nephew Al-Qaasim ibn Muhammad ibn Abi Bakr (رضي الله عنه) make a grammatical mistake, when he and his (paternal) cousin were talking in front of her, and she told him off for this mistake. Imam Muslim commented on this incident: "Ibn 'Ateeq said,

> 'Al-Qaasim and I were talking in front of 'Aa'ishah, and Al-Qaasim was one who made frequent mistakes in grammar, as his mother was not an Arab. 'Aa'ishah said to him, 'Why do you not speak like this son of my

[34] *Al-Istee'aab*, 4/1883; *Al-Iṣaabah*, 8/140.

[35] *Taarikh aṭ-Ṭabari*: *Ḥawaadith Sanat* 58; *As-Samṭ ath-Thameen*, 82; *Al-Istee'aab*, 4/1885.

> brother? I know where the problem comes from: he was brought up by his mother, and you were brought up by your mother...’”’”[36]

Among the reports in which the books of literature speak of the vast knowledge of ‘Aa’ishah, is that which describes how ‘Aa’ishah bint Ṭalḥah was present in the circle of Hishaam ibn ‘Abdul-Malik, where the *shaykhs* (scholars) of Banu Umayyah were present. They did not mention any point of Arab history, wars and poetry but she did not contribute to the discussion, and no star appeared but she did not name it. Hishaam said to her,

> “As for the first (i.e., knowledge of history etc.), I find nothing strange (in your knowing about it), but where did you get your knowledge about the stars?” She said, “I learnt it from my (maternal) aunt ‘Aa’ishah.”[37]

‘Aa’ishah (رضي الله عنها) had a curious mind and was always eager to learn. Whenever she heard about something she did not know, she would ask about it until she understood it. Her closeness to the Messenger of Allah (ﷺ) meant that she was like a vessel full of knowledge.

Imam Bukhari reports from Abu Mulaykah that ‘Aa’ishah, the wife of the Prophet (ﷺ) never heard anything that she did not know, but she would keep going over it until she understood it. The Prophet said,

> “Whoever is brought to account will be punished.”
> ‘Aa’ishah said: ‘I said, ‘But does Allah not say,
> “*Soon his account will be taken by an easy reckoning.*”
> *(Qur’an 84: 8)*

---

[36] Muslim, 5/47, *Kitaab al-Masaajid, baab karaahat aṣ-ṣalaat bi haḍrat aṭ-ṭa‘aam.*

[37] *Al-Aghaani*, 10/57.

> He said, "That refers to *al-'arḍ* (presentation, when everyone is brought before Allah on the Day of Judgement); but whoever is examined in detail is doomed."[38]

In addition to her great knowledge, 'Aa'ishah was also very eloquent in her speech. When she spoke, she captured the attention of her audience and moved them deeply. This is what made Al-Aḥnaf ibn Qays say:

> "I heard the speeches of Abu Bakr, 'Umar, 'Uthmaan, 'Ali and the *khulafa'* who came after them, but I never heard any speech more eloquent and beautiful than that of 'Aa'ishah."

Moosa ibn Ṭalḥah said: "I never saw anyone more eloquent and pure in speech than 'Aa'ishah."[39]

Another of these brilliant women who achieved high level of knowledge was the daughter of Sa'eed ibn al-Musayyab, the scholar of his age, who refused to marry his daughter to the *khaleefah*, 'Abdul-Malik ibn Marwaan, and instead married her to one of his righteous students, 'Abdullah ibn Wadaa'ah. 'Abdullah went in to his wife, who was one of the most beautiful of people, and one of the most knowledgeable in the Qur'an, Sunnah and the rights and duties of marriage. In the morning, 'Abdullah got up and was preparing to go out. His wife asked him, "Where are you going?" He said, "To the circle of your father Sa'eed ibn al-Musayyab, so that I may learn." She said, "Sit down; I will teach you what Sa'eed knows." For one month, 'Abdullah did not attend Sa'eed's circle, beacuse the knowledge that this beautiful young girl had learned from her father (and was passing on to him) was sufficient.

---

[38] *Fatḥ al-Baari*, 1/196, *Kitaab al-'Ilm, baab man sami'a shay'an fa raaja' ḥatta ya'rifahu.*

[39] Tirmidhi, 5/364, *Kitaab al-Manaaqib, baab min faḍl 'Aa'ishah*; he said that it is *ḥasan ṣaḥeeḥ ghareeb.*

Another of these prominent female scholars was Faṭimah, the daughter of the author of *Tuḥfat al-Fuqahaa'*, 'Ala' ad-Deen as-Samarqandi (d. 539 AH). She was a *faqeehah* (female jurist) and scholar in her own right: she had learned *fiqh* from her father and had memorized his book *At-Tuḥfah*. Her father married her to his student 'Ala' ad-Deen al-Kaasaani, who was highly distinguished in the fields of *al-uṣool* (main issues of Islamic jurisprudence) and *al-furoo'* (sub issues). He wrote a commentary on *Tuḥfat al-Fuqahaa'* entitled *Bada'ai' aṣ-Ṣana'ai'*, and showed it to his *shaykh*, who was delighted with it and accepted it as a *mahr* for his daughter, although he had refused offers of marriage for her from some of the (Muslim) kings of Byzantium. The *fuqaha'* of his time said, "He commentated on his *Tuḥfah* and married his daughter."

Before her marriage, Faṭimah used to issue *fatwa* along with her father, and the *fatwa* would be written in her handwriting and that of her father. After she married the author of *Al-Bada'ai'*, the *fataawa* would appear in her handwriting and that of her father and her husband. Her husband would make mistakes, and she would correct them.[40]

'Aa'ishah, the other wives of the Prophet (ﷺ), the daughter of Sa'eed ibn al-Musayyab, Faṭimah as-Samarqandi and other famous women scholars were not something unique or rare among Muslim women. There were innumerable learned women, who studied every branch of knowledge and became prominent in many fields. Ibn Sa'd devoted a chapter of *Aṭ-Ṭabaqaat* to reports of hadith transmitted by women, in which he mentioned more than seven hundred women who reported hadith from the Prophet (ﷺ), or from the trustworthy narrators among the *Ṣaḥaabah*; from these women in turn, many prominent scholars and Imams also narrated hadith.

Ḥaafiẓ ibn 'Asaakir (d. 571 AH), one of the most reliable narrators of

---

40 *Tuḥfat al-Fuqahaa'*, 1/12.

hadith, who was so trustworthy that he was known as *ḥaafiẓ al-ummah*, counted over eighty women among his *shaykhs* and teachers.[41] If we bear in mind that this scholar never left the eastern part of the Islamic world, and never visited Egypt, North Africa or Andalusia — which were even more crowded with women of knowledge — we will see that the number of learned women he never met was far greater than those from whom he did receive knowledge.

One of the phrases used by scholars in the books of Ḥadith is: "The pious, scholar and trustworthy in the chains of narrations. — so-and-so, the daughter of so-and-so told me..."

Among the names mentioned by Imam Bukhari are: Sitt al-Wuzara' Wazeerah bint Muhammad ibn 'Umar ibn As'ad ibn al-Munajji al-Tunukhiyah and Kareemah bint Aḥmad al-Marooziyah. They are also mentioned by Ibn Ḥajar al-'Asqallani in the introduction to *Fatḥ al-Baari*.[42]

The position of these great women is enhanced by the fact that they were sincere and truthful, far above any hint of suspicion or doubt — a status that many men could not reach. This was noted by Imam al-Ḥaafiẓ adh-Dhahabi in *Mizaan al-I'tidaal*, where he states that he found four thousand men about whose reports he had doubts, then follows that observation with the comment:

> "I have never known of any woman who was accused (of being untrustworthy) or whose hadith was rejected."[43]

The modern Muslim woman, looking at the magnificent heritage of women in Islamic history, is filled with the desire for knowledge, as these prominent women only became famous and renowned throughout history by virtue of their knowledge. Their minds can

---

41 *Ṭabaqaat ash-Shaafi'iyah*, 4/273.

42 *Fatḥ al-Baari*, 1/7.

43 *Mizaan al-I'tidaal*, 3/395.

only be developed, and their characters can only grow in wisdom, maturity and insight, through the acquisition of useful, beneficial and correct knowledge.

She is not superstitious

The knowledgeable Muslim woman avoids all the foolish superstitions and nonsensical myths that tend to fill the minds of ignorant and uneducated women. The Muslim woman, who understands the teachings of her religion, believes that consulting and accepting the words of fortune-tellers, soothsayers, magicians and other purveyors of superstition and myths is one of the major sins that annul the good deeds of the believer and spell doom for him or her in the Hereafter. Muslim reports from some of the wives of the Prophet (ﷺ) that he said:

> "Whoever goes to a fortune-teller and asks him about anything, his prayers will not be accepted for forty days."[44]

Abu Dawood reports the hadith of Abu Hurayrah (رضي الله عنه) in which the Prophet (ﷺ) said:

> "Whoever goes to a fortune-teller and believes in what he says, has disbelieved in that which was revealed to Muhammad."[45]

She never stops reading and studying

The Muslim woman does not let her household duties and the burdens of motherhood prevent her from reading widely, because she

---

44 Muslim, 14/227, *Kitaab as-Salaam, baab taḥreem al-kahanah wa ityan al-kuhhaan.*

45 A *ḥasan* hadith narrated by Abu Dawood, 4/21, *Kitaab aṭ-Ṭibb, baab fil-kaahin.*

understands that reading is the source which will supply her mind with nourishment and knowledge which it needs in order to flourish and grow.

The Muslim woman, who understands that seeking knowledge is a duty required of her by her faith, can never stop nourishing her mind with knowledge, no matter how busy she may be with housework or taking care of her children. She steals the odd moment, here and there, to sit down with a good book, or a useful magazine, so that she may broaden her horizons with some useful academic, social or literary knowledge, thus increasing her intellectual abilities.

Her Soul

The Muslim woman does not neglect to polish her soul through worship, *dhikr* (remembrance of Allah), and reading the Qur'an; she never neglects to perform acts of worship at the appointed times. Just as she takes care of her body and mind, she also takes care of her soul, as she understands that the human being is composed of a body, a mind and a soul, and that all three deserve appropriate attention. A person may be distinguished by the balance he or she strikes between body, mind and soul, so that none is cared for at the expense of another. Striking this balance guarantees the development of a sound, mature and moderate character.

She performs acts of worship regularly and purifies her soul

The Muslim woman pays due attention to her soul and polishes it through worship, doing so with a pure and calm approach that will allow the spiritual meanings to penetrate deep into her being. She removes herself from the hustle and bustle of life, and concentrates on her worship as much as she is able to. When she prays, she does so with calmness of heart and clearness of mind, so that her soul may be refreshed by the meaning of the words of Qur'an, *dhikr* and *tasbeeḥ* that she is mentioning. Then she sits alone for a little while, praising and glorifying Allah, and reciting some *ayat* from His Book, and meditating upon the beautiful meanings of the words she is reciting. She checks her attitude and behaviour every now and then, correcting herself if she has done anything wrong or fallen short in some way. Thus her worship will bring about the desired results of purity of soul, cleansing of her sins, and freeing from the bonds of *Shayṭaan* whose constant whispering may destroy a person. If she makes a mistake or stumbles from the Straight Path, the true Muslim woman soon puts it right, seeks forgiveness from Allah (ﷻ), renounces her sin or error, and repents sincerely. This is the attitude of righteous, Allah-fearing Muslim women:

> "*Those who fear Allah, when a thought of evil from Shayṭaan assaults them, bring Allah to remembrance, when lo! They see aright.*" *(Qur'an 7: 201)*

Therefore, the Prophet (ﷺ) used to tell his Companions:

> "Renew your faith." He was asked, "O' Messenger of Allah, how do we renew our faith?" He said, "By frequently repeating *Laa ilaha ill-Allah* (there is no god except Allah)."[46]

The Muslim woman always seeks the help of Allah in strengthening and purifying her soul by constantly worshipping and remembering Allah (ﷻ), checking herself, and keeping in mind, at all times, what will please Allah. So whatever pleases Him, she does, and what angers Him, she refrains from. Thus, she will remain on the Straight Path, never deviating from it or doing wrong.

---

[46] Aḥmad, 2/359, with a *jayyid* isnad.

She keeps company with righteous people and joins religious gatherings

In order to attain this high status, the Muslim woman chooses righteous, Allah-fearing friends, who will be true friends and offer sincere advice, and will not betray her in word or deed. Good friends have a great influence in keeping a Muslim woman on the Straight Path, and helping her to develop good habits and refined characteristics. A good friend — in most cases — mirrors one's behaviour and attitudes:

> "Do not ask about a man: ask about his friends, for every friend follows his friends."[47]

Mixing with decent people is an indication of one's good lineage and noble aims in life:

> "By mixing with noble people you become one of them, so you should never regard anyone else as a friend."[48]

So it is as essential to choose good friends as it is to avoid doing evil:

> "If you mix with people, make friends with the best of them, do not make friends with the worst of them lest you become like them."[49]

The Muslim woman is keen to attend gatherings where there is discussion of Islam and the greatness of its teachings regarding the individual, family and society, and where those present think of the power of Almighty Allah (ﷻ) and His bountiful blessings to His creation, and encourage one another to obey His commandments, heed His prohibitions and seek refuge with Him. In such gatherings, hearts are softened, souls are purified, and a person's whole being is

---

[47] *'Adiy ibn Zayd al-'Ibaadi* by the author, 172.

[48] Anonymous.

[49] *'Adiy ibn Zayd al-'Ibaadi* by the author, 172.

filled with the joy of faith.

So, 'Abdullah ibn Rawaaḥah (🙲), whenever he met one of the Companions of the Prophet, used to say, "Come, let us believe in our Lord for a while." When the Prophet (🙵) heard about this, he said,

> "May Allah have mercy on Ibn Rawaaḥah, for he loves
> the gatherings that the angels feel proud to attend."[50]

The rightly-guided *khaleefah* 'Umar al-Farooq (🙲) used to make the effort to take a regular break from his many duties and the burden of his position as ruler. He would take the hand of one or two men and say,

> "Come on, let us go and increase our faith," then they would
> remember Allah.[51]

Even 'Umar (🙲), who was so righteous and performed so many acts of worship, felt the need to purify his soul from time to time. He would remove himself for a while from the cares and worries of life, to refresh his soul and cleanse his heart. Likewise, Mu'aadh ibn Jabal (🙲) would often say to his companions, when they were walking, "Let us sit down and believe for a while."[52]

The Muslim is responsible for strengthening his soul and purifying his heart. He must always push himself to attain a higher level, and guard against slipping down:

> *"By the Soul, and the proportion and order given to it;*
> *and by its enlightenment as to its wrong and its right —*
> *truly he succeeds that purifies it, and he fails that*
> *corrupts it!"*   (Qur'an 91: 7-10)

---

[50] Aḥmad, 3/265, with a *ḥasan* isnad.

[51] *Ḥayaat aṣ-Ṣaḥaabah*, 3/329.

[52] Ibid.

So, the Muslim woman is required to choose with care the best friends and attend the best gatherings, so that she will be in an environment which will increase her faith and *taqwa*:

> "*And keep your soul content with those who call on their Lord morning and evening, seeking His Face; and let not your eyes pass beyond them, seeking the pomp and glitter of this Life; nor obey any whose heart We have permitted to neglect the remembrance of Us, one who follows his own desires, whose case has gone beyond all bounds.*" *(Qur'an 18: 28)*

She frequently repeats du'aa' (supplications) described in Ḥadith

Another way in which the Muslim woman may strengthen her soul and connect her heart to Allah (ﷻ) is by repeating the supplications which it is reported that the Prophet (ﷺ) used to say on various occasions. There is a *du'aa'* (supplication) for leaving the house, and others for entering the house, starting to eat, finishing a meal, wearing new clothes, lying down in bed, waking up from sleep, saying farewell to a traveller, welcoming a traveller back home, etc. There is hardly anything that the Prophet (ﷺ) did, that he did not have a *du'aa'* for, through which he asked Allah to bless him in his endeavour, protect him from error, guide him to the truth, decree good for him and safeguard him from evil, as is explained in the books of hadith narrated from the Prophet (ﷺ).[53] He used to teach these *ad'iyah* (supplications) and *adhkaar* (rememberance of Allah)

---

[53] See, for example, *Al-Adhkaar* by An-Nawawi and *Al-Maa'thuraat* by Ḥasan al-Banna'. (Translator's note: English-speaking Muslims who wish to learn *du'aa'* may consult *Selected Prayers* by Jamaal Badawi, which is based largely on *Al-Ma'thuraat* and includes transliterations and translations of many *du'aa'*.)

to his Companions, and encouraged them to repeat them at the appropriate times.

The true Muslim woman is keen to learn these *du'aa'* and *adhkaar*, following the example of the Prophet (ﷺ) and his distinguished Companions, and she keeps repeating them at the appropriate times, as much as she is able. In this way, her heart will remain focused on Allah, her soul will be cleansed and purified, and her *Eemaan* will increase.

The modern Muslim woman is in the utmost need of this spiritual nourishment, to polish her soul and keep her away from the temptations and unhealthy distractions of modern life, that could spell doom for women in societies which have deviated from the guidance of Allah and sent groups of women to Hell, as the Prophet (ﷺ) indicated:

> "I looked into Hell, and saw that the majority of its inhabitants were women."[54]

The Muslim woman who understands the teachings of her religion looks where she is going and strives to increase her good deeds, so that she may be saved from the terrifying trap into which the devils among mankind and jinn in all times and places try to make women fall.

---

[54] Muslim, 17/53, *Kitaab ar-Riqaaq, baab akthar ahl al-jannah al-fuqara' wa akthar ahl an-naar an-nisa'*.

CHAPTER THREE

The Muslim Woman and Her Parents

She treats them with kindness and respect (birr)

One of the main distinguishing characteristics of the true Muslim woman is her respectful and kind treatment to her parents. Islam encourages respect towards and kind treatment of parents in many definitive texts of the Qur'an and Sunnah; any Muslim woman who reads these texts has no choice but to adhere to their teachings and treat her parents with kindness and respect, no matter what the circumstances or the state of the relationship between daughter and parents.

She recognizes their status and knows her duties towards them

From her reading of the Qur'an, the Muslim woman understands the high status to which Allah (ﷻ) has raised parents, and that it is a status which mankind has never known except in Islam, which has placed respect for parents just one step below belief in Allah and true worship of Him. Many *ayat* of the Qur'an describe pleasing one's parents as coming second only to pleasing Allah, and confirm that treating parents well is the best of good deeds after having faith in Allah (ﷻ).

> "*Worship Allah, and join not any partners with Him; and do good to parents...*" *(Qur'an 4: 36)*

So the Muslim woman who truly understands the teachings of her religion is kinder and more respectful towards her parents than any other woman in the world; this does not stop when she leaves the home after marriage and start her own family, and has her own, independent, busy life. Her respect and kindness towards her parents are ongoing and will remain an important part of her behaviour until the end of her life, in accordance with the Qur'anic teaching which has enjoined kind treatment of parents for life, especially when they reach old age and become incapacitated and are most in need of kind words and good care:

> "*Your Lord has decreed that you worship none but Him, and that you be kind to parents. Whether one or both of them attain old age in your life, say not to them a word of contempt, nor repel them, but address them in terms of honour. And, out of kindness, lower to them the wing of humility, and say, 'My Lord! Bestow on them Your Mercy even as they cherished me in childhood.'*"
>
> *(Qur'an 17: 23-24)*

The Muslim woman whose heart has been illuminated with the light of the Qur'anic guidance is always receptive and responsive to this divine instruction, which she reads in the *ayat* (verses) that enjoin good treatment of parents. So her kindness and respect towards them will increase, and she will be even more devoted to serving them. She will do her utmost to please them, even if she has a husband, house, children and other responsibilities of her own:

> "*Worship Allah, and join not any partners with Him; and do good to parents...*" *(Qur'an 4: 36)*

> "*We have enjoined on man kindness to parents...*"
>
> *(Qur'an 29: 8)*

> "*And We have enjoined on man [to be good] to his parents: in travail upon travail did his mother bear him...*" *(Qur'an 31: 14)*

Anyone who looks into the Islamic sources regarding the kind treatment of parents will also find plenty of hadith that reinforce the message of the *ayat* (verses) quoted above and reiterate the virtue of kindness and respect towards one's parents, as well as warning against disobedience or mistreatment of them for any reason whatsoever.

'Abdullah ibn Mas'ood (ﷺ) said:

> "I asked the Prophet, 'Which deed is most liked by Allah?' He said, 'Prayer offered on time.' I asked him, 'Then what?' He said, 'Kindness and respect towards parents.' I asked him, 'Then what?' He said, 'Jihad for the sake of Allah.'"[1]

The Prophet (ﷺ), the great educator, placed kindness and respect towards parents between two of the greatest deeds in Islam: prayer offered on time and jihad for the sake of Allah. Prayer is the pillar or foundation of the faith, and jihad is the pinnacle of Islam. What a high status the Prophet (ﷺ) has given to parents!

A man came to the Prophet (ﷺ) to "make *bay'ah*" and to pledge to undertake *hijrah* and jihad in the hope of receiving reward from Allah (ﷻ). The Prophet (ﷺ) did not rush to accept his *bay'ah*, but asked him,

> "Are either of your parents alive?" The man said, "Yes, both of them." The Prophet asked, "And do you wish to receive reward from Allah?" The man replied, "Yes." So the kind-hearted and compassionate Prophet told him, "Go back to your parents and keep them company in the best possible way."[2]

---

[1] Bukhari and Muslim, See *Sharḥ as-Sunnah*, 2/176, *Kitaab aṣ-Ṣalaat, baab faḍl aṣ-ṣalawaat al-khams.*

[2] Bukhari and Muslim, See *Riyaaḍ uṣ-Ṣaaliḥeen*, 191, *baab birr al-waalidayn.*

According to a report narrated by Bukhari and Muslim, a man came and asked the Prophet (ﷺ) for permission to participate in jihad. He asked him,

> "Are your parents alive?" The man said, "Yes," so the Prophet told him, "So perform jihad by taking care of them."[3]

In the midst of preparing his army for jihad, the Prophet (ﷺ) did not forget the weakness of parents and their claims on their children, so he gently discouraged this volunteer and reminded him to take care of his parents, despite the fact that he needed all the manpower he could get for the forthcoming jihad. This is because he understood the importance of respect and kind treatment of parents, and knew its position in the overall Islamic framework that Allah (ﷻ) has designed for the well being and happiness of mankind.

When the mother of Sa'd ibn Abi Waqqaaṣ objected to her son's embracing Islam, she told him. "Give up Islam, or I will go on hunger strike until I die. Then you will feel shame before the Arabs, as they will say that he killed his mother." Sa'd told her, "You should know that, by Allah, even if you had a hundred souls, and they left your body one by one, I would never give up Islam." Then Allah (ﷻ) revealed an *aayah* (verse) which the Prophet (ﷺ) recited to the Muslims, in which Sa'd was rebuked for the harshness of his reply to his mother:

> "*But if they strive to make you join in worship with Me things of which you have no knowledge, obey them not; yet bear them company in this life with justice [and consideration]...*" *(Qur'an 31: 15)*

The story of the devoted worshipper Jurayj (an ascetic of the children of Israel), which was told by the Prophet (ﷺ), is a vivid illustration of

---

[3] *Riyaaḍ uṣ-Ṣaaliḥeen*, 191, *baab birr al-waalidayn.*

the importance of respecting one's parents and being quick to obey them. One day his mother called him whilst he was praying, and he wondered, "My Lord, my mother or my prayer?" He chose to continue his prayer (rather than answering his mother). She called him a second time, but he continued praying and did not answer her. Then she called him a third time, and when he did not respond she prayed to Allah (ﷻ) not to let him die until he had seen the face of a prostitute. There was a prostitute in that locality who had committed adultery with a shepherd and became pregnant. When she realised that she was with child, the shepherd told her: "If you are asked about the father of the baby, say it is Jurayj, the devoted worshipper." This is what she said, so the people went and destroyed the place where he used to pray. The ruler brought him to the public square, and on the way Jurayj remembered his mother's prayer and smiled. When he was brought forth to be punished, he asked for permission to pray two *rak'ahs* (units), then he asked for the infant to be brought forth and whispered in his ear, "Who is your father?" The infant said, "My father is so-and-so, the shepherd."[4] The people exclaimed "*Laa ilaha illa-Allah*" and "*Allahu Akbar!*" They told Jurayj, "We will rebuild your prayer-place with silver and gold!" He said, "No, just rebuild it as it was, with bricks and mortar."

Concerning this story, which is reported by Bukhari, the Prophet (ﷺ) said:

> "If Jurayj had had sound knowledge, he would have known that answering his mother was more important than continuing his prayer."[5]

---

[4] This child is one of the three who spoke in the cradle. The other two are 'Eesa ibn Maryam (Jesus the son of Mary) and the child who was with his mother among the people of *Al-Ukhdud* (the ditch). (Author)

[5] *Fatḥ al-Baari*, 3/78, *Kitaab al-'Amal fiṣ-Ṣalaah, baab idha da'at al-umm waladaha fiṣ-ṣalaat*, and 5/136, *Kitaab al-Maẓaalim, baab idha hadama ḥaa'iṭan falyabni ghayrahu.*

Hence, the *fuqahaa'* suggested that if one is praying a *nafl* prayer and any of his/her parents calls, he/she is obliged to stop the prayer and answer them.

The duty to treat one's parents with kindness and respect sunk into the consciousness of the Muslims, so they hastened to treat their parents well both during their lives and after their deaths. There are many reports and hadiths that indicate this, for example the report that describes how a woman of Juhaynah came to the Prophet (ﷺ) and said:

> "My mother made a vow (*nadhr*) to perform Ḥajj but she did not perform Ḥajj before she died. May I perform Ḥajj on her behalf?" He said, "Yes, go and perform Ḥajj on her behalf. If you knew that your mother had a debt, would you not pay it off for her? Pay off what is due to Allah, for Allah has more right to be paid off."[6]

According to another report given by Muslim, she asked,

> "She owed a month's fasting, so may I fast on her behalf?" The Prophet said, "Fast on her behalf." She said, "She never performed Ḥajj, so may I perform Ḥajj on her behalf?" He said, "Perform Ḥajj on her behalf."[7]

She is kind and respectful towards her parents even if they are not Muslims

The Prophet (ﷺ) raised his teachings to a new peak when he enjoined his followers to treat their parents with kindness and respect, even if they were adherents of a religion other than Islam. This is clear from

---

6 *Fatḥ al-Baari*, 4/64, *Kitaab Juz' aṣ-ṣayd, baab al-ḥajj wan-nudhoor.*

7 Muslim, 8/25, *Kitaab aṣ-Ṣiyaam, baab qaḍa' aṣ-ṣawm 'an al-mayyit.*

the hadith of Asma' bint Abi Bakr aṣ-Ṣiddeeq, who said:

> "My mother came to me, and she was a *mushrik* (pagan, unbeliever) at the time of the Prophet. I asked the Prophet, 'My mother has come to me and needs my help, so should I help her?' He said, 'Yes, keep in touch with your mother and help her.'"[8]

The true Muslim, who understands the meaning of this Qur'anic guidance and the teachings of the Prophet (ﷺ), cannot but be the best and kindest of all people towards his parents at all times. This is the practice of the *Ṣaḥaabah* (Companions of the Prophet) and those who followed them sincerely. A man asked Sa'eed ibn Musayyab (رضي الله عنه): "I understood all of the *aayah* about kindness and respect towards parents, apart from the phrase '*but address them in terms of honour.*' How can I address them in terms of honour?" Sa'eed replied: "It means that you should address them as a servant addresses his master." Ibn Sireen (رضي الله عنه) used to speak to his mother in a soft voice, like that of a sick person, out of respect for her.

She is extremely reluctant to disobey them

Just as the Muslim woman hastens to treat her parents with kindness and respect, she is also afraid to commit the sin of disobeying them, because she realises the enormity of this sin which is counted as one of the major sins (*al-kabaa'ir*). She is aware of the frightening picture which Islam paints of the one who disobeys her parents, and this stirs her conscience and softens any hardness of heart or harsh feelings that she might be harbouring.

Islam draws a comparison between disobedience towards one's parents and the crime of associating partners with Allah, just as it

---

[8] Bukhari and Muslim, See *Sharḥ as-Sunnah*, 13/13, *Kitaab al-Birr waṣ-Ṣilah, baab ṣilat al-waalid al-mushrik.*

establishes a link between true faith in Allah and respectful treatment of parents. Disobedience to one's parents is a heinous crime, which the true Muslim woman is loath to commit, for it is the greatest of major sins and the worst of errors.

Abu Bakrah Nufay' ibn al-Ḥarith said:

> "The Messenger of Allah asked us three times, 'Shall I tell you the greatest sins?' We said, 'Yes, O' Messenger of Allah.' He said, 'Associating partners with Allah and disobeying one's parents.'"[9]

Her mother comes first, then her father

Islam has encouraged respect and kindness towards parents. Some texts deal with the mother and father separately, but taken all together, the texts enjoin a healthy balance in children's attention to their parents, so that respect to one parent will not be at the expense of the other. Some texts further confirm that the mother should be given precedence over the father.

So, as we have seen, when a man came to give *bay'ah* and pledge to take part in jihad, the Prophet (ﷺ) asked him, "Are either of your parents alive?" This indicates that the Muslim is obliged to treat both parents equally well. Similarly, Asma' was ordered to keep in contact with her *mushrikah* (idolateress) mother.

A man came to the Prophet (ﷺ) and asked him,

> "O' Messenger of Allah, who among people is most deserving of my good company?" He said, "Your mother." The man asked, "Then who?" The Prophet said, "Your mother." The man asked, "Then who?" The

---

[9] Bukhari and Muslim, See *Sharḥ as-Sunnah*, 13/15, *Kitaab al-Birr waṣ-Ṣilah, baab taḥreem al-'uqooq.*

> Prophet said, "Your mother." The man asked, "Then who?" The Prophet said, "Then your father."[10]

This hadith confirms that the Prophet (ﷺ) gave precedence to kind treatment of one's mother over kind treatment of one's father, and the *Ṣaḥaabah* used to remind the Muslims of this after the death of the Prophet (ﷺ). Ibn 'Abbaas, a great scholar and *faqeeh* of this ummah, considered kind treatment of one's mother to be the best deed to bring one closer to Allah. A man came to him and said, "I asked for a woman's hand in marriage, and she refused me. Someone else asked for her hand and she accepted and married him. I felt jealous, so I killed her. Will my repentance be accepted?" Ibn 'Abbaas asked, "Is your mother still alive?" He said, "No." So he told him, "Repent to Allah and do your best to draw close to Him."

'Aṭaa' ibn Yasaar, who narrated this report from Ibn 'Abbaas, said:

> "I went and asked Ibn 'Abbaas, 'Why did you ask him if his mother was still alive?' He said, 'Because I know of no other deed that brings people closer to Allah than kind treatment and respect towards one's mother.'"[11]

Imam Bukhari opens his book *Al-Adab al-Mufrad* with a chapter on respect and kindness towards parents (*birr al-waalidayn*), in which he places the section on good treatment of the mother before that on good treatment of the father, consistent with the teachings of the Prophet (ﷺ).

The Qur'an evokes feelings of love and respect in the heart of the child, and encourages him or her to treat parents well. It refers to the mother being given precedence because of pregnancy and breast-feeding, and the pains and trials that she suffers during these two

---

[10] Bukhari and Muslim, See *Sharḥ as-Sunnah*, 13/4, *Kitaab al-Birr waṣ-Ṣilah, baab birr al-waalidayn.*

[11] Bukhari: *Al-Adab al-Mufrad*, 1/45, *baab birr al-umm.*

stages, in a most gentle and compassionate way. It recognizes her noble sacrifice and great tenderness and care:

> "*And We have enjoined on man [to be good] to his parents: in travail upon travail did his mother bear him, and in years twain was his weaning: [hear the command]: 'Show gratitude to Me and to your parents: to Me is [your final] Goal.*" *(Qur'an 31: 14)*

What a supreme teaching! What humane, compassionate direction: "*Show gratitude to Me and to your parents.*" Showing gratitude to parents for what they have done for their child comes second only to showing gratitude to Allah, and is one of the best righteous deeds. What a high status this religion gives to parents!

Ibn 'Umar saw a Yemeni man circumambulating the Ka'bah, carrying his mother. The man said to him,

> "I am like a tame camel for her: I have carried her more than she carried me. Do you think I have paid her back, O' Ibn 'Umar?" He replied, "No, not even one contraction!"[12]

Every time 'Umar ibn al-Khaṭṭab (ﷺ) saw the reinforcements from Yemen, he asked them, "Is Uways ibn 'Aamir among you?" — until he found Uways. He asked him, "Are you Uways ibn 'Aamir?" Uways said, "Yes." 'Umar asked, "Are you from the clan of Muraad in the tribe of Qaran?" Uways said, "Yes." 'Umar asked, "Did you have leprosy, then you were cured of it except for an area the size of a *dirham*? Uways said, "Yes." 'Umar asked, "Do you have a mother?" Uways said, "Yes." 'Umar said: "I heard the Messenger of Allah (ﷺ) say:

[12] Bukhari: *Al-Adab al-Mufrad*, 1/62, *baab jaza' al-waalidayn.*

'There will come to you with the reinforcements from Yemen a man called Uways ibn 'Aamir of the clan of Muraad from the tribe of Qaran. He had leprosy but has been cured of it except for a spot the size of a *dirham*. He has a mother, and he has always treated her with kindness and respect. If he prays to Allah, Allah will fulfil his wish. If you can ask him to pray for forgiveness for you, then do so.' So ask Allah to forgive me. Uways asked Allah to forgive him, then 'Umar asked him, "Where are you going?" Uways said, "To Koofah." 'Umar said, "Shall I write a letter of recommendation for you to the governor there?" Uways said, "I prefer to be anonymous among the people."[13]

What a high status Uways reached by virtue of his kindness and respect towards his mother, so that the Prophet (ﷺ) recommended his *Ṣaḥaabah* to seek him out and ask him to pray for them!

All of this indicates the high status to which Islam has raised the position of motherhood, and given the mother precedence over the father. At the same time, Islam has given importance to both parents, and has enjoined kindness and respect to both.

A woman may enjoy a life of ease and luxury in her husband's home, and may be kept so busy with her husband and growing children that she has little time to spare for her parents, and neglects to check on them and treat them well.

But the true Muslim woman is safe from such errors, as she reads the recommendations of the Qur'an and Sunnah concerning parents. So she pays attention to them, constantly checking on them and

---

[13] Muslim, 16/95, *Kitaab Faḍaa'il aṣ-Ṣaḥaabah, baab min faḍaa'il Uways al-Qarani.*

hastening to treat them well, as much as her energy, time and circumstances permit, and as much as she can.

She treats them kindly

The Muslim woman who has embraced the values of Islam is kind and respectful towards her parents, treating them well and choosing the best ways to speak to them and deal with them. She speaks to them with all politeness and respect, and surrounds them with all honour and care, lowering to them the wing of humility, as commanded by Allah (ﷻ) in the Qur'an. She never utters a word of contempt or complaint to them, no matter what the circumstances, always heeding the words of Allah:

> "*Your Lord has decreed that you worship none but Him, and that you be kind to parents. Whether one or both of them attain old age in your life, say not to them a word of contempt, nor repel them, but address them in terms of honour. And, out of kindness, lower to them the wing of humility, and say: 'My Lord! Bestow on them Your mercy even as they cherished me in childhood.'*"
>
> *(Qur'an 17: 23-24)*

If one or both parents are deviating from true Islam in some way, the dutiful Muslim daughter should, in this case, approach them in a gentle and sensitive manner, so as to dissuade them from their error. She should not condemn them harshly, but should try to convince them with solid proof, sound logic, wise words and patience, until they turn to the truth in which she believes.

The Muslim woman is required to treat her parents well, even if they are *mushrikeen*. She does not forget that she is obliged to treat them well in spite of their *shirk*. Although she knows that *shirk* is the worst of major sins, this does not prevent her from treating her parents well according to the uniquely tolerant shari'ah of Islam:

> *"And We have enjoined on man [to be good] to his parents: in travail upon travail did his mother bear him, and in years twain was his weaning: [hear the command], 'Show gratitude to Me and to your parents: to Me is [your final] Goal.' But if they strive to make you join in worship with Me things of which you have no knowledge, obey them not; yet bear them company in this life with justice [and consideration], and follow the way of those who turn to Me [in love]: in the End the return of you all is to Me, and I will tell you the truth [and meaning] of all that you did."*
>
> *(Qur'an 31: 14-15)*

Kindness and respect towards parents is an important matter in Islam, because it springs from the strongest of human ties, the bond of a child to his or her mother and father. But this bond, great as it is, must come second to the bonds of faith. If the parents are *mushrikeen*, and order their son or daughter to join them in their *shirk*, then the child must not obey them. There is no obedience to a created being in disobeying the Creator; no other bond may supersede that of faith and belief in Allah. However, children are still obliged to honour and take care of their parents.

The Muslim woman is kind and respectful towards her parents in all circumstances, and she spares no effort to make them happy, as much as she can and within the limits of Islam. So she checks on them from time to time, offers her services, visits them often and greets them with a cheerful smile, a loving heart, delightful gifts and words of kindness.

This is how she cares for them during their lives. After their death, she shows her love and respect by praying for them, giving charity on their behalf, and paying off whatever debts they may owe to Allah (سبحانه وتعالى) or to other people.

Treating parents with kindness and respect is one of the essential attitudes of Muslim men and women. This noble attitude should be ongoing and should continue, no matter how complicated life becomes, no matter how high the cost of living rises, and no matter how many burdens or responsibilities a person has.

This attitude is an indication of the rich emotions that still exist in Muslim lands, *Al-Ḥamdu-lillah* (Praise Be to Allah), and it is a proof of the gratitude which Muslim men and women feel towards the older generation, which has made so many sacrifices for them when they themselves were most in need of kind words, consolation and a helping hand.

This attitude will protect a person, man or woman, from hard-heartedness and ingratitude. What is more, it will open to them the gates of Paradise.

CHAPTER FOUR

The Muslim Woman and Her Husband

Marriage in Islam

In Islam, marriage is a blessed contract between a man and a woman, in which each becomes "permitted" to the other, and they begin the long journey of life in a spirit of love, co-operation, harmony and tolerance, where each feels at ease with the other, and finds tranquillity, contentment and comfort in the company of the other. The Qur'an has described this relationship between men and women, which brings love, harmony, trust and compassion, in the most moving and eloquent terms:

> "*And among His Signs is this, that He created for you mates from among yourselves, that you may dwell in tranquillity with them, and He has put love and mercy between your [hearts]...*" *(Qur'an 30: 21)*

This is the strongest of bonds, in which Allah (ﷻ) unites the two Muslim partners, who come together on the basis of love, understanding, co-operation and mutual advice, and establish a Muslim family in which children will live and grow up, and they will develop the good character and behaviour taught by Islam. The Muslim family is the strongest component of a Muslim society when its members are productive and constructive, helping and encouraging one another to be good and righteous, and competing with one another in good works.

The righteous woman is the pillar, cornerstone and foundation of the Muslim family. She is seen as the greatest joy in a man's life, as the Prophet (ﷺ) said:

> "This world is just temporary conveniences, and the best comfort in this world is a righteous woman."[1]

A righteous woman is the greatest blessing that Allah can give to a man, for with her he can find comfort and rest after the exhausting struggle of earning a living. With his wife, he can find incomparable tranquillity and pleasure.

How can a woman be the best comfort in this world? How can she be a successful woman, true to her own femininity, and honoured and loved? This is what will be explained in the following pages.

She chooses a good husband

One of the ways in which Islam has honoured woman is by giving her the right to choose her husband. Her parents have no right to force her to marry someone she dislikes. The Muslim woman knows this right, but she does not reject the advice and guidance of her parents when a potential suitor comes along, because they have her best interests at heart, and they have more experience of life and people. At the same time, she does not forego this right because of her father's wishes that may make him force his daughter into a marriage with someone she dislikes.

There are many texts that support the woman in this sensitive issue, for example the report quoted by Imam Bukhari from Al-Khansaa' bint Khidaam:

> "My father married me to his nephew, and I did not like this match, so I complained to the Messenger of Allah. He said to me: 'Accept what your father has arranged.' I said, 'I do not wish to accept what my father has arranged.' He said, 'Then this marriage is invalid, go

---

[1] Muslim, 10/56, *Kitaab ar-Riḍa', baab istiḥbaab nikaah al-bikr.*

> and marry whomever you wish.' I said, 'I have accepted what my father has arranged, but I wanted women to know that fathers have no right in their daughter's matters (i.e. they have no right to force a marriage on them).'"[2]

At first, the Prophet (ﷺ) told Al-Khansaa' to obey her father, and this is as it should be, because the concern of fathers for their daughters' well-being is well-known. But when he realized that her father wanted to force her into a marriage she did not want, he gave her the freedom to choose, and saved her from the oppression of a father who wanted to force her into an unwanted marriage.

Islam does not want to impose an unbearable burden on women by forcing them to marry a man they dislike, because it wants marriages to be successful, based on compatibility between the partners; there should be common ground between them in terms of physical looks, attitudes, habits, inclinations and aspirations. If something goes wrong, and the woman feels that she cannot love her husband sincerely, and fears that she may commit the sin of disobeying and opposing the husband whom she does not love, then she may ask for a divorce. This is confirmed by the report in which the wife of Thaabit ibn Qays ibn Shammaas, Jameelah the sister of 'Abdullah ibn Ubayy, came to the Prophet (ﷺ) and said: "O' Messenger of Allah, I have nothing against Thaabit ibn Qays as regards his religion or his behaviour, but I hate to commit any act of *kufr* when I am a Muslim. The Prophet (ﷺ) said:

> "Will you give his garden back to him?" — her *mahr* (dower) had been a garden. She said, "Yes." So the Messenger of Allah sent word to him: "Take back your

---

[2] *Fatḥ al-Baari*, 9/194, *Kitaab an-Nikaah, baab ikraah al-bint 'ala az-zawaaj*; Ibn Maajah, 1/602, *Kitaab an-Nikaah, baab man zawwaja ibnatahu wa hiya kaarihah; Al-Mabsooṭ* 5/2.

> garden, and give her one pronouncement of divorce."[3]

According to another report given by Bukhari from Ibn 'Abbaas, she said,

> "I do not blame Thaabit for anything with regard to his religion or his behaviour, but I do not like him."

Islam has protected woman's pride and humanity, and has respected her wishes with regard to the choice of a husband with whom she will spend the rest of her life. It is not acceptable for anyone, no matter who he is, to force a woman into a marriage with a man she does not like.

There is no clearer indication of this than the story of Bareerah, an Ethiopian slave-girl who belonged to 'Utbah ibn Abu Lahab, who forced her to marry another slave whose name was Mugheeth. She would never have accepted him as a husband if she had been in control of her own affairs. 'Aa'ishah (ﷺ) took pity on her, so she bought her and set her free. Then this young woman felt that she was free and in control of her own affairs, and that she could take a decision about her marriage. She asked her husband for a divorce. Her husband used to follow her, weeping, whilst she rejected him. Bukhari quotes Ibn 'Abbaas describing this freed woman who insisted on the annulment of her marriage to someone she did not love; the big-hearted Prophet (ﷺ) commented on this moving sight, and sought to intervene. Ibn 'Abbaas said:

> "Bareerah's husband was a slave, who was known as Mugheeth. I can almost see him, running after her and crying, with tears running down onto his beard. The Prophet said to 'Abbaas, 'O 'Abbaas, do you not find it strange, how much Mugeeth loves Bareerah, and how much Bareerah hates Mugheeth?' The Prophet said (to

---

[3] *Fatḥ al-Baari*, 9/395, *Kitaab aṭ-Ṭalaaq, baab al-khul'*.

> Bareerah), 'Why do you not go back to him?' She said, 'O' Messenger of Allah, are you commanding me to do so?' He said, 'I am merely trying to intervene on his behalf.' She said, 'I have no need of him.'"[4]

The Prophet (ﷺ) was deeply moved by this display of human emotion: deep and overwhelming love on the part of the husband, and equally powerful hatred on the part of the wife. He could not help but remind the wife, and ask her why she did not go back to him, as he was her husband and the father of her child. This believing woman asked him whether he was ordering her to do so: was this a command, a binding obligation? The Prophet (ﷺ), this great law-giver and educator, replied that he was merely trying to intercede and bring about reconciliation if possible; he was not trying to force anybody to do something they did not wish to.

Let those stubborn, hard-hearted fathers who oppress their own daughters listen to the teaching of the Prophet (ﷺ)!

The Muslim woman who understands the teachings of her religion has wise and correct standards when it comes to choosing a husband. She does not concern herself just with good looks, high status, a luxurious lifestyle or any of the other things that usually attract women. She looks into his level of religious commitment and his attitude and behaviour, because these are the pillars of a successful marriage, and the best features of a husband. Islamic teaching indicates the importance of these qualities in a potential husband, as Islam obliges a woman to accept the proposal of anyone who has these qualities, lest *fitnah* and corruption become widespread in society:

> "If there comes to you one with whose religion and attitude you are satisfied, then give your daughter to him

---

[4] *Fatḥ al-Baari*, 9/408, *Kitaab aṭ-Ṭalaaq, baab shafa'at an-Nabi fi zawj Bareerah.*

> in marriage, for if you do not do so, *fitnah* and mischief will become widespread on earth."[5]

Just as the true Muslim young man will not be attracted to the pretty girls who have grown up in a bad environment, so the Muslim young woman who is guided by her religion will not be attracted to stupid "play-boy" types, no matter how handsome they may be. Rather, she will be attracted to the serious, educated, believing man who is clean-living and pure of heart, whose behaviour is good and whose understanding of religion is sound. No-one is a suitable partner for the good, believing woman except a good, believing man; and no-one is a suitable partner for the wayward, immoral woman but a wayward, immoral man, as Allah (ﷻ) has said:

> "*Women impure are for men impure, and men impure for women impure, and women of purity are for men of purity, and men of purity are for women of purity...*"
>
> *(Qur'an 24: 26)*

This does not mean that the Muslim woman should completely ignore the matter of physical appearance, and put up with unattractiveness or ugliness. It is her right — as stated above — to marry a man for whom her heart may be filled with love, and who is pleasing to her both in his appearance and in his conduct. Appearance should not be neglected at the expense of inner nature, or vice versa. A woman should choose a man who is attractive to her in all aspects, one who will gain her admiration and respect. The true Muslim woman is never dazzled by outward appearances, and she never lets them distract her from seeing the essence of a potential spouse.

The Muslim woman knows that the man has the right of *qiwaamah* over her, as the Qur'an says:

---

[5] A *ḥasan* hadith narrated by Tirmidhi, 2/274, *Abwaab an-Nikaaḥ*, 3; Ibn Maajah, 1/633, *Kitaab an-Nikaaḥ, baab al-akfaa'*.

> "*Men are the protectors and maintainers [qawwaa-moon] of women, because Allah has given the one more [strength] than the other, and because they support them from their means...*" *(Qur'an 4: 34)*

Hence, she wants to marry a man of whose *qiwaamah* over her she will feel proud, one whom she will be happy to marry and never regret it. She wants a man who will take her hand in his and set out to fulfil their life's mission of establishing a Muslim family and raising a new generation of intelligent and caring children, in an atmosphere of love and harmony, which will not be impeded by conflicting attitudes or religious differences. Believing men and believing women are supposed to walk side-by-side in the journey of life, which is a serious matter for the believer, so that they may fulfil the great mission with which Allah (ﷻ) has entrusted mankind, men and women alike, as the Qur'an says:

> "*For Muslim men and women — for believing men and women, for devout men and women, for true men and women, for men and women who are patient and constant, for men and women who humble themselves, for men and women who give in charity, for men and women who fast [and deny themselves], for men and women who guard their chastity, and for men and women who engage much in Allah's praise — for them has Allah prepared forgiveness and great reward.*"
>
> *(Qur'an 33: 35)*

In order to achieve this great goal of strengthening the marriage bond, and establishing a stable family life, it is essential to choose the right partner in the first place.

Among the great Muslim women who are known for their strength of character, lofty aspirations and far-sightedness in their choice of a husband, is Umm Sulaym bint Milḥaan, who was one of the first

Anṣaar women to embrace Islam. She was married to Maalik ibn Naḍar, and bore him a son, Anas. When she embraced Islam, her husband Maalik was angry with her, and left her, but she persisted in her Islam. Shortly afterwards, she heard the news of his death, and she was still in the flower of her youth. She bore it all with the hope of reward, for the sake of Allah, and devoted herself to taking care of her ten-year-old son Anas. She took him to the Prophet (ﷺ), so that he could serve him (and learn from him).

One of the best young men of Madeenah, one of the best-looking, richest and strongest, came to seek her hand in marriage. This was Abu Ṭalḥah — before he became Muslim. Many of the young women of Yathrib liked him because of his wealth, strength and youthful good looks, and he thought that Umm Sulaym would joyfully rush to accept his offer. But to his astonishment, she told him, "O' Abu Ṭalḥah, do you not know that your god whom you worship is just a tree that grew in the ground and was carved into shape by the slave of Bani so-and-so." He said, "Of course." She said, "Do you not feel ashamed to prostrate yourself to a piece of wood that grew in the ground and was carved by the slave of Bani so-and-so?" Abu Ṭalḥah was stubborn, and hinted to her of an expensive dowry and luxurious lifestyle, but she persisted in her point of view, and told him frankly: "O' Abu Ṭalḥah, a man like you could not be turned away, but you are a disbelieving man, and I am a Muslim woman. It is not permitted for me to marry you, but if you were to embrace Islam, that would be my dowry (*mahr*), and I would ask you for nothing more."[6]

He returned the following day to try to tempt her with a larger dowry and more generous gift, but she stood firm, and her persistance and maturity only enhanced her beauty in his eyes. She said to him, "O'

---

[6] An-Nasaa'i with a *ṣaḥeeḥ* isnad, 6/114, *Kitaab an-Nikaaḥ, baab at-tazweej 'ala al-Islam.*

Abu Ṭalḥah, do you not know that your god whom you worship was carved by the carpenter slave of so-and-so? If you were to set it alight, it would burn." Her words came as a shock to Abu Ṭalḥah, and he asked himself, 'Does the Lord burn?' Then he uttered the words: "*Ashhadu an laa ilaha ill-Allah wa ashhadu anna Muhammadan rasool-Allah.*"

Then Umm Sulaym said to her son Anas, with joy flooding her entire being, "O' Anas, marry me to Abu Ṭalḥah." So Anas brought witnesses and the marriage was solemnized.

Abu Ṭalḥah was so happy that he was determined to put all his wealth at Umm Sulaym's disposal, but hers was the attitude of the selfless, proud, sincere believing woman. She told him, "O' Abu Ṭalḥah, I married you for the sake of Allah, and I will not take any other dowry." She knew that when Abu Ṭalḥah embraced Islam, she did not only win herself a worthy husband, but she also earned a reward from Allah (ﷻ) that was better than owning red camels (the most highly-prized kind) in this world, as she had heard the Prophet (ﷺ) say:

> "If Allah were to guide one person to Islam through you, it is better for you than owning red camels."[7]

Such great Muslim women are examples worthy of emulation, from whom Muslim women may learn purity of faith, strength of character, soundness of belief and wisdom in choosing a husband.

She is obedient to her husband and shows him respect

The true Muslim woman is always obedient to her husband, provided that no sin is involved. She is respectful towards him and is always eager to please him and make him happy. If he is poor, she does not complain about his being unable to spend much. She does not

---

7 *Fatḥ al-Baari*, 7/476, *Kitaab al-Maghaazi, baab ghazwat Khaybar.*

complain about her housework, because she remembers that many of the virtuous women in Islamic history set an example of patience, goodness and a positive attitude in serving their husbands and taking care of their homes despite the poverty and hardships they faced. One of the foremost of these exemplary wives is Faṭimah az-Zahra' (رضي الله عنها), the daughter of Muhammad (ﷺ) and the wife of 'Ali ibn Abi Ṭaalib (رضي الله عنه). She used to complain of the pain in her hands caused by grinding grain with the hand-mill. Her husband 'Ali ibn Abi Ṭaalib said to her one day, "Your father has brought some female slaves, so go and ask him for one of them to come and serve you." She went to her father, but she felt too shy to ask him for what she wanted. 'Ali went and asked him to provide a servant for his beloved daughter, but the Prophet (ﷺ) could not respond to those who were dearest to him whilst ignoring the needs of the poor among the Muslims, so he came to his daughter and her husband and said:

> "Shall I not teach you something that is better than that for which you asked me? When you go to bed at night, say, '*Subḥaan Allah*' thirty-three times, '*Al-Ḥamdu lillah*' thirty-three times, and '*Allahu Akbar*' thirty-four times. This is better for you than a servant."

Then he bid them farewell and left, after instilling in them this divine help which would make them forget their tiredness and help them to overcome their exhaustion.

> 'Ali began to repeat the words that the Prophet had taught him. He said, 'I never stopped doing that after he had taught me these words.' One of his companions asked him, 'Not even on the night of Ṣiffeen?' He said, 'Not even on the night of Ṣiffeen.'[8]

---

[8] *Fatḥ al-Baari*, 7/71, *Kitaab Faḍaa'il aṣ-Ṣaḥaabah, baab manaaqib 'Ali ibn Abi Ṭaalib*; Muslim, 17/45, *Kitaab adh-Dhikr wad-du'aa', baab at-tasbeeḥ awwal an-nahaar wa 'ind an-nawm.*

Asma' bint Abi Bakr aṣ-Ṣiddeeq served her husband Az-Zubayr, and took care of the house. Her husband had a horse, which she took care of, feeding it and exercising it. She also repaired the water-bucket, made bread, and carried dates on her head from far away. Bukhari and Muslim report this in her own words:

> "Az-Zubayr married me, and he had no wealth, no slaves, nothing except his horse. I used to feed his horse, looking after it and exercising it. I crushed date-stones to feed his camel. I used to bring water and repair the bucket, and I used to make bread but I could not bake it, so some of my Anṣaari neighbours, who were kind women, used to bake it for me. I used to carry the dates from the garden that the Prophet had given to Az-Zubayr on my head, and this garden was two-thirds of a *farsakh* (more than a kilometre) away. One day I was coming back with the dates on my head. I met the Messenger of Allah, who had a group of his Companions with him. He called me, then told his camel to sit down so that I could ride behind him. I told (Az-Zubayr), 'I felt shy, because I know that you are a jealous man.' He said, 'It is worse for me to see you carrying the dates on your head than to see you riding behind him.' Later, Abu Bakr sent me a servant, who relieved me of having to take care of the horse; it was as if I had been released from slavery."[9]

The true Muslim woman devotes herself to taking care of her house and husband. She knows her husband's rights over her, and how great they are, as was confirmed by the Prophet's words:

> "No human being is permitted to prostrate to another,

---

9 *Fatḥ al-Baari*, 9/319, *Kitaab an-Nikaaḥ, baab al-ghirah.*

> but if this were permitted I would have ordered wives to prostrate to their husbands, because of the greatness of the rights they have over them."[10]

And:

> "If I were to order anyone to prostrate to anyone else, I would have ordered women to prostrate to their husbands."[11]

'Aa'ishah (ﷺ) asked the Messenger of Allah (ﷺ):

> "Who has the greatest rights over a woman?" He said, "Her husband." She asked, "And who has the greatest rights over a man?" He said, "His mother."[12]

> "A woman came to ask the Prophet about some matter, and when he had dealt with it, he asked her, 'Do you have a husband?' She said, 'Yes.' He asked her, 'How are you with him?' She said, 'I never fall short in my duties, except for that which is beyond me.' He said, 'Pay attention to how you treat him, for he is your Paradise and your Hell.'"[13]

How can the Muslim woman complain about taking care of her house and husband when she hears these words of Prophetic guidance? She should fulfil her household duties and take care of her husband in a spirit of joy, because she is not carrying a tiresome burden, she is

---

[10] Aḥmad and Al-Bazzaar; the men of its isnad are *rijaal aṣ-ṣaḥeeḥ*. See *Majma' az-Zawaa'id*, 9/4, *baab ḥaqq az-zawj 'ala al-mar'ah*.

[11] A *ḥasan ṣaḥeeḥ* hadith, by Tirmidhi, 2/314, in *Abwaab ar-Riḍaa'*, 10.

[12] Al-Bazzaar with a *ḥasan* isnad. *Majma' az-Zawaa'id*, 4/308, *baab ḥaqq az-zawj 'ala al-mar'ah*.

[13] Aḥmad and Nasaa'i with *jayyid* isnads, and by Al-Ḥaakim, who said that its isnad was *ṣaḥeeḥ*. See Al-Mundhiri, *At-Targheeb wat-Tarheeb*, 3/52, *Kitaab an-Nikaaḥ*.

doing work in her home that she knows will bring reward from Allah.

The *Ṣaḥaabah*, may Allah be pleased with them, and those who followed them understood this Islamic teaching and transmitted it from the Prophet (ﷺ). When a bride was prepared for marriage, she would be told to serve her husband and take care of his rights. Thus the Muslim woman knew her duties towards her husband, and down through the ages, caring for her husband and being a good wife were established womanly attributes. One example of this is what was said by the *faqeeh* Al-Ḥanbali ibn al-Jawzi in his book *Aḥkaam an-Nisa'* (p. 331):

> "In the second century AH there was a righteous man called Shu'ayb ibn Ḥarb, who used to fast and spend his nights in prayer. He wanted to marry a woman, and told her humbly, 'I am a bad-tempered man.' She replied, tactfully and cleverly, 'The one who makes you lose your temper is worse than you.' He realized that there stood before him a woman who was intelligent, wise and mature. He immediately said to her, 'You will be my wife.'"

This woman had a clear understanding of how to be a good wife, which confirmed to the man who had come to seek her hand that she was a woman who would understand the psychology and nature of her husband and would know what would please him and what would make him angry. She would be able to win his heart and earn his admiration and respect, and would close the door to every possible source of conflict that could disrupt their married life. The woman who does not understand these realities does not deserve to be a successful wife. Through her ignorance and shortcomings she may provoke her husband to lose his temper, in which case, she would be worse than him, for being the direct cause of his anger.

The tactful Muslim woman is never like this. She helps her husband to be of good character, by displaying different types of intelligence, cleverness and alertness in the way she deals with him. This opens his heart to her and makes him fond of her, because being a good wife is not only a quality that she may boast about among her friends, but it is also a religious obligation for which Allah (ﷻ) will call her to account: if she has done well, she will be rewarded, but if she has fallen short she will have to pay the penalty.

One of the most important ways in which the Muslim woman obeys her husband is by respecting his wishes with regard to the permissible pleasures of daily life, such as social visits, food, dress, speech, etc. The more she responds to his wishes in such matters, the happier and more enjoyable the couple's life becomes, and the closer it is to the spirit and teachings of Islam.

The Muslim woman does not forget that her obedience to her husband is one of the things that may lead her to Paradise, as the Prophet (ﷺ) said:

> "If a woman prays her five daily prayers, fasts her month (of Ramaḍaan), obeys her husband and guards her chastity, then it will be said to her: 'Enter Paradise through whichever of its gates you wish.'"[14]

Umm Salamah (رضي الله عنها) said: "The Messenger of Allah (ﷺ) said:

> 'Any woman who dies, and her husband is pleased with her, will enter Paradise.'"[15]

The Prophet (ﷺ) draw a clear and delightful picture of the well-behaved, easy-going, loving, righteous Muslim wife, the one who will be happy in this world and the next:

---

[14] Aḥmad and Ṭabaraani; its narrators are *thiqat*. *Majma' az-Zawaa'id*, 4/306, *baab ḥaqq az-zawj 'ala al-mar'ah*.

[15] Ibn Maajah, 1/595, *Kitaab an-Nikaaḥ, baab ḥaqq az-zawj 'ala al-mar'ah*; Al-Ḥaakim, 4/173, *Kitaab al-Birr waṣ-Ṣilah*; he said its isnad is *ṣaḥeeḥ*.

> "Shall I not tell you about your wives in Paradise?" We said, "Of course, O' Messenger of Allah." He said, "They are fertile and loving. If she becomes angry or is mistreated, or her husband becomes angry, she says, 'My hand is in your hand; I shall never sleep until you are pleased with me.'"[16]

The true Muslim woman knows that Islam, which has multiplied her reward for obeying her husband and made it a means of her admittance to Paradise, has also warned every woman who deviates from the path of marital obedience and neglects to take care of her husband, that she will be guilty of sin, and will incur the wrath and curses of the angels.

Bukhari and Muslim report from Abu Hurayrah that the Prophet (ﷺ) said:

> "If a man calls his wife to his bed and she does not come, and he goes to sleep angry with her, the angels will curse her until the morning."[17]

Muslim reports from Abu Hurayrah that the Prophet (ﷺ) said:

> "By the One in Whose hand is my soul, there is no man who calls his wife to his bed, and she refuses him, but the One Who is in heaven will be angry with her, until the husband is pleased with her once more."[18]

The angels' curse will befall every woman who is rebellious and

---

[16] Ṭabaraani. Its narrators are those whose reports are accepted as *ṣaḥeeḥ*. *Majma' az-Zawaaa'id*, 4/312.

[17] *Fatḥ al-Baari*, 9/294, *Kitaab an-Nikaaḥ, baab idha baatat al-mar'ah muhaajirah firaash zawjiha*; Muslim, 10/8, *Kitaab an-Nikaaḥ, baab taḥreem imtinaa' al-mar'ah min firaash zawjiha.*

[18] Muslim, 10/7, *Kitaab an-Nikaaḥ, baab taḥreem imtinaa' al-mar'ah min firaash zawjiha.*

disobedient; this does not exclude those who are too slow and reluctant to respond to their husbands:

> "Allah will curse those procrastinating women who, when their husbands call them to their beds, say 'I will, I will...' until he falls asleep."[19]

Marriage in Islam is intended to protect the chastity of men and women alike, therefore it is the woman's duty to respond to her husband's requests for conjugal relations. She should not give silly excuses and try to avoid it. For this reason, several hadiths urge a wife to respond to her husband's needs as much as she is able, no matter how busy she may be or whatever obstacles there may be, so long as there is no urgent or unavoidable reason not to do so. In one of these hadiths, the Prophet (ﷺ) said:

> "If a man calls his wife to his bed, let her respond, even if she is riding her camel (i.e., very busy)."[20]

And:

> "If a man calls his wife, then let her come, even if she is busy at the oven."[21]

The issue of protecting a man's chastity and keeping him away from temptation is more important than anything else that a woman can do, because Islam wants men and women alike to live in an environment which is entirely pure and free from any motive of *fitnah* or *ḥaraam*

---

[19] A *ṣaḥeeḥ* hadith narrated by Ṭabaraani in *Al-Awsaṭ* and *Al-Kabeer. Majma' az-Zawaa'id*, 4/296, *baab fi man yad'ooha zawjaha fa ta'ttalla.*

[20] Al-Bazzaar, whose narrators are *rijaal aṣ-ṣaḥeeḥ*. *Majma' az-Zawaa'id*, 4/312.

[21] A *ḥasan ṣaḥeeḥ* hadith narrated by Tirmidhi, 2/314, *Abwaab ar-riḍaa',* 10, and by Ibn Ḥibbaan, *Ṣaḥeeḥ*, 9,473, *Kitaab an-Nikaaḥ*.

pleasures. The flames of sexual desire and thoughts of pursuing them through *ḥaraam* means can only be extinguished by means of discharging that natural energy in natural and lawful ways. This is what the Prophet (ﷺ) meant in the hadith narrated by Muslim from Jaabir:

> "If anyone of you is attracted to a woman, let him go to his wife and have intercourse with her, for that will calm him down."[22]

The warning given to the woman whose husband is angry with her reaches such an extent that it would shake the conscience of every righteous wife who has faith in Allah and the Last Day. She is told that her prayer and good deeds will not be accepted, until her husband is pleased with her again.

This is stated in the hadith narrated by Jaabir from 'Abdullah: "The Messenger of Allah (ﷺ) said:

> 'There are three people whose prayers will not be accepted, neither their good works: a disobedient slave until he returns to his masters and puts his hand in theirs; a woman whose husband is angry with her, until he is pleased with her again; and the drunkard, until he becomes sober.'"[23]

When these hadiths refer to the husband being angry with his wife, they refer to cases in which the husband is right and the wife is wrong. When the opposite is the case, and the husband is wrong, then his anger has no negative implications for her; in fact, Allah (ﷻ) will

---

[22] Muslim, 9/178, *Kitaab an-Nikaaḥ, baab nadab man raa'a imra'atan fa waqa'at fi nafsihi ila an yaa'ti imra'tahu.*

[23] Ibn Ḥibbaan in his *Ṣaḥeeḥ*, 12/178, *Kitaab al-Ashribah*, 2, *faṣl fil-ashribah.*

reward the wife for her patience. But the wife is still required to obey her husband, so long as no sin is involved, because there should be no obedience to a created being if it entails disobedience to the Creator. Concerning this, the Prophet (ﷺ) said:

> "It is not permitted for a woman who believes in Allah to allow anyone into her husband's house whom he dislikes; or to go out when he does not want her to; or to obey anyone else against him; or to forsake his bed; or to hit him. If he is wrong, then let her come to him until he is pleased with her, and if he accepts her then all is well, Allah will accept her deeds and make her position stronger, and there will be no sin on her. If he does not accept her, then at least she will have done her best and excused herself in the sight of Allah."[24]

Another aspect of wifely obedience is that she should not fast at times other than Ramaḍaan except with his permission, that she should not allow anyone to enter his house without his permission, and that she should not spend any of his earnings without his permission. If she spends anything without him having told her to do so, then half of the reward for that spending will be given to him. The true Muslim woman takes heed of this teaching which was stated by the Prophet (ﷺ) in the hadith:

> "It is not permitted for a woman to fast when her husband is present, except with his permission; or to allow anyone into his house except with his permission; or to spend any of his earnings unless he has told her to do so, otherwise half of the reward will be given to him."[25]

---

[24] Al-Ḥaakim, 2/190, *Kitaab an-Nikaaḥ*; he said its isnad is *ṣaḥeeḥ*.

[25] *Fatḥ al-Baari*, 9/295, *Kitaab an-Nikaaḥ, baab la taa'dhan al-mar'ah fi bayt zawjiha li aḥad illa bi idhnihi.*

According to another report given by Muslim, he (ﷺ) said:

> "A woman should not fast if her husband is present, except with his permission. She should not allow anyone to enter his house when he is present without his permission. Whatever she spends of his wealth without him having told her to do so, half of the reward for it will be given to him."[26]

The point here is the permission of the husband. If a wife gives some of his money in voluntary charity without his permission, then she will not receive any reward; on the contrary, it will be recorded as a sin on her part. If she wants to spend in his absence, and she knows that if he knew about it he would give his permission, then she is allowed to do so, otherwise it is not permitted.

Mutual understanding and harmony between husband and wife cannot be achieved unless there is understanding between them on such matters, so that neither of them will fall into such errors and troubles as may damage the marriage which Islam has built on a basis of love and mercy, and sought to maintain its purity, care and harmony.

If the husband is a miser, and spends too little on her and her children, then she is allowed to spend as much as she needs from his wealth on herself and her children, in moderation, without his knowledge. The Prophet (ﷺ) stated this to Hind bint 'Utbah, the wife of Abu Sufyan, when she came to him and said,

> "O' Messenger of Allah, Abu Sufyan is a stingy man. What he gives me is not enough for me and my child, unless I take from him without his knowledge." He told

[26] Muslim, 7/115, *Kitaab az-Zakaah, baab ajr al-khaazin wal-mar'ah idha taṣaddaqat min bayt zawjaha.*

> her, "Take what is enough for you and your child, in moderation."[27]

Thus Islam has made women responsible for good conduct in their running of the household affairs.

The Muslim woman understands the responsibility that Islam has given her, to take care of her husband's house and children by making her a "shepherd" over her husband's house and children. She has been specifically reminded of this responsibility in recognition of her role, in the hadith in which the Prophet (ﷺ) made every individual in the Islamic society responsible for those under his or her authority in such a way that no-one, man or woman, may evade responsibility:

> "Each of you is a shepherd, and each is responsible for those under his care. A ruler is a shepherd; a man is the shepherd of his family; a woman is the shepherd of her husband's house and children. For each of you is a shepherd and each of you is responsible for those under his care."[28]

The true Muslim woman is always described as being loving towards her children and caring towards her husband. These are two of the most beautiful characteristics that a woman of any time or place may possess. The Prophet (ﷺ) praised these two characteristics, which were embodied by the women of Quraysh, who represented the best women among the Arabs in terms of loving their children, caring for their husbands, respecting their rights and looking after their wealth with care, honesty and wisdom:

> "The best women who ride camels are the women of Quraysh. They are the most compassionate towards

---

[27] Bukhari and Muslim. See *Sharḥ as-Sunnah*, 9/327, *Kitaab al-'Iddah, baab nafaqah al-awlaad wal-aqaarib.*

[28] Bukhari and Muslim. See *Sharḥ as-Sunnah*, 9/327, *Kitaab al-Imaarah wal-Qaḍa': baab ar-ra'ee mas'ool 'an ra'iyatihi.*

> their children when they are small, and the most careful with regard to their husbands' wealth."[29]

This is a valuable testimony on the part of the Prophet (ﷺ), attesting to the psychological and moral qualities of the women of Quraysh which enhanced their beauty and virtue. This testimony respresents a call to every Muslim woman to emulate the women of Quraysh in loving her children and taking care of her husband. These two important characteristics contribute to the success of a marriage, make individuals and families happy, and help a society to advance.

It is a great honour for a woman to take care of her husband every morning and evening, and wherever he goes, treating him with gentleness and good manners which will fill his life with joy, tranquillity and stability. Muslim women have the best example in 'Aa'ishah (رضي الله عنها), who used to accompany the Prophet (ﷺ) on Ḥajj, surrounding him with her care, putting perfume on him with her own hands before he entered *iḥraam*, and after he finished his *iḥraam*, before he performed *ṭawaaf al-ifaaḍah*.[30] She chose for him the best perfume that she could find. This is stated in a number of *ṣaḥeeḥ* hadith reported by Bukhari and Muslim, for example:

> "I applied perfume to the Messenger of Allah with my own hands before he entered the state of *iḥraam* and when he concluded it before circumambulating the House."[31]
>
> "I applied perfume to the Messenger of Allah with these two hands of mine when he entered *iḥraam* and when

---

[29] Muslim, 16/81, *Kitaab faḍaa'il aṣ-Ṣaḥaabah, baab min faḍaa'il nisaa' Quraysh.*

[30] *Ṭawaaf al-ifaaḍah* is one of the important rites of Ḥajj. It is done on the tenth day of *Dhu'l-Ḥijjah* after sacrificing an animal and shaving one's head. (Translator)

[31] Muslim, 8/99, *Kitaab al-Ḥajj, baab istiḥbaab aṭ-ṭeeb qabl al-iḥraam.*

> he concluded it, before he performed *ṭawaaf*," — and she spread her hands.[32]

'Urwah said:

> "I asked 'Aa'ishah, 'With what did you perfume the Messenger of Allah at the time when he entered *iḥraam*?' She said, 'With the best of perfume.'"[33]

According to another report also given by Muslim, 'Aa'ishah (ﷺ) said:

> "I applied the best perfume I could find to the Messenger of Allah before he entered *iḥraam* and when he concluded it, before he perfomed *ṭawaaf al-ifaaḍah*."[34]

When the Prophet (ﷺ) was in seclusion (*i'tikaaf*), he would lean his head towards 'Aa'ishah, and she would comb and wash his hair. Bukhari and Muslim both report this in *ṣaḥeeḥ* hadith narrated from 'Aa'ishah (ﷺ), such as:

> "When the Messenger of Allah was in *i'tikaaf*, he inclined his head towards me and I combed his hair, and he did not enter the house except to answer the call of nature."[35]

> "I used to wash the Prophet's head when I was menstruating."[36]

---

32 *Fatḥ al-Baari*, 3/585, *Kitaab al-Ḥajj, baab aṭ-ṭeeb.*

33 Muslim, 8/100, *Kitaab al-Ḥajj, baab istiḥbaab aṭ-ṭeeb qabl al-iḥraam.*

34 Ibid.

35 Muslim, 3/208, *Kitaab al-Ḥayḍ, baab jawaaz ghusl al-ḥaa'iḍ ra'as zawjiha wa tarjeeluhu.*

36 *Fatḥ al-Baari*, 1/403, *Kitaab al-Ḥayḍ, baab mubashirah al-ḥaa'iḍ*; Muslim, 3/209, *Kitaab al-Ḥayḍ, baab jawaaz ghusl al-ḥaa'iḍ ra'as zawjiha.*

'Aa'ishah urged women to take good care of their husbands and to recognize the rights that their husbands had over them. She saw these rights as being so great and so important that a woman was barely qualified to wipe the dust from her husband's feet with her face, as she stated:

> "O' womenfolk, if you knew the rights that your husbands have over you, every one of you would wipe the dust from her husband's feet with her face."[37]

This is a vivid expression of the importance of the husband's rights over his wife. 'Aa'ishah wanted to bring this to women's attention, so as to remove from the hearts of arrogant and stubborn women all those harsh, obstinate feelings that all too often destroy a marriage and turn it into a living hell.

Honouring and respecting one's husband is one of the characteristic attitudes of this ummah. It is one of the good manners known at the time of *jaahiliyah* that were endorsed by Islam and perpetuated by the Arabs after they embraced Islam. Our Arab heritage is filled with texts that eloquently describe the advice given by mothers to their daughters, to care for, honour and respect their husbands; these texts may be regarded as invaluable social documents.

One of the most famous and most beautiful of these texts was recorded by 'Abdul-Malik ibn 'Umayr al-Qurashi, who was one of the outstanding scholars of the second century AH. He quotes the words of advice given by Umamah bint al-Ḥaarith, one of the most eloquent and learned women, who was possessed of wisdom and great maturity, to her daughter on the eve of her marriage. These beautiful words deserve to be inscribed in golden ink.

---

37 Ibn Ḥibbaan, and with a *jayyid* isnad by Al-Bazzaar; its narrators are well-known and are *thiqaat*. See Ibn al-Jawzi, *Aḥkaam an-Nisa'*, p. 311.

'Abdul-Malik said:

> " 'Awf ibn Muḥallim ash-Shaybaani, one of the most highly respected leaders of the Arab nobility during the *jaahiliyah*, married his daughter Umm Iyaas to Al-Ḥaarith ibn 'Amr al-Kindi. She was made ready to be taken to the groom, then her mother Umamah came in to her, to advise her, and said:
>
> 'O' my daughter, if it were deemed unnecessary to give you this advice because of good manners and noble descent, then it would have been unnecessary for you, because you possess these qualities, but it will serve as a reminder to those who are forgetful, and will help those who are wise.
>
> O' my daughter, if a woman were able to do without a husband by virtue of her father's wealth and her need for her father, then you of all people would be most able to do without a husband, but women were created for men just as men were created for them.
>
> O' my daughter, you are about to leave the home in which you grew up, where you first learned to walk, to go to a place you do not know, to a companion with whom you are unfamiliar. By marrying you, he has become a master over you, so be like a servant to him, and he will become like a servant to you. Take from me ten qualities, which will be a provision and a reminder for you.
>
> <u>The first and second</u> of them are: be content in his company, and listen to and obey him, for contentment brings peace of mind, and listening to and obeying one's husband pleases Allah.
>
> <u>The third and fourth</u> of them are: make sure that you smell good and look good; he should not see anything ugly in you, and he should not smell anything but a pleasant smell from you. *Koḥl* is the best kind of beautification to be found, and water is better than the rarest perfume.

The fifth and the sixth of them are: prepare his food on time, and keep quiet when he is asleep, for raging hunger is like a burning flame, and disturbing his sleep will make him angry.

The seventh and eighth of them are: take care of his servants (or employees) and children, and take care of his wealth, for taking care of his wealth shows that you appreciate him, and taking care of his children and servants shows good management.

The ninth and tenth of them are: never disclose any of his secrets, and never disobey any of his orders, for if you disclose any of his secrets, you will never feel safe from his possible betrayal, and if you disobey him, his heart will be filled with hatred towards you.

Be careful, O' my daughter, of showing joy in front of him when he is upset, and do not show sorrow in front of him when he is happy, because the former shows a lack of judgement, whilst the latter will make him unhappy.

Show him as much honour and respect as you can, and agree with him as much as you can, so that he will enjoy your companionship and conversation.

Know, O' my daughter, that you will not achieve what you would like to until you put his pleasure before your own, and his wishes before yours, in whatever you like and dislike. May Allah choose what is best for you and protect you.'"[38]

She was taken to her husband, and the marriage was a great success; she gave birth to kings who ruled after him.

This advice clearly included everything that one could think of as regards the good manners that a young girl needs to know about in order to treat her husband properly and be a suitable companion for

[38] *Jamharah Khuṭab al-'Arab*, 1/145.

him. The words of this wise mother deserve to be taken as the standard for every young girl who is about to get married.

If she is rich, the true Muslim woman does not let her wealth and financial independence make her blind to the importance of respecting her husband's rights over her. She still takes care of him and honours him, no matter how rich she is or may become. She knows that she is obliged to show gratitude to Allah for the blessings He has bestowed upon her, so she increases her charitable giving for the sake of Allah. The first person to whom she should give generously is her own husband, if he is poor; in this case she will receive two rewards, one for taking care of a family member, and another for giving charity, as the Prophet (ﷺ) stated in the hadith narrated by Zaynab ath-Thaqafiyah, the wife of 'Abdullah ibn Mas'ood (رضي الله عنه): "The Prophet (ﷺ) told us:

> 'O' women, give in charity even if it is some of your jewellery.' She said, 'I went back to 'Abdullah ibn Mas'ood and told him. 'You are a man of little wealth, and the Prophet has commanded us to give charity, so go and ask him whether it is permissible for me to give you charity. If it is, I will do so; if it is not, I will give charity to someone else.' 'Abdullah said, 'No, you go and ask.' So I went, and I found a woman of the Anṣaar at the Prophet's door, who also had the question. We felt too shy to go in, out of respect, so Bilal came out and we asked him, 'Go and tell the Messenger of Allah that there are two women at the door asking you: Is it permissible for them to give *ṣadaqah* to their husbands and the orphans in their care? But do not tell him who we are.' So Bilal went in and conveyed this message to the Prophet, who asked, 'Who are they?' Bilal said, 'One of the women of the Anṣaar, and Zaynab.' The Prophet asked, 'Which Zaynab is it?' Bilal said, 'The

> wife of 'Abdullah.' The Prophet said: 'They will have two rewards, the reward for upholding the relationship, and the reward for giving charity.'"[39]

According to another report by Bukhari, he said,

> "Your husband and your child are more deserving of your charity."[40]

The true Muslim woman is always careful to give thanks for Allah's blessings if her life is easy, and she never loses her patience if she encounters difficulty. She never forgets the warning that the Prophet (ﷺ) issued to women in general, when he saw that most of the inhabitants of Hell will be women. She thus seeks refuge with Allah from becoming one of them.

Bukhari and Muslim narrated from Ibn 'Abbaas (رضي الله عنه) that the Prophet (ﷺ) said:

> "O' women, give charity, for I have surely seen that you form the majority of the inhabitants of Hell." They asked, "Why is this so, O' Messenger of Allah?" He said, "Because you curse too much, and are ungrateful for good treatment (on the part of your husbands)."[41]

According to another report given by Bukhari, he said,

> "Because they are ungrateful for good and kind treatment. Even if you treated onc of them (these ungrateful women) well for an entire lifetime, and when

---

[39] *Fatḥ al-Baari*, 3/328, *Kitaab az-Zakaat, baab az-zakaat 'ala az-zawj wal-aytaam fil-ḥijr*; Muslim, 7/86, *Kitaab az-Zakaat, baab az-zakaat 'ala al-aqaarib.*

[40] *Fatḥ al-Baari*, 3/325, *Kitaab az-Zakaat, baab az-zakaat 'ala al-aqaarib.*

[41] Ibid; Muslim, 2/65, *Kitaab al-Eemaan, baab bayaan naqṣaan al-eemaan bi naqṣ aṭ-ṭa'aat wal-'asheer az-zawj.*

> she saw one fault in you, she would say, 'I have never seen anything good from you!'"[42]

According to yet another report by Aḥmad, a man said,

> "O' Messenger of Allah, are they not our mothers and sisters and wives?" He said, "Of course, but when they are treated generously they are ungrateful, and when they are tested, they do not have patience."[43]

When the true Muslim woman thinks about these *ṣaḥeeḥ* (authentic) hadiths which describe the fate of most women in the Hereafter, she is always on the alert lest she fall into the sins of ingratitude towards her husband, or frequent cursing, or denying her husband's good treatment of her, or forgetting to give thanks for times of ease, or failing to be patient at times of difficulty. In any case, she hastens to give charity as the Prophet (ﷺ) urged all women to do, in the hope that it may save them from that awful fate which will befall most of those women who deviate from truth and let trivial matters distract them from remembering Allah and the Last Day, and whose bad qualities will ultimately lead them into the Fire of Hell. The Muslim woman, on the other hand, sets the highest example of respecting her husband and pointing out his good qualities. This is the attitude of loyalty that befits the true Muslim woman who respects her husband's rights and does not ignore his virtues.

Muslim women's history is full of stories which reflect this loyalty and recognition of the good qualities of the husband. One of these stories is that of Asma' bint 'Umays, who was one of the great women in Islam, and one of the first women to migrate to Madeenah. She was married to Ja'far ibn Abi Ṭaalib, then to Abu Bakr aṣ-Ṣiddeeq, then to 'Ali, may Allah be pleased with them all. On one

---

42 *Fatḥ al-Baari*, 1/83, *Kitaab al-Eemaan, baab kufraan al-'asheer.*

43 Aḥmad, 3/428; its narrators are *rijaal aṣ-ṣaḥeeḥ*.

occasion, her two sons Muhammad ibn Ja'far and Muhammad ibn Abi Bakr were competing with one another, each of them saying. "I am better than you, and my father is better than your father." 'Ali said to her, "Judge between them, O' Asma'." She said, "I have never seen a young man among the Arabs who was better than Ja'far, and I have never seen a mature man who was better than Abu Bakr." 'Ali said, "You have not left anything for me. If you had said anything other than what you have said, I would have hated you!" Asma' said:

> "These are the best three, and you are one of them even if you are the least of them."[44]

What a clever and eloquent answer this wise woman gave! She gave each of her three husbands the respect he deserved, and pleased 'Ali, even though he was the least of them, because she included all of them in that group of the best.

She treats his mother and family with kindness and respect

One of the ways in which a wife expresses her respect towards her husband is by honouring and respecting his mother.

The Muslim woman who truly understands the teachings of her religion knows that the person who has the greatest right over a man is his mother, as we have seen in the hadith of 'Aa'ishah (﷿) quoted above. So she helps him to honour and respect his mother, by honouring and respecting her herself. In this way she will do herself and her husband a favour, as she will be helping him to do good deeds and fear Allah, as commanded by the Qur'an. At the same time, she will endear herself to her husband, who will appreciate her honour and respect towards his family in general, and towards his mother in particular. Nothing could please a decent, righteous and

---

[44] *At-Tabaqaat al-Kubra*, 7/208-209.

respectful man more than seeing strong ties of love and respect between his wife and his family, and nothing could be more hateful to a decent man than to see those ties destroyed by the forces of evil, hatred and conspiracy. The Muslim family which is guided by faith in Allah (سبحانه وتعالى) and follows the pure teachings of Islam is unlikely to fall into the trap of such *jaahili* behaviour, which usually flourishes in an environment that is far removed from the true teachings of this religion.

A Muslim wife may find herself being tested by her mother-in-law and other in-laws, if they are not of good character. If such is the case, she is obliged to treat them in the best way possible, which requires a great deal of cleverness, courtesy, diplomacy and repelling evil with that which is better. Thus she will maintain a balance between her relationship with her in-laws and her relationship with her husband, and she will protect herself and her marriage from any adverse effects that may result from the lack of such a balance.

The Muslim woman should never think that she is the only one who is required to be a good and caring companion to her spouse, and that nothing similar is required of her husband or that there is nothing wrong with him mistreating her or failing to fulfil some of the responsibilities of marriage. Islam has regulated the marital relationship by giving each partner both rights and duties. The wife's duties of honouring and taking care of her husband are balanced by the rights that she has over him, which are that he should protect her honour and dignity from all kinds of mockery, humiliation, trials or oppression. These rights of the wife comprise the husband's duties towards her. He is obliged to honour them and fulfil them as completely as possible.

One of the Muslim husband's duties is to fulfil his role of *qawwam* (maintainer and protector) properly. This is a role that can be properly fulfilled only by a man who is a successful leader in his home and family, one who possesses likeable masculine qualities. Such a man has a noble and worthy attitude, is tolerant, overlooks minor errors, is in control of his married life, and is generous without being extravagant. He respects his wife's feelings and makes her feel that she shares the responsibility of running the household affairs, bringing up the children, and working with him to build a sound Muslim family, as Islam wants it to be.

She endears herself to her husband and is keen to please him

The true Muslim woman is always keen to win her husband's love and to please him. Nothing should spoil his happiness or enjoyment of life. So she speaks kind words to him, and refrains from saying anything hurtful or upsetting. She brings him good news and keeps bad news from him as much as she can, or postpones telling it until a suitable time when it will not upset him so much. If she finds that she has no alternative but to tell him upsetting news, she looks for the most suitable way to convey it, so that it is not be so hard on him. This is the wise approach and good conduct of the clever woman, but it is very difficult to attain and only a very few virtuous women ever do so.

One of those who did reach this high level was the great Muslim woman Umm Sulaym bint Milḥaan, the wife of Abu Ṭalḥah al-Anṣaari. Her son passed away while Abu Ṭalḥah was travelling, and her attitude was so unique that if Imam Muslim had not reported this story, we would have taken it to be a mere myth. Let us hear her son Anas ibn Maalik tell the story of his remarkable mother and her unique attitude:

> "A son of Abu Ṭalḥah by Umm Sulaym died. Umm Sulaym told her family, 'Do not tell Abu Ṭalḥah about his son until I tell him about it.' Abu Ṭalḥah came home,

so she prepared dinner for him, and he ate and drank. Then she beautified herself in a way that she had never done before, and he had sex with her. When she saw that he was satisfied, she said, 'O' Abu Ṭalḥah, what do you think if somebody lent something to someone, then ask it back?, Will it be right not to return it?' He said, 'No.' She said, 'Then resign yourself about your son (i.e., he died).' Abu Ṭalḥah became angry and said, 'You let me indulge myself and then you tell me about my son!' He went to the Messenger of Allah and told him what had happened. The Messenger of Allah said, 'May Allah bless both of you for this night!' Umm Sulaym became pregnant. The Messenger of Allah went on a journey, and she accompanied him. Whenever the Messenger of Allah came back from a journey, he never entered Madeenah at night. When they (the travelling-party) approached Madeenah, her labour-pains started. Abu Ṭalḥah stayed with her, and the Messenger of Allah proceeded ahead to Madeenah. Abu Ṭalḥah said, 'O' Lord, You know how I love to go out with Your Messenger when he goes out, and to come back with him when he comes back, and I have been detained, as You see.' Umm Sulaym said, 'O' Abu Ṭalḥah, I do not feel as much pain as I did before, so let us go on.' When they reached Madeenah, her labour-pain started again, and she gave birth to a boy. My mother said to me, 'O' Anas, nobody should feed him until you take him to the Messenger of Allah in the morning.' I therefore took the baby to the Messenger of Allah next morning. When I reached him he was carrying an iron tool. He saw me, then said, 'I hope that Umm Sulaym has given birth.' I said, 'Yes.' So he put down the tool and I brought the child to him and placed him in his (Prophet's) lap. The

Messenger of Allah called for some of the dates of Madeenah. He chewed it until it became soft, then he put it in the baby's mouth and the baby began to smack his lips. The Messenger of Allah said: 'See how much the Anṣaar love dates!' Then he wiped the baby's face and named him 'Abdullah.'"[45]

How great was Umm Sulaym's faith, and how magnificent her patience and virtue! How bravely she hid her pain from her husband and endeared herself to him. She managed to conceal her grief at the loss of her beloved son and spent that time with her husband patiently hoping that by being a good wife to her husband she might earn the pleasure of Allah. This is true, deep and sincere faith.

Allah (ﷻ) answered the Prophet's prayer for Umm Sulaym and her husband, and she became pregnant from that night. When she was heavily pregnant, she saw her husband Abu Ṭalḥah preparing to set out on another military campaign with the Messenger of Allah (ﷺ). She insisted on partaking of the honour of jihad with him alongside the Messenger of Allah (ﷺ), even though she was in the later stages of pregnancy. Her husband took pity on her because of the difficulties of the journey and the heat of the desert, yet he asked the Prophet for permission to let her come with him. The Prophet granted the permission because he knew her strength of character and love of jihad.

Umm Sulaym was present when the Muslims were triumphant at Makkah, and when they were sorely tested at Ḥunayn. She stood firm, as solid as a rock, alongside her husband and the small group of believers around the Prophet (ﷺ), even though she was pregnant. At the time when many others had fled, she remained there until Allah (ﷻ) brought victory to the believers.

---

[45] Muslim, 16/11, *Kitaab Faḍaa'il aṣ-Ṣaḥaabah, baab faḍaa'il Umm Sulaym.*

She suffered labour pain on the way when the victorious *mujaahideen* (fighters in the cause of Allah) were close by Madeenah in their return journey. When the pains became intense, she and her husband stayed behind for a while, but her husband prayed to his Lord in the still of night because he loved to enter Madeenah with the Prophet. Suddenly the pains ceased and she told her husband to follow the army that had proceeded ahead. They caught up with them, and after they entered Madeenah, Umm Sulaym's labour pain began anew. She gave birth to a boy, and his brother on his mother's side, Anas, brought him to the Prophet, who fed him a small amount of chewed dates (*taḥneek*) and named him 'Abdullah. The prayer of the Prophet (ﷺ) for this baby was fulfilled, as among his descendents were ten great scholars.

No doubt Allah, the Almighty, the All-Knower, knew the sincerity of Umm Sulaym's faith, and conveyed the good news of Paradise to her via His Prophet (ﷺ):

> "I entered Paradise, and heard footsteps. I said, 'Who is this?' They told me, 'It is Al-Ghumaysa', the daughter of Milḥaan, the mother of Anas ibn Maalik.'"[46]

Another example of the ways in which a wife may endear herself to her husband may be found in the words of 'Aa'ishah (رضي الله عنها).

> "She spoke to the Prophet (ﷺ) when he came back to his wives after he had kept away from them for a month. He had said, 'I will not go to them for a month,' because he was very angry with them. When twenty-nine days passed, he came to 'Aa'ishah first. 'Aa'ishah said to him, 'You swore to stay away from us for a month, and only twenty-nine days have passed; I have been counting them.' The Prophet said, 'This month has

---

46 Muslim, 16/11, *Kitaab Faḍaa'il aṣ-Ṣaḥaabah, baab fadaa'il Umm Sulaym.*

twenty-nine days.' That particular month had only twenty-nine days."[47]

'Aa'ishah's telling the Prophet (ﷺ) that she had counted twenty-nine days was a clear indication of her love towards her husband and of how she had waited, day after day, hour after hour, for him to come back to her. It shows how she loved and missed her husband. This approach made her even dearer to him, so when he came back to his wives, he started with her.

The sincere Muslim woman recognizes her husband's likes, dislikes and habits, and tries to accommodate them as much as she can, in the best interests of mutual understanding and marital harmony, and to protect the marriage from the boredom of routine. This is what every wise and intelligent wife does. It is narrated that the *qaaḍi* (judge) and *faqeeh* (jurist), Shurayh married a woman from Bani Ḥandhalah. On their wedding night, each of them prayed two *rak'ahs* (units of prayer) and asked Allah (ﷻ) to bless them. Then the bride turned to Shurayh and said, "I am a stranger, and I do not not know much about you. Tell me what you like, and I will do it, and tell me what you do not like so that I may avoid it." Shurayh said, "She stayed with me for twenty years, and I never had to tell her off for anything, except on one occasion, and I was in the wrong then."

This is the respectful and loving wife as Islam wants her to be, responsible for her home and loyal to her husband, and always careful to maintain good relationship between them. If anything happens to upset their marriage, she hastens to calm the situation with her sincere love and wise understanding. She does not listen to the whispering of the *Shayṭaan* which calls her to do wrong. She never

---

[47] From a lengthy hadith narrated by Bukhari and Muslim. See *Fatḥ al-Baari*, 5/116, *Kitaab al-Maẓaalim, baab al-ghurfah wal-'aleeyah al-mushrifah*; Muslim, 7/195, *Kitaab aṣ-Ṣiyaam, baab bayan an ash-shahr yakoon tis'an wa 'ishreen.*

hastens to ask her husband for a divorce. The marriage bond should be too strong to be undone by temporary arguments or occasional misunderstandings. The Prophet (ﷺ) warned those foolish women who ask their husbands for a divorce with no legitimate reason that they would be denied even the scent of Paradise:

> "Any woman who asks her husband for a divorce with no good reason will be deprived of even smelling the scent of Paradise."[48]

She does not disclose his secrets

The chaste Muslim woman does not disclose her husband's secrets, and does not talk to anyone about whatever secrets and other matters there may be between them. The serious Muslim woman is above that, she would never sink to the level of such cheap and shameless talk as goes on amongst the lowest type of people. Her time is too precious to be wasted in such vulgar behaviour. She would never accept for herself to be counted as one of those people whom the Prophet (ﷺ) described as one of the worst types:

> "Among the worst type of people in the sight of Allah on the Day of Judgement is a man who enjoys his wife's intimate company, and she enjoys his intimate company, then one of them goes and discloses the secret of the other."[49]

Disclosing secrets of the intimate and private affairs between a husband and wife is the most disgusting thing. It is done only by the

---

[48] Tirmidhi, 2/329, *Abwaab aṭ-Ṭalaaq*, 11; Ibn Ḥibbaan, 9/490, *Kitaab an-Nikaaḥ, baab ma'aashirat az-zawjayn.*

[49] Muslim, 10/8, *Kitaab an-Nikaaḥ, baab taḥreem ifsha' sirr al-mar'ah*; *At-Targheeb wal-Tarheeb*, 3/86, *Kitaab an-Nikaaḥ, baab at-tarheeb min ifsha' as-sirr bayna al-zawjayn.*

wicked of the worst type. There are some secrets the disclosure of which is not as bad as disclosing this secret. Revealing secrets in any case is bad and unpleasant. Keeping secrets in itself is a worthy and virtuous deed, whilst disclosing them is very bad. Nobody can be immune from faults and shortcomings except the infallible Prophet (ﷺ). The disclosure of a secret entrusted by the Prophet (ﷺ) to Ḥafsah, who told it to 'Aa'ishah, led to the plotting and intrigue in his household. This caused him to keep away from his wives for a month, because he was much upset with them.[50] Concerning this, the following *aayah* was revealed:

> "*When the Prophet disclosed a matter of confidence to one of his consorts, and she then divulged it [to another], and Allah made it known to him, he confirmed part thereof and repudiated a part. Then when he told her thereof, she said, 'Who told you this?' He said, 'He told me Who knows and is well-acquainted [with all things].*'" *(Qur'an 66: 3)*

The two women concerned are then confronted with their error, and called to repent, so that they might draw closer to Allah after having distanced themselves by their deed; otherwise, Allah would be his (the Prophet's) Protector, and Jibreel (Gabriel) (عليه السلام) and the righteous believers and the Angels would also support him:

> "*If you two turn in repentance to Him, your hearts are indeed so inclined; but if you back up each other against him, truly Allah is his Protector, and Gabriel, and [every] righteous one among those who believe —*

---

[50] The story of the Prophet's keeping away from his wives is narrated by Bukhari, Muslim and others. *Fatḥ al-Baari*, 5/116, *Kitaab al-Maẓaalim, baab al-ghurfah wal-'aleeyah al-mushrifah*, and 8/656, *Kitaab at-Tafseer, Soorah at-Taḥreem*; Muslim, 7/195, *Kitaab aṣ-Ṣiyaam, baab bayan an ash-shahr yakoon tis'an wa 'ishreen.*

> *and furthermore, the angels — will back [him] up.”*
> *(Qur'an 66: 4)*

Then they are issued with a stern warning and the terrifying prospect that if they persist in their error, they may lose the honour of being the wives of the Prophet:

> *“It may be, if he divorced you [all], that Allah will give him in exchange Consorts better than you — who submit [their wills], who believe, who are devout, who turn to Allah in repentance, who worship [in humility], who travel [for Faith] and fast, — previously married or virgins.”* *(Qur'an 66: 5)*

This incident presents a valuable lesson to the Muslim woman on the importance of keeping her husband's secrets, and the effect this confidentiality has on the stability of the individual and the home. One of the greatest blessings that Allah has bestowed on the Muslims in particular, and on mankind in general, is that he has made the public and private life of His Messenger (ﷺ) like an open book, in which can be read the teachings of this *'aqeedah* and its practical application in real life. Nothing is secret or hidden: matters and events that people usually keep secret are discussed openly in the Qur'an and Sunnah, even unavoidable human weaknesses. All of these issues are presented in order to teach people right from wrong.

The *Ṣaḥaabah*, may Allah be pleased with them all, understood that the Prophet's life was entirely devoted to Allah and His message, so why should they keep secret or conceal any aspect of his life? The stories that have been narrated about his life, his household and his wives represent a practical application of the words he preached, and for this reason, the *Ṣaḥaabah* (may Allah reward them with all good) transmitted the most precise details of his life, and did not fail to record any aspect of his daily life, whether it was major or minor. This is part of the way in which Allah caused the life of his Prophet to be recorded, including details of the precise way in which Islamic teachings were applied in his life. This is in addition to the Qur'anic references to the Prophet's life, which form a record that will remain until heaven and earth pass away.

She stands by him and offers her advice

One of the laws that Allah has decreed for this life is that men and women should work together to cultivate and populate the earth and run the affairs of life therein. Man cannot do without woman, and vice versa. Hence the laws of Islam teach men and women to co-operate in all matters. Islam encourages a man to help his wife, as much as he is able; the Prophet (ﷺ), who is the example for all Muslims, used to help and serve his family until he went out to pray, as the Mother of the Believers 'Aa'ishah said.[51]

Just as Islam expects a man to help his wife with housework and running household affairs, so the woman is also expected to help him in dealing with the outside world and to play her role in life by offering her opinions and advice, and supporting him in practical terms.

History tells us that Muslim women engaged in jihad side by side with men, marching with them in the battles, bringing water to the thirsty, tending the wounded, setting broken bones, stemming the flow of blood, encouraging the soldiers, and sometimes joining in the actual fighting, running back and forth between the swords and spears, standing firm when some of the brave men had fled. Their courageous conduct in battle was praised by the Prophet (ﷺ), as we have described previously.

However, women's contribution to public life did not confine to the battlefield. Women stood by men, side-by-side, also at times of

---

[51] *Fatḥ al-Baari*, 2/162, *Kitaab al-Adhaan, baab man kaana fi ḥaajat ahlihi.*

peace, offering their valuable opinions, soothing their hearts at times of stress and supporting them during times of hardship.

History has recorded many names of great Muslim men who used to seek and follow the advice of their wives, foremost among whom is the Prophet (ﷺ) himself, who sometimes followed the advice of Khadeejah, Umm Salaamah, 'Aa'ishah and others among his wives. 'Abdullah ibn az-Zubayr used to follow the advice of his mother Asma', Al-Waleed ibn 'Abdul-Malik used to follow the advice of his wife Umm al-Baneen bint 'Abdul 'Aziz ibn Marwaan, and Haroon ar-Rasheed used to follow the advice of his wife Zubaydah, and there are many other such examples in the history of Islam.

The true, sincere Muslim woman understands the heavy burden that Islam has placed on her shoulders, by obliging her to be a good wife to her husband, to surround him with care and meet his every need, to please his heart, satisfy his sentiments and to renew his energy so that he may fulfil his mission in life. She does not withhold her advice when she sees that he needs it, and she never hesitates to stand by his side, encouraging him, supporting him and offering advice and consolation.

The first Muslim woman, Khadeejah bint Khuwaylid (رضي الله عنها) is the best example of a woman who influenced her husband. The Prophet (ﷺ) came to her on the day of the first Revelation, anxious, trembling and shaking all over. He told her, 'Cover me, cover me!' She hastened to offer her help and support, advising him and thinking of a practical way of helping him. Bukhari and Muslim report the story related by 'Aa'ishah of how the Revelation commenced, and the marvellous way in which Khadeejah responded to by supporting her husband:

> "The Revelation started in the form of a dream that came true, he never saw a dream but it would clearly come to pass. Then he was made to like seclusion, so he would go and stay alone in the cave of Hira', praying

and worshipping for many nights at a time, before coming back to his family to collect supplies for another period of seclusion. Then the truth came suddenly, when he was in the cave of Hira'. The angel came to him and said 'Read!' He said, 'I am not a reader.' (The Prophet said:) 'The angel embraced me and squeezed me until I nearly passed out, then released me, and said, 'Read!' I said, 'I am not a reader.' The angels embraced me a second time, squeezed me until I nearly passed out, then released me and said, 'Read!' I said, 'I am not a reader.' The angel embraced me a third time and squeezed me until I nearly passed out, then released me and said:

"*Read! In the name of your Lord and Cherisher, who created — created man, out of a [mere] clot of congealed blood: Read! And your Lord is Most Bountiful — He Who taught [the use of] the Pen — taught man that which he knew not.*" *(Qur'an 96: 1-5)*"

The Messenger of Allah came back to Khadeejah, trembling all over, and said, 'Cover me, cover me!' They covered him up until he calmed down, then he said to Khadeejah, 'O' Khadeejah, what is wrong with me?' He told her what had happened, then said, 'I fear for myself.' Khadeejah said: 'No, rather be of good cheer, for by Allah, Allah would never forsake you. By Allah, you uphold the ties of kinship, speak the truth, spend money on the needy, give money to the penniless, honour your guests and help those beset by difficulties. She took him to Waraqah ibn Nawfal ibn Asad ibn 'Abdul 'Uzza, who was her cousin, the son of her father's brother. He was a man who had become a Christian during the time of *jaahiliyah*. He could write

> the Arabic script and he had written as much of the Gospel in Arabic as Allah willed. He was an old man who had become blind. Khadeejah said to him, 'O' Uncle, listen to your nephew.' Waraqah ibn Nawfal said, 'O' son of my brother, what has happened?' The Messenger of Allah told him what had happened. Waraqah said, 'This is *An-Namoos* (i.e., Jibreel), who was sent down to Moosa (Moses), upon whom be peace. I wish that I were a young man, and could be alive when your people cast you out.' The Messenger of Allah asked, 'Will they really cast me out?' Waraqah said, 'Yes. No man has ever come with what you have brought, but his people were hostile towards him. If I live to see that day I will give you all the support I can.'"[52]

This report is strong evidence of Khadeejah's wifely perfection, wisdom, strength of character, steadfastness, understanding and deep insight. She knew the Prophet's outstanding character, good conduct and purity of heart, and this made her certain that Allah (ﷻ) would never forsake a man such as Muhammad (ﷺ) or permit any bad fate to befall him. She knew that behind this remarkable new event that had overwhelmed the Messenger of Allah (ﷺ) lay something great that Allah had prepared for His Messenger. She therefore spoke to him in kind and sweet words of encouragement, filling him with confidence, tranquillity and firm conviction:

> "Be of good cheer, O' cousin, and stand firm. By the One in Whose hand is the soul of Khadeejah, I hope that you will be the Prophet of this nation."[53]

---

[52] *Fatḥ al-Baari*, 1/23, *Kitaab Bada' al-Waḥy, baab ḥadeeth 'Aa'ishah awwal ma bade'a bihi al-waḥy*; Muslim, 2/197, *Kitaab al-Eemaan, baab bada' al-waḥy.*

[53] Ibn Hisham, *As-Seerah*, 1/254.

Then she took him to her cousin Waraqah ibn Nawfal, who had knowledge of the Torah and Gospel, and told him what had happened to the Prophet.

The first Mother of the Believers, Khadeejah (رضي الله عنها), was a sincere adviser in the way of Islam to the Prophet (ﷺ). She had already earned the great status and lasting fame of being the first person to believe in Allah and His Messenger, and she stood by her husband, the Prophet, supporting him and helping him to bear the worst oppression and persecution that he faced at the beginning of his mission. She endured along with him every hardship and difficulty that he was confronted with. Ibn Hisham says in his *Seerah*:

> "Khadeejah had faith, and believed in what he brought from Allah. In this way, Allah helped His Prophet (ﷺ). Whenever he heard any hateful words of rejection or disbelief that upset him, Allah would cause to put his spirits high (and revived) when he would come back to her. She would encourage him and advise him to be patient, believe in him and make it easier for him to bear whatever the people said or did. May Allah have mercy on her."[54]

She was a woman who always spoke the truth, and carried this burden sincerely. It is no surprise that she earned the pleasure of Allah and deserved to be honoured by Him. The Almighty conveyed the greeting of *salaam* to her through His Messengers Jibreel (Gabriel) and Muhammad, and gave her glad tidings of a house in Paradise, as is stated in the hadith narrated by Abu Hurayrah:

> "Jibreel came to the Prophet and said: 'O' Messenger of Allah, Khadeejah is coming to you with vessels containing food and drink. When she comes to you,

---

54 Ibid., 1/257.

convey to her the greeting of *salaam* from her Lord and from me, and give her the glad tidings of a house of pearls in Paradise, in which there is no noise or hard work."[55]

The true Muslim woman puts her mind to good work, thinks deep and gives advice to her husband at times when he may be most in need of advice. By doing so, she does a great favour to her husband, and this is one of the ways in which she may treat him well.

Another of these great stories which feature correct and timely advice given by a woman is during the reaction of the Muslims to the treaty of Ḥudaybiyah. It came from the mother of the believers Umm Salamah, which demonstrates her deep insight and great wisdom.

Umm Salamah (رضي الله عنها) was one of those who were with the Prophet (ﷺ) when he went to Makkah to perform *'Umrah* in 6 AH. This journey was interrupted by Quraysh. They prevented the Prophet (ﷺ) and his Companions from entering the Grand House — *Bayt al-Ḥaraam*, the Ka'bah. The treaty of Ḥudaybiyah was drawn up between the Prophet and Quraysh. This was a peace-treaty intended to put an end to the fighting for ten years. It was also agreed that if anyone from Quraysh reached Muhammad without the permission of his guardian, he would be returned, but if any of the Muslims reached Quraysh, he would not be returned and that the Muslims would go back that year without entering Makkah, etc.

By virtue of his deep understanding that was derived from the guidance of Allah, the Prophet understood that this treaty, which appeared to be quite unfair to the Muslims, was in fact something good and represented a great victory for Islam and the Muslims. The *Ṣaḥaabah*, however, were dismayed when they learned the

---

55 Bukhari and Muslim. See *Sharḥ as-Sunnah*, 14/155, *Kitaab Faḍaa'il aṣ-Ṣaḥaabah, baab manaaqib Khadeejah.*

content of the treaty. They saw it as unfair and unjust, especially as they had the upper hand at that time. 'Umar ibn al-Khaṭṭab (رضي الله عنه) expressed the angry feelings of the *Ṣahaabah* when he went to Abu Bakr (رضي الله عنه) and asked him: "Is he not the Messenger of Allah?" Abu Bakr said, "Of course, he is." "Are we not Muslims?" "Yes, we are." "Are they not *mushrikeen*?" "Yes, they are so." "Why should we accept this deal which is so humiliating to our religion?" Abu Bakr warned him, "O' 'Umar!, follow his orders. I bear witness that he is the Messenger of Allah." 'Umar said, "And I bear witness that he is the Messenger of Allah." Then 'Umar went to the Messenger of Allah (ﷺ), and asked him similar questions he had asked Abu Bakr. But when he asked, "Why should we accept this deal which is so humiliating to our religion?" the Prophet (ﷺ) replied,

> "I am the slave of Allah and His Messenger; I will never disobey His command, and He will never forsake me."[56]

Then 'Umar realized that his haste to oppose the treaty was a mistake. He used to say,

> "I kept giving charity, fasting, praying and freeing slaves because of what I did and said on that day, until I hoped that ultimately it would be good for me (because it made me perform so many good deeds)."[57]

When the Prophet (ﷺ) had ratified the treaty, he commanded his Companions to get up, slaughter their sacrificial animals, and shave their heads, but none of them got up. He told them three times to do this, but none of them seemed responding. He went to his wife Umm

---

[56]   Ibn Hisham, *As-Seerah*, 3/331; see also *Fatḥ al-Baari*, 6/281, *Kitaab al-Jizyah wal-mawaadi'ah, baab ḥadeeth Sahl ibn Ḥaneef*; Muslim, 12/141, *Kitaab al-Jihaad was-Siyar, baab ṣulh al-Ḥudaybiyah*.

[57]   Ibid.

Salamah, and told her what he was facing from the people. At this point the wisdom and intelligence of Umm Salamah became quite clear: she told him, "O' Messenger of Allah, go out and do not speak to any of them until you have sacrificed your animal and shaved your head."

The Prophet (ﷺ) took her advice, and did as she suggested. When the *Çaḥaabah* saw that, they rushed to sacrifice their animals, pushing one another aside, and some of them began to shave one another's heads, until they were almost fighting with one another because of their distress and grief, and their regret for having disobeyed the Prophet.[58]

After that, the Muslims came back to their senses, and they understood the Prophet's great wisdom in agreeing to this treaty, which in fact was a manifest victory, because many more people entered Islam after it than had before. Muslim narrated that the *aayah* (verse),

> "*Verily We have granted you a manifest Victory.*"
> *(Qur'an 48: 1),*

> — referred to the treaty of Ḥudaybiyah. The Prophet sent for 'Umar and recited this *aayah* to him. 'Umar said, 'Is it really a victory O' Messenger of Allah?' He said, 'Yes.' 'Umar then felt at peace and consoled himself."[59]

She encourages her husband to spend for the sake of Allah

Another way in which the true Muslim woman supports her husband is by encouraging him to spend and give charity for the sake of Allah,

---

58 *Zaad al-Ma'ad*, 3:295, Ṭabari, 2/124.

59 Muslim, 12/141, *Kitaab al-Jihaad waṣ-Ṣiyar, baab ṣulh al-Ḥudaybiyah.*

and not to waste money in extravagance and ostentatious purchases, as we see so many ignorant and misguided women doing.

The alert Muslim woman always wants goodness and success for her husband, she, therefore, urges him to do good deeds, and to do more of them, because she believes that by doing this, she will increase her honour in this world and her reward in the next.

One of the beautiful stories narrated about woman encouraging her husband to spend for the sake of Allah is about Umm ad-Daḥdaḥ.

> "When her husband came to her and told her that he had given in charity the garden in which she and her children were living, in the hope of receiving a bunch of dates[60] in Paradise, she said, 'You have got a good deal, you have got a good deal.' The Prophet commented, 'How many bunches of dates Abu ad-Daḥdaḥ will have in Paradise!' and he repeated this several times.[61]

She helps him to obey Allah

One of the qualities of the good Muslim wife is that she helps her husband to obey Allah in various ways, especially to stay up and pray at night (*qiyaam al-layl*). By doing this, she does him an immense favour, because she reminds him to do something he might otherwise forget or neglect. Thus she causes him, and herself, to be covered by the mercy of Allah.

What a beautiful picture the Prophet (ﷺ) drew of the married couple helping one another to obey Allah and do good deeds, and entering into the mercy of Allah together. This comes in the hadith narrated by

---

[60] Muslim, 8/33, *Kitaab al-Janaa'iz, baab al-laḥd wa naṣab al-laban 'alal-mayyit.*

[61] Aḥmad and Ṭabaraani; its narrators are *rijaal aṣ-ṣaḥeeḥ*. See also *Majma' az-Zawaa'id*, 9/324, *Kitaab al-Manaaqib, baab ma jaa' fi Abi ad-Daḥdaḥ.*

Abu Hurayrah (رضي الله عنه), who said: "The Messenger of Allah (ﷺ) said:

> 'May Allah have mercy on the man who gets up at night to pray and wakes up his wife to pray, and if she refuses, he sprinkles water in her face. And may Allah have mercy on the woman who gets up at night to pray, and wakes her husband up to pray, and if he refuses, she sprinkles water in his face.'"[62]

She fills his heart with joy

The clever and sensitive Muslim woman does not forget that one of the greatest deeds she can do in life, after worshipping Allah, is to be successful in endearing herself to her husband and filling his heart with joy, so that he feels in the depths of his heart that he is happy to be married to her, and enjoys living with her and being in her company. She uses her intelligence to find ways and means of opening his heart and filling it with joy and happiness, so that she may become the queen of his heart.

She understands that she is the greatest joy of a man in this world, as is stated in the hadith narrated by 'Abdullah ibn 'Amr ibn al-'Aaṣ (رضي الله عنه), in which the Prophet (ﷺ) is reported to have said:

> "This world is nothing but temporary conveniences, and the greatest joy in this world is a righteous woman."[63]

She does not forget that she is the greatest joy in this life for a man, if she knows how to endear herself to him. If she does not know how to

---

[62] Abu Dawood, 2/45, in *Kitaab aṣ-Ṣalaah*: *baab qiyaam al-layl*, and by Al-Ḥaakim 1/309, *Kitaab Ṣalaat at-Taṭawwu'*; he said that it is *ṣaḥeeḥ* according to the conditions of Muslim.

[63] Muslim, 10/56, *Kitaab ar-Riḍaa', baab istiḥbaab nikaaḥ al-bikr.*

endear herself to him, then in most cases she will be a source of unhappiness and misery to her husband, as was confirmed by the Prophet (ﷺ):

> "Three things make the son of Adam happy, and three make him miserable. Among the things that make the son of Adam happy are a good wife, a good home and a good means of transport; the things that make him miserable are a bad wife, a bad home and a bad means of transport."[64]

Hence, being a good wife, and endearing oneself to one's husband, are a part of religion. This offers protection to a man by helping him to remain chaste, and strengthens the foundations of the family, thus bringing happiness to her husband and children.

The Muslim woman by nature likes to endear herself to her husband. By doing so she finds a way of fulfilling her femininity and her inclinations to make herself attractive. But for the Muslim woman, the matter goes even further. By seeking to win her husband's heart, she is also seeking to earn the pleasure of Allah (ﷻ), Who has made the excellent behaviour with her spouse a part of religion and about which she will be questioned in the Hereafter. She therefore does not spare any effort in her loving treatment of her husband. She presents pleasing appearance, speaks pleasantly and kindly, and is a clever and likeable companion.

She makes herself beautiful for him

She makes herself beautiful for her husband by means of make-up, clothing, etc., in order to appear more beautiful and attractive, to please her husband. This was the practice of the righteous women of the *salaf* (predecessors), who used to devote their time to

---

[64] Aḥmad, 1/168; its narrators are *rijaal aṣ-ṣaheeḥ*.

worshipping Allah and reading the Qur'an. Foremost among them were 'Aa'ishah (ﷺ) and others. They used to wear fine clothes and jewellery at home and when travelling with their husbands, in order to make themselves look beautiful and attractive to them.

Bakrah bint 'Uqbah visited 'Aa'ishah (may Allah be pleased with them) and asked her about using henna. 'Aa'ishah said, "It comes from a good tree and pure water." She also asked her about removing body hair, and she said, "If you have a husband, and you are to remove your eyes and replace them with something better for him, then do it."[65]

Let the careless women who neglect their appearance in front of their husbands listen to the advice of 'Aa'ishah, and realize that their beauty should be primarily for their husbands, and not for their friends and peers. Those women who are failing to make themselves beautiful for their husbands are sinners, because they are falling short in one of the greatest duties of marriage. Their negligence in beautifying themselves for their husbands may be the cause of their (husbands) staying away from them (wives) and looking at other women.

The wife whose husband always finds her with unkempt hair, pale looking, wan and wearing shabby old clothes, is a foolish and disobedient wife. It will be of no help to her if she rushes to beautify herself only when receiving guests, or going to a women's party, but remains looking shabby most of the time in front of her husband. I think that the Muslim woman who is truly guided by the teachings of Islam will be safe from such shortcomings, because she treats her husband properly, and a woman who treats her husband properly is most unlikely to fail in fulfilling her duty towards him.

It is one of the teachings of Islam that a woman should make herself

---

65 Ibn al-Jawzi, *Aḥkaam an-Nisa'*, 343.

look bcautiful for her husband, so that her husband sees her in the manner he loves to see. This is the reason that it is forbidden for a woman to dress in mourning for more than three days, except in the case of her husband's death, when she is permitted to mourn for four months and ten days. We find proof of this in the hadith narrated by Bukhari from Zaynab, the daughter of Umm Salamah. She said, "I came to Zaynab bint Jaḥsh, the wife of the Prophet (ﷺ) when her brother had died. She called for perfume and applied it to herself, then said, "I am not using perfume because I need to, but because I heard the Messenger of Allah (ﷺ) say from the *minbar* (pulpit):

> "It is not permitted for a woman who believes in Allah and the Last Day to grieve for more than three days, except for her husband, (for whom she may grieve) four months and ten days."[66]

She is cheerful and grateful when she meets him

One of the ways in which the Muslim woman makes herself attractive to her husband is by being happy, cheerful, friendly and gentle, thus flooding her husband's life with joy. When he comes home exhausted from his work, she greets him with a smiling face and kind words. She puts her own concerns to one side for a while, and helps him to forget some of his worries. She appears as cheerful and serene as she can, and expresses her gratitude to him every time he does something good for her.

The true Muslim woman is fair-minded, and is never ungrateful to any person, because the teachings of her religion protect her from falling into the error of bad behaviour and ingratitude for favours. How then could she be ungrateful to her husband, her beloved lifelong

---

[66] *Fatḥ al-Baari*, 9/484, *Kitaab aṭ-Ṭalaaq, baab iḥdaad al-mutawaffa 'anha zawjuha.*

companion? She knows well the teaching of the Prophet (ﷺ):

> "He does not thank Allah who does not thank people."[67]

She understands from this that every person who does good deeds and favours deserves thanks and recognition, so how could she hesitate or fail to show gratitude to her husband, especially when she hears the words of the Prophet (ﷺ):

> "Allah will not look at the woman who does not thank her husband at the time when she cannot do without him."[68]

She shares his joys and sorrows

Another way in which a woman may endear herself to her husband is by sharing his joys and sorrows. She joins him in some of his pastimes, and his daily work, such as reading, exercise, and attending useful talks and gatherings, and so on, so that her husband feels that he is not alone in his enjoyment of good things in life. He is sharing these pleasures with a loving, intelligent and loyal wife.

The fact that the Prophet (ﷺ) raced with 'Aa'ishah more than once indicates the fact that Islam urges both the spouses to share their partner's joy and happiness in life, because this sharing has a powerful impact in deepening their feelings for one another and strengthening the bonds between them.

Just as she shares his joys, she also shares his worries and concerns, and comes to him with kind words of consolation, mature and sensible advice and sincere emotional support.

---

67 Bukhari in *Al-Adab al-Mufrad*, 1/310, *baab man la yashkur an-naas.*

68 Al-Ḥaakim in *Al-Mustadrak*, 2/190, *Kitaab an-Nikaah.*

She does not look at other men

The true Muslim woman avoids looking at men other than her husband. She does not stare at men who are not related to her (i.e. who are not her *mahram*), in obedience to the command of Allah:

> "*And say to the believing women that they should lower their gaze...*" *(Qur'an 24: 31).*

By refraining from looking at other men, she attains the (Qur'anic) quality of chaste women who restrain their glances, a quality men love most in women. It is indicative of their purity, decency and fidelity. This is the excellent characteristic of the chaste, decent, pure Muslim woman, referred to in the Qur'an when it speaks of the women of Paradise and their qualities that are loved by men:

> "*In them will be [Maidens] chaste, restraining their glances, whom no man or jinn before them has touched.*" *(Qur'an 55: 56)*

She does not describe other women to him

Another characteristic of the intelligent Muslim woman is that she does not describe any of her (female) friends or acquaintances to him, because this is forbidden in Islam as the Prophet (ﷺ) said:

> "No woman should talk about another woman, or describe her to her husband (so that it is) as if he sees her."[69]

Islam wants people's hearts to be at peace, put a stop to provocative thoughts and overactive imaginations, so that people may live their lives in a decent and calm fashion, free from such thoughts and able

---

69 *Fatḥ al-Baari*, 9/338, *Kitaab an-Nikaaḥ, baab tabaashir al-mar'at al-mar'ah fatana'at-ha li zawjiha.*

to go about the tasks and duties for which they were created. No man should let his mind be occupied with cheap thoughts of comparing his wife with the woman she describes, or let himself become crazy with her imaginative beauty. He should not let such foolish talk stop him from going about his work and usual pastimes, or lead him to temptation and make him go astray.

She tries to create an atmosphere of peace and tranquility for him

The Muslim woman does not only make herself beautiful for her husband and share his work and pastimes, but she also tries to create an atmosphere of peace and tranquillity in the home. She tries to keep a clean and tidy home, in which he will see order and good taste, and clean, well-mannered, polite children, and where good meals are prepared regularly. The clever woman also does whatever else she can, based on her knowledge and good taste. All of this is part of being a good Muslim wife as enjoined by Islam.

The true Muslim woman does not forget that, according to Islam, marriage is one of the signs of Allah. Islam has made the wife a source of tranquillity, rest and consolation for her husband:

> "*And among His Signs is this, that He created for you mates from among yourselves, that you may dwell in tranquillity with them, and He has put love and mercy between your [hearts]...*" *(Qur'an 30: 21)*

Marriage is the deepest of bonds which Allah (سبحانه وتعالى) ties between one soul and another, so that they may enjoy peace, tranquillity, stability and permitted pleasures. The wife is a source of refuge, security and rest for her husband in a marital home that is filled with sincere love and compassionate mercy. The truly-guided Muslim woman is the best one to understand this lofty meaning and to translate it into a pleasant and cheerful reality.

She is tolerant and forgiving

The Muslim woman is tolerant and forgiving, overlooking any errors on the part of her husband. She does not bear a grudge against him for such errors or remind him about them every now and then. There is no quality that will endear her to her husband like the quality of tolerance and forgiveness, and there is nothing that will turn her husband against her like resentment, counting faults and reminding him about his mistakes.

The Muslim woman who is following the guidance of Islam obeys the command of Allah (ﷻ):

> "...*Let them forgive and overlook, do you not wish that Allah should forgive you?...* *(Qur'an 24: 22)*

Such a woman deserves to be the queen of her husband's heart and to fill his soul with joy and happiness.

She is strong in character and wise

Among the most prominent characteristics of the Muslim woman are her strength of character, mature way of thinking, and serious conduct. These are the qualities that a Muslim woman possesses both before and after marriage, because they are the result of her understanding of Islam and awareness of her mission in life.

She exhibits this strength of character when she is choosing a husband. She does not give way to her father's whims if he has deviated from the right way and is seeking to force her into a marriage that she does not want. Neither does she give in to the man who comes to seek her hand in marriage, no matter how rich or powerful he may be, if he does not have the qualities of a true Muslim husband.

After marriage, her character remains strong, even though she is distinguished by her easy-going nature, mild-tempered behaviour and loving obedience to her husband. Her strength of character comes to the fore especially when she has to take a stand in matters concerning her religion and *'aqeedah*, as we have seen in some of the narratives referred to previously, such as Umm Sulaym bint Milḥaan, who insisted on adhering to Islam along with her son Anas, although her husband Maalik ibn an-Naḍar remained a *mushrik*, opposed to his wife being Muslim; and Umm Habeebah bint Abi Sufyan who remained steadfast in her Islam when her husband 'Ubaydullah ibn Jaḥsh al-Asadi became an apostate and joined the religion of the Abyssinians; and Barirah who was determined to separate from her husband whom she did not love, even though the Prophet (ﷺ) tried to intervene on his behalf; and the wife of Thabit ibn Qays ibn Shammaas, who demanded a divorce from her husband whom she did not love either, and the Prophet (ﷺ) accepted her request.

The primary motive of these women in taking up such a strong stance was their concern to adhere to Islam, to keep their belief (*'aqeedah*) pure, and ultimately to please Allah (ﷺ).

Each of them was seeking that which is *ḥalaal* (lawful) in her married life, and feared committing any *ḥaraam* (forbidden, unlawful) deed, either because she was married to a man who did not share her religious beliefs, or she was falling short in her duties towards a husband whom she did not love or could not live with. If it were not for their strength of character and dignity, consciousness of themselves and their faith, they would have followed the commands of their misguided husbands and would have found themselves going astray, choking on the misery of living with a husband they could not truly accept. The courage of these women shows how the true Muslim women should be, no matter where or when she lives.

But the Muslim woman's strength of character should not make her forget that she is required to obey her husband and treat him with honour and respect. Her strength of character should make her strike a wise balance in the way she speaks and acts towards him, with no inconsistency or carelessness. Even in those moments of anger which are unavoidable in married life, she should control herself and restrain her tongue, lest she say anything that could hurt her husband's feelings. This is the quality of a strong, balanced character.

'Aa'ishah (ﷺ) represents the highest example of this good quality, and every Muslim woman should follow her example. The way in which she swore an oath when she was happy with her husband, the Prophet (ﷺ), was different from the way she spoke when she was upset with him. This is an example of good manners and respect. It was something that the Prophet (ﷺ) noticed, as she narrated that he said:

> "I know when you are happy with me and when you are upset with me." She said, "How do you know that?" He said, "When you are happy with me, you say, 'No, by the Lord of Muhammad,' and when you are upset with me, you say, 'No, by the Lord of Ibraheem.' She said, 'Yes, that is right. By Allah, O' Messenger of Allah, I only keep away from your name.'"[70]

What a refined manner and sincere love!

'Aa'ishah's strength of character became even more prominent when she was tried with the slander (*al-ifk*) which Allah made a test for His Messenger (ﷺ) and for all the ummah, raising the status of some and lowering that of others, increasing the faith of those who were guided and increasing the loss of those who went astray.

Her strength of character and deep faith in Allah became apparent, and her trust in Him alone to prove her innocence was quite clear. I can find no more beautiful description of the deep and sincere faith of 'Aa'ishah and her trust in the justice of Allah, than that given by Ibn

---

[70] Muslim, 15/203, *Kitaab Faḍaa'il aṣ-Ṣaḥaabah, baab faḍaa'il Umm al-Mu'mineen 'Aa'ishah.*

Qayyim al-Jawziyah, who said:

"The test was so severe that the Revelation ceased for a month because of it, and nothing at all concerning this issue was revealed to the Messenger of Allah during that period, so that the wisdom behind what had happened might become completely apparent and the sincere believers might be increased in faith and adherence to justice and might think well of Allah, His Messenger, the Messenger's family and those believers who spoke the truth. The *munafiqeen* — hypocrites, meanwhile, would be increased only in sins and hypocrisy, and their true nature would be exposed to the Prophet and the believers. 'Aa'ishah, the one who had spoken the truth, and her parents would be shown to be true servants of Allah who had received His full blessing. Their need for Allah and desire to draw closer to Him would increase; they would feel humble before Him and would put their hope and trust in Him, instead of hoping for the support of other people. 'Aa'ishah would despair of receiving help from any created being, and she passed this most difficult test when her father said, 'Get up and thank him,' after Allah had sent down a Revelation confirming her innocence. She said, 'By Allah, I will not get up and thank him; I will only give thanks to Allah Who has revealed my innocence.'

Another aspect of the wisdom behind the Revelation being suspended for a month was that people would focus solely on this issue and examine it closely; the believers would wait with eager anticipation to hear what Allah would reveal to His Messenger concerning this matter. The Revelation came like rain on parched land, when it was most needed by the Messenger of Allah and his family, by Abu Bakr and his family and, by the *Ṣaḥaabah*. It brought them great relief and joy. If Allah had revealed the truth of the matter from the first instant, then the wisdom behind this event would have been obscured and a great lesson would have been lost.

Allah wanted to demonstrate the status of His Prophet and his family in His sight, and the honour which He had bestowed upon them. He Himself was to defend His Messenger and rebuke his enemies, in such a way that the Prophet (ﷺ) had nothing to do with it. Allah alone would avenge His Prophet and his family.

The Messenger of Allah (ﷺ) was the target of this slander, and the one who was accused was his wife. It was not appropriate for him to declare her innocence, although he knew that she was indeed innocent, and never thought otherwise. When he asked people to avenge him of those who had spread the slander, he said: 'Who could blame me if I were to punish those who slandered my family? By Allah, I have never known anything but good from my family, and they have told me about a man from whom I have never known anything but good, and he never came in my house except with me.' He had more proof than the believers had of 'Aa'ishah's innocence, but because of his high level of patience, perseverance and deep trust in Allah, he acted in the appropriate manner until the Revelation came that made his heart rejoice and raised his status, showing to his ummah that Allah was taking care of him.

Whoever examines 'Aa'ishah's response, when her father told her to get up and thank the Messenger of Allah, and she said, 'No, I will give thanks only to Allah,' will realize the extent of her knowledge and the depth of her faith. She attributed this blessing to Allah alone, and gave thanks only to Him. She had a sound grasp of *Tawḥeed*, and demonstrated great strength of character and confidence in her innocence. She was not curious or anxious about the outcome when she spoke thus, because she was sure that she had done nothing wrong.

> Because of her faith in the Prophet's love for her, she said what she said. She became even dearer to him when she said, 'I will not give thanks except to Allah, for He is the One Who has revealed my innocence.' She displayed remarkable maturity and steadfastness when her dearly beloved husband, whom she could not bear to be apart from, kept away from her for a month; then when the matter was resolved and he wished to come back to her, she did not rush to him, despite her great love for him. This is the highest level of steadfastness and strength of character."[71]

It is indeed the highest level of maturity and strength of character. The true Muslim woman is humble, kind, loving and obedient to her husband, but she does not allow her character to weaken before him, even if he is the most beloved of all people to her, and the most noble and honourable of all human beings, so long as she is in the right and is adhering to the way of Allah. 'Aa'ishah (رضي الله عنها) set the highest example of the strength of character of the Muslim woman who is proud of her religion and understands what it is to be a true servant, a true slave of Allah alone.

The Muslim woman should not interpret 'Aa'ishah's attitude as an attitude of superiority or arrogance, pushing her husband away. We have already explained the duties of the Muslim woman towards her husband i.e., obedience, loving kindness and seeking to please him, in accordance with Islamic teachings. What we learn from the attitude of 'Aa'ishah is the esteem and honour with which Islam regards woman, so long as she adheres to the laws and teachings of Islam. This is what gives her character strength, pride, honour and wisdom.

Islam gives women rights and recognition which are envied by Western women when they hear about them. This has been freely admitted by women's liberation activists in Arab countries, as we

---

[71] Ibn al-Qayyim, *Zaad al-Ma'ad*, 3/261-264.

have seen. Many of them have retracted their claims that Muslim women need to be liberated; one such activist is Dr. Nawaal El Sa‘adawi, who was interviewed for the Kuwaiti newspaper *Al-Waṭan* (mid-August 1989).

Dr. El Sa‘adaawi was asked, “Do you think that the European women are an example to be copied?” She replied,

> “No, not at all. European women have advanced in some fields, but are backward in others. The marriage laws in Europe oppress women, and this is what led to the development of women’s liberation movements in those countries and in America, where this movement is very strong and is even at times quite vicious.”

Then she remarked:

> “Our Islamic religion has given women more rights than any other religion has, and has guaranteed her honour and pride, but what has happened is that men have sometimes used certain aspects of this religion to create a patriarchal class system in which males dominate females.”

Clearly this “patriarchal oppression” mentioned by Dr. El Sa‘adaawi, which has led to the oppression of women, has been caused by ignorance of the true teachings of Islam.

She is one of the most successful wives

This discussion above concerning the intellectual, psychological, social and aesthetic characteristics of a smart and Islamically conscious Muslim woman demonstrates that she is a successful wife, rather most successful one. Most of them are the great blessing, good fortunes and source of happiness for their respective men.

By virtue of her understanding of Islamic teaching, and fulfilling duties towards her husband, she becomes the greatest source of happiness in her husband's life. When he comes home, she greets him with a warm and friendly smile, speaking kindly and sweetly, looking attractive and smart, with a clean and tidy house, pleasant conversation, and a table full of good food, pleasing him and making him happy.

She is obedient, kind and loving towards her husband, ever eager to please him. She does not disclose his secrets or upset his plans. She stands by him at times of hardship, offering her support and wise advice. She shares his joys and sorrows. She endears herself to him by the way she looks and behaves, and fills his life with joy and happiness. She encourages him to obey Allah in various ways, and motivates him by joining him in numerous activities. She respects his mother and family. She refrains from looking at other men. She keeps away from foolish and worthless talk. She is keen to provide an atmosphere of peace, tranquillity and stability for her husband and children. She is strong of character without being rude or aggressive, and is kind and gentle without being weak. She earns the respect of those who speak to her. She is tolerant and forgiving, overlooking errors and never bearing grudges.

Thus, the Muslim wife deserves to be the most successful wife. She is the greatest blessing that Allah may bestow upon a man, and an incomparable source of joy in this life. The Prophet (ﷺ) indeed spoke the truth when he said:

> "This world is nothing but temporary conveniences, and the greatest joy in this world is a righteous woman."[72]

---

[72] Muslim, 10/56, *Kitaab ar-Riḍaa', baab istiḥbaab nikaaḥ al-bikr.*

CHAPTER FIVE

The Muslim Woman and Her Children

Introduction

Undoubtedly, children are a source of great joy and delight; they make life sweet, bring more *rizq* (sustenance) into a family's life and give hope. A father sees his children as a future source of help and support, as well as an increase in number and perpetuation of the family. A mother sees her children as a source of hope, consolation and joy in life, and as hope for the future. All of these hopes rest on the good upbringing of the children and giving them a sound training and education for life, so that they become active and constructive elements in society, a source of goodness for their parents, community and society as a whole. They then will be as Allah (ﷻ) described them:

> "*Wealth and sons are allurements of the life of this world...*" *(Qur'an 18: 46)*

If their education and upbringing are neglected, they will become bad characters, a burden on their parents, family, community and humanity at large.

She understands the great responsibility that she has towards her children

The Muslim woman never forgets that the mother's responsibility in bringing up the children and forming their characters is greater than that of the father, because children tend to be closer to their mother and spend more time with her. She knows all about their behavioural, emotional and intellectual development during their childhood and the difficult years of adolescence.

Hence the woman who understands the teachings of Islam and her own educational role in life, knows her full responsibility for the upbringing of her children, as is referred to in the Qur'an:

> "*O' you who believe! Save yourselves and your families from a Fire whose fuel is Men and Stones...*"
>
> *(Qur'an 66: 6)*

The Prophet (ﷺ) also referred to this responsibility in the hadith:

> "Beware! Each of you is a shepherd and each of you is responsible and answerable for his flock. The leader and the ruler is a shepherd over the people and shall be questioned about his subjects (as to how he conducted their affairs); a man is a guardian over his family and shall be questioned about them (as to how he looked after their physical and moral well-being); a woman is the guardian over the household of her husband and his children and shall be questioned about them (as to how she managed the household and brought up the children); a servant is the shepherd of his master's property and shall be questioned about it (as to how he safeguarded his trust). Beware! Everyone of you is a guardian and everyone of you shall be questioned with regard to his trust."[1]

Islam places responsibility on the shoulders of every individual; no one person is left out. Parents — especially mothers — are made responsible for providing their children with a solid upbringing and sound Islamic education, based on the noble characteristics that the

---

[1] Bukhari and Muslim, See *Sharḥ as-Sunnah*, 10/61, *Kitaab al-Imarah wal-qaḍa', baab ar-ra'ee mas'ool 'an ra'iy 'atihi.*

Prophet (Blessings and Peace be upon him) declared that he had been sent to complete and spread among people:

> "I have only been sent to make righteous behaviour complete."[2]

Nothing is more indicative of the greatness of the parents' responsibility towards their children and their duty to give them a suitable Islamic upbringing than the verdict of the *'ulama* that every family should pay heed to the words of the Prophet (ﷺ):

> "Instruct your children to pray when they are seven and hit them if they do not do so when they are ten."[3]

Any parents who are aware of this hadith but do not teach their children to pray when they reach seven or do not hesitate even to hit them if they do not do so when they reach ten, are parents who are sinners and failing in their duty; they would be answerable to Allah (ﷻ) for their failure.

The family home is a microcosm of society in which the children's mentality, intellect, attitudes and inclinations are formed when they are still very small and are ready to receive sound words of guidance. Hence the parents' important role in forming the minds of their sons and daughters and directing them towards truth and good deeds is quite clear.

Muslim women have always understood their responsibility in raising their children, and they have a brilliant record in producing and influencing great men, and instilling noble values in their hearts. Intelligent and brilliant women did produce far more noble sons than intelligent and brilliant men did, so much so that you can hardly find

---

[2] Bukhari in *Al-Adab al-Mufrad*, 1/371, *baab ḥusn al-khulq*.

[3] Aḥmad, 2/187, and by Abu Dawood with a *ḥasan* isnad, 1/193, *Kitaab aṣ-Ṣalaat, baab mata yu'mar al-ghulaam biṣ-ṣalaat.*

any among the great men of our ummah who have controlled the course of events in history who is not indebted to his mother.

Zubayr ibn al-'Awaam was indebted for his greatness to his mother Ṣafiyah bint 'Abdul Muṭṭalib, who instilled in him the good qualities and distinguished nature.

'Abdullah, Mundhir and 'Urwah, the sons of Zubayr were the products of the values instilled in them by their mother, Asma' bint Abi Bakr. Each of them attained high status and left their respective impact in history.

'Ali ibn Abi Taalib (رضي الله عنه) received wisdom, virtue and good character from his distinguished mother, Faṭimah bint Asad.

'Abdullah ibn Ja'far, the chief of the Arab generosity and the noble of the youths, lost his father at an early age. It was his mother Asma' bint 'Umays who took care of him and instilled in him the virtues and noble characteristics, and she herself became one of the great women of Islam.

Mu'aawiyah ibn Abi Sufyaan inherited his strength of character and intelligence from his mother, Hind bint 'Utbah, and not from his father Abu Sufyaan. When he was a baby, she noticed that he possessed intelligent and clever features. Someone said to her, "If he lives, he will become the leader of his people." She responded, "May he not live if he is only to become the leader of his people!"

Mu'awiyah was unable to instill his cleverness, patience and skills in his own son and heir, Yazeed, because the boy's mother was a simple Bedouin woman whom he had married for her beauty and for the status of her tribe and family.

Mu'aawiyah's brother Ziyad ibn Abi Sufyaan, who was a prime example of intelligence, shrewdness and quick-wittedness, was similarly unable to pass these qualities on to his son 'Ubaydullah, who grew up to be stupid, clumsy, incapable and superficial. His mother was Marjanah, a Persian woman who possessed none of the qualities that might entitle her to be the mother of a great man.

History records the names of two great men of Bani Umayyah, the first known for his strength of character, capability, intelligence, wisdom and decisiveness, and the second took the path of justice, goodness, piety and righteousness.

The first was 'Abdul Malik ibn Marwan. His mother was 'Aa'ishah bint al-Mughirah ibn Abi al-'Aaṣ ibn Umayyah. She was well-known for her strength of character, resolution and intelligence. The second was 'Umar ibn 'Abdul 'Aziz (رضي الله عنه), the fifth of the *Khulafa' ar-Rashideen* (The four Caliphs right after Prophet Muhammad). His mother was Umm 'Aasim bint 'Aasim ibn 'Umar ibn al-Khaṭṭab. She was the most noble in character of the women of her time. Her mother was the God-fearing, righteous worshipper of Allah whom Caliph 'Umar had selected to marry his son 'Aasim, when he found her an embodiment of honesty and integrity, because she did not agree to add water to milk as her mother asked her to do, saying that Allah was watching whatever she did.

If we turn towards Andalusia, we find the brilliant, ambitious ruler 'Abdur Raḥmaan an-Naaṣir who, having started life as an orphan, went on to establish an empire in the West, to which the leaders and kings of Europe surrendered and to whose institutes of learning the scholars and philosophers of all nations flocked to seek knowledge. This state made great contribution to the worldwide Islamic culture. If we were to examine the secret of this man's greatness, we would find that it lay in the greatness of his mother who knew how to instill in him the dynamic spirit of ambition.

During the 'Abbasid period, there were two great women who planted the seeds of ambition, distinction and ascendancy in their sons. The first was the mother of Ja'far ibn Yaḥya, who was the *wazeer* (the Prime minister) of the *Khaleefah* Ḥaroon ar-Rasheed.

The second was the mother of Imam Ash-Shafi'ee. He never saw his father who died whilst he was still a babe in arms; it was his mother who took care of his education.

There are many such examples of brilliant women in our history, women who instilled in their sons nobility of character and the seeds of greatness, and who stood behind them in everything they achieved of power and status.

She uses the best methods in bringing them up

The intelligent Muslim woman understands the psychology of her children, and is aware of their differences in attitudes and inclination. She tries to penetrate their innocent world and plant the seeds of noble values and worthy characteristics, using the best and most effective methods of parenting.

The mother is naturally close to her children, and she endears herself to them so that they will be open with her and will share their thoughts and feelings with her. She hastens to correct them and refine their thoughts and feelings, taking into account each child's age and mental level. She plays and jokes with them sometimes, complimenting them and letting them hear words of love, affection, compassion and self-denial. Thus, their love for her increases, and they accept her words of guidance and correction eagerly. They obey her out of love for her, for there is a great difference between sincere obedience that comes from the heart, which is based on love, respect and trust, and insincere obedience that is based on oppression, violence and force. The former is lasting obedience, strong and fruitful, whilst the latter is shallow and baseless, and quickly vanishing when the violence and cruelty reach extreme levels.

She demonstrates her love and affection for them

The Muslim woman is not ignorant of the fact that her children need her warm lap, deep love and sincere affection in order to develop soundly, with no psychological problems, crises or complexes. This sound upbringing fill them with optimism, trust, hope and ambition. Thus the caring Muslim mother demonstrates her love and affection for her children on every occasion, flooding their lives with joy and happiness and filling their hearts with confidence and security.

The true Muslim woman is compassionate towards her children, for compassion is a basic Islamic characteristic, one that was encouraged by the Prophet (ﷺ) in words and deeds as Anas (رضي الله عنه) tells us:

> "I never saw anyone who was more compassionate towards children than the Messenger of Allah. His son Ibraheem was in the care of a wet-nurse in the hills around Madeenah. He would go there, and we would go with him, he would enter the house, pick up his son and kiss him, then come back."[4]

The Prophet's compassion and love towards Muslim children included little ones at play. He would flood them with his compassion and affection. Anas reported that,

> "Whenever the Prophet passed by a group of boys he would smile fondly and greet them."[5]

An example of the Prophet's enduring wisdom with regard to the upbringing of children is the hadith:

> "He is not one of us who does not show compassion to our little ones and recognize the rights of our elders."[6]

---

[4] Muslim, 15/75, *Kitaab al-Faḍaa'il, baab raḥmatihi wa tawaaḍu'ihi.*

[5] Bukhari and Muslim, See *Sharḥ as-Sunnah*, 12/264, *Kitaab al-Isti'dhaan, baab at-tasleem 'ala aṣ-ṣubyaan.*

[6] Aḥmad, 2/185, and by Al-Ḥaakim, 1/62, *Kitaab al-Eemaan*; its isnad is *ṣaḥeeḥ*.

Abu Hurayrah (رضي الله عنه) narrated that the Prophet (ﷺ) kissed Al-Ḥasan ibn 'Ali. Al-Aqra' ibn Ḥaabis said, "I have ten children and I have never kissed any of them." The Prophet (ﷺ) said:

> "He who does not show mercy will not be shown mercy."[7]

The Prophet (ﷺ), the great educator, always sought to instill the quality of mercy and compassion in people's hearts, and to awaken their potential for love and affection, which are the most basic of human characteristics.

One day a Bedouin came and asked the Prophet (ﷺ), "Do you kiss your sons? We do not." The Prophet (ﷺ) said,

> "What can I do for you if Allah has removed mercy from your heart?"[8]

'Aa'ishah (رضي الله عنها) reported:

> "Whenever Faṭimah came into the room, the Prophet (ﷺ) would stand up, welcome her, kiss her and offer her his seat, and whenever he came into the room, she would stand up, take his hand, welcome him, kiss him and offer him her seat. When she came to see him during his final illness, he welcomed her and kissed her."[9]

The Prophet (ﷺ) praised the women of Quraysh, because they were the most compassionate women towards their children, the most

---

[7] Bukhari and Muslim, *Sharḥ as-Sunnah*, 13/34, *Kitaab al-Birr waṣ-Ṣilah, baab raḥmat al-walad wa taqbeelihi.*

[8] *Fatḥ al-Baari*, 10/426, *Kitaab al-Adab, baab raḥmat al-walad wa taqbeelihi.*

[9] *Fatḥ al-Baari*, 8/135, *Kitaab al-Maghaazi, baab maraḍuhu wa wafatuhu*; Abu Dawood, 4/480, *Kitaab al-Adab, baab ma jaa' fil-qiyaam.*

concerned with raising them properly and making sacrifices for them, in addition to taking good care of their husbands. This may be seen in the words narrated by Bukhari from Abu Hurayrah (رضي الله عنه), who said:"I heard the Messenger of Allah (ﷺ) say:

> 'The women of Quraysh are the best women ever to ride camels. They are compassionate towards their children and the most careful with regard to their husbands' wealth."[10]

In the light of this guidance, the true Muslim woman cannot be stern towards her children and treat them in a rough or mean fashion, even if there is austerity and harshness in her nature, because this religion, with its enlightenment and guidance, softens hearts and awakens feelings of love and affection. Our children are part of us, going forth into the world, as the poet Ḥiṭṭaan ibn al-Mu'alla said:

> "Our children are our hearts, walking among us on the face of the earth, if even a little breeze touches them, we cannot sleep for worrying about them."[11]

Parents should be filled with love, affection and care, willing to make sacrifices and do their best for their children.

Undoubtedly the wealth of emotion that the Muslim mother feels for her children is one of the greatest causes of her happiness in life. This is something which has been lost by Western women, who are overwhelmed by materialism and exhausted by the daily grind of work, which has caused them to lose the warmth of family feelings. This was vividly expressed by Mrs. Salma al-Ḥaffar, a member of the Syrian women's movement, after she visited America:

"It is truly a shame that women lose the most precious thing

---

[10] *Fatḥ al-Baari*, 6/472, *Kitaab Aḥaadeeth al-Anbiya', baab qawlihi ta'ala*, 45-48 *min Aal 'Imran* (Qur'an 3: 45-48).

[11] Abu Tammam, *Al-Ḥamaasah*, 1/167.

> that nature[12] has given them, i.e. their femininity, and then their happiness, because the constant cycle of exhausting work has caused them to lose the small paradise which is the natural refuge of women and men alike, one that can only flourish under the care of a mother who stays at home. The happiness of individuals and society as a whole is to be found at home, in the lap of the family. The family is the source of inspiration, goodness and creativity."[13]

She treats her sons and daughters equally

The wise Muslim woman treats all her children fairly and equally. She does not prefer one of them to another in any way, because she knows that Islam forbids such actions on the part of the parents, and because of the negative psychological impact that this may have over the child whose sibling is preferred to him. The child who feels that he is not treated equally with his brothers and sisters will grow up with complexes and anxiety, eating his heart out with jealousy and hatred. In contrast, the child who grows up feeling that he and his siblings are treated equally will grow up healthy and free from jealousy and hatred; he will be content, cheerful, tolerant and willing to put others before himself. This is what Islam requires of parents and urges them to do.

Bukhari, Muslim and others report that,

> "The father of An-Nu'man ibn Basheer (رضي الله عنه) brought him to the Prophet (ﷺ) and said, 'I have given this son of mine a slave I have.' The Prophet asked, 'Have you given each of your children the same?' He said, 'No.'

---

[12] In fact it is Allah Who gives these things, not nature. This expression is one of the effects of Westernization. (Author)

[13] From an article by Salma al-Ḥaffar in the Damacus newspaper *Al-Ayyaam*, 3/9/1962.

The Prophet told him, 'Then take the slave back.'"

According to another report:

> "The Prophet (ﷺ) asked, 'Have you done the same for all your children?' (My father) said, 'No', so the Prophet said, 'Fear Allah and treat all of your children equally.'"

According to a third report:

> "The Prophet (ﷺ) asked, 'O' Basheer, do you have any other children?' He said, 'Yes.' The Prophet asked, 'Will you give a similar gift to each of them?' He said, 'No.' So the Prophet said, 'Do not ask me to be witness to this, because I do not want to be a witness to unfairness.' Then he added, 'Would you not like all your children to treat you with equal respect?' (Basheer) said, 'Of course.' The Prophet told him, 'So do not do it.'"[14]

So the Muslim woman who truly fears Allah treats all her children with equal fairness, and does not favour one above the other in giving gifts, spending money on them, or in the way she treats them. Then all of them will love her, will pray for her and will treat her with kindness and respect.

She does not discriminate between sons and daughters in her affection and care

The true Muslim woman does not discriminate between her sons and daughters in her affection and care, as do some women who are not free from the effects of a *jaahili* mentality. She is fair to all her

---

[14] Bukhari and Muslim, See *Sharḥ as-Sunnah*, 8/296, *Kitaab al-'Ataaya wal-hadaaya, baab ar-rujoo' fi hibbat al-walad wat-taswiyah bayna al-awlaad fin-naḥl.*

children, boys and girls alike, and cares for them all with compassion and love. She understands that children are a gift from Allah, and that Allah's gift, be it sons or daughters, are without any replacement:

> "*...He bestows [children] male or female according to His Will [and Plan], or He bestows both males and females, and He leaves barren Whom He will: for He is full of knowledge and power.*" *(Qur'an 42: 49-50)*

The Muslim woman who is truly guided by her religion does not forget the great reward that Allah (ﷻ) has prepared for the one who brings up daughters and takes care of them properly, as is stated in numerous *ṣaḥeeḥ* hadiths, for example the hadith narrated by Bukhari and Muslim from 'Aa'ishah (رضي الله عنها) in which she says:

> "A woman came to me with her two daughters and asked me (for charity). She found that I had nothing except for a single date, which I gave to her. She took it and divided it between her two daughters, and did not eat any of it herself, then she got up and left with her daughters. The Prophet (ﷺ) came in and I told him what had happened. The Prophet said, 'Whoever is tested with daughters and treats them well, they will be for him/her a shield against the Fire of Hell.'"[15]

According to another report narrated by Muslim from 'Aa'ishah (رضي الله عنها), she said:

> "A poor woman came to me carrying her two daughters. I gave her three dates to eat. She gave each child a date, and raised the third to her own mouth to eat it. Her daughters asked her to give it to them, so she split the

[15] Bukhari and Muslim, See *Sharḥ as-Sunnah*, 6/187, *Kitaab az-Zakah, baab faḍl aṣ-ṣadaqah 'ala al-awlaad wal-aqaarib.*

> date that she had wanted to eat between them. I was impressed by what she had done, and told the Messenger of Allah (ﷺ) about it. He said, 'Allah has decreed Paradise for her because of it,' or said, 'She was saved from Hell because of it.'"[16]

Abu Hurayrah (رضي الله عنه) reported that the Prophet (ﷺ) said:

> "Whoever has three daughters, and shelters them, bearing their joys and sorrows with patience, Allah will admit him/her to Paradise by virtue of his/her compassion towards them." A man asked, "What if one has only two, O' Messenger of Allah?" He said, "Even if they are only two." Another man asked, "What if one has only one, O' Messenger of Allah?" He said, "Even if one has only one."[17]

Ibn 'Abbas (رضي الله عنه) narrated that the Messenger of Allah (Blessings and Peace be upon him) said:

> "Whoever had a daughter born to him, and he did not bury her alive or humiliate her, and he did not prefer his son over her, Allah will admit him to Paradise because of her."[18]

The Prophet's compassion extended to females, and included sisters as well along with daughters, as is seen in the hadith narrated by Bukhari in *Al-Adab al-Mufrad* from Abu Sa'eed al-Khudri, saying that the Prophet (ﷺ) said:

---

16 Muslim, 16/179, *Kitaab al-Birr waṣ-ṣilah, baab al-iḥsaan ila al-banaat.*

17 Aḥmad, 2/335 and Al-Ḥaakim, 4/176, *Kitaab al-Birr waṣ-ṣilah*. He said: its isnad is *ṣaḥeeḥ.*

18 Al-Ḥaakim *Al-Mustadrak* 4/177, *Kitaab al-Birr waṣ-Ṣilah*. He said its isnad is *ṣaḥeeḥ.*

> "There is no one who has three daughters, or three sisters, and he treats them well, but Allah will admit him to Paradise."[19]

According to a report by Ṭabaraani, the Prophet (ﷺ) said:

> "There is no one among my ummah who has three daughters, or three sisters, and he supports them until they are grown up, but he will be with me in Paradise like this — and he held up his index and middle fingers together."[20]

No wise mother complains about bringing up daughters, or prefers her sons over them, if she listens to the teachings of the Prophet (ﷺ) which raise the status of daughters and promise Paradise as wide as heaven and earth and the company of the Prophet to the one who brings them up and treats them properly!

In the Muslim family, and in the true Islamic society, girls are protected, loved and respected. In the warm bosom of her parents — especially her mother — a girl will always find protection and care, no matter how long she stays in the home of her parents, brothers or other family members who support her, whether she is married or not. Islam has guaranteed girls a life of protection, pride and support, and has spared them from a life of humiliation, need, want and being lost, such as is the lot of women living in societies that have gone astray from the guidance of Allah. In those countries, when a girl reaches the age of eighteen, she is bereft of the warm parental guardianship and protection to face the hardships of a life filled with difficulties and risks at the time when she is most in need of protection, compassion and care.

---

[19] Bukhari in *Al-Adab al-Mufrad*, 1/162, *baab man 'ala thalaatha ihkwaat.*

[20] Ṭabaraani in *Al-Awsaṭ* with two isnads; the narrators of the first isnad are *rijaal aṣ-ṣaḥeeḥ*. See *Majma' az-Zawaa'id*, 8/157.

There is a great difference between the laws of Allah, which came to bring happiness to mankind, and the imperfect man-made laws which cause nothing but misery.

It comes as no surprise that in the West, as a result of these materialistic laws, we see armies of promiscuous young men and hordes of unfortunate, miserable, unmarried young mothers, the numbers of which are increasing exponentially day by day.

She does not invoke against her children

The wise Muslim woman does not invoke against her own children, heeding the words of the Prophet (ﷺ) who forbade such invocations for fear that they are answered by Allah. This was stated in the lengthy hadith narrated by Jaabir in which the Prophet said:

> "Do not invoke against yourselves, or against your children, or against your wealth, in case you say such words at a time when Allah will answer your invocation."[21]

Invocation against one's own children is not a good habit. No mother does so at a time of anger, but she will regret it later on after she has calmed down. I do not think that a mother who has truly sought the guidance of Islam would lose her mind and her equilibrium to such an extent that she would invoke against her own children, no matter what they did. Such a woman would not allow herself to indulge in something that is done only by foolish, hot-tempered women.

She is alert to everything that may have an influence on them

The smart Muslim mother keeps her eyes open as far as her children are concerned. She knows what they are reading and writing, the

[21] Muslim, 18/139, *Kitaab az-Zuhd, baab ḥadeeth Jaabir aṭ-ṭaweel.*

hobbies and activities they persue, the friends they have chosen, and the places they go to in their free time. She knows all of this without her children feeling that she is watching them. If she finds anything objectionable in their hobbies, reading-materials, etc., or if she sees them hanging around with undesirable friends, or going to unsuitable places, or taking up bad habits such as smoking, or wasting time and energy on *ḥaraam* (forbidden) games that teach them to get used to trivialities, she hastens to correct her children in a gentle and wise manner, and persuades them to return to the straight path. The mother is more able to do this than the father, because she spends much more time with the children, and they are more likely to open up and share their thoughts and feelings with her than with their father. Hence it is quite clear that the mother has a great responsibility to bring up her children properly and form their characters in a sound fashion, in accordance with Islamic principles, values and traditions.

Every child is born in a state of *fitrah* (the natural, good, disposition of mankind), and it is the parents who raise him into a Jew, a Christian or a Magian, as the Prophet (ﷺ) said in the *ṣaḥeeḥ* hadith narrated by Bukhari.

There is no secret about the enormous impact the parents have on the personality and psychological development of their child from the earliest years until the child attains the age of maturity.

The books that children read should open their minds and form their personalities well, giving them the highest examples to follow; they should not corrupt their minds and extinguish the light of goodness in their souls.

Hobbies should help to develop the positive aspects of a child's nature and reinforce good tastes, and not encourage any negative tendancies.

Friends should be of the type that lead one to Paradise, not to Hell; they should influence a child in a positive way and encourage him/

her to do good, to strive to improve himself/herself and to succeed, rather than drag him/her down into sin, disobedience and failure. How many people have been brought to the slippery slope of destruction and perdition by their friends, whilst their mothers and fathers were unaware of what was happening to their own children! How wise are the words of the poet 'Adiyy ibn Zayd al-'Ibaadi concerning friends:

> "If you are among people, then make friends with the best of them.
> Do not make friends with the worst of them lest you become as bad as he is.
> Do not ask about the man, but ask about his friends, for every person is influenced by his friends."[22]

The true Muslim mother takes notice of her children's books, magazines, hobbies, school, teachers, clubs, media interests, and everything that may have an impact on their personalities, minds, souls and faith. She intervenes when necessary, either to encourage or to put a stop to something, so that the children's upbringing will not be affected by corruption or sickness.

Successful upbringing of children depends on a mother who is alert and intelligent, and understands her responsibility towards her children, so that she does a good job and raises children to be a boon to their parents and society in general. Families that fail to raise their children properly, usually do so because the mother does not understand her responsibility towards her children. She neglects them and they become a source of evil and a torment to their parents and others.

Children would not become a source of evil if their parents, especially the mother, knew their responsibility and took it seriously.

---

[22] Adiyy ibn Zayd al-'Ibaadi: *Ash-Shaa'ir al-Mubtakir*, by the author, Pp. 171-172.

She instills good behaviour and attitudes in them

The Muslim woman tries hard to instill in her children's hearts the best qualities, such as loving others, upholding the ties of kinship, caring for the weak, respecting elders, showing compassion to little ones, deriving satisfaction from doing good, being sincere in word and deed, keeping promises, judging fairly, and all other good and praiseworthy characteristics.

The wise Muslim woman knows how to reach her children's hearts and instill these worthy qualities, using the best and most effective methods, such as setting a good example, coming down to their level, treating them well, encouraging them, advising and correcting them, and being compassionate, kind, tolerant, loving, and fair. She is gentle without being too lenient, and is strict without being harsh. Thus the children receive a proper upbringing, and grow up open-minded, mature, righteous, sincere, good, able to give and prepared to make a constructive contribution in all aspects of life. Not surprisingly, the Muslim mother's upbringing produces the best results, for she is the first school and the first teacher, as the poet said:

> "The mother is a school: if you prepare her properly, you will prepare an entire people of good character;
> The mother is the first teacher, foremost among them, and the best of teachers."[23]

---

[23] *Diwaan Ḥaafiẓ Ibraheem*, 282. Published by Daar al-Kuṭub al-Miṣriyah.

CHAPTER SIX

The Muslim Woman and Her Sons and Daughters-in-Law

Her Daughter-in-Law

Her attitude towards her daughter-in-law

The Muslim woman who understands the teachings of her religion and who is of a high character, regards her daughter-in-law as she regards her own daughters. Fate has made this woman the wife of her son, and she has joined the family and become one of its members. Similarly, when the young Muslim woman, brought up with Islamic values and attitudes, leaves her parents' home and goes to her husband and begins the new matrimonial life, she regards her mother-in-law as her own mother.

She knows how to make a good choice in selecting a daughter-in-law

Thus, before any marriage takes place, it is very important for both parties (both potential mothers-in-law and potential daughters-in-law) to be very careful in making the right choice. When seeking spouses for her sons and/or daughters, a mother must examine each candidate's religious commitment and character, and look for a sound upbringing and good reputation.

When the wise Muslim woman looks for a wife for her son, she always bears in mind the fact that this will be a new daughter joining her family, one who should enjoy the same respect and love as her own daughters, and will share their duties within the framework of the greater family. She should want for her new daughter-in-law nothing but success, happiness and stability in marriage. So the wise mother will not be attracted only by the apparent physical beauty of the proposed girls. She will also require her future daughter-in-law first and foremost to be strong in her commitment to Islam, and to be of a good and balanced character. This is in accordance with the teaching of the Prophet (ﷺ):

> "A woman may be married for four reasons: her wealth, her lineage, her beauty or her religion; choose the one who is religious, may your hands be rubbed with dust (i.e., let you be successful)!"[1]

She knows her place

On the basis of this correct understanding of the daughter-in-law's position in marriage and her position in her new family, the mother-in-law treats her daughter-in-law properly and fairly in all circumstances and at all times.

It never crosses the mind of the Muslim mother-in-law who is filled with Islamic values, that this woman has stolen the son whom she spent long years bringing up only to be taken away, when he reached the age of manhood and became able to work and make sacrifices, by a wife who would lead him into a happy home where he would forget everything that his mother ever did for him. Such evil thoughts never occur to the righteous Muslim woman, because she understands the laws of Allah that apply in this life, and she knows that her son, to whom she taught Islamic values from early childhood, cannot be made to forget his mother by his beautiful wife, just as the daughter-in-law whom she chose for her son from among the good, believing

---

[1] Bukhari and Muslim, See *Sharḥ as-Sunnah*, 9/8, *Kitaab an-Nikaaḥ, baab ikhtiyaar dhat ad-deen.*

young women, would never accept for her husband to forget his mother in this way, which is precise disobedience, forbidden by Islam.

If she feels any stirrings of jealousy at some moment of human weakness, she seeks refuge in her faith and fear of Allah. She sheds these hateful feelings and returns to a proper opinion of her daughter-in-law. This is the attitude of the righteous believers, men and women alike, when they are struck by some evil thought, they turn to Allah:

> "*Those who fear Allah, when a thought of evil from Satan assaults them, bring Allah to remembrance, when lo! they see [aright]!*" *(Qur'an 7: 201)*

Hence, a balance is struck between the daughter-in-law, the mother-in-law and the husband, and matters may run their natural, peaceful course unaffected by misguided whims and desires and governed instead by religion, reason and wisdom.

She gives advice but does not interfere in their private life

From the moment her daughter-in-law is brought as a bride to her son, the wise Muslim woman remembers that her daughter-in-law has the right to live her married life in all aspects - so long as it remains within the limits of Islamic teaching - and that no-one has the right to interfere in the private life of the spouses except in cases where it is essential to do so, as every Muslim is required to give sincere advice in accordance with the Prophet's words:

> "Religion is sincere advice (*naṣeeḥah*)..."[2]

The Muslim mother-in-law's standard in her behaviour towards her daughter-in-law is similar to her behaviour towards her own daughter.

---

[2] Muslim, 2/37, *Kitaab al-Eemaan, baab bayan un ad-deen an-naṣeeḥah.*

Just as she wants her daughter to have a happy, successful and indepen-dent matrimonial life, undisturbed by any interference in her private life, she wishes the same for her daughter-in-law, with no exceptions.

She respects her and treats her well

The good Muslim mother-in-law respects her daughter-in-law and treats her well; she makes her feel that she is loved and appreciated. She listens to her thoughts and opinions, approving and encouraging those that are good, and gently correcting those that are mistaken. In all of this, the mother-in-law's aim is to be fair and just. She judges her daughter-in-law exactly as she would judge her daughter if she were in her place and where there is an opinion to her daughter as her mother and in accordance with the words of the Qur'an:

> "*O' you who believe! Fear Allah, and [always] say a word directed to the Right.*" *(Qur'an 33: 70)*

She does not omit to express the joy that she feels from time to time, when she sees that her son is happy with his wife. This adds to the best feelings that her son and daughter-in-law feel. Similarly, she does not forget to include her daughter-in-law on various occasions, just as she thinks of her daughters, so she lets her accompany them, and makes her feel that she is one of them, and that she is a beloved member of the family since she is married to her beloved son.

In this way, the mother-in-law becomes dear to her daughter-in-law, because she shows that her daughter-in-law is dear to her. This is in direct contrast to the practice in those backward, *jaahili* societies that have deviated from the guidance of Allah, where hatred and despicable plots between mothers-in-law and daughters-in-law are the norm, to such an extent that this enmity has become a traditional, inevitable phenomenon, about which there are many folk sayings and popular songs. None of this could have happened if both mothers-in-law and daughters-in-law had really respected one another's rights as outlined by Islam, and had stayed within the limits prescribed by Allah (ﷻ). This is why the traditional enmity between the mother-in-law and her daughter-in-law disappeared in those societies that truly embraced Islam and adhered to its teachings and values.

She is wise and fair in her judgement of her daughter-in-law

A mother-in-law may find herself being tested by a daughter-in-law who is not of good character, one who does not treat others well. Here we see the need for the mother-in-law to exercise wisdom and sophistication by repelling evil with something better, as stated in the Qur'an:

> "*Nor can Goodness and Evil be equal. Repel [Evil] with what is better: then will he between whom and you was hatred become as it were your friend and intimate!And no one will be granted such goodness except those who exercise patience and self-restraint — none but persons of the greatest good fortune.*" *(Qur'an 41: 34-35)*

One way in which a mother-in-law may repel evil with something better is by concealing her daughter-in-law's negative qualities and mistakes from her son as much as possible, advising her daughter-in-law on her own and explaining how keen she is for the marriage to continue on the basis of love and good works. The mother-in-law should continue to advise her daughter-in-law until she rids herself of those negative qualities, or at least minimizes them. Thus the daughter-in-law will feel that she has a sincere, loving mother-in-law, not a fearsome enemy who is just waiting for her to stumble.

The wise Muslim mother-in-law remains fair and just when she judges between her daughter-in-law and her son, if she sees her son mistreating her daughter-in-law. Her awareness and fear of Allah prevent her from siding with her son at the expense of the truth, so she does not support him in oppressing his wife or in doing wrong. This is in accordance with the words of the Qur'an:

> "*...Whenever you speak, speak justly, even if a near relative is concerned...*" *(Qur'an 6: 152)*
>
> "*...And when you judge between man and man, that you judge with justice...*" *(Qur'an 4: 58)*

The Muslim woman who is truly following this guidance will never commit the sin of oppression, and will never be content to give any judgement except that which is fair, even if this means judging in favour of her daughter-in-law and against her son.

Her Son-in-Law

Her attitude towards her son-in-law

The attitude of the truly-guided Muslim woman towards her sons-in-law is no different than her attitude towards her daughters-in-law. She treats her daughter-in-law as if she were one of her own daughters, similarly she treats her son-in-law as if he were one of her own sons. Just as she wants her own son to be one of the best of people, so she also wants her son-in-law to be one of the best of people too.

She knows how to make a good choice in selecting a son-in-law

She makes a good choice when selecting a son-in-law, accepting none but one who is religious, well-mannered and has a good reputation, as the Prophet encouraged Muslims to do in the hadith:

> "If there comes to you one with whose religious commitment and character you are pleased, then marry

your daughter to him; if you do not do so, it will be a cause of *fitnah* and widespread mischief on earth."[3]

In seeking a spouse for her daughter, she is not attracted only by a smart appearance, high status or plentiful wealth, because she knows that by marrying her daughter to this man she is going to gain a son, to whom she will entrust her daughter's honour, life and happiness, none of which may be protected or properly taken care of except by a man who is well-mannered, religious, noble, chivalrous and moral.

She respects and honours him

Not surprisingly, her son-in-law is on the receiving end of her honour, respect and appreciation. At every opportunity she makes him feel that he has become a member of the family by marrying her daughter, so she wishes him and her daughter happiness and success in their life together. She lets him know that he is the one to whom she has entrusted the precious honour of her daughter, and in whom she places her hopes for the achievement of her daughter's fondest wishes. She makes him feel that she is a second mother to him, so she does not withhold any advice, or spare any effort to do whatever will bring happiness to him, his wife and his children.

She helps her daughter to be a good wife to her husband

The wise Muslim woman never ceases to offer advice to her daughter in ways that will be of benefit to her in running her household and taking care of her husband and children. She always points out to her daughter anything that will please her husband and make him happy, and encourages her to undertake the duties of a wife and mother in

---

[3] A *ḥasan* hadith narrated by Tirmidhi, 2/274, *Abwaab an-Nikaaḥ*, 3; Ibn Maajah, 1/633, *Kitaab an-Nikaaḥ, baab al-akfaa'*.

the best way possible. If she notices any shortcoming, negligence or carelessness on the part of her daughter, she hastens to correct and advise her, and helps her to make up for the shortcoming, so that there will be no reason for her son-in-law to look down on her daughter. She does not neglect to mention her son-in-law's good characteristics from time to time, so that her daughter becomes more fond of him, and more content with what Allah has given her. In this way, a mother becomes the greatest help to her daughter in consolidating her marriage and making it happy.

She is fair, and is never biased in favour of her daughter

The Muslim mother-in-law is always fair in her opinions and judgements if any misunderstanding arises between her daughter and son-in-law, or if she notices any failure on her daughter's part to be a good wife or to perform her domestic duties or to take care of her husband's legitimate desires. She does not stand by her daughter, rather she speaks words of fairness and truth, as commanded by Allah (ﷻ) in the Qur'an:

> "*...Whenever you speak, speak justly, even if a near relative is concerned...*" *(Qur'an 6: 152)*

> "*...And when you judge between man and man, that you judge with justice...*" *(Qur'an 4: 58)*

If she notices that her daughter tends to take a lot of money from her husband or spends extravagantly, and that her words of advice to her daughter are not heeded, then she speaks out, explaining to her daughter the error of her ways and pointing out how she has transgressed the limits laid down by Islam with regard to spending, as has been outlined in the Qur'anic description of the honoured, truly-guided slaves of Allah:

> "*Those who, when they spend, are not extravagant and not niggardly, but hold a just [balance] between those [extremes].*" *(Qur'an 25: 67)*

If what she notices on her daughter's part is excessive power and a tendency to undermine her husband's honour and *qawwaamah*, she hastens to explain to her daughter in the clearest terms that men are *qawwaamoon* over women, as the Qur'an says:

> "*Men are the protectors and maintainers of women, because Allah has given the one more [strength] than the other, and because they support them from their means...*" *(Qur'an 4: 34)*

And that men have been given this role of protecting and maintaining women for two essential reasons which women should never forget: the precedence given to men, and the wealth that they spend on women:

> "*...but men have a degree [of advantage] over them.*" *(Qur'an 2: 228)*

The mother-in-law who is adhering to Islam and who is wise and fair does not differentiate between her son and her son-in-law. Just as she wants her son to fulfil his role as *qawwaam* over his wife and to conduct his marriage wisely, seriously and in a manly fashion, so she wants the same thing for her son-in-law too, even if that means that her daughter has to face some strictness, because justice demands that of every woman who believes in Allah and the Last Day.

Just as the Muslim mother-in-law will criticize her daughter-in-law if necessary for any extravagance that she may notice, out of compassion towards her son, she will also criticize her own daughter if she oversteps the limits, in order to be fair and just, and in obedience to the words of the Qur'an:

> "...*Whenever you speak, speak justly, even if a near relative is concerned...*" *(Qur'an 6: 152)*

She deals with problems wisely

A son-in-law may be of a certain mentality with which his wife and mother-in-law do not feel at ease, which may result in mutual dislike and arguments. In such cases, the duty of the mother-in-law who understands the teachings of Islam is to approach her son-in-law in a diplomatic manner, taking into account his particular mentality and nature, to deal with him wisely, and never to despair of reaching her goal with a measure of patience and persistence.

She is always very careful never to exaggerate her son-in-law's negative points to her daughter; rather, so long as those negative aspects do not affect his religion or moral character and do not warrant the end of the marriage, she tries to make them look as small as possible, whilst striving to deal with them by legitimate means and wise methods.

Thus, the mother-in-law who is truly guided by Islam becomes a blessing and a source of goodness for her daughter and her husband, offering solid support to their marriage and proving by her fairness and piety that she is indeed a second mother to the husband, not the traditional enemy of the couple, as she is often described in backward, *jaahili* societies where comedians tell funny stories of that everlasting enmity which in fact is the result of the Muslims' failure to properly apply the laws and values of their religion.

We may well imagine the great happiness felt by both families — her son's family and her daughter's family — towards this wise, sensitive and pious mother-in-law, when she is sincere and loved by both her son-in-law and her daughter-in-law, and this love is reflected in the happiness of both families.

By virtue of her *taqwa*, fairness and goodness to her son and daughter-in-law, she increases the happiness of her daughter and son, and contributes to the comfort and tranquillity of their families.

How beautiful are the deeds of the intelligent, believing mother-in-law, and how great is the need of her sons' and daughters' families for her!

dignified way, she intends the happiness of her daughter and son, and contributes to the comfort and tranquility of their families.

How beautiful are the deeds of the intelligent, believing mother-in-law, and how great is the respect of her sons' and daughters' families for her!

CHAPTER SEVEN

The Muslim Woman and Her Relatives

The Muslim woman who is guided by the teachings of her religion never forgets that her relatives have rights over her, and that she is required to uphold the ties of kinship and to treat them well. The relatives (in Arabic *Arḥaam*, which literally means "wombs") are those to whom a person is linked by ties of blood, whether they are his/her heirs or not.

Islamic view of kinship ties

Islam has recognized the ties of kinship in a way that is unparalleled in other religions or "isms"; it enjoins Muslims to uphold the ties of kinship and condemns the one who breaks this tie.

There is no greater proof of the emphasis placed by Islam on the ties of kinship than the vivid picture painted by the Messenger of Allah (ﷺ), who described kinship (*raḥm*) as standing in the vast arena of creation and seeking refuge with Allah from being cut off. Allah answers its prayer, taking care of those who maintain the ties of kinship, and cutting off those who cut off these ties.

This is seen in the *ṣaḥeeḥ* hadith narrated by Abu Hurayrah (رضي الله عنه) who said that the Prophet (ﷺ) said:

> "Allah created the universe, and when He finished, kinship (*raḥm*) stood up and said, 'This is the standing up of one who seeks Your protection from being cut off.' Allah said, 'Yes, would it please you if I were to take care of those who take care of you and cut off those who cut you off?' It said, 'Of course.' Allah said, 'Then

your prayer is granted.'

Then the Prophet said, 'Recite, if you wish:

> "*Then, is it to be expected of you, if you were put in authority, that you will do mischief, in the land, and break your ties of kith and kin? Such are the men whom Allah has cursed for He has made them deaf and blinded their sight.*" *(Qur'an 47: 22-23)*'[1]

Many *ayat* (verses) of the Qur'an reiterate and affirm the position of *arḥaam* in Islam, encouraging people to uphold the ties of kinship and instilling a strong sense of the importance of recognizing kinship rights and avoiding neglect of those rights, and warning against abuse of them. One of these *ayat* is:

> "*...Fear Allah, through Whom you demand your mutual [rights], and [reverence] the wombs [that bore you]...*" *(Qur'an 4: 1)*

This *aayah* commands man to fear Allah (ﷻ) first and foremost, then places respect for *arḥaam* second to that *taqwa* in order to emphasize its importance.

For the true Muslim, the fact that *raḥm* is often mentioned in conjunction with belief in Allah and good treatment of parents, is enough to confirm its status and importance:

> "*Your Lord has decreed that you worship none but Him, and that you be kind to parents...*" *(Qur'an 17: 23)*

> "*And render to the kindred their due rights, as [also] to those in want, and to the wayfarer: but squander not [your wealth] in the manner of a spendthrift.*" *(Qur'an 17: 26)*

---

[1] Bukhari and Muslim, See *Sharḥ as-Sunnah*, 13/20, *Kitaab al-Birr waṣ-Ṣilah, baab thawaab ṣilat ar-raḥm wa ithm man qaṭa'aha.*

> "*Worship Allah, and join not any partners with Him; and do good — to parents, kinsfolk, orphans, those in need. Neighbours who are near, neighbours who are strangers, the companion by your side, the wayfarer [you meet]...*" *(Qur'an 4: 36)*

Hence kind treatment of relatives comes one degree below kind treatment of parents on the scale of human relationships as defined by the Qur'an; from there, kindness and respect extends to encompass all those needy members of the greater human family. This suits human nature, which is more inclined to start with kind treatment of those who are closer; it is also in harmony with the overall Islamic system of social organization and mutual responsibility which starts with the family then is readily extended first to relatives and then to society at large, in a spirit of mercy and friendship which makes life more pleasant and beautiful for mankind.

Upholding the ties of kinship is one of the major principles of Islam, one of the fundamentals that this religion has promoted from the first day the Messenger of Allah (ﷺ) began to preach his message. It is one of the most characteristic features of Islamic law. It is evident from the long conversation recorded in history between the Roman Emperor Heraculius and the Makkan leader Abu Sufiyan. When the emperor asked Abu Sufyan, "What does your Prophet order you to do?" He answered, "He (the Prophet) tells us:

> 'Worship Allah alone and do not associate anything with Him. Give up the religion of your forefathers.' He tells us to pray, to tell only truth, to be chaste and to uphold the ties of kinship."[2]

Upholding the ties of kinship is counted as one of the major characteristics of this religion, along with pure monotheistic belief in

---

[2] Bukhari and Muslim, See *Riyaaḍ uṣ-Ṣaaliḥeen*, 51, *baab aṣ-ṣidq.*

Allah, establishing prayer, and adherence to truthfulness and chastity. Abu Sufiyan put it as a distinctive feature of Islam when he answered the querries of Heraclius eager to understand Islam for the very first time.

In the lengthy hadith of 'Amr ibn 'Abasah (ﷺ), which includes many of the basic teachings of Islam, he said:

> "I met the Prophet (ﷺ) in Makkah (that is, at the beginning of his Prophethood), and asked him, 'What are you?' He said, 'A Prophet.' I asked, 'What is a Prophet?' He said, 'Allah has sent me.' I asked, 'With what has He sent you?' He said, 'He has sent me to uphold the ties of kinship, to break the idols and to teach that Allah is One and has no partner whatsoever..."[3]

In this summary of the most important principles of Islam, the Prophet clearly gave precedence to upholding the ties of kinship and mentioned this among the foremost features of the faith. This is indicative of its high status in the framework of this religion which Allah (ﷻ) has revealed as a mercy to the Worlds.

The sources of Islam go to great lengths to encourage upholding the ties of kinship, and warn against cutting them off. Abu Ayyoob al-Anṣaari (ﷺ) said:

> "A man said, 'O' Messenger of Allah, tell me of a good deed that will grant me entrance to Paradise.' The Prophet said: 'Worship Allah and do not associate anything with Him, establish regular prayer, pay zakah, and uphold the ties of kinship.'"[4]

---

[3] Muslim, 6/115, *Kitaab Ṣalaat al-Musaafireen, baab al-awqaat allati nuhiya 'an aṣ-ṣalaat feeha.*

[4] Bukhari and Muslim, See *Riyaaḍ uṣ-Ṣaaliḥeen*, 195, *baab birr al-waalidayn wa ṣilat al-arḥaam.*

How great is the tie of kinship, and how heavily will it weigh in the balance of a person's deeds (on the Day of Judgement)! For it appears in the same context as worshipping Allah (ﷻ), believing in His absolute unity, establishing regular prayer and paying zakah. Hence, it is one of the best righteous deeds that will guarantee Paradise and save one from Hell. Anas (رضي الله عنه) reported that the Prophet (ﷺ) said,

> "Whoever would like his *rizq* (provision) to be increased and his life to be extended, should uphold the ties of kinship."[5]

So, it is a blessing for the one who upholds the ties of kinship, a blessing which affects both his *rizq* and his life: his wealth will increase and he will live a longer and more blessed life.

Ibn 'Umar used to say: "Whoever fears his Lord and upholds the ties of kinship, his life will be extended, his wealth will increase and his family will love him more."[6]

The Muslim woman does not forget that upholding the ties of kinship is a duty required of women just as it is required of men, and that the words concerning it are addressed to every Muslim, whether man or woman, as is the case with all the general duties of Islam. So the Muslim woman upholds the ties of kinship sincerely and earnestly, and does not let her busy life of responsibilities distract her from doing so.

The Muslim woman who understands the teachings of her religion realizes that upholding the ties of kinship brings blessing in a woman's *rizq* and in her life, mercy from Allah in this world and the next, and makes people love her and praise her. In contrast, breaking

---

[5] Bukhari and Muslim, See *Sharḥ as-Sunnah*, 13/19, *Kitaab al-Birr waṣ-Ṣilah, baab thawaab ṣilat ar-raḥm.*

[6] Bukhari: *Al-Adab al-Mufrad*, 1/140, *baab man waṣala raḥmahu aḥabbahu Allah.*

those ties will spell disaster and misery for her, earning her the dislike of Allah and the people, and keeping her far from Paradise in the Hereafter. It is misery and deprivation enough for such a woman to hear the words of the Prophet (ﷺ):

> "The person who breaks the ties of kinship will never enter Paradise."[7]

It is sufficient to know that the mercy of Allah will be denied to the one who breaks the ties of kinship; moreover, it will be denied to the group wherein is a person who breaks the ties of kinship, as in the hadith reported by Bukhari in *Al-Adab al-Mufrad*:[8]

> "Mercy will not descend upon a people among whom is one who breaks the ties of kinship."

Hence, the great *Ṣaḥaabi* Abu Hurayrah (رضي الله عنه) never liked to make supplication to Allah in a gathering in which a person who had broken the ties of kinship was present, because that would prevent mercy from descending and the *du'aa'* from being answered. On one Thursday night gathering, he said: "I urge everyone who has broken the ties of kinship to get up and leave us." No-one got up until he had said this three times. Then a young man got up and went to see a paternal aunt of his whom he had forsaken for two years. When he entered, she said, "O son of my brother, what brings you here?" He said, "I heard Abu Hurayrah say such-and-such." She told him, "Go back to him and ask him why he said that." (Abu Hurayrah) said: "I heard the Prophet (ﷺ) say:

> 'The deeds of the sons of Adam are shown to Allah

7 Bukhari and Muslim, See *Sharḥ as-Sunnah*, 13/26, *Kitab al-Birr waṣ-Ṣilah, baab thawaab ṣilah ar-raḥm wa ithm man qaṭa'aha.*

8 *Al-Adab al-Mufrad*, 1/144, *baab la tanzeel ar-raḥmah 'ala qawm feehim qaaṭi' raḥm.*

> every Thursday evening, night preceding Friday, and the deeds of the one who breaks the ties of kinship are not accepted."[9]

The sensitive Muslim woman who is hoping to earn the pleasure of her Lord and attain salvation in the Hereafter will be deeply shaken by the news given in these texts, that breaking the ties of kinship will cause mercy to be withheld from her and her *du'aa'* not to be answered. It will be a source of great misery to her to be in such a position, to do deeds which are of no avail, to seek the mercy of her Lord and not receive it. It is unimaginable that a true Muslim woman would ever break the ties of kinship.

Breaking the ties of kinship is a sin which the Muslim woman whose heart is filled with true guidance and the desire to obey Allah and earn His pleasure would never commit, because it is one of the sins that Allah (سبحانه وتعالى) has said will bring punishment; indeed, it is one of the foremost sins for which Allah will punish the one who is guilty of them both in this world and the next, as is stated in the hadith:

> "There is no worse sin for which Allah will hasten the punishment of one who commits it in this world — in addition to what awaits him in the Hereafter — than oppressing others and breaking the ties of kinship."[10]

The acts of oppressing others and breaking the ties of kinship are akin to each other. The Messenger of Allah (ﷺ) mentioned them together in this hadith. For breaking the ties of kinship is a kind of *ẓulm* (wrongdoing, oppression), and what *ẓulm* can be worse than breaking off relations with one's own kin and destroying the ties of love and affection?

---

[9] Bukhari: *Al-Adab al-Mufrad*, 1/142, *baab birr al-aqrab fal-aqrab.*

[10] Aḥmad, 5/38, and Ibn Maajah, 2/37, *Kitaab az-Zuhd, baab al-baghy.* Its isnad is *ṣaḥeeḥ.*

The Messenger of Allah (ﷺ) described the oppression that befalls the ties of kinship when they are cut off:

> "The tie of kinship (*raḥm*) is a close-knit relationship that comes from Allah, the Most Merciful (*Ar-Raḥmaan*).[11] It says: 'O' my Lord! I have been oppressed, O' my Lord! I have been cut off.' He answers, 'Will you not be content if I cut off the one who cuts you off and take care of the one who takes care of you?'"[12]

Allah (ﷻ) raised the status of the tie of kinship and honoured it by deriving its name, *raḥm*, from one of His own names, *Ar-Raḥmaan*. For He said (in a hadith *qudsi*):

> "I am *Ar-Raḥmaan* (the Most Merciful) and I have created *raḥm* and derived its name from My name. Whoever takes care of it, I will take care of him, and whoever cuts it off, I will forsake him."[13]

These texts clearly confirm that the one who upholds the ties of kinship will be happy, loved and honoured and will enjoy the cool shade of his Lord's mercy. The one who breaks those ties will be denied that shade, and will be forsaken and abandoned, denied the mercy, forgiveness and pleasure of his Lord.

The Muslim woman upholds the ties of kinship according to the teachings of Islam

The Muslim woman who is truly guided by the teachings of her religion does not neglect to uphold the ties of kinship, and never lets

---

[11] The connection is clearer in Arabic, as *raḥm* and *Ar-Raḥmaan* are derived from the same root. (Translator)

[12] Bukhari: *Al-Adab al-Mufrad*, 1/146, *baab ithm qaaṭi' ar-raḥm.*

[13] Bukhari: *Al-Adab al-Mufrad*, 1/132, *baab faḍl ṣilat ar-raḥm.*

the responsibilities of motherhood or the burden of caring for her house and husband distract her from always upholding these ties. She organizes her time so that she may visit her relatives, following Islamic teaching, which regulates these relationships and ranks them in order of priority and degree of closeness, starting with the mother, then moving on to the father, then other relatives, from the most closely-related to others who are more distantly related.

A man came to the Prophet (ﷺ) and asked, "O' Messenger of Allah! Who is most deserving of my good company?" He said,

> "Your mother, then your mother, then your mother, then your father, then those who are most closely related to you."[14]

The Muslim woman earns two rewards when she treats her relatives with kindness and respect: one reward for maintaining the relationship, and another reward for giving charity, if she is rich and can spend money on them. This gives her a greater incentive to give to her relatives, if they are in need. By doing so, she will earn two rewards from Allah (ﷻ), and will also win the affection of her relatives. This is what the Prophet (ﷺ) encouraged Muslims to do, in the hadith narrated by Zaynab ath-Thaqafiyah, the wife of 'Abdullah ibn Mas'ood (رضي الله عنه), who said that the Messenger of Allah said:

> "O' women, give in charity even if it is some of your jewellery." She said, I went back to 'Abdullah ibn Mas'ood and told him, 'You are a man of little wealth, and the Prophet has commanded us to give charity, so go and ask him whether it is permissible for me to give you charity. If it is, I will do so; if not, I will give charity to someone else.' 'Abdullah said, 'No, you go and ask.' So

---

14 Bukhari and Muslim, See *Riyaaḍ uṣ-Ṣaaliḥeen*, 189, *baab birr al-waalidayn waṣ-ṣilat ar-raḥm.*

> I went, and I found a woman of the Anṣaar at the Prophet's door, who also had the same question. We felt too shy to go in, out of respect, so Bilaal came out and we asked him, 'Go and tell the Messenger of Allah that there are two women at the door asking: Is it permissible for them to give *ṣadaqah* to their husbands and the orphans in their care? But do not tell him who we are.' So Bilaal went in and conveyed this message to the Messenger of Allah, who asked, 'Who are they?' Bilaal said, 'One of the women of the Anṣaar, and Zaynab.' The Messenger of Allah asked, 'Which Zaynab is it?' Bilaal said, 'The wife of 'Abdullah.' The Messenger of Allah said, 'They will have two rewards, the reward for upholding the relationship, and the reward for giving charity.'"[15]

The Prophet (ﷺ) said:

> "Charity given to a poor person is charity, and charity given to a relative earns two rewards: one for giving charity and one for upholding the ties of kinship."[16]

Ummul Mu'mineen Maymoonah bint Umm al-Ḥaarith (رضي الله عنها) narrated that she freed her slave but did not seek permission. When the Prophet visited her on her turn she said,

> "Did you notice O' Messenger of Allah that I have freed my slave?" He said, "Did you do that?" She replied, "Yes, I did." He said, "Had you gifted him to any one of your maternal uncle you would have received greater reward."[17]

---

[15] Bukhari and Muslim, See *Sharḥ as-Sunnah*, 6/187, *Kitaab az-Zakah*, *baab faḍl aṣ-ṣadaqah 'ala al-awlaad wal-aqaarib.*

[16] Tirmidhi, 2/84, *Abwaab az-Zakah*, 26; he said it is a *ḥasan* hadith.

[17] Bukhari and Muslim, See *Sharḥ as-Sunnah*, 6/195, *Kitaab az-Zakah, baab faḍl aṣ-ṣadaqah 'ala al-aqaarib.*

The Prophet (ﷺ) used to stress the preference and excellence of kind treatment to relatives at every opportunity. When the *aayah*:

> "*By no means shall you attain righteousness unless you give [freely] of that which you love...*" *(Qur'an 3: 92),*

— was revealed, Abu Ṭalḥah went to the Prophet (ﷺ) and said: "O' Messenger of Allah, Allah says, "*By no means shall you attain righteousness unless you give [freely] of that which you love...*" *(Qur'an 3: 92),* — the most beloved of my properties is Bayraḥa' (a date orchard), which I now donate as *ṣadaqah* to Allah, hoping to store up reward with Him. O' Messenger of Allah, dispose it of as you wish." The Prophet (ﷺ) said:

> "Bravo! You have got the best deal for your property. I have heard what you said, and I think that you should divide it among your relatives.' Abu Ṭalḥah said, 'I will do so, O' Messenger of Allah.'"

He divided it among his relatives and (paternal) cousins.[18]

The Prophet (ﷺ) looked far back into history and evoked ties of kinship going back centuries, when he enjoined good treatment of the people of Egypt, as is recorded in the hadith narrated by Muslim. He said:

> "You will conquer Egypt, which is known as the land of *al-qeeraaṭ* (i.e. where coins are minted) so when you conquer it, treat its people well, for they have protection (*dhimmah*) and the ties of kinship (*raḥm*)." Or he said: "...protection and the relationship by marriage (*siḥr*)."[19]

---

[18] Bukhari and Muslim, See *Sharḥ as-Sunnah*, 6/189, *Kitaab az-Zakah, baab faḍl aṣ-ṣadaqah 'ala al-aqaarib.*

[19] Muslim, 16/97, *Kitaab faḍaa'il aṣ-Ṣaḥaabah, baab waṣiyah an-Nabi bi ahl miṣr.*

The *'ulama'* explained that *raḥm* here referred to Haajar, the mother of Ismaa'eel (Ishmael), and *siḥr* referred to Maaryah, the mother of the Prophet's son Ibraheem — both of whom came from Egypt.

What a display of loyalty, faithfulness and good treatment, which extends to the kinsfolk and countrymen of those two noble women down throughout the ages! The Muslim woman who hears these wise teachings of the Prophet (ﷺ) cannot but uphold her ties with her relatives, offering them her sincere love, keeping in constant contact with them and treating them with kindness and respect.

She maintains the ties even with non-Muslim relatives

When the Muslim woman looks into the guidance of Islam, she sees that it reaches new heights of gentleness and humanity by enjoining its followers to uphold the ties of kinship even if one's relatives follow a religion other than Islam. 'Abdullah ibn 'Amr ibn al-'Aaṣ (رضي الله عنه) said: I heard the Prophet (ﷺ) openly saying:

> "The family of Abu so-and-so are not my friends, for my friends are Allah and the righteous believers. But they have ties of kinship with me, which I will recognize and uphold."[20]

When the *aayah*:

> "*And admonish your nearest kinsmen*"
>
> *(Qur'an 26: 214)*

— was revealed, the Messenger of Allah (ﷺ) summoned Quraysh. They gathered and he addressed them both in general and specific terms:

---

20 Bukhari and Muslim, See *Sharḥ as-Sunnah*, 13/29, *Kitaab al-Birr waṣ-ṣilah, baab thawaab ṣilat ar-raḥm.*

"O' Banu Ka'b ibn Lu'ayy, save yourselves from the Fire. O' Banu Murrah ibn Ka'b, save yourselves from the Fire. O' Banu 'Abd Shams, save yourselves from the Fire. O' Banu 'Abd Manaaf, save yourselves from the Fire. O' Banu Haashim, save yourselves from the Fire. O' Banu 'Abdul Muṭṭalib, save yourselves from the Fire. O' Faṭimah, save yourself from the Fire. I cannot do anything to protect you from the punishment of Allah, but there are ties of kinship between us that I will recognize and uphold."[21]

These sublime prophetic teachings reached the ears of the first Muslim generation with great impact in their dealings with their non-Muslim relatives. They were very kind to them. Among the evidences related by Ibn 'Abdul Barr in *Al-Isti'aab* and Ibn Ḥajar in *Al-Iṣaabah* is one that says that a female slave of *Umm al-Mu'mineen* Ṣafiyah (رضي الله عنها) came to the *khaleefah* 'Umar ibn al-Khaṭṭab (رضي الله عنه) and said, "O' *Ameer al-Mu'mineen*, Ṣafiyah loves the *Sabbath* (Saturday) and treats the Jews well." 'Umar sent for Ṣafiyah and questioned her about that. She replied: "As far *Sabbath* is concerned, I have not loved it since Allah replaced it with *Juma'ah* (Friday) for me. As for the Jews, I have relatives among them with whom I uphold the ties of kinship." Then she turned to her slave and asked her what had made her tell such a lie. The slave woman answered, "*Shayṭaan*." Ṣafiyah's response was to tell her: "Go, you are free."[22]

Similarly, 'Umar did not see anything wrong with giving a garment that the Messenger had sent him to his half-brother (through his mother), who was a *mushrik*.[23]

---

21 Muslim, 3/79, *Kitaab al-Eemaan, baab man maata 'ala al-kufr la talḥaquhu ash-shafaa'ah.*

22 Ibn 'Abdul-Barr, *Al-Isti'aab*, 4/1872; Ibn Ḥajar, *Al-Iṣaabah*, 8/127.

23 *Fatḥ al-Baari*, 10/414, *Kitaab al-Adab, baab ṣilat al-akh al-mushrik.*

Hence, the Muslim woman sees that the spring of human emotion does not dry up when a person utters the *Shahaadah*, rather his or her heart overflows with love and good treatment towards his or her relatives, even if they are not Muslim. The expression of the noble Messenger (ﷺ), "but there are ties of kinship between us which I will recognize and uphold (literally 'moisten')" is an example of Arabic eloquence, a metaphor in which the kinship tie (*raḥm*) is likened to the earth, and is "irrigated" by upholding it, so that it bears fruits of love and purity; if it is cut off, it becomes barren and produces only hatred and animosity. The true Muslim is on good terms with everyone and is liked by everyone, as they see good characteristics embodied in him/her.

Islam encourages treating parents with kindness and respect, even if they are *mushrikeen* as it encourages treating relatives equally well, even if they are not Muslims, based on the gentleness, humanity and mercy which this religion brings to the whole of mankind.

Allah (سبحانه وتعالى) says:

> "*We sent you not, but as a Mercy for all creatures.*"
> *(Qur'an 21: 107)*

She understands the broad meaning of upholding the tie of kinship

For the Muslim woman, the tie of kinship is multi-faceted. Sometimes it may involve spending money to ward off poverty and relieve hardship; at other times it may mean making visits to strengthen the ties of love; or speaking and smiling kindly and offering a warm welcome; or giving advice, showing compassion or making a selfless gesture..., i.e. acts of goodness which will awaken and increase human feelings of love, compassion and mutual support among those who are related to one another.

Hence, the Prophet (ﷺ) urged Muslims to uphold the ties of kinship even in the simplest of ways:

> "Maintain your ties of kinship even if it is merely with a greeting (i.e. saying *As-Salaam 'alaykum*)."[24]

She maintains the ties of kinship even if her relatives fail to do so

The Muslim woman whose soul is infused with the true teachings of this religion upholds the ties of kinship and does not break them. She does not treat like with like, upholding the tie if her relatives uphold it and breaking it if they break it. The Muslim woman is one who always upholds the ties of kinship, because by doing so she is seeking the pleasure and reward of Allah, and not equal treatment in return. In this way, she sets the highest example of that refined human behaviour which Islam is always keen to instill in the souls of Muslim men and women. It is, in fact, a most difficult level to achieve, except for those whom Allah has guided and who have devoted themselves to seeking His pleasure. The Muslim woman who is truly guided by the teachings of her religion is among this noble group of women who are eager to treat their relatives well in accordance with the teachings of the Prophet (ﷺ) who said:

> "The one who maintains a relationship with his/her relatives only because they maintain a relationship with him/her is not truly upholding the ties of kinship. The one who truly upholds those ties is the one who does so even if they break off the relationship."[25]

---

[24] Al-Bazzaar from Ibn 'Abbaas, as stated by Al-Ḥaythami in *Kashf al-Astaar*, 2/373; its isnads strengthen one another, as stated by As-Sakhaawi in *Al-Maqaaṣid al-Ḥasanah*, p. 146.

[25] *Fatḥ al-Baari*, 10/423, *Kitaab al-Adab, baab laysa al-waaṣil bil-mukaafi'*.

This is the refined human attitude to which Islam wants all Muslim men and women to aspire in their dealings with their relatives. Hence, the Prophet (ﷺ) reinforced the attributes of kindness, patience and tolerance in the Muslims, especially in the case of the one who upholds the ties of kinship and receives nothing in return but harshness, mistreatment and cruelty. He (ﷺ) stated that Allah is with the one who upholds the ties of kinship and does not receive similar treatment in return, and he (ﷺ) drew a frightening picture of the punishment that awaits the hard-hearted person who harshly denies and breaks the ties of kinship. A man came to the Prophet (ﷺ) and said, "O' Messenger of Allah, I have relatives with whom I try to keep in touch, but they cut me off. I treat them well, but they abuse me; I am patient and kind towards them, but they insult me." The Prophet (ﷺ) said:

> "If you are as you say, then it is as if you are putting hot dust in their mouths. Allah will continue to support you as long as you continue to do that."[26]

How important is the tie of kinship, and how heavily will it weigh in the balance of the believer! How unfortunate are those who neglect it and cut off the ties of love and kinship! How great will be the reward of the woman who upholds the ties of kinship and bears her relatives' harshness with patience, so that Allah Himself will support her against them, filling her heart with patience when they treat her badly and helping her to persevere in her noble attitude. How great is the sin of those men and women who break the ties of kinship, that the Prophet (ﷺ) likened such a person to one who eats hot dust as punishment for breaking the ties of kinship when others are seeking to maintain it.

---

26 Muslim, 16/115, *Kitaab al-Birr waṣ-Ṣilah wal-Aadaab, baab taḥreem at-taḥaasud wat-tabaaghuḍ.*

The true Muslim woman is one who upholds the ties of kinship no matter what the circumstances; she does not cut them off even if they cut her off. Thus she seeks the pleasure of her Lord, rising above the petty issues that may arise between relatives from time to time, and avoiding the insignificant matters that occupy the minds of lesser people and fill their hearts with hatred. She believes that she is above going down to the level of insignificant, foolish issues that cancel out good deeds and affect the purity of the kinship tie. It never occurs to her to sink to such a level when she listens to the words of the Prophet (ﷺ):

> "The tie of kinship (*raḥm*) is suspended from the throne of Allah, and says, 'Whoever supports me, Allah will support him, and whoever cuts me off, Allah will cut him off.'"[27]

[27] Bukhari and Muslim, See *Riyaaḍ uṣ-Ṣaaliḥeen*, 191, *baab birr al-waalidayn waṣ-ṣilat ar-raḥm.*

CHAPTER EIGHT

The Muslim Woman and Her Neighbours

The Muslim woman is kind and friendly towards her neighbours

One of the attributes of the Muslim woman who understands the teachings of her religion is that she treats her neighbours well and respects them.

She adheres to the Islamic teachings regarding good treatment of neighbours

The true Muslim woman understands the teachings of Islam which strongly urge good treatment of neighbours and gives the neighbour such a high status in the scale of human relationships, such as has never been equalled in any other religion or system before or since.

Allah (ﷻ) has clearly commanded the good treatment of neighbours in the Qur'an:

> "*Serve Allah, and join not any partners with Him; and do good — to parents, kinsfolk, orphans, those in need, neighbours who are near, neighbours who are strangers, the companion by your side, the wayfarer [you meet], and what your right hands possess...*"
>
> *(Qur'an 4: 36)*

The "neighbour who is near" is one with whom one shares ties of kinship or religion; the "neighbour who is a stranger" is one with whom one shares no such ties; and the "companion by your side" is a friend, colleague or travelling-companion.

Everyone whose home neighbours yours has the rights of a neighbour over you, even if you are not connected by kinship or religion. This honouring of the neighbour is an example of the tolerance promoted by Islam.

There are many hadiths of the Prophet (ﷺ) which enjoin good treatment of neighbours in general, regardless of kinship or religious factors, and confirm the importance of the neighbourly relationship in Islam. For example he (ﷺ) said:

> "Jibreel (Gabriel) kept on enjoining the good treatment of neighbours to such an extent that I thought he would include neighbours as heirs."[1]

Islam gives such a high status to neighbours that when Jibreel reiterated the importance of treating them well, the Prophet (ﷺ) thought that he would raise neighbours to the level of kinship and give them similar rights of inheritance.

The Prophet (ﷺ) followed Jibreel's urging, and encouraged Muslims to honour neighbours and treat them well. In his historical *khuṭbah* (sermon) during the Farewell Pilgrimage, in which he summarized the most important points of his teachings, he did not forget to mention neighbours and emphasized their rights to such an extent that the eminent *Ṣaḥaabi* [Companion of the Messenger of Allah (ﷺ)] Abu Umamah also thought that the Prophet would make neighbours heirs:

> "I heard the Prophet, when he was seated on his she-camel during the Farewell Pilgrimage, saying, 'I enjoin you to treat your neighbours well,' and urging their

---

[1] Bukhari and Muslim. See *Sharḥ as-Sunnah*, 13/71, *Kitaab al-Birr waṣ-Ṣilah, baab ḥaqq al-jaar.*

> good treatment so much that I thought, he is going to give them the rights of inheritance."[2]

The Prophet (ﷺ) sometimes used to stir up the emotions of the *Ṣaḥaabah* when he encouraged them to do good deeds, so he would start by saying, "Whoever believes in Allah and the Last Day, let him do such-and-such..." He would use this emotive phrase to command or encourage some good deed or desirable characteristic. Among the hadiths that use this method of conveying a message is:

> "Whoever believes in Allah and the Last Day, let him treat his neighbour well; whoever believes in Allah and the Last Day, let him honour his guest; whoever believes in Allah and the Last Day, let him speak good or else remain silent."[3]

According to a report given by Bukhari, he (ﷺ) said:

> "Whoever believes in Allah and the Last Day, let him not harm or annoy his neighbour..."[4]

Good treatment of neighbours is enjoined at the beginning of the hadith, and is identified as one of the signs and most beneficial results of belief in Allah and the Last Day.

She likes for her neighbours what she likes for herself

The Muslim woman who is truly open to the teachings of her religion is soft-hearted, easy-going and tolerant. She is loving towards her neighbours, sensitive to everything that could disturb, annoy or

---

[2] Ṭabaraani with a *jayyid* isnad. See *Majma' az-Zawaa'id*, 8/165.

[3] Bukhari and Muslim. See *Riyaaḍ uṣ-Ṣaaliḥeen*, 185, *baab fi ḥaqq al-jaar wal-waṣiyah bihi.*

[4] *Fatḥ al-Baari*, 10/445, *Kitaab al-Adab, baab man kaana yu'min billah wal-yawm al-aakhir fa laa yu'dhi jaarahu.*

offend them. She wishes them well, just as she wishes herself well, and she shares their joys and sorrows, in accordance with the teachings of the Prophet (ﷺ):

> "None of you truly believes until he likes for his brother what he likes for himself."[5]

According to a report given by Muslim from Anas, the Prophet (ﷺ) said:

> "By the One in Whose hand is my soul, no slave truly believes until he likes for his neighbour or, he said, his brother what he likes for himself."[6]

The true Muslim woman does not fail to think of her neighbours who may be faced with difficulties from time to time, so she gives them gifts occasionally. She recognizes that they may be affected by the smell of cooking or barbecues emanating from her house, and she understands their desire for delicious food which they may not be able to afford, so she sends some of it to them, thereby fulfilling the spirit of social responsibility which the Prophet (ﷺ) encouraged in his words to Abu Dharr:

> "O' Abu Dharr, if you cook some broth, add extra water to it, and take care of your neighbour."[7]

According to another report, he (ﷺ) said:

> "If you cook some broth, add extra water to it, then think of the families in your neighbourhood and send some of it to them."[8]

---

[5] Bukhari and Muslim. See *Sharḥ as-Sunnah*, 13/60, *Kitaab al-Birr waṣ-Ṣilah, baab ḥaqq al-jaar.*

[6] Muslim, 2/17, *Kitaab al-Eemaan, baab min khiṣaal al-eemaan an tuḥibb li akheeka ma tuḥibbu li nafsika.*

[7] Muslim, 2/177, *Kitaab al-Adab, baab al-waṣiyah bil-jaar wal-iḥsaan ilayhi.*

[8] Ibid.

The Muslim woman's conscience will not let her ignore her neighbour's poverty and difficulty without making the effort to do good and offer some generous gifts of food and other things, especially if she is well-off and living a life of ease, enjoying the bounties that Allah (ﷻ) has bestowed upon her. How can she do otherwise, when the words of the Prophet (ﷺ) are ringing in her ears?

> "He does not believe in me, who eats his fill while his neighbour beside him is hungry, and he knows about it."[9]
>
> "He is not a believer, who eats his fill while his neighbour is hungry."[10]

She treats her neighbour in the best way

The Muslim woman who truly understands the teachings of her religion never thinks that any favour is too small to be worth doing for her neighbour; she does whatever favours she can for her, no matter how insignificant they may appear. She does not let shyness or her desire to show off, prevent her from doing the little that she can afford, or make her withhold it on the basis that it is not good enough, so that she waits until she is able to offer more. Such an attitude deprives both her and her neighbour of much good, because by waiting for some hoped-for bounty that may never arrive, she wastes the opportunity to do good. The Prophet (ﷺ) drew the attention of women in particular to the importance of even the smallest gifts and favours between neighbours:

> "O' Muslim women, do not think that any gift is too

---

[9] Ṭabaraani and Al-Bazzaar with a *ḥasan* isnad. See *Majma' az-Zawaa'id*, 8/167.

[10] Ṭabaraani and Abu Ya'la; its narrators are *thiqaat*. See *Majma' az-Zawaa'id*, 8/167.

> insignificant to give to a neighbour, even if it is only a sheep's foot."[11]

A sheep's foot is a thing of little value, but it is better than nothing, and no woman should feel that any gift is not worth giving to a neighbour. Allah (ﷻ) says:

> "*Then shall anyone who has done an atom's-weight of good, see it!*" *(Qur'an 99: 7)*

And the Prophet (ﷺ) said:

> "Save yourself from the Fire even by giving half a date in charity, and if you do not find (half a date), then by saying a good word."[12]

But this hadith, which is general in application, may also be taken to mean that the recipient should not look down at the gift. The meaning then is: No (female) neighbour should scorn the gift given to her by another (female) neighbour, even if it is just a sheep's foot. Rather, she should thank her for it, because gratitude engenders friendship among neighbours and encourages mutual support and help. This is in addition to the fact that thanking people for favours is a basic Islamic trait which the Prophet (ﷺ) strongly encouraged:

> "The one who does not give thanks to people does not give thanks to Allah."[13]

Islam wants to spread mutual love and affection among neighbours. The ways in which people may achieve this are many, and include the exchange of gifts. Hence the Prophet (ﷺ) forbade women, in

---

[11] Bukhari and Muslim. See *Sharḥ as-Sunnah*, 6/141, *Kitaab az-Zakaat*, *baab at-taṣadduq bish-shay' al-yaseer.*

[12] Bukhari and Muslim. See *Sharḥ as-Sunnah*, 6/140, *Kitaab az-Zakaat, baab at-taṣadduq bish-shay' al-yaseer.*

[13] Bukhari: *Al-Adab al-Mufrad*, 1/310, *baab man lam yashkur an-naas.*

particular, to look down at any gift that she may give to or receive from her neighbour, no matter how small, because women are very sensitive in such matters and this may affect her feelings towards her neighbours. Thus he drew women's attention to the fact that what matters is the noble and worthy thought behind the gift, not the material value of the gift itself. The Muslim woman should not forget this and think of any gift as too insignificant, because in Islam thoughts and intentions are more important than material values.

She treats her neighbours well even if they are not Muslims

The true Muslim woman does not restrict her good treatment only to neighbours who are related to her or who are Muslims, but she extends it to non-Muslim neighbours too, in accordance with the tolerant teachings of Islam which encourage kindness towards all people, regardless of their race or religion, so long as they do not commit any acts of hostility or aggression towards Muslims:

> "*Allah forbids you not, with regard to those who fight you not for [your] Faith nor drive you out of your homes, from dealing kindly and justly with them: for Allah loves those who are just.*" *(Qur'an 60: 8)*

On the basis of this, the great *Ṣaḥaabi* 'Abdullah ibn 'Amr asked his slave, after slaughtering a sheep, "Did you give some to our Jewish neighbour? Did you give some to our Jewish neighbour? For I heard the Messenger of Allah (ﷺ) say,

> 'Jibreel (Gabriel) kept on enjoining the good treatment of neighbours to such an extent that I thought he would include neighbours as heirs.'"[14]

---

[14] Bukhari and Muslim. See *Sharḥ as-Sunnah*, 13/71, *Kitaab al-Birr waṣ-Ṣilah, baab ḥaqq al-jaar.*

How great is the mercy of Islam towards all people, and how kind is its concern towards those who live under its shade! History bears witness to the fact that the People of the Book have lived alongside Muslims in many regions of the Islamic world, secure in the knowledge that they, their honour and their wealth were safe, enjoying a good neighbourly relationship, good treatment and freedom of worship. Their ancient churches still exist in Muslim villages clinging to mountaintops, surrounded by thousands of Muslims who uphold the well-being of their Jewish and Christian neighbours.

She starts with the neighbour whose home is closest to her own

The true Muslim woman does not forget the precise system that Islam set out when it enjoined the good treatment of neighbours. Islam has told her to give priority to the one whose house is closest, then the one who is next closest, and so on. This takes into account the closeness of the neighbours whose homes are beside one another, the issues which may frequently arise between them, and the importance of maintaining friendship and harmony.

'Aa'ishah (رضي الله عنها) said:

> "O' Messenger of Allah! I have two neighbours, so to which one should I send a gift?" He said, "To the one whose door is closest to yours."[15]

This system of priority in the good treatment of neighbours does not mean that the Muslim woman should ignore the neighbours who are further away from her home. Everyone around her home is considered to be a neighbour and thus enjoys the rights of a neighbour. This system is merely the matter of organization, by

[15] Bukhari: *Al-Adab al-Mufrad*, 1/198, *baab tahdi ila aqrabahim baaban.*

means of which the noble Prophet (ﷺ) encouraged taking care of the closest neighbour because he or she is the one with whom there is usually ongoing contact and interaction.

The true Muslim woman is the best neighbour

It comes as no surprise that the Muslim woman who truly understands the teachings of her religion is the best of neighbours, because good treatment of neighbours is a basic Islamic attitude that is deeply engrained in the conscience of the Muslim woman who has been brought up with the teachings of Islam, which state that the one who is kindest to her neighbour is the best neighbour in the sight of Allah (ﷻ). It is reported:

> "The best of companions in the sight of Allah is the one who is best to his companion, and the best of neighbours in the sight of Allah is the one who is best to his neighbour."[16]

The noble Prophetic guidance has stressed that a good and righteous neighbour is a pillar of happiness in a Muslim's life. It is because the neighbour — male or female — guarantees comfort, security and safety. A hadith says:

> "Among the things that bring happiness to a Muslim in this life are a righteous neighbour, a spacious house and a good steed."[17]

The *salaf* (pious predecessors) appreciated the value of good neighbours so much that they considered having a good neighbour to be a precious blessing. One story which reflects this tells that the neighbour of Sa'eed ibn al-'Aaṣ wanted to sell his house for 100,000

---

[16] Tirmidhi, 3/224, *Abwaab al-birr waṣ-Ṣilah, baab ma jaa' fi ḥaqq al-jiwaar.*

[17] Al-Ḥaakim, 4/166, in *Kitaab al-Birr waṣ-Ṣilah.*

dirhams, and told the would-be purchaser, "This is the price of the house, but what would you give for having Sa'eed as a neighbour?" When Sa'eed heard about this, he sent his neighbour the price of the house and told him to stay there.

This is the status of neighbours in Islam, and the attitude and behaviour of a good Muslim neighbour. But what about bad neighbours?

Bad neighbours

Having a bad neighbour is something which is so appalling that the sensitive Muslim woman cannot think of it without shuddering and being filled with a sense of fear, loathing and dread.

The bad neighbour is a person who is deprived of the blessing of faith

It is sufficient misery for a bad neighbour to know that she is deprived of the blessing of faith, which is the greatest blessing in a person's life. The Messenger of Allah (ﷺ) confirmed the fact that this blessing is stripped away from every person who persists in mistreating his or her neighbour to the extent that he or she is counted as a bad neighbour, and stated in certain terms when he swore by Allah three times that such a person would be stripped of the blessing of faith. He said:

> "By Allah, he does not believe. By Allah, he does not believe. By Allah, he does not believe." He was asked, "Who, O' Messenger of Allah?" He said, "The one from whose evils (or troubles) his neighbour does not feel safe."[18]

---

[18] Bukhari and Muslim. See *Riyaaḍ uṣ-Ṣaaliḥeen*, 185, *baab fi ḥaqq al-jaar wal-waṣiyah bihi.*

According to a report by Muslim:

> "He will not enter Paradise whose neighbour is not safe from his evil (or trouble)."[19]

How great must be the crime of the bad neighbour, if his/her mistreatment of his/her neighbour is depriving him/her of the blessings of faith and denying him/her entrance to Paradise!

The true Muslim woman who is pure of heart contemplates the meaning of these texts and the deep impression they leave in her mind concerning bad neighbours. It never occurs to her to mistreat her neighbour, no matter what the circumstances, because mistreating neighbours or becoming involved in disputes and conspiracies is not a thing to be taken lightly: it is a major sin which destroys faith and places one's ultimate fate in jeopardy. This would be the greatest loss, and the mere thought of it makes the true Muslim woman tremble.

The bad neighbour is a person whose good deeds are not accepted

The bad neighbour is a person who has lost her faith, as stated in the hadith quoted above; she is also a person whose good deeds are put to vain. No act of obedience or righteousness will be of any benefit to her, so long as she persists in her mistreatment of her neighbour. Good deeds are essentially based on faith in Allah, and faith in Allah is not the matter of mere words: what counts is the practical implementation of that which Allah (تعالى) requires of His servants. If a bad neighbour has lost her faith by persisting in her mistreatment of her neighbour, then there is no hope that Allah will accept her good deeds, no matter how great or how many they may be. They will be utterly wiped out, even if she spends her nights and days performing good deeds (prayer and fasting etc.).

---

[19] Muslim, 2/18, *Kitaab al-Eemaan, baab bayaan taḥreem idha' al-jaar.*

The Prophet (ﷺ) was asked:

> "O' Messenger of Allah, such-and-such a woman spends her nights in prayer, fasts during the day, and so on, and she gives in charity, but she offends her neighbours with her sharp tongue. The Prophet said: 'Her good deeds will be of no avail: she is among the people of Hell.' They said, 'And so-and-so prays only the obligatory prayers, gives charity in the form of left-over curds, but does not offend anyone.' The Prophet said: 'She is among the people of Paradise.'"[20]

The Prophet (ﷺ) described the bad neighbour as being one of the worst types of people:

> "There are three worst types of people: a ruler who, if you do well, does not appreciate it, and if you do wrong, he does not forgive you for it; a bad neighbour who, if he sees something good, he conceals it, and if he sees something bad he broadcasts it; and a wife who, when you are present she annoys you and if you go away, she betrays you."[21]

The hadith paints such an ugly picture of the bad neighbour that the true Muslim woman would be so shaken that she will avoid committing the sin of mistreating a neighbour and it will be most unlikely that she will let any dispute or hostility arise between her and her neighbour, or become involved in schemes and plots. The Prophet's warning against harming or arguing with neighbours is always echoing in her ears, and she never forgets it any time she feels the stirrings of anger or hostility towards a neighbour:

---

[20] Bukhari: *Al-Adab al-Mufrad*, 1/210, *baab laa yu'dhi jarahu.*

[21] Ṭabaraani in *Al-Kabeer*, 18/267; its narrators are *thiqaat.*

> "The first two disputing parties to appear before Allah on the Day of Judgement will be two neighbours."[22]

Her good treatment with her neighbour is not lacking

Not only does the Muslim woman refrain from harming or disturbing her neighbour, she also does not spare any effort to help her neighbour, opening wide the doors of care, friendship and generosity. She is careful not to fall short in her duties whenever she is called upon to take care of her neighbours, and to honour them and treat them well, lest the words of the Prophet (ﷺ) concerning the miserly, unhelpful neighbour should become applicable to her:

> "How many people will be hanging on to their neighbours on the Day of Judgement, saying: 'O' my Lord! He shut his door in my face and denied me his kind treatment and help!'"[23]

What a miserable position the miserly, uncaring neighbour will be in on the Day of Judgement!

According to Islam, the Muslim men and women are like a high wall, whose bricks are the people of this ummah. Each brick must be sound, and strongly bonded with the others, to make this wall sturdy and durable, otherwise it will become weak and prone to collapse. Thus, Islam surrounds this wall with strong spiritual ties, to preserve its integrity and strength, so that it will not be shaken no matter what events befall it.

The Prophet (ﷺ) gave a marvellous metaphor of the solidarity and mutual support among Muslim men and women:

---

[22] Aḥmad and Ṭabaraani. See *Majma' az-Zawaa'id*, 8/170.

[23] Bukhari: *Al-Adab al-Mufrad*, 1/200, *baab man aghlaqa al-baab 'ala al-jaar.*

> "Believers are like a structure, parts of which support other parts."[24]

> "The believers, in their mutual friendship, mercy and affection, are like one body: if any part of it complains, the rest of the body will also stay awake in pain."[25]

If a religion places such an amazing emphasis on the solidarity of its followers, it is natural that it should strengthen neighbourly ties and base them on a solid foundation of friendship, kindness, mutual support and good treatment.

She puts up with her neighbour's mistakes and bad treatment

The Muslim woman who is guided by her religion is patient with her neighbour and does not get angry or bear a grudge if she makes a mistake or has some shortcomings. She is tolerant and forgiving towards her, thus hoping to earn reward from Allah (ﷻ) and to attain His love and pleasure. This is proven by the hadith of Abu Dharr: when Muṭarrif ibn 'Abdullah met him, he said, "O' Abu Dharr! I heard about what you said and wanted to meet you." Abu Dharr said, "Your father was a great man! Now you have met me." Muṭarrif said: "I heard that you have said that the Messenger of Allah (ﷺ) said: 'Allah loves three and hates three.'" Abu Dharr said, "I do not think that I would tell lies about the Messenger of Allah." Muṭarrif said, "Then who are the three whom Allah loves?" Abu Dharr [quoting the Prophet (ﷺ)] said:

> "A man who fights for the sake of Allah, with perseverance and hoping for reward from Him, and

---

[24] Bukhari and Muslim. See *Sharḥ as-Sunnah*, 13/47, *Kitaab al-Birr waṣ-Ṣilah, baab ta'aawun al-mu'mineen wa taraḥumuhum.*

[25] Ibid.

fights until he is killed, and you find this in the Book of Allah. He then recited:

'*Truly Allah loves those who fight in His cause in battle array, as if they were a solid cemented structure.*'
(*Qur'an 61: 4*)"

Muṭarrif asked, "Then who (is next)?" He said,

"A man who has a bad neighbour who annoys and disturbs him, but he bears it with patience and forbearance until Allah ends the matter either during his lifetime or upon the death of either of them."[26]

One of the characteristics of the Muslim woman whose soul has truly been cleansed and moulded by Islam is that she patiently bears the annoyances caused by her neighbours, as much as she is able. She repels their bad treatment with something that is better, and by being patient and behaving properly she sets the highest example of good treatment of one's neighbours and removes the roots of evil and hatred from their souls. Even more importantly, she acts in accordance with the teachings of the Prophet (ﷺ):

"Whoever believes in Allah and the Last Day, let him not harm or annoy his neighbour..."[27]

Let them hear this, those women who lose their minds when their child fights with the neighbours' children so that they turn a blind eye to their own child's faults and insult their neighbours with bad language and hurtful accusations, thus destroying the ties of neighbourliness and friendship in a moment of anger. Let them know that they are going against all the Islamic teachings regarding the

---

26 Aḥmad and Ṭabaraani. See *Majma' az-Zawaa'id*, 8/171.

27 *Fatḥ al-Baari*, 10/445, *Kitaab al-Adab, baab man kaana yu'min billahi wal-yawm al-aakhir fa laa yu'dhi jaarahu.*

good treatment of neighbours and that they are showing themselves to be content to be bad neighbours.

Let those women who are wise, polite and forbearing neighbours and who respond kindly to their neighbours' good treatment rejoice, because they are among the righteous neighbours with whose wise and rightly-guided conduct Allah (ﷻ) is pleased.

CHAPTER NINE

The Muslim Woman and Her Friends and Sisters in Islam

She loves them as sisters for the sake of Allah

The way in which the true Muslim woman relates to her friends and sisters in Islam is different from the way in which other women conduct their social affairs. Her relationship with her sisters is based on *taakhi* (brotherhood or sisterhood) for the sake of Allah. This love for the sake of Allah is the highest bond that may exist between one human being and another, whether man or woman. It is the bond of faith in Allah which Allah (ﷻ) established between all believers when He, the Almighty, All-Merciful, said:

> "*The Believers are but a single brotherhood...*"
> *(Qur'an 49: 10)*

The brotherhood of faith is the strongest of bonds between hearts and minds. It comes as no surprise to see that Muslim sisters enjoy a strong, enduring relationship that is based on love for the sake of Allah, the Exalted, which is the noblest and purest form of love between human beings. This is a love which is untainted by any worldly interest or ulterior motive. It is the love in which Muslim men and women find the sweetness of faith:

> "There are three things that whoever attains them will find the sweetness of faith: if Allah and His Messenger are dearer to him than anyone or anything else; if he loves a person solely for the sake of Allah; and if he would hate to return to *kufr* (disbelief) after Allah has

rescued him from it, as much as he would hate to be thrown into the Fire."[1]

The status of two who love one another for the sake of Allah

Many hadiths describe the status of two people who love each other for the sake of Allah, whether they are men or women, and describe the high position in Paradise which Allah (ﷻ) has prepared for them and the great honour which He will bestow upon them on the Day when mankind is resurrected to meet the Lord of the Worlds.

It is sufficient honour for those who love one another for the sake of Allah, men and women alike, to know that their Almighty Lord will take care of them on the Day of Judgement and will say:

> "Where are those who loved one another for My glory? Today I will shade them in My shade on the Day when there is no shade but Mine."[2]

Such is the magnificent honour and tremendous reward that will be bestowed upon those who truly loved one another for the sake of Allah, on that awesome Day.

Love for the sake of Allah, and not for the sake of anything else in life, is very difficult, and none can attain it except the one who is pure of heart, for whom this world and all its pleasures are as nothing in comparison with the pleasure of Allah. It is not surprising that Allah (ﷻ) should give them a status and blessing which is commensurate with their position in this world, above whose concerns they have risen. We see proof of this in the hadith of Mu'aadh, who said that the

---

[1] Bukhari and Muslim. See *Sharḥ as-Sunnah*, 1/49, *Kitaab al-Eemaan, baab ḥalawat al-eemaan.*

[2] Muslim, 16/123, *Kitaab al-Birr waṣ-Ṣilah wal-Adab, baab faḍl al-ḥubb fi Allah.*

Prophet (ﷺ) said:

> "Allah said: 'Those who love one another for My glory will have *minbars* [pulpits] of light, and the Prophets and martyrs will wish that they had the same."[3]

Allah (ﷻ) bestows upon those who love one another for His sake a gift which is even greater than this status and blessing, that is, His precious love which is very difficult to attain. This is proven by the hadith of Abu Hurayrah (رضي الله عنه) in which the Prophet (ﷺ) said:

> "A man went to visit a brother of his in another village. Allah sent an angel to wait for him on the road. When the man came along, the angel asked him, 'Where are you heading to?' He said, 'I am going to visit a brother of mine who lives in this village.' The angel asked, 'Have you done him any favour (for which you are now seeking repayment)?' He said, 'No, I just love him for the sake of Allah.' The angel told him, 'I am a messenger to you from Allah, sent to tell you that He loves you as you love your brother for His sake.'"[4]

What a great love, that raises a person to a position where Allah (ﷻ) loves him and is pleased with him!

The Prophet (ﷺ) understood the impact of this strong, pure love in building societies and nations, so he never let any occasion pass without advocating this love and commanding the Muslims to announce their love for one another, in order to open hearts and spread love and purity among the ranks of the ummah.

---

[3] Tirmidhi, 4/24, *baab maa jaa' fil-ḥubb fi-Allah*; he said, it is a *ṣaḥeeḥ ḥasan* hadith.

[4] Muslim, 16/124, *Kitaab al-Birr waṣ-Ṣilah wal-Adab, baab faḍl al-ḥubb fi-Allah.*

> Anas (ﷺ) said that a man was with the Prophet (ﷺ), when another man passed by. The first man said, "O' Messenger of Allah, indeed I truly love this man." The Prophet (ﷺ) asked him, "Have you let him know that?" He said, "No." The Prophet said, "Tell him." He caught up with him and told him, "Truly I love you for the sake of Allah," and the man said, "May Allah love you who loves me for His sake."[5]

The Prophet (ﷺ) used to do the same thing himself, teaching the Muslims how to build a society based on pure love and brotherhood. One day he took Mu'aadh by the hand and said,

> "O' Mu'aadh, by Allah I love you, so I advise you, O' Mu'aadh, never forget to recite, after every prayer, 'O' Allah, help me to remember You and to give thanks toYou and to worship You properly (*Allahumma, a'inni 'ala dhikrika wa shukrika wa ḥusni 'ibaadatika*).'"[6]

Mu'aadh began to spread this pure love among the Muslims throughout the Muslim lands, telling them what he had learned from the Prophet (ﷺ) about the great reward that Allah had prepared for those who love one another for His sake, and about His great love for them. In *Al-Muwaṭṭa'*, Imam Maalik gives a report with a *ṣaḥeeḥ isnad* (authentication) from Abu Idris al-Khawlaani who said:

> "I entered the mosque of Damascus, where I saw a young man who had a bright smile, and I saw the people gathered around him. When they disagreed on some matter, they referred it to him, and accepted his opinion. I asked who he was, and they told me, 'This is Mu'aadh ibn Jabal (ﷺ).' Early the next day,

---

[5] Abu Dawood, 4/452, *Kitaab al-Adab, baab ikhbaar ar-rajul bi maḥabbatihi ilayh.*

[6] Reported with a *ṣaḥeeḥ* isnad by Aḥmad, 5/245.

I went to the mosque but I found that he had arrived even earlier than I. He was praying, so I waited until he had finished, then I approached him from the front side, greeted him and said, 'By Allah, I love you.' He asked, 'For the sake of Allah?' I said, 'For the sake of Allah.' He repeated his question, 'For the sake of Allah?' And I said, 'For the sake of Allah.' So he took hold of my collar, pulled me towards him and said, 'I have good news for you. I heard the Prophet (ﷺ) say:

'Allah says: 'My love is granted to those who love one another for My sake, who visit one another for My sake, and who spend on one another for My sake.''''[7]

The effect of love for the sake of Allah on the life of Muslim men and women

Islam came to build an ideal society based on sincere love and brotherhood, so it had to plant the seeds of love in the hearts of the individuals of which society is composed. Therefore, it made this love among believing men and among believing women one of the conditions of faith that will grant admittance to Paradise. This may be seen in the hadith narrated by Imam Muslim from Abu Hurayrah (رضي الله عنه) in which the Prophet (ﷺ) said:

"By the One in Whose hand is my soul, you will not enter Paradise until you believe, and you will not believe until you love one another. Shall I not tell you of something that if you do it, you will love one another? Spread *salaam* amongst yourselves."[8]

---

[7] Maalik: *Al-Muwaṭṭa*, 2/953, *Kitaab ash-Shi'r, baab maa jaa' fil-mutḥaabbayn fi-Allah.*

[8] Muslim, 2/35, *Kitaab al-Eemaan, baab bayaan annahu la yadkhul al-jannah illa al-mu'mineen.*

The Prophet (ﷺ), with his brilliant and deep insight, understood that nothing could eliminate hatred, jealousy and rivalry from people's hearts but true brotherhood, based on sincere love, friendship and mutual advice, and free of feuds, hatred, insincerity and envy. The way to achieve this is through spreading *salaam*, so that hearts may be opened to sincere love and friendship.

So the Prophet (ﷺ) frequently repeated this teaching to his *Ṣaḥaabah*, aiming to sow the seed of love in their hearts and nurture them until they bore fruits of that great love that Islam wants for the Muslims, men and women alike.

With this sincere love, the Prophet (ﷺ) built the first generation of Muslims, who formed the solid foundation on which the great structure of Islam was built and lit the way for the rest of humanity to follow.

With this sincere love, the Prophet (ﷺ) was able to build a model human society, based on the brotherhood of faith, a society that was remarkable both in its strength, durability and ability to make sacrifices in the cause of jihad to spread Islam throughout the world, and in the solidarity of its members, which the Prophet (ﷺ) described in the most marvellous way:

> "Believers are like a structure, parts of which support other parts."[9]
>
> "The believers, in their mutual friendship, mercy and affection, are like one body: if any part of it complains, the rest of the body will also stay awake in pain."[10]

From the very beginning and throughout history, the Muslim woman

---

[9] Bukhari and Muslim. See *Sharḥ as-Sunnah*, 13/47, *Kitaab al-Birr waṣ-Ṣilah, baab ta'aawun al-mu'mineen wa taraaḥumuhum.*

[10] Ibid.

has always participated in the building of the Islamic society that is based on the brotherhood of faith, and she is still doing her share of the efforts to spread the blessed virtue of love for the sake of Allah in Muslim society, turning to her sisters and friends with an overflowing heart to strengthen the ties of love and sisterhood for the sake of Allah.

She does not forsake or abandon her sister

The Muslim woman who truly understands the teachings of Islam does not ignore the fact that Islam, which encourages brotherly love and mutual affection, is also the religion that has forbidden brothers and sisters in faith to hate or abandon one another. Islam has explained that two people who truly love one another for the sake of Allah will not be separated by the first minor offence that either of them may commit, because the bond of love for the sake of Allah is too strong to be broken by such minor matters. The Prophet (ﷺ) said:

> "No two people who love one another for the sake of Allah, or for the sake of Islam, will let the first minor offence of either of them come between them."[11]

Anger may strike a woman in moments of human weakness, and she may hurt her sister, which could provoke harsh feelings and conflicts. In such cases, the Muslim woman should not forget that Islam does not ignore human nature and its vulnerability to changing emotions. For this reason, Islam has defined the length of time during which anger may subside. This time is considered to be three days. After this time has passed, it is forbidden for the two conflicting parties to refuse to seek a reconciliation. The Prophet (ﷺ) said:

> "It is not permissible for a Muslim to be estranged from his brother for more than three days, both of them turning away from one another when they meet. The

[11] Bukhari: *Al-Adab al-Mufrad*, 1/493, *baab ḥijrat al-Muslim.*

better of them is the one who is first to greet the other."[12]

The word "Muslim" obviously includes both men and women when it occurs in hadith like this, which set out the regulations governing the lives of individuals, families and societies in the world of Islam.

Hence, we can see that the Muslim woman whose soul has been shaped by Islam does not persist in ignoring her sister, no matter what the reason. Rather, she will hasten to bring about a reconciliation and greet her with *salaam*, because she knows that the better of them is the one who is the first to greet the other. If her sister returns her *salaam*, both of them will share the reward for the reconciliation, but if she does not return the greeting, then one who gave the greeting will be absolved of the sin of forsaking her sister, while the one who refused to return the *salaam* will have to bear the burden of that sin alone. This is made clear by the hadith in which Abu Hurayrah (رضي الله عنه) said that he heard the Messenger of Allah (ﷺ) say:

> "It is not permissible for a man to be estranged from a believer for more than three days. If three days have passed, then he should go and give *salaam* to him; if he returns the *salaam*, then both of them will have share in the reward, and if he does not respond then the one who gave the *salaam* will be absolved of the sin of estrangement."[13]

It goes without saying that the word "man" in the context of this hadith refers to both men and women. The longer the period of estrangement lasts, the greater the sin of both parties becomes, as the Prophet (ﷺ) said:

---

[12] Bukhari and Muslim. See *Sharḥ as-Sunnah*, 13/100, *Kitaab al-Birr waṣ-Ṣilah, baab an-nahy 'an ḥijraan al-ikhwaan.*

[13] Bukhari: *Al-Adab al-Mufrad*, 1/505, *baab innas salaam yujzi' min aṣ-ṣarm.*

> "Whoever forsakes his brother for a year, it is as if he had shed his blood."[14]

How evil is the crime of forsaking one's brother or sister, according to Islam! How heavy is the burden of the one who is guilty of this crime that is likened to the shedding of blood! The Islamic system of education is based on mutual love and affection, and ongoing contact. Therefore Islam wants Muslim men and women to eliminate hatred and envy from their lives, and not to give any room to those evil characteristics that contradict the brotherhood of faith. Hence, Islam is filled with teachings that describe the best ethics ever known since man first walked on the face of the earth:

> "Do not break off ties with one another, do not turn away from one another, do not hate one another, do not envy one another. Be brothers, as Allah has commanded you."[15]

> "Beware of suspicion, for speaking on the basis of suspicion is the worst kind of lie. Do not seek out one another's faults, do not spy on one another, do not compete with one another, do not envy one another, do not hate one another, and do not turn away from one another. O' servants of Allah, be brothers."[16]

> "Do not envy one another, do not outbid one another (in order to inflate prices), do not hate one another, do not turn away from one another, and do not enter into a

---

[14] Bukhari: *Al-Adab al-Mufrad*, 1/497, *baab man hajara akhaahu sanah.*

[15] Muslim, 16/120, *Kitaab al-Birr waṣ-Ṣilah wal-Adab, baab taḥreem aẓ-ẓann wat-tajassus wat-tanaafus.*

[16] Bukhari and Muslim. See *Sharḥ as-Sunnah*, 13/109, *Kitaab al-Birr waṣ-Ṣilah, baab maa la yajooz min aẓ-ẓann.*

> transaction when others have already entered into it. O' servants of Allah, be brothers. A Muslim is the brother of a Muslim. He does not oppress him, humiliate him or look down upon him. *Taqwa* (piety) is here" — and so saying, he pointed to his chest (heart) three times. "It is evil enough for a man to look down upon his Muslim brother. The whole of a Muslim's being is sacred to another Muslim — his blood, his wealth and his honour are inviolable."[17]

The Muslim woman who has received a sound Islamic education thinks deeply about these teachings of the Prophet (ﷺ), which contain all the most noble characteristics such as love, friendship, brotherhood, sincerity, compassion and selflessness. She will not be able to persist in her hatred, for nobody can do so except the one who is mean and narrow-minded, or has a diseased heart or twisted nature. The true Muslim woman is far removed from such evil characteristics.

Therefore, Islam issues a stern warning to those hard-hearted people, men and women alike, who are deviating from true Islam and its spirit of tolerance by insisting on remaining estranged. They are risking an awful fate in the Hereafter: their actions may prevent them from attaining the mercy and forgiveness of Allah, and may close the doors of Paradise against them. The Prophet (ﷺ) said:

> "The doors of Paradise are opened on Monday and Thursday, and every servant who does not associate anything with Allah will be forgiven, except for the man who bears a grudge against his brother. It will be said, 'Wait for these two until they reconcile, wait for these

---

[17] Muslim, 16/120, *Kitaab al-Birr waṣ-Ṣilah wal-Aadaab, baab taḥreem ẓulm al-Muslim wa khadhaluhu wa iḥtiqarahu.*

two until they reconcile, wait for these two until they reconcile.'"[18]

The great *Ṣaḥaabi* Abu ad-Darda' (ﷺ) used to say: "Shall I not tell you about something that is better for you than charity and fasting? Reconcile between your brothers, for hatred diminishes reward."[19]

How important it is for women to understand and meditate upon this great *Ṣaḥaabi's* penetrating insight into the spirit of this religion, which is based on brotherhood and love, when they have arguments and conflicts. Abu ad-Darda', whose intelligence and good sense the Prophet (ﷺ) used to trust, understood that hatred cancels out good deeds and destroys rewards, so reconciling the estranged Muslim with his brother is better for him than charity and fasting, because if he were to continue bearing a grudge against his brother, this would negate any reward he might receive for those acts of worship.

She is tolerant and forgiving towards them

The Muslim woman who is truly guided by Islam is tolerant towards her friends and sisters, and does not bear grudges against them. If she becomes angry with one of her sisters, she restrains her anger and freely forgives the one who has committed an error, without seeing any shame in doing so. In fact, she sees this as a good deed which will bring her closer to Allah (ﷻ):

> "*...[those] who restrain anger and pardon [all] men — for Allah loves those who do good.*"*(Qur'an 3: 134)*

If a person suppresses his or her seething anger, and does not forgive, that anger will turn into resentment and malice, which are more

---

[18] Muslim, 16/122, *Kitaab al-Birr waṣ-Ṣilah wal-Aadaab, baab an-nahy 'an ash-shaḥnaa'.*

[19] Bukhari: *Al-Adab al-Mufrad*, 1/505, *baab ash-shaḥnaa'.*

dangerous than anger. When a person forgives and forgets, the flames of anger are extinguished, and his or her soul is cleansed of the effects of anger and hatred. This is the level of *iḥsaan* which earns Allah's love for those who attain it:

> *"...for Allah loves those who do good." (Qur'an 3: 134)*

The Muslim woman who truly adheres to the teachings of Islam is one of this group of *muḥsineen* (good doers). She does not allow anger to continue boiling in her heart, because suppressed resentment is a very heavy burden on the soul; rather, she hastens to forgive and forget, thus freeing herself from this burden, and filling her soul with tranquillity and peace of mind.

Something that may help the Muslim woman to reach this difficult level of *iḥsaan* is the knowledge that forgiving one's sister is not a source of humiliation or shame, rather it will raise her in status and honour in the sight of Allah, as the Prophet (ﷺ) described:

> "Allah will not increase His servant when he forgives except in honour. No-one humbles himself for the sake of Allah but Allah will raise his status."[20]

If we compare this honour and status with the status of *iḥsaan* reached by the woman who is tolerant and forgiving, we will realize what an honour she has attained, for in the sight of Allah she is one of the *muḥsinaat*, and in the sight of people she is a respected, beloved example.

The Muslim woman who has truly understood the teachings of Islam cannot have any trace of hatred or resentment in her heart towards anybody, because she understands precisely the value of forgiveness and purity of heart, and their importance if she seeks Allah's forgiveness and pleasure, as the Prophet (ﷺ) explained:

---

[20] Muslim, 16/141, *Kitaab al-Birr waṣ-Ṣilah wal-Aadaab, baab istiḥbaab al-'afw wat-tawaaḍu'.*

"There are three sins, whoever dies free of these sins will be forgiven for anything else, if Allah wills: associating anything with Allah; practising magic or witchcraft; and bearing resentment towards his brother."[21]

She meets them with a smiling face

The true Muslim woman is cheerful of countenance, always greeting her sisters with warmth and smiles, as the Prophet (ﷺ) said:

"Do not think little of any good deed, even if it is just greeting your brother with a cheerful countenance."[22]

Having a cheerful and friendly face is a good characteristic which Islam encourages and considers to be a good deed which will bring reward, because a cheerful face mirrors a pure soul. This inward and outward purity is one of the distinguishing features of the sincere Muslim. Hence the Prophet (ﷺ) said:

"Your smiling at your brother is an act of charity (*ṣadaqah*)."[23]

The Prophet (ﷺ) was cheerful of countenance, always greeting his *Ṣaḥaabah* with warmth and smiles whenever he saw them, as the great *Ṣaḥaabi* Jareer ibn 'Abdullah described: "From the time I embraced Islam, the Messenger of Allah never refused to see me and he never saw me except with a smile on his face."[24]

---

[21] Bukhari: *Al-Adab al-Mufrad*, 1/505, *baab ash-shaḥnaa'*.

[22] Muslim, 16/177, *Kitaab al-Birr waṣ-Ṣilah wal-Aadaab, baab istiḥbaab ṭalaqat al-wajh 'ind alliqaa'*.

[23] Tirmidhi, 3/228, *Abwaab al-Birr*, 36. He said it is *ḥasan ghareeb*.

[24] *Fatḥ al-Baari*, 10/504, *Kitaab al-Adab, baab at-tabassum waḍ-Ḍaḥk*; Muslim, 16/35, *Kitaab Faḍaa'il aṣ-Ṣaḥaabah, baab faḍaa'il Jareer ibn 'Abdullah*.

Islam wants the ties of friendship and brotherhood/sisterhood to remain strong among the Muslims, so it encouraged them to spread *salaam*, to be cheerful of countenance, to speak gently and to greet one another warmly, so that hearts will remain pure and open, ready to work together in kindness to do good deeds, and capable of carrying out the duties of Islam no matter what effort and sacrifices may be required.

She is sincere towards them

One of the virtues of the true Muslim woman is that she is completely sincere, towards Allah, His Prophet, and to the leaders and the masses of the Muslims, as is stated in the *ṣaḥeeḥ* hadith:

> "Religion is sincerity."[25] We (the *Ṣaḥaabah*) asked, "To whom?" He (the Prophet) said: "To Allah (by obeying Him, attributing to Him what He deserves and performing jihad for His sake); to His Book (by reading it, understanding it and applying it to one's daily life); to His Prophet (by respecting him greatly and fighting on his behalf both in his lifetime and after his death, and by following his sunnah); to the rulers of the Muslims (by helping them in their task of leading Muslims to the right path and alerting them if they are heedless); and to their common folk (by being merciful towards them)."[26]

---

[25] *Naṣeeḥah* is an Arabic word that may be translated by a number of words in English. The most common translation is "good advice," but it also carries connotations of sincerity, integrity, and "doing justice to a person or situation." (Translator)

[26] Muslim, 2/37, *Kitaab al-Eemaan, baab bayaan an ad-deen naṣeeḥah*. The explanations in brackets are adapted from those given in the English translation of *Ṣaḥeeḥ* Bukhari by Dr. Muhammad Muḥsin Khan, Vol. 1, p. 48. (Translator)

This attitude makes the Muslim woman sincere towards her sisters. She does not cheat them, mislead them, or conceal anything good from them. When she is always sincere towards them it is not merely for the sake of courtesy or to show off her social manners; she behaves in this way because sincerity is one of the fundamental bases of Islam which the first believers used to pledge to observe in their oath of allegiance (*bay'ah*) to the Prophet (ﷺ), as Jareer ibn 'Abdullah stated:

> "I gave allegiance to the Prophet and pledged to observe regular prayer, to pay zakah, and to be sincere towards every Muslim."[27]

In the hadith quoted above, we see that the Prophet (ﷺ) summed up Islam in one word, *naṣeeḥah* [advice], showing that sincerity is the central foundation of the faith. For without sincerity, a person's faith is invalid and his or her Islam is worthless. This is the meaning of the hadith of the Prophet (ﷺ):

> "None of you truly believes until he likes for his brother what he likes for himself."[28]

This is impossible to achieve unless one loves one's brother with all sincerity.

A person's liking for his brother what he likes for himself is no easy matter. It is very difficult to attain, and no man or woman can attain it except the one who has received a sound Islamic education, whose heart has been cleansed of all selfishness, hatred, envy and malice, and who is infused with love for others.

---

[27] Bukhari and Muslim. See *Sharḥ as-Sunnah*, 1/63, *Kitaab al-Eemaan, baab al-bay'ah 'al al-Islam.*

[28] Bukhari and Muslim. See *Sharḥ as-Sunnah*, 13/60, *Kitaab al-Birr waṣ-Ṣilah, baab yuḥibbu li akheehi maa yuḥibbu li nafsihi.*

The true Muslim woman who feels in the depths of her soul that her love for her sister is one of the conditions of true faith and that her religion is based on sincerity, is more likely to attain that difficult level; indeed, it is something that comes naturally to her in her dealings with her friends and sisters, and she becomes a truthful mirror to them, advising and correcting them, and wishing them nothing but good, as Abu Hurayrah (رضي الله عنه) used to say: "The believer is the mirror of his brother. If he sees any fault in him, he corrects it."[29]

In these words, Abu Hurayrah (رضي الله عنه) was echoing the hadith of the Prophet (ﷺ):

> "The believer is the mirror of his brother. The believer is the brother of a believer: he protects him from ruin and guards his back."[30]

It is natural that the true Muslim woman should have this noble attitude towards her sister. She could not do otherwise, even if she wanted to: the person who is living on such an exalted level of purity, love, loyalty and sisterhood cannot come down to the level of hatred, betrayal, malice, selfishness and jealousy. A vessel will leak out whatever is in it; musk cannot but smell beautiful; and good soil cannot but bring forth good produce. How beautifully the poet Zuhayr ibn Abi Sulma expressed this:

> "Does any plant produce large flowers but the *washeej* (a plant with spear-like leaves)?
> Are palm-trees planted anywhere except in the soil which is suitable for them?"[31]

---

[29] Bukhari: *Al-Adab al-Mufrad*, 1/333, *baab al-Muslim mir'atu akheehi.*

[30] Ibid.

[31] *Sharḥ Diwan Zuhayr*, 115, published by Daar al-Kuṭub al-Miṣriyah.

She is faithful and kind towards them

Islam does not stop at encouraging its followers to respect and be kind to their friends; it also encourages them to be kind to their parents' friends too, in recognition of the virtue of kindness and loyalty and in order to establish these values as an essential part of Islamic life. The books of our heritage are filled with reports of loyalty and kindness that the *salaf* embodied in their daily lives, so that they became a fine example for all of mankind.

An example of this is the hadith narrated by Imam Muslim in his *Ṣaḥeeḥ* from Ibn 'Umar, in which the Prophet (ﷺ) said:

> "The best kind of goodness (*birr*) is that a man should keep in touch with and respect his father's friend."[32]

The Prophet (ﷺ) used to nurture the souls of the Muslims and plant the seeds of faithfulness in them whenever he found an opportunity to tell them something of his guidance. A man of Banu Salamah came to him and asked: "O' Messenger of Allah, is there any deed of kindness and respect that I can do for my parents after they die?" He (ﷺ) said,

> "Yes, pray for them, ask forgiveness for them, fulfil their promises after they die, keep in contact with your relatives — for you have no relatives except through them — and honour their friends."[33]

The Prophet (ﷺ) set the highest example of faithfulness and kindness by taking care of Khadeejah's friends after she died. He never forgot them or neglected to treat them kindly. The Prophet's concern for the friends of Khadeejah (رضي الله عنها) upset 'Aa'ishah (رضي الله عنها), who felt jealous of

---

[32] Muslim, 16/110, *Kitaab al-Birr waṣ-Ṣilah wal-Aadaab, baab faḍl ṣilah aṣdiqaa' al-abb wal-umm.*

[33] Ibn Ḥibbaan in his *Ṣaḥeeḥ*, 2/162, *Kitaab al-Birr wal-iḥsaan, baab ḥaqq al-waalidayn.*

her. This is clear from the words of 'Aa'ishah:

> "I never felt jealous of any of the wives of the Prophet as I did of Khadeejah, although I had never seen her. But he used to mention her often, and sometimes he would slaughter a sheep, butcher the meat, and send it to Khadeejah's friends. One time I said to him, 'It is as if there were no other woman in the world but Khadeejah!' He said, 'She was such-and-such, and I had children by her.'"[34]

According to another report:

> "He used to slaughter a sheep and send to her [khadeejah's] friends a goodly amount of it."[35]

By this example, the Prophet (ﷺ) expanded the concept of faithfulness and kindness to include the distant friends of deceased parents and wives. So what about our own friends who are still alive!

She is kind to them

The Muslim woman who is truly guided by Islam is never arrogant towards her sisters and friends; she is never sullen towards them, and never uses harsh words with them. She is always kind, gentle and friendly towards them, treating them well and speaking nicely to them. The words of Allah describing the believers, men and women, as being,

> "*...lowly [or humble] with the believers, mighty against the kaafiroon...*" *(Qur'an 5: 54)*

---

[34] *Fatḥ al-Baari*, 7/133, *Kitaab Manaaqib al-Anṣaar, baab tazweej an-Nabi Khadeejah wa faḍliha*; Muslim, 15/201, *Kitaab al-Faḍaa'il, baab faḍaa'il Khadeejah.*

[35] Ibid.

— are sufficient to give her the most vivid picture of how the Muslim woman should be with her friends and sisters. The ideal situation is to be so gentle and kind that it almost looks like humility.

When the Muslim woman hears the Prophet's teachings she finds strong evidence in support of kindness towards others; it is described as something that may adorn every aspect of life, as the Prophet (ﷺ) said:

> "There is no kindness in a thing but it adds beauty to it, and there is no absence of kindness but it disfigures a thing."[36]

When the Muslim woman studies the life of the Prophet (ﷺ), she is impressed by the magnificent nature of his character, his overwhelming gentleness and his utmost kindness in his dealings with people. He was never known to scowl at anybody, or to speak harshly, or to be severe or harsh-hearted. Allah (ﷻ) indeed spoke the truth when He said:

> "*...Were you severe or harsh-hearted, they would have broken away from about you...*" *(Qur'an 3: 159)*

Anas (رضي الله عنه), his servant and constant companion, described his noble character thus:

> "I served the Messenger of Allah for ten years, and he never said to me 'Uff! (The smallest word of contempt). If I did something, he never said, 'Why did you do that?' and if I did not do something, he never said, 'Why did you not do that?'"[37]

---

[36] Muslim, 16/146, *Kitaab al-Birr waṣ-Ṣilah wal-Aadaab, baab faḍl ar-rifq.*

[37] Bukhari and Muslim. See *Riyaaḍ uṣ-Ṣaaliḥeen*, 336, *baab ḥusn al-khalq.*

Anas also said:

> "The Prophet never used obscene language, or uttered curses and insults. If he wanted to rebuke someone, he would say, 'What is the matter with him, may his forehead be covered with dust![38]'"[39]

She does not gossip about them

The alert Muslim woman does not allow herself to be drawn into gossip or to attend gatherings where gossip takes place. She restrains her tongue and refrains from gossiping in general, and avoids backbiting about her friends and sisters in particular. She regards it as her duty to prevent gatherings from sinking to the level of cheap gossip, because gossip (back-biting) is clearly *haraam* according to the words of the Qur'an:

> " *Nor speak ill of each other behind their back. Would any of you like to eat the flesh of his dead brother? Nay, you would abhor it. But fear Allah, for Allah is Oft-Returning, Most Merciful.*" *(Qur'an 49: 12)*

The Muslim woman always refrains from indulging in any talk that could lead to gossip. From her understanding of Islam, she knows that it is the tongue that may lead its owner to Hell, as stated in the hadith in which the Prophet (ﷺ) warned Mu'aadh ibn Jabal.

> "He (the Prophet) took hold of his tongue and said, 'Restrain this.' Mu'aadh said, 'O' Messenger of Allah, will we be held responsible for what we say?' The

---

[38] It has been suggested that what was meant by this expression was that the Prophet was praying that the person would increase his *sujood*, i.e. pray more, as this would guide and reform him. (Author)

[39] *Fatḥ al-Baari*, 10/452, *Kitaab al-Adab, baab lam yakun an-Nabi faaḥishan wa laa mutafhishan.*

> Prophet said: 'May your mother be bereft of you! Is there anything that causes people to be thrown into Hell on their faces (or he said: on their noses) but the harvest of their tongues?'"[40]

Gossip is an evil characteristic which does not befit the Muslim woman who has been guided by Islam. Such a woman refuses to be two-faced, hypocritical or fickle, gossiping about her friends and sisters in their absence, then when she meets them, she smiles warmly and makes a display of friendship. She knows that such fickleness is *ḥaraam* according to Islam, which is based on straightforwardness, honesty and frankness. Such good qualities come naturally to believing men and women, for Islam has made them despise inconsistency, fickleness and hypocrisy. These characteristics are regarded as so loathsome by Islam that the one who possesses them is described as being two-faced, and those who are two-faced, men and women alike, are among the worst of people in the sight of Allah, as the Prophet (ﷺ) said:

> "You will find among the worst people in the sight of Allah on the Day of Judgement, the one who is two-faced, who approaches some people in one way and some in another."[41]

The true Muslim woman is straightforward and consistent, never two-faced. She is always bright and cheerful, and treats all people in the same, noble, manner. She never forgets that the woman who is two-faced is a hypocrite: Islam and hypocrisy do not go together, and the woman who is a hypocrite will be in the lowest level of Hell.

---

[40] A *ṣaḥeeḥ ḥasan* hadith narrated by Ibn Maajah, 2/1315, *Kitaab al-fitan.*

[41] *Fatḥ al-Baari*, 10/474, *Kitaab al-Adab, baab maa qeela fee dhil-wajhayn*; Muslim, 16/157, *Kitaab al-Birr waṣ-Ṣilah wa al-Aadaab, baab dhamm dhil-wajhayn.*

She avoids arguing with them, making hurtful jokes and breaking promises

Among the good manners of the true Muslim woman are a sense of moderation, wisdom and tact. She does not exhaust her friends with irritating arguments, she does not annoy them with hurtful jokes, and she does not break a promise that she has made to them. In this, she follows the guidance of the Prophet (ﷺ):

> "Do not argue with your brother, do not joke excessively with him, do not make a promise to him then break it."[42]

Excessive arguing is a repulsive habit that fills people's hearts with hatred and disgust; making hurtful jokes destroys the purity of a friendship between two sisters; and breaking promises weakens the ties of sisterhood and friendship, and destroys mutual respect. The alert Muslim woman avoids behaving in such a way that makes a person despicable.

She is generous and honours her sisters

The Muslim woman who understands the teachings of her religion is generous and gives freely to her friends and sisters. Her approach is friendly and sincere. When she invites them, she welcomes them warmly and offers them food generously.

Friendly gatherings over food strengthen the ties of sisterhood and friendship between sisters, filling their lives with the sense of noble human emotions that have been lost by the Western woman raised in a materialistic culture, who has been filled with the spirit of opportunism, selfishness and individualism. The Western woman is

42 Bukhari: *Al-Adab al-Mufrad*, 1/485, *baab laa ta'id akhaaka shay'an fa tukhlifahu.*

suffering from spiritual emptiness and emotional dryness which result in a feeling of being deprived of true friendship and sincere friends. This is the situation of Westerners in general, and Western women in particular, and they compensate for it by devoting themselves to caring for their dogs, to make up for the lack of human emotional warmth drained from them by their materialistic philosophy. A French report states that there are seven million dogs in France, a country whose population is fifty-two million. These dogs live with their owners like one of the family. It is no longer strange in French restaurants to see a dog and its owner eating together at the same table. When an official of the animal welfare organization in Paris was asked, "Why do the French treat their dogs like they treat themselves?" He answered, "Because they want someone to love, but they cannot find any person to love."[43]

The materialistic man, whether in the West or in the East, can no longer find a true, sincere friend in his own society on whom to bestow his love and affection. So he turns to these animals in whom he finds more gentleness and faithfulness than in the people around him. Can man become any more emotionally degenerate than this extreme love for animals when he has lost the blessing of faith and guidance?

This emotional degeneration from which Westerners are suffering and which has dried up the human feelings in their souls, is one of the first things that attracted the attention of emigrant Arab writers, both Muslim and non-Muslim. They noticed that the materialistic lifestyle that has overtaken Western societies has made men into machines who know nothing in life but work, productivity and fierce

---

43 Prof. Waheeduddin Khan, *Wujoob taṭbeeq ash-shari'ah al-Islamiyah fi kulli zamaan wa makaan* (The necessity of applying Islamic shari'ah in every time and place), in *Al-Mujtama'*, No. 325, Kuwait, 24 Dhu'l-Qai'dah 1396/16 November 1976.

competition, who do not know what it is to smile warmly at a friend. They are overwhelmed by the haste and crowds of this machine-like existence. Seeing all of this alarmed those Arab writers, who had grown up in the Islamic world and breathed its spirit of tolerance, and whose hearts were filled with brotherly love. So they began earnestly calling the Westerners towards the values of love and brotherhood. One of them was Naseeb 'Areeḍah, who raised the banner of this humane call to the Westerner whose heart was stained with materialism and who had been blinded and deafened by the roar of the machines:

> "O' my friend, O' my companion, O' my colleague,
> My love for you is not out of curiosity or a desire to impose on you.
> Answer me with the words 'O' my brother!' O' my friend,
> And repeat it, for these are the sweetest words.
> If you wish to walk alone,
> Or if you grow bored of me,
> Then go ahead, but you will hear my voice,
> Calling 'O' my brother,' bearing the message,
> And the echo of my love will reach you wherever you are,
> So you will understand its beauty and its glory."[44]

The burden of materialistic life in the West became too much for Yusuf As'ad Ghaanim to bear, and he could no longer stand this life which was full of problems and sinking in the ocean of materialism, and was devoid of the fresh air of spirituality, brotherhood and affection. So he began to long for the Arab countries of the Islamic world, the lands of Prophethood and spirituality, the home of love, brotherhood and purity. He wished that he could live in an Arab tent, and leave behind the civilized world with all its noise and glaring lights:

---

[44] *Diwaan al-arwaaḥ al-ḥa'irah, qism an-naz'ah al-insaaniyah.*

> "If I were to live a short life in any Arab land, I would thank Allah for a short but rich life in a world where He is loved in the hearts of its people. I got so tired of the West that tiredness itself got bored of me. Take your cars and planes, and give me a camel and a horse. Take the Western world, land, sea and sky, and give me an Arab tent which I will pitch on one of the mountains of my homeland Lebanon, or on the banks of Barada or the shores of the Tigris and Euphrates, in the suburbs of 'Amman, in the deserts of Saudi Arabia, in the unknown regions of Yemen, on the slopes of the Pyramids, in the oases of Libya... Give me an Arab tent, and I will weigh it against the entire world and emerge a winner..."[45]

Many writings by emigrant Arab writers share the same tone, but it is sufficient to give just a few examples here. All of their writings express the emigrants' longing for the emotional richness that they missed when they came to the West, an experience which awoke in them feelings of longing for the East where Islam had spread love, brotherhood, mutual affection and solidarity.

Islam planted the seeds of love and brotherhood in the souls of its followers, and encouraged them to make friends and exhange invitations and visits. Those who invite others to these kinds of gatherings are described as being among the best of people:

> "The best of you is the one who offers food freely and returns the greeting of *salaam*."[46]

The Prophet (ﷺ) gave good news to those who are generous, men and women alike, that they will be among those who will enter Paradise in peace:

> "Spread *salaam*, offer food generously, uphold the ties

---

[45] 'Eesa an-Na'uri: *Adab al-Mahjar*, Daar al-Ma'arif, Egypt, p. 527.

[46] A *ḥasan* hadith narrated by Aḥmad, 6/16.

of kinship, stand in prayer at night when people are sleeping, and enter Paradise in peace."[47]

The Prophet (ﷺ) further encouraged these generous people with the promise of special chambers in Paradise:

> "In Paradise there are rooms whose outside can be seen from the inside, and whose inside can be seen from the outside. Allah has prepared them for those who feed others generously, who are gentle in speech, who fast continuously, and who stand in prayer at night when people are sleeping."[48]

She prays for her sisters in their absence

The sincere Muslim woman whose heart is filled with the sweetness of faith likes for her Muslim sister what she likes for herself. So she never forgets to pray for her in her absence, a *du'aa'* that is filled with the warmth of sincere love and sisterhood. She knows that such *du'aa'* (supplications) are the quickest to be answered because of their sincerity and warmth of feeling and the noble intention behind them. This is confirmed by the words of the Prophet (ﷺ):

> "The quickest prayer to be answered is a man's supplication for his brother in his absence."[49]

The *Ṣaḥaabah* understood this and used to ask their brothers to pray for them whenever they were in a situation where their prayers would be answered. Men and women alike shared this virtue, which is indicative of the high level of the entire society during that golden

---

[47] Aḥmad, 2/295, and Al-Ḥaakim 4/129, *Kitaab al-At'amah.*

[48] Aḥmad, 5/343 and Ibn Ḥibban, 2/262, *Kitaab al-Birr wal-Iḥsaan, baab ifsha' as-salaam wa iṭ'aam aṭ-ṭa'aam.*

[49] Bukhari: *Al-Adab al-Mufrad*, 2/83, *baab du'aa' al-akh bi ẓahr al-ghayb.*

period of our history. Bukhari reports, in *Al-Adab al-Mufrad*, from Ṣafwaan ibn 'Abdullah ibn 'Ṣafwaan, whose wife was Darda' bint Abu ad-Darda'. He said: "I came to visit them in Damascus, and found Umm ad-Darda' in the house, but Abu ad-Darda' was not there. She said, 'Do you want to go for Ḥajj?' I said, 'Yes.' She said, 'Pray for me, for the Prophet (ﷺ) used to say,

> 'The Muslim's prayer for his absent brother will be answered. There is an angel at his head who, whenever he prays for his brother, says, *'Ameen*, and you shall have likewise.'"'

He (Ṣafwaan) said, "I met Abu ad-Darda' in the market and he told me something similar, reporting from the Prophet."[50]

The Prophet (ﷺ) instilled team spirit in the souls of Muslim men and women at every opportunity, strengthening the ties of love for the sake of Allah between them, spreading an attitude of selflessness, and uprooting the inclination towards individualism and selfishness, in order that the Muslim society should be infused with feelings of love, close ties, solidarity and selflessness.

One of the brilliant ways in which he (ﷺ) instilled this team spirit was his response to the man who prayed out loud:

> "O' Allah, forgive me and Muhammad only." He told him, "You have denied it to many people."[51]

In this way, the Prophet (ﷺ) did not just correct this man alone, but he effectively instilled team spirit in the entire ummah of Islam, and taught every Muslim, man and women, no matter when or where they lived, that it is not right for anyone who has uttered the words of the *Shahaadah* to keep goodness to himself, because the believer should

---

[50] Ibid, 2/84.

[51] Ibid, 2/85.

always like for his brother what he likes for himself.

In conclusion, then, this is how the Muslim woman who has received a sound Islamic education should be: she loves her sisters for the sake of Allah, and her sisterly love towards them is sincere and in their best interests; she likes for them what she likes for herself; she is keen to maintain the ties of love and sisterhood between them, and she does not cut them off or forsake them; she is tolerant and forgiving of their mistakes and faults; she does not bear any hatred, envy or malice towards them; she always greets them with a cheerful, smiling face; she is kind and loyal towards them; she does not gossip about them; she does not hurt their feelings by being hostile or arguing with them; she is generous to them; she prays for them in their absence.

It is no surprise that the Muslim woman whose personality has been cleansed and moulded by Islam should have such noble characteristics. This is the miracle that Islam has wrought in the education and forming of human character, no matter where or when a man or woman lives.

CHAPTER TEN

The Muslim Woman and Her Community/Society

Introduction

When it comes to Islamic duties, the Muslim woman is just like a man: she has a mission in life, and so she is required to be as effective, active and social as her particular circumstances and capabilities allow, mixing with other women as much as she can and dealing with them in accordance with the worthy Islamic attitudes and behaviour that distinguish her from other women.

Wherever the Muslim woman is found, she becomes a beacon of guidance, and a positive source of correction and education, through both her words and her deeds.

The Muslim woman who has been truly guided by the Qur'an and Sunnah has a refined social personality of the highest degree, which qualifies her to undertake her duty of calling other women to Islam, opening their hearts and minds to the guidance of this great religion which elevated the status of women at a remarkably early stage in their history and furnished them with a vast range of the best of characteristics which are outlined in the Qur'an and Sunnah. Islam has made the acquisition of these characteristics a religious duty for which a person will be rewarded, and will be called to account if he or she fails to attain them. These texts succeeded in making the personality of the woman who is sincere towards Allah (ﷻ) into a brilliant example of the decent, chaste, polite, God-fearing, refined, sociable woman.

The Muslim woman who understands the teachings of Islam stands out in every women's gathering she attends, as she demonstrates the true values of her religion and the practical application of those values by her attaining of those worthy attributes. The make-up of her distinct social character represents a huge store of those Islamic values, which can be seen in her social conduct and dealings with people. From this rich, pure source, the Muslim woman draws her own customs, habits and ways of dealing with others and she cleanses her soul and forms her own Muslim, social personality from the same source.

She has a good attitude towards others and treats them well

The Muslim woman is of good and noble character, friendly, humble, gentle of speech and tactful. She likes others and is liked by them. By doing so, she is following the example of the Prophet (ﷺ) who, as his servant Anas (رضي الله عنه) reported, was,

> "The best of people in his attitude towards others."[1]

Anas (رضي الله عنه) saw more than anyone else of the Prophet's good attitude, and witnessed such good attitudes that no-one could imagine it existed in any human being. He told us of one aspect of that noble attitude of the Prophet (ﷺ):

> "I served the Messenger of Allah for ten years, and he never said to me 'Uff!' (the smallest word of contempt). If I did anything, he never said, 'Why did you do that?' And if I did not do something, he never said, 'Why did you not do such-and-such?'"[2]

---

[1] Bukhari and Muslim. See *Sharḥ as-Sunnah*, 13/235, *Kitaab al-Faḍaa'il, baab ḥusn al-khulqihi.*

[2] Bukhari and Muslim. See *Riyaaḍ aṣ-Ṣaaliḥeen*, 336, *baab ḥusn al-khulq.*

The Prophet (ﷺ) was of the best character, as Allah, the Almighty, All-High, said:

> "*And you [stand] on an exalted standard of character.*"
> *(Qur'an 68: 4)*

He (ﷺ) repeatedly told his *Ṣaḥaabah* of the effect a good attitude would have in forming an Islamic personality and in raising a person's status in the sight of Allah and of other people. He told them:

> "Among the best of you are those who have the best attitude (towards others)."[3]

> "The most beloved to me and the closest to me on the Day of Resurrection will be those of you who have the best attitudes. And the most hateful to me and the furthest from me on the Day of Resurrection will be the prattlers and boasters and *al-mutafayhiqoon*." The *Ṣaḥaabah* said, "O' Messenger of Allah, we understand who the prattlers and boasters are, but who are *al-mutafayhiqoon?*" He said, "The proud and arrogant."[4]

The *Ṣaḥaabah* — men and women alike — used to hear the Prophet's noble moral teachings, and they would see with their own eyes the excellent way in which he used to deal with people. So they would obey his words and follow his example. Thus was established their society which has never been equalled by any other in the history of mankind.

Anas (رضي الله عنه) said:

> "The Prophet was merciful. Nobody came to him without receiving a promise of his help, which he would

---

[3] *Fatḥ al-Baari*, 10/456, *Kitaab al-Adab, baab ḥusn al-khulq*; Muslim, 15/78, *Kitaab al-Faḍaa'il, baab kathrat ḥaya'ihi.*

[4] Tirmidhi, 3/249, in *Abwaab al-Birr*, hadith no. 70. He said it is a *ḥasan* hadith.

> fulfil if he had the means to do so. On one occasion, the *iqamah* for prayer had been given, when a Bedouin came to him, took hold of his cloak, and said, 'I still have some matter outstanding, and I do not want to forget it.' So the Prophet went with him and resolved the matter, then he came back and prayed."[5]

The Prophet (ﷺ) did not see anything wrong with listening to the Bedouin and resolving his issue, even though the *iqamah* had already been given. He did not get upset with the man for pulling on his cloak, nor did he object to resolving the matter before the prayer, because he was building a just society, teaching the Muslims by his example how a Muslim should treat his brother, and showing them the moral principles that should prevail in a Muslim community.

If good attitudes and manners among non-Muslims are the result of a good upbringing and solid education, then among Muslims such good attitudes come, above all, from the guidance of Islam, which makes good attitudes a basic characteristic of the Muslim, one which will raise his status in this world and will weigh heavily in his favour in the Hereafter. No deed will count for more on the Day of Judgement than a man's good attitude, as the Prophet (ﷺ) said:

> "Nothing will weigh more heavily in the balance of the believing servant on the Day of Resurrection than a good attitude (towards others). Verily Allah hates those who utter vile words and obscene speech."[6]

Islam has made this good attitude towards others an essential part of faith, and those who have the best attitude towards others are the most complete in faith, as the Prophet (ﷺ) said:

---

5 Bukhari: *Al-Adab al-Mufrad*, 1/375, *baab sakhaawat an-nafs.*

6 Tirmidhi 3/244, in *Abwaab al-Birr, baab ḥusn al-khulq*. He said it is a *ḥasan ṣaḥeeḥ hadith.*

> "The most perfect in faith among the believers are those who are best in their attitude towards others."[7]

Islam also describes those who have the best attitude towards others as being the most beloved to Allah (ﷻ) of His servants. This is seen in the hadith of Usaamah ibn Shurayk, who said:

> "We were sitting with the Prophet as if there were birds on our heads [silently]: none of us were talking. Some people came to him and asked, 'Who is the most beloved to Allah of His Servants?' He said, 'Those who are the best in attitude towards others.'"[8]

It comes as no surprise that the person who has the best attitude towards others should also be the one who is most beloved to Allah (ﷻ), for good treatment of others is an important feature of Islamic law. It is the most significant deed that can be placed in the balance of the Muslim on the Day of Judgement, as we have seen. It is equivalent to prayer and fasting, the two greatest bases of Islam, as the Prophet (ﷺ) said:

> "No greater deed will be placed in the balance than a good attitude towards others. A good attitude towards others will bring a person up to the level of fasting and prayer."[9]

According to another report, he (ﷺ) said:

> "By virtue of his good attitude towards others, a person may reach the level of one who habitually fasts (during the day) and stands in prayer (at night)."

---

[7] Tirmidhi, 2/315, in *Abwaab ar-Riḍa'*, 11. He said it is a *ḥasan ṣaḥeeḥ* hadith.

[8] Ṭabaraani: *Al-Kabeer*, 1/181, 183. The men of its isnad are trustworthy.

[9] Tirmidhi, 3/245, *Abwaab al-Birr waṣ-Ṣilah*, 61. The men of its isnad are *thiqaat.*

So the Prophet (ﷺ) repeatedly emphasized the importance of a good attitude and encouraged his Companions to adopt it, using various methods to instill it in their hearts by his words and deeds. He understood the great impact this good attitude would have in purifying their souls and enhancing their morals and manners. For example, he told Abu Dharr:

> "O' Abu Dharr, shall I not tell you of two qualities which are easy to attain but which will weigh more heavily in the balance?" He said, "Of course, O' Messenger of Allah." He said, "You should have a good attitude towards others and remain silent for lengthy periods. By the One in Whose hand is my soul, nothing that people have ever attained is better than these two."[10]

And he (ﷺ) said:

> "A good attitude is a blessing and a bad attitude is a calamity. Piety (*birr*) lengthens life, and charity will prevent a bad death."[11]

One of his *du'aa'* was:

> "*Allahumma aḥsanta khalqi fa aḥsin khulqi* (O' Allah, You have made my physical constitution good, so make my attitude and behaviour good also)."[12]

The prayer of the Prophet (ﷺ), asking Allah to make his attitude good when Allah had described him in the Qur'an as being,

---

[10] Abu Ya'la and Ṭabaraani: *Al-Awsaṭ*; the men of Abu Ya'la are *thiqaat*. See *Majma' az-Zawaa'id*, 8/22.

[11] Aḥmad, 3/502; its men are *thiqaat.*

[12] Aḥmad, 1/403; its men are trustworthy.

"...*on an exalted standard of character*" *(Qur'an 68: 4)*,

— is a clear indication of his deep concern and earnest desire that the Muslims should continue to seek to increase in good attitudes, no matter what heights they had already scaled, just as their Prophet (ﷺ) continued to seek to increase in good attitudes through this *du'aa'*. "Good attitudes" is a comprehensive term which includes all the good characteristics that human beings may acquire, such as modesty, patience, gentleness, forgiveness, tolerance, cheerfulness, truthfulness, trustworthiness, sincerity, straightforwardness, purity of heart, and so on.

The one who sets out to explore the Islamic teachings on social issues will find himself confronted with a host of teachings that encourage every single one of these noble attitudes. This is an indication of the intense concern that Islam has to form the social personality of the Muslim in the most precise fashion. So it does not stop at mentioning generalities, but it also deals with every minor moral issue that may form individual aspects of the integrated social personality. This comprehensiveness does not exist in other social systems as it does in Islam.

The researcher who sets out to explore the character of the Muslim woman has no alternative but to examine all these texts, and to understand the guidance and legislation contained therein. Only then will he be able to fully comprehend the noble social personality that is unique to the true Muslim, man and/or woman.

She is truthful

The Muslim woman is truthful with all people, because she has absorbed the teachings of Islam which encourages truthfulness and regards it as the chief of virtues, whilst lying is forbidden and regarded as the source of all evils and bad deeds. The Muslim woman believes that truthfulness naturally leads to goodness, which will admit the one who practices it to Paradise, while falsehood leads to iniquity which will send the one who practices it to Hell. The Prophet (ﷺ) said:

> "Truthfulness leads to piety (*birr*), and piety leads to Paradise. A man continues to speak the truth until he is recorded in the sight of Allah as a sincere lover of truth (*ṣiddeeq*). Falsehood leads to iniquity and iniquity leads to Hell. A man will continue to speak falsehood until he is recorded in the sight of Allah as a liar."[13]

Therefore, the Muslim woman is keen to be a sincere lover of truth (*ṣiddeeqah*), striving to be true in all her words and deeds. This is a sublime status which is achieved only by God-fearing Muslim women by means of truthfulness, purity of heart and by virtue of which she is recorded in the sight of Allah as an honoured lover of truth.

She avoids giving false statements

The true Muslim woman whose personality has been moulded by the teachings and guidance of Islam does not give false statements, because to do so is *ḥaraam* (forbidden):

> "*...And shun the word that is false.*" *(Qur'an 22: 30)*

Bearing false witness,[14] besides being *ḥaraam*, does not befit the Muslim woman. It damages her honour and credibility, and marks a person as twisted and worthless in the sight of others. So the Qur'an completely forbids this attitude for the chosen servants of Allah, men

---

[13] Bukhari and Muslim. See *Riyaaḍ aṣ-Ṣaaliḥeen*, 50, *baab aṣ-ṣidq*.

[14] *Shahaadat az-Zoor* may be interpreted in the following ways: bearing false witness by giving evidence that is false; assisting in something which implies fraud or falsehood; attending the gatherings of the *kuffaar* on the occasion of their festivals. (Translator)

and women alike, just as it forbids other major sins:

> "*Those who witness no falsehood and, if they pass by futility, they pass it by with honourable [avoidance].*"
>
> *(Qur'an 25: 72)*

Nothing is more indicative of the enormity of this sin than the fact that the Prophet (ﷺ) mentioned it as coming after the two most serious sins on the scale of major sins: associating partners with Allah, and disobedience to parents. Then he repeated it to the Muslims, warning them with the utmost fervour. He (ﷺ) said:

> "Shall I not tell you of the most serious of the major sins?" We said: "Of course, O' Messenger of Allah." He said: "Associating anything with Allah, and diobeying parents." He was reclining, but then he sat up and said: "And bearing false witness," and he kept repeating this until we wished that he would stop (i.e., so that he would not exhaust himself with his fervour)."[15]

She gives sincere advice

The true Muslim woman does not only strive to free herself of negative characteristics; she also seeks to offer sincere advice to every woman she comes into contact with who has deviated from the guidance of Allah — and how many women there are who have wronged themselves and are in great need of someone to offer them sincere advice and guide them back towards the straight path which Allah (ﷻ) has commanded all of us to follow.

For the true Muslim woman, offering sincere advice is not just the

---

[15] Bukhari and Muslim. *Riyaaḍ aṣ-Ṣaaliḥeen*, 689, *baab ghalaẓ taḥreem shahaadat az-zoor.*

matter of volunteering to do good out of generosity; it is a duty enjoined by Islam, as the Prophet (ﷺ) said:

> "Religion is sincerity (or sincere advice)." The *Ṣaḥaabah* (Companions of the Prophet) asked, "To whom?" He said, "To Allah, to His Book, to His Messenger, to the leaders of the Muslims and to their common folk."[16]

When the *Ṣaḥaabah* swore allegiance (*bay'ah*) to the Prophet (ﷺ), they would pledge to observe *ṣalaah* and zakah, and to be sincere towards every Muslim, as is shown in the statement of Jareer ibn 'Abdullah (رضي الله عنه):

> "I swore allegiance to the Prophet with the pledge that I would establish regular prayer, pay zakah and be sincere to every Muslim."[17]

How brilliantly the Prophet (ﷺ) expressed the meaning of *naṣeeḥah* when he said, "Religion is sincerity (or sincere advice)!" He summed up the entire religion in just one word, "*naṣeeḥah*," indicating to every Muslim the value of sincerity and sincere advice, and the great impact that sincere advice has on the lives of individuals, families and societies. When sincerity spreads among a people, they are guided to the straight path; if sincerity is withheld, they will go far astray.

Therefore, *naṣeeḥah* was one of the most important matters that Muslims pledged to observe when they swore allegiance to the Prophet (ﷺ): it comes after *ṣalaah* and zakah, as we have seen in the hadith of Jareer ibn 'Abdullah quoted above.

---

16 Muslim, 2/37, *Kitaab al-Eemaan, baab bayaan 'an ad-deen an-naṣeeḥah.*

17 Bukhari and Muslim. See *Sharḥ as-Sunnah*, 13/92, *Kitaab al-Birr waṣ-Ṣilah, baab an-naṣeeḥah.*

The fact that sincere advice is mentioned in conjunction with *ṣalaah* and zakah in the oath of allegiance given by the great *Ṣaḥaabi* Jareer ibn 'Abdullah to the Prophet (ﷺ) is an indication of its importance in the Islamic scheme of things and in deciding a person's fate in the Hereafter. It is therefore a basic characteristic of the true Muslim who is concerned about his destiny on the Day of Judgement.

In Islam, responsibility is a general duty that applies to men and women alike, each person has responsibilities within his or her own social sphere, as the Prophet (ﷺ) explained:

> "Each of you is a shepherd and each of you is responsible for his flock. The leader is a shepherd and is responsible for his flock; a man is the shepherd of his family and is responsible for his flock; a woman is the shepherd in the house of her husband and is responsible for her flock; a servant is the shepherd of his master's wealth and is responsible for it. Each of you is a shepherd and is responsible for his flock."[18]

If we understand this, we will realize that the woman's responsibility includes offering sincere advice to everyone around her who can benefit from it.

She guides others to righteous deeds

The Muslim woman whose soul has been purified by Islam and cleansed of the stains of selfishness and love of show guides others to righteous deeds when she knows of them, so that goodness will come to light and people will benefit from it. It is all the same to her whether the good deed is done by herself or by others, because she knows that the one who guides others to do righteous deeds will be

---

[18] Bukhari and Muslim. See *Sharḥ as-Sunnah*, 10/61, *Kitaab al-Imaarah wal-qaḍa', baab ar-raa'ee mas'ool 'an raiy'atihi.*

rewarded like the one who does the actual deed, as the Prophet (ﷺ) said:

> "Whoever guides others to do good will have a reward like that of the person who does the good deed."[19]

The Muslim woman is the least likely to keep goodness to herself, or to boast to others about doing good, which is the attitude of selfish women who love to show off. It is enough for the Muslim woman who guides others to do good to know that she will be rewarded by Allah (ﷻ) in either case, and for the true Muslim woman, storing up reward with Allah is more important than fame and a good reputation. In this way, goodness spreads throughout the community, and every person will have the opportunity to do whatever Allah helps him or her to do.

How many of these deadly psychological disorders are preventing good from being spread in society! For the people who are suffering from them hope that they alone will undertake good deeds to the exclusion of others, but circumstances prevent them from doing so. So goodness and benefits remain locked up waiting for the opportunity that never comes. The true Muslim, man or woman, who seeks to please Allah and earn reward from Him is free from such disorders. The true Muslim guides people to do good deeds as soon as he or she is aware of an opportunity, and thus he or she earns a reward from Allah (ﷻ) equal to the reward of the one who does the good deed itself.

She does not cheat, deceive, or stab in the back

The sincere Muslim woman for whom truthfulness has become a deeply-rooted characteristic does not cheat, deceive or stab in the

---

[19] Muslim, 13/38, *Kitaab al-Imarah, baab faḍl i'aanat al-ghaazi fi sabeelillah.*

back, because these worthless characteristics are beneath her personality. They contradict the values of truthfulness, and do not befit the Muslim woman. Truthfulness requires an attitude of sincerity, straightforwardness, loyalty and fairness, which leaves no room for cheating, lying, trickery, deceit or betrayal.

The Muslim woman who is filled with the guidance of Islam is truthful by nature, and has a complete aversion from cheating, deceiving and back-stabbing, which she sees as a sign of a person's being beyond the pale of Islam, as the Prophet (ﷺ) stated in the hadith narrated by Muslim:

> "Whoever bears arms against us is not one of us, and whoever cheats us is not one of us."[20]

According to another report, also narrated by Muslim,

> "The Prophet (ﷺ) passed by a pile of food (in the market), put his hand in it and felt dampness (although the surface of the pile was dry). He said, 'O' owner of the food, what is this?' The man said, 'It was damaged by rain, O' Messenger of Allah.' He said, 'And you did not put the rain-damaged food on top so that people could see it! Whoever cheats us is not one of us.'"[21]

Muslim society is based on purity of human feeling, sincerity towards every Muslim, and fulfilment of promises to every member of the society. If any cheats or traitors are found in that society, they are most certainly alien elements whose character is in direct contrast to the noble character of true Muslims.

Islam views cheating, deception and back-stabbing as heinous crimes

---

[20] Muslim, 2/108, *Kitaab al-Eemaan, baab qawl an-Nabi man ghashshana fa laysa minna.*

[21] Muslim, 2/109, *Kitaab al-Eemaan, baab man ghashshana fa laysa minna.*

which will be a source of shame to the guilty party both in this world and the next. The Prophet (ﷺ) announced that on the Day of Resurrection, every traitor would be raised carrying the flag of his betrayal and a caller will cry out in the vast arena of judgement, pointing to him and drawing attention to him:

> "Every traitor will have a banner on the Day of Resurrection, and it will be said: 'This is the betrayer of so-and-so.'"[22]

How great will be the shame of those traitors, men and women, who thought that their betrayal was long since forgotten, and now here it is, spread out for all to see and carried aloft on banners held by their own hands.

Their shame on the Day of Judgement will increase when they will see the Prophet (ﷺ), who is the hope of intercession on that great and terrible Day, standing in opposition to them, because they have committed the heinous crime of betrayal, which is a crime of such enormity that it will deprive them of the mercy of Allah (ﷻ) and the intercession of the Prophet (ﷺ):

> "Allah, may He be exalted, said: 'There are three whom I will oppose on the Day of Resurrection: a man who gave his word, and then betrayed; a man who sold a free man into slavery and kept the money; and a man who hired someone, benefitted from his labour, then did not pay his wages."[23]

The Muslim woman who has been truly guided by Islam steers clear of all forms of deceit and back-stabbing which exist in many forms in

---

[22] Bukhari and Muslim. See *Sharḥ as-Sunnah*, 10/71-73, *Kitaab al-Imaarah wal-qaḍa', baab wa'eed al-ghadr*; *Riyaaḍ aṣ-Ṣaaliḥeen*, 705, *baab taḥreem al-ghadr.*

[23] *Fatḥ al-Baari*, 4/417, *Kitaab al-Buyu', baab ithm man ba'a hurran.*

the world of modern women, but the Muslim woman values herself too highly to include herself among those cheating, deceiving women whom the Prophet (ﷺ) considered to be hypocrites:

> "There are four features, whoever has all of them is a true hypocrite, and whoever has one of them has one of the qualities of a hypocrite until he gives it up: when he is trusted, he is unfaithful; when he speaks, he tells lies; when he make a promise, he proves treacherous; and when he disputes, he resorts to slander."[24]

She keeps her promises

One of the noble attitudes of the true Muslim woman is that she keeps her promises. This attitude is the companion of truthfulness, and indeed, stems naturally from it.

Keeping promises is a praiseworthy attitude, one that indicates the high level of civility attained by the woman who exhibits it. It helps her to succeed in life, and earns her the love, respect and appreciation of others.

The effects of this attitude in instilling moral and psychological virtues in girls and boys are not unknown; if they see their mothers always keeping their promises, this is the best example that they can be given.

For the Muslim woman, keeping promises is not just the matter of social niceties, something to boast about among her friends and peers; it is one of the basic Islamic characteristics and one of the clearest indicators of sound faith and true Islam. Many texts of the Qur'an and Sunnah emphasize the importance of this quality:

---

[24] Bukhari and Muslim. See *Sharḥ as-Sunnah*, 1/74, *Kitaab al-Eemaan, baab 'alaamaat an-nifaaq.*

"O' you who believe! Fulfil all obligations."
(Qur'an 5: 1)

"And fulfil every engagement, for [every] engagement will be enquired into [on the Day of Reckoning]."
(Qur'an 17: 34)

This is a definitive command from Allah (ﷻ) to His believing servants, men and women alike, to keep their promises and to fulfil whatever obligations those promises entail. There is no room for escaping or dodging this responsibility. It does not befit the Muslim who has committed himself or herself to, then tries to get out of keeping the promise. It is his duty to keep his word. In some *ayat*, the word for "promise" is connected by the grammatical structure of *idaafah* (genitive) to Allah (ﷻ) Himself, as an indication of its dignity and sanctity, and of the obligation to keep promises:

"Fulfil the Covenant of Allah, when you have entered into it..." *(Qur'an 16: 91)*

Islam dislikes those prattlers who carelessly make promises without following through and keeping their word:

"O' you who believe! Why say you that which you do not? Grievously odious is it in the sight of Allah that you say that which you do not." *(Qur'an 61: 2-3)*

Allah (ﷻ) does not like His believing slaves, male or female, to sink to the level of empty words, promises made with no intention of fulfilment, and all manner of excuses to avoid upholding the commitments made. Such conduct does not befit believing men and women. The tone of the question asked in this *aayah* is an expression of the extreme disapproval incurred by those believers who commit the sin of saying that which they do not do.

The Prophet (ﷺ) said:

> "The signs of a hypocrite are three: when he speaks, he lies; when he makes a promise, he breaks it; and when he is entrusted with something, he betrays that trust."[25]

According to a report given by Muslim, he (ﷺ) added:

> "Even if he fasts, prays and thinks that he is a Muslim."[26]

The level of a woman's Islam is not determined only by acts of worship and rituals, but also the extent to which her character is influenced by the teachings and high values of Islam. She does only that which will please Allah. The Muslim woman who understands and adheres to the teachings of Islam does not break her promises, or cheat others, or betray them, because such acts contradict the morals and values of true Islam, and such attitudes are only found among men and women who are hypocrites.

Let them know this, those women who tell lies to their own children, who make promises then go back on their word, thus planting the seeds of dishonesty and promise-breaking in their children's hearts. Let them know this, those women who make empty, meaningless promises and attach no importance to the word of honour to which they have committed themselves, lest by such carelessness they become hypocrites themselves and earn the punishment of the hypocrites which, as is well known, is a place in the lowest level of Hell.

---

[25] Bukhari and Muslim. See *Sharḥ as-Sunnah*, 1/72, *Kitaab al-Eemaan, baab 'alaamaat an-nifaaq.*

[26] Muslim, 2/48, *Kitaab al-Eemaan, baab bayan khiṣaal al-munaafiq.*

She is not a hypocrite

The true Muslim woman is frank and open in her words and opinions, and is the furthest removed from hypocrisy, flattery and false praise, because she knows from the teachings of Islam that hypocrisy is *ḥaraam*, and does not befit the true Muslim.

The Prophet (ﷺ) has protected us from falling into the mire of hypocrisy and flattery. "When Banu 'Amir came to him and praised him, saying, 'You are our master,' he (ﷺ) said,

> 'The only Master is Allah.' When they said, 'You are the most excellent and greatest of us,' he said, 'Say what you want, or a part of it, but do not speak like agents of *Shayṭaan* (Satan). I do not want you to raise me above the status to which Allah has appointed me. I am Muhammad ibn 'Abdullah, His Servant and Messenger.'"[27]

The Prophet (ﷺ) prevented people from exaggerating in their praise of others, some of whom may not even be deserving of praise, when he forbade them to describe him as "master," "excellent" and "great," at the time when he was without doubt the greatest of the Messengers, the master of the Muslims and the greatest and most excellent of them. He did this because he understood that if the door of praise was opened to its fullest extent, it might lead to dangerous types of hypocrisy which are unacceptable to a pure Islamic spirit and the truth on which this religion is based. He forbade the *Ṣaḥaabah* to praise a man to his face, lest the one who spoke the words crossed the boundary of hypocrisy, or the object of his admiration be filled with feelings of pride, arrogance, superiority and self-admiration.

Bukhari and Muslim narrate that Abu Bakrah (رضي الله عنه) said:

---

[27] *Ḥayaat aṣ-Ṣaḥaabah*, 3/99.

> "A man praised another man in the presence of the Prophet, who said: 'Woe to you! You have cut your companion's throat!' several times. Then he said: 'Whoever of you insists on praising his brother, let him say: 'I think So-and-so is such-and-such, and Allah knows the exact truth, and I do not confirm anyone's good conduct before Allah, but I think him to be such-and-such,' if he knows that this is the case.'"[28]

If praising a person cannot be avoided, then it must be sincere and based on truth. The praise should be moderate, reserved and without any exaggeration. This is the only way in which a society can rid itself of the diseases of hypocrisy, lies, deceit and sycophancy.

In *Al-Adab al-Mufrad*, Bukhari reports from Rajaa' from Miḥjan al-Aslami that:

> "The Prophet (ﷺ) and Miḥjan were in the mosque when the Prophet saw a man praying, bowing and prostrating, and asked, 'Who is that?' Miḥjan began to praise the man, saying, 'O' Messenger of Allah, he is So-and-so, and is such-and-such.' The Prophet said: 'Stop. Do not let him hear you, or it will be his downfall!'"[29]

According to a report given by Aḥmad, Miḥjan said:

> "O' Messenger of Allah, this is so-and-so, one of the best people of Madeenah," or "one of the people who prays the most in Madeenah." The Prophet said: "Do not let him hear you, or it will be his downfall!" — two or three times — "You are an ummah for whom I wish ease."[30]

---

[28] *Fatḥ al-Baari*, 10/476, *Kitaab al-Adab, baab maa yukrah min at-tamaaduḥ*; Muslim, 18/126, *Kitaab az-Zuhd, baab an-nahi 'an ifraaṭ fil-madḥ.*

[29] *Al-Adab al-Mufrad*, 1/433, *baab yuḥtha fi wujooh al-maddaaḥeen.*

[30] Aḥmad, 5/32; its isnad is *ṣaḥeeḥ*.

The Prophet (ﷺ) described hearing praise as being a person's downfall, because of its profound psychological impact on the human mind which by nature loves to hear such words. So the one who is praised begins to feel superior to and to look down on other people. If such praise is repeated by the hypocrites and flatterers — and how many of them there are surrounding those in positions of power and authority! — this will satisfy a strong desire in his heart and will become something he wants to hear regularly. Then he will hate to hear criticism and advice, and will only accept praise, thanks and adulation. No wonder, then, that truth will be lost, justice will be eliminated, morality will be destroyed and society will be corrupted.

For this reason the Prophet (ﷺ) ordered his Companions to throw dust in the faces of those who praise others, lest their number, and hence flattery and hypocrisy, increase, which would have had disastrous consequences for the whole Muslim society.

The *Ṣaḥaabah*, may Allah be pleased with them all, used to feel upset when they heard others praising them, although they were the most deserving of such praise, because they feared its disastrous consequences and adhered to the basic principles of Islam that abhor such cheap, empty expressions. Nafi'(رضي الله عنه) and others said:

> "A man said to Ibn 'Umar: 'O' you who are the best of people!' or 'O' son of the best of people!' Ibn 'Umar said: 'I am not the best of people, neither am I the son of the best of people. I am just one of the servants of Allah: I hope for His (mercy) and I fear His (wrath). By Allah, you will continue to pursue a man (with your praise) until you bring about his downfall (and destruction).'"[31]

This is a wise statement from a great *Ṣaḥaabi* of the utmost Islamic sensibilities, who adhered to Islamic teachings both in secret and

---

[31] *Ḥayaat aṣ-Ṣaḥaabah*, 3/103.

openly.

The *Ṣaḥaabah* (may Allah be pleased with them all) understood precisely the Prophet's guidance telling them that their words and deeds should be free from hypocrisy. The great difference between that which is done sincerely for the sake of Allah and that which is merely hypocrisy and flattery was abundantly clear to them.

Ibn 'Umar said that some people said to him:

> "When we visit our rulers we tell them something different from what we say when we have left them."
> Ibn 'Umar said: "At the time of the Prophet, we used to consider this to be hypocrisy."[32]

The true Muslim woman is protected by her religion from sinking to the dangerous level of hypocrisy to which many women today have sunk, thinking that they have not overstepped the bounds of polite flattery. They do not realize that there is a type of flattery that is *ḥaraam* and that they could sink so low without realizing it and fall into the sin of that despised hypocrisy which may lead to their ultimate doom. This happens when they keep quiet and refrain from telling the truth, or when they praise those who do not deserve it.

She is characterized by shyness (ḥaya')

Women are shy by nature, and what I mean here by shyness is the same as the definition of the *'ulama'* (scholars): the noble attitude that always motivates a person to keep away from what is abhorrent and to avoid falling short in one's duties towards those who have rights over him/her. The Prophet (ﷺ) was the highest example of shyness, as the great *Ṣaḥaabi* Abu Sa'eed al-Khudri described him:

---

[32] *Fatḥ al-Baari*, 13/170, *Kitaab al-Aḥkaam, baab maa yukrah min thanaa' as-sulṭaan.*

"The Messenger of Allah was more shy than the virgin hiding away in her own room. If he saw something he disliked, we would know it only from his facial expression."[33]

The Prophet (ﷺ) praised the attitude of shyness in a number of *aḥaadeeth*, and explained that it is pure goodness, both for the one who possesses this virtue and for the society in which he lives.

'Imran ibn Huṣayn (رضي الله عنه) narrated that the Prophet (ﷺ) said:

"Shyness brings nothing but good."[34]

According to a report given by Muslim, he (ﷺ) said:

"Shyness is all good."[35]

Abu Hurayrah (رضي الله عنه) narrated that the Prophet (ﷺ) said:

"Faith has seventy-odd (over seventy) branches. The greatest of them is saying *Laa ilaaha ill-Allah* (there is no god but Allah), and the least of them is removing something harmful from the road. Shyness is one of the branches of faith."[36]

The true Muslim woman is shy, polite, gentle and sensitive to the feelings of others. She never says or does anything that may harm people or offend their dignity.

The attitude of shyness that is deeply-rooted in her nature is supported by her understanding of the Islamic concept of shyness,

---

[33] Bukhari and Muslim. See *Riyaaḍ aṣ-Ṣaaliḥeen*, 364, *Kitaab al-Adab, baab fil-ḥaya' wa faḍluhu.*

[34] Bukhari and Muslim. See *Riyaaḍ aṣ-Ṣaaliḥeen*, 363, *Kitaab al-Adab, baab fil-ḥaya' wa faḍluhu.*

[35] Muslim, 2/7, *Kitaab al-Eemaan, baab al-ḥaya' shu'bah min al-eemaan.*

[36] Bukhari and Muslim. See *Riyaaḍ aṣ-Ṣaaliḥeen*, 363, *Kitaab al-Adab.*

which protects her against going wrong or deviating from Islamic teachings in her dealings with others. She does not only feel shy in front of people, but she also feels shy before Allah (ﷻ). She is careful not to let her faith become contaminated by wrongdoing, because shyness is one of the branches of faith. This is the highest level that may be reached by the woman who is characterized by shyness. In this way she is distinguished from the Western woman who has lost the characteristic of shyness.

She is proud and does not beg

One of the features that distinguish the Muslim woman who has truly understood the guidance of Islam is the fact that she is proud and does not beg. If she is faced with difficulties or is afflicted with poverty, she seeks refuge in patience and self-pride, whilst redoubling her efforts to find a way out of the crisis of poverty that has befallen her. It never occurs to her to put herself in the position of begging and asking for help, because Islam thinks too highly of the true Muslim woman to allow her to put herself in such a position. The Muslim woman is urged to be proud, independent and patient — then Allah (ﷻ) will help her and give her independence and patience:

> "Whoever refrains from asking from people, Allah will help him. Whoever tries to be independent, Allah will enrich him. Whoever tries to be patient, Allah will give him patience, and no-one is given a better or vaster gift than patience."[37]

The Muslim woman who understands the teachings of Islam knows that Islam has given the poor some rights over the wealth of the rich, who should give freely without reminders or insults. But at the same time, Islam wants the poor to be independent and not to rely on this

---

[37] Bukhari and Muslim. See *Riyaaḍ aṣ-Ṣaaliḥeen*, 35, *baab aṣ-ṣabr.*

right. The higher hand is better than the lower hand, so all Muslims, men and women, should always work so that their hand will not be the lower one. That is more befitting and more honouring to them. So those men and women who have little should increase their efforts and not be dependent on charity and hand-outs. This will save them from losing face. Whenever the Messenger of Allah (ﷺ) delivered any sermon from the *minbar* about charity and refraining from begging, he would remind the Muslims that,

> 'the higher hand is better than the lower, the higher hand is the one that spends, whilst the lower hand is the one that begs.'"[38]

She does not interfere in that which does not concern her

The true Muslim woman is wise and discerning; she does not interfere in that which does not concern her, nor does she concern herself with the private lives of the women around her. She does not poke her nose into their affairs or force herself on them in any way, because this could result in sin or blame on her part. By seeking to avoid interfering in that which does not concern her, she protects herself from vain and idle talk, as she is adhering to a sound Islamic principle that raises the Muslim above such foolishness. It furnishes him with the best of attitudes, and guides him towards the best way of dealing with others:

> "A sign of a person's being a good Muslim is that he should leave alone that which does not concern him."[39]

---

[38] Muslim, 7/124, *Kitaab az-Zakah, baab bayaan an al-yad al-'uliya khayr min al-yad as-sufla.*

[39] Tirmidhi, 3/382, *Abwaab az-Zuhd*, 8; Ibn Maajah, 2/1316, *Kitaab al-Fitan, baab kaff al-lisaan 'an al-fitnah.*

Abu Hurayrah (رضي الله عنه) reported that the Prophet (ﷺ) said:

> "Allah likes three things for you and dislikes three
> things. He likes for you to worship Him, not to associate
> anything with Him, and to hold fast, all together, by the
> Rope which He (stretches out for you), and not to be
> divided among yourselves *(cf. Aal 'Imraan 3: 103).*
> And He dislikes for you to pass on stories and gossip, to
> ask too many questions, and to waste money."[40]

The divinely-guided society which has been formed by Islam has no
room for passing on stories and gossip, asking too many questions, or
interfering in the private affairs of others, because the members of
such a society are too busy with something much more important,
which is the establishing of the word of Allah on earth, taking the
banner of Islam to the four corners of the earth, and spreading its
values among mankind. Those who are engaged in such great
missions do not have the time to indulge in such sins.

She refrains from slandering the honour of others and seeking out their faults

The God-fearing Muslim woman restrains her tongue and does not
seek out people's faults or slander their honour, and she hates to see
such talk spread in the Muslim community. She acts in accordance
with the guidance of the Qur'an and Sunnah, which issue a severe
warning to those corrupt and misguided men and women who
indulge in slandering the honour of others, that they will suffer a
terrible punishment in this world and the next:

> *"Those who love [to see] scandal published broadcast
> among the Believers, will have a grievous Penalty in*

---

[40] Muslim, 12/10, *Kitaab al-Aqdiyah, baab an-nahi 'an kathrat al-masaa'il
min ghayri ḥaajah.*

> *this life and in the Hereafter: Allah knows, and you
> know not."*   *(Qur'an 24: 19)*

The one who indulges in the slander of people's honour, and spreads news of scandal throughout the community is just like the one who commits the scandalous deed, as 'Ali ibn Abi Ṭaalib (رضي الله عنه) stated:

> "The one who tells the news of scandals and the one
> who spreads the news of scandals are equally sinful."[41]

The true Muslim woman understands that the human shortcomings of some weak or careless women cannot be dealt with by seeking out their faults and mistakes and broadcasting them throughout the community. The way to deal with them is by offering sound advice to the women concerned, encouraging them to obey Allah (جل جلاله), and teaching them to hate disobedience themselves, always being frank without hurting their feelings or being confrontational.

Kind words and gentle approach in explaining the truth opens hearts and minds, and leads to complete spiritual and physical submission. For this reason, Allah (جل جلاله) forbids the Muslims to spy on one another and seek out one another's faults:

> *"...And spy not on each other..."*   *(Qur'an 49: 12)*

Exposing people's shortcomings, seeking out their faults, spying on them and gossiping about them are actions which not only hurt the people concerned; they also harm the greater society in which they live. Therefore the Qur'an issued a stern warning to those who love to spread scandal in the community, because whenever scandal is spread in a community, people's honour is insulted, and rumours, plots and suspicions increase, then the disease of promiscuity becomes widespread, people become immune to acts of disobedience

---

[41]   Bukhari: *Al-Adab al-Mufrad*, 1/419, *baab man sami'a bi faaḥishah fa afshāhā.*

and sin, the bonds of brotherhood are broken, and hatred, enmity, conspiracies and corruption are on rise. This is what the Prophet (ﷺ) referred to when he said:

> "If you seek out the faults of the Muslims, you will corrupt them, or you will nearly corrupt them."[42]

So the Prophet (ﷺ) issued a stern warning to the Muslims against the danger of slandering people's honour and exposing their faults. He threatened that the one who takes such matters lightly would himself be exposed, even if he were hiding in the innermost part of his home:

> "Do not hurt the feelings of the servants of Allah; do not embarrass them; do not seek to expose their faults. Whoever seeks to expose the faults of his Muslim brother, Allah will seek to expose his faults and expose him, even if he hides in the innermost part of his home."[43]

The Prophet (ﷺ) was deeply offended by those who were nosey, suspicious or doubtful, or who sought to undermine people's reputation and honour. He would become very angry whenever he heard any news of these aggressors who hurt others. Ibn 'Abbaas (رضي الله عنه) described the anger of the Prophet (ﷺ) and his harshness towards those who slandered the honour of others:

> "The Prophet gave a speech that even reached the ears of virgins in their private rooms. He said: 'O' you who have spoken the words of faith, but faith has not penetrated your hearts! Do not hurt the feelings of the believers and do not seek out their faults. Whoever seeks out the faults of his Muslim brother, Allah will

---

42 Abu Dawood, 4/375, *Kitaab al-Adab, baab fi an-nahi 'an at-tajassus.*

43 Reported with a *ḥasan* isnad by Aḥmad, 5/279.

> seek out his faults, and whoever's faults are sought out by Allah will be exposed, even if he is in the innermost part of his house."[44]

These harsh words, which were even heard by the virgins secluded in their private rooms, reflect the anger felt by the Prophet (ﷺ). He started his speech with the words "O' you who have spoken the words of faith, but faith has not penetrated your hearts!" How great is the sin of those who are included among those whose hearts are deprived of the blessings of faith!

She does not show off or boast

The Muslim woman does not slip into the error of pride, boasting and showing off, because her knowledge of Islam protects her from such errors. She understands that the very essence of this religion is sincerity towards Allah (ﷻ) in word and deed; any trace of a desire to show off will destroy reward, cancel out good deeds, and bring humiliation on the Day of Judgement.

Worshipping Allah (ﷻ) is the goal behind the creation of mankind and jinn, as the Qur'an says:

> "*I have only created jinns and men, that they may serve Me.*" *(Qur'an 51: 56)*

But this worship cannot be accepted unless it is done sincerely for the sake of Allah:

> "*And they have been commanded no more than this: to worship Allah, offering Him sincere devotion, being True [in faith]...*" *(Qur'an 98: 5)*

When a Muslim woman's deeds are contaminated with the desire to

---

44 Ṭabaraani; the men of its isnad are *thiqaat*. See *Majma' az-Zawaa'id,* 8/94.

boast or show off or seek fame and reputation, the good deeds will be invalidated. Her reward will be destroyed and she will be in a clear state of loss. The Qur'an issues a clear and stern warning to those who spend their wealth then remind the beneficiaries of their charity, or of their gifts in a way that hurts their feelings and offends their dignity:

> *"O' you who believe! Cancel not your charity by reminders of your generosity or by injury — like those who spend their substance to be seen of men, but believe neither in Allah nor the Last Day. They are in Parable like a hard, barren rock, on which is a little soil; on it falls heavy rain, which leaves it [just] a bare rock. They will be able to do nothing with aught they have earned. And Allah guides not those who reject faith."*
>
> *(Qur'an 2: 264)*

Reminding the poor of one's generosity cancels out the reward of the acts of charity, just as pouring water washes away all traces of soil on a smooth stone. The last part of the *aayah* presents the frightening admonition that those who show off do not deserve the guidance of Allah and are counted as *kaafirs*: "*And Allah guides not those who reject faith.*"

Such people's main concern is to appear to people to be doing good works; they are not concerned with earning the pleasure of Allah. Allah (سبحانه وتعالى) has described them as doing apparently good deeds:

> *"To be seen of men, but little do they hold Allah in remembrance."* *(Qur'an 4: 142)*

Thus their deeds will be thrown back in their faces, because they associated something or someone else with Allah, and Allah (سبحانه وتعالى) does not accept any deeds except those which are done purely for His sake, as is stated in the hadith of Abu Hurayrah (رضي الله عنه), in which he reports that he heard the Messenger of Allah (ﷺ) say:

> "Allah said: 'I am so self-sufficient that I am in no need of having an associate. Thus he who does an action for someone else's sake as well as Mine shall have that action renounced by Me to the one whom he associated with Me.'"[45]

The true Muslim woman is cautious, when doing good deeds, to avoid falling into the dangerous trap into which so many women who seek to do good have fallen, without even realizing it, by seeking praise for their efforts and honourable mention on special occasions. Theirs is a terrible fall indeed.

The Prophet (ﷺ) has clearly explained this issue and has referred to the terrible humiliation that those who show off will suffer on that awful Day,

> "*whereon neither wealth nor sons will avail, but only he [will prosper] that brings to Allah a sound heart.*"
>
> *(Qur'an 26: 88-89).*

This is mentioned in another hadith in which Abu Hurayrah (رضي الله عنه) said: "I heard the Prophet (ﷺ) say:

> 'The first person to be judged on the Day of Resurrection will be a man who was martyred. He will be brought forth and Allah will remind him of His blessings, and he will recognize them. Then he will be asked, 'What did you do with them?' He will say, 'I fought for Your sake until I was martyred.' Allah will say, 'You have lied. You only fought so that people would say, 'He is courageous and brave,' and they did

---

45 Muslim, 18/115, *Kitaab az-Zuhd, baab taḥreem ar-riya'.*

> say it.' Then He will order that he be dragged on his face and thrown into the Fire. Then there will be a man who studied much and taught others, and recited the Qur'an. He will be brought forth and Allah will remind of His blessings, and he will recognize them. Then he will be asked, 'What did you do with them?' He will say, 'I studied much, and taught others, and recited the Qur'an for Your sake. Allah will say, 'You have lied. You studied so that people would say, 'He is a great scholar,' and you recited the Qur'an so that they would say, 'He is a *qaari'*,' and they did say it.' Then He will order that he be dragged on his face and thrown into the Fire. Then there will be a man to whom Allah gave all types of wealth in abundance. He will be brought forth and Allah will remind him of His blessings and he will recognize them. Then he will be asked, 'What did you do with them?' He will say, 'I have never seen any way in which You would like money to be spent for Your sake without spending it.' Allah will say, 'You have lied. You did that so people would say, 'he is generous,' and they did say it.' Then He will order that he be dragged on his face and thrown into the Fire.''''[46]

The intelligent Muslim woman who is truly guided by the Qur'an and Sunnah carefully avoids slipping into the sin of boasting in any of its many forms. She is ever keen to devote all of her deeds exclusively to Allah (ﷻ), seeking His pleasure, and whenever the appalling spectre of pride and boasting looms before her, she remembers and adheres to the teaching of the Prophet (ﷺ):

---

[46] Muslim, 13/50, *Kitaab al-Imaarah, baab man qaatala lir-riyaa' was-sum'ah.*

"Whoever makes a show of his good deeds so that people will respect him, Allah will show what is truly in his heart."[47]

She is fair in her judgements

The Muslim woman may be put in a position where she is required to form an opinion or judgement on some person or matter. This is where her faith, common sense and *taqwa* reveal themselves. The true Muslim woman judges fairly, and is never unjust, biased or influenced by her own whims, no matter what the circumstances, because she understands from the teachings of Islam that being just and avoiding unfairness are at the very heart of her faith, as stated by clear and unambiguous texts of the Qur'an and Sunnah and expressed in commandments that leave no room for prevarication:

> "*Allah does command you to render back your Trusts to whom they are due; and when you judge between man and man, that you judge with justice...*" *(Qur'an 4: 58)*

Justice as known by the Muslim and the Islamic society is aboslute and pure justice. It is not influenced by friendship, hatred or blood ties:

> "*O' you who believe! Stand out firmly for Allah, as witnesses to fair dealing, and do not let the hatred of others to you make you swerve to wrong and depart from justice. Be just: that is next to Piety: and fear Allah. For Allah is well-acquainted with all that you do.*" *(Qur'an 5: 8)*

---

[47] Bukhari and Muslim. See *Sharḥ as-Sunnah*, 10/323, *Kitaab ar-Riqaaq, baab ar-riyaa' was-sum'ah.*

> "...*Whenever you speak, speak justly, even if a near relative is concerned...*" *(Qur'an 6: 152)*

The Prophet (ﷺ) set the highest example of justice when Usaamah ibn Zayd came to intercede for the Makhzoomi woman who had committed theft, and the Prophet (ﷺ) had decided to cut off her hand. He said:

> "Do you intercede concerning one of the punishments decreed by Allah, O' Usaamah? By Allah, even if Faṭimah the daughter of Muhammad had committed theft, I would have cut off her hand."[48]

This is absolute, universal justice which is applied to great and small, prince and commoner, Muslims and non-Muslims. None can escape its grasp, and this is what differentiates justice in Islamic societies from justice in other societies.

History records the impressive story that earns the respect of the institutions of justice throughout the world and at all times: the *khaleefah* 'Ali ibn Abi Ṭaalib (رضي الله عنه) stood side by side in court with his Jewish opponent, who had stolen his shield, on equal terms. The *qaaḍi* (judge), Shurayh, did not let his great respect for the *khaleefah* prevent him from asking him to produce evidence that the Jew had stolen his shield. When the *khaleefah* could not produce such evidence, the *qaaḍi* ruled in favour of the Jew, and against the *khaleefah*. Islamic history is full of such examples which indicate the extent to which truth and justice prevailed in the Muslim society.

Therefore, the Muslim woman who truly adheres to the teachings of her religion, is just in word and deed, and this attitude of hers is reinforced by the fact that truth and justice are an ancient part of her heritage and fairness is a sacred part of her belief.

---

[48] Bukhari and Muslim. See *Sharḥ as-Sunnah*, 10/328, *Kitaab al-Ḥudood, baab qat' yad ash-shareef wal-mar'ah wa'sh-shafaa'ah fil-ḥadd.*

She does not oppress or mistreat others

To the extent that the Muslim woman is keen to adhere to justice in all her words and deeds, she also avoids oppression (*ẓulm*), for oppression is darkness in which male and female oppressors will become lost, as the Prophet (ﷺ) explained:

> "Keep away from oppression, for oppression is darkness on the Day of Resurrection."[49]

The following hadith *qudsi* definitively and eloquently expresses Allah's prohibition of oppression in a way that leaves no room for prevarication:

> "O' My servants, I have forbidden oppression for Myself and have made it forbidden amongst you, so do not oppress one another."[50]

If Allah (ﷻ), the Creator, the Sovereign, the Most Holy, the Exalted in Might, the Omnipotent, the Almighty, may He be glorified, has forbidden oppression for Himself, and forbidden it for His servants, does it then befit His weak, mortal servant to commit the sin of oppression against his human brother?

The Prophet (ﷺ) forbade Muslim men and women to commit the sin of oppression against their brothers and sisters in faith, no matter what the motives, reasons or circumstances might be. It is unimaginable that a Muslim who is adhering to the strong bonds of brotherhood could commit such a sin:

> "A Muslim is the brother of another Muslim: he does not oppress him or forsake him when he is oppressed.

---

49 Muslim, 16/134, *Kitaab al-Birr waṣ-Ṣilah wal-Aadaab, baab taḥreem aẓ-ẓulm.*

50 Op. cit, 16/132.

> Whoever helps his brother, Allah will help him; whoever relieves his brother from some distress, Allah will relieve him of some of his distress on the Day of Resurrection; whoever covers (the fault of) a Muslim, Allah will cover his faults on the Day of Resurrection."[51]

The Prophet (ﷺ) did not stop at forbidding oppression against another Muslim, man or woman; he also forbade Muslims to forsake a brother in faith who was being oppressed, because this act of forsaking an oppressed brother is in itself a terrible form of oppression. He encouraged Muslims to take care of their brothers' needs and to ease their suffering and conceal their faults, as if indicating that the neglect of these virtues constitutes oppression, failure and injustice with regard to the ties of brotherhood that bind the Muslim and his brother.

We have quoted above the texts that enjoin absolute justice which cannot be influenced by love, hatred, bias or ties of blood, and other texts that forbid absolute injustice. This means that justice is to be applied to all people, and that injustice to any people is to be avoided, even if the people concerned are not Muslim. Allah (ﷻ) commands justice and good treatment to all, and forbids oppression and wrongdoing to all:

> "*Allah forbids you not, with regard to those who fight you not for [your] Faith nor drive you out of your homes, from dealing kindly and justly with them: For Allah loves those who are just.*" *(Qur'an 60: 8)*

---

[51] *Fatḥ al-Baari*, 5/97, *Kitaab al-Maẓaalim. baab laa yaẓlum al-Muslimu al-Muslimah wa laa yuslimuhu.*

She is fair even to those whom she does not like

Life sometimes imposes on a Muslim woman the burden of having to live or mix with women whom she does not like, such as living in the same house with one of her in-laws or other women with whom she has nothing in common and does not get along well. This is something which happens in many homes, a fact which cannot be denied, for souls are like conscripted soldiers: if they recognize one another, they will become friends, and if they dislike one another, they will go their separate ways, as the Prophet (ﷺ) explained in the hadith whose authenticity is agreed upon. How should the Muslim woman who has received a sound Islamic education conduct herself in such a situation? Should she be negative in her dealings, judgements and reactions, or should she be gentle, tactful, fair and wise, even with those whom she does not like?

The answer is that the Muslim woman who is truly guided by Islam should be fair, wise, gentle and tactful. She should not expose her true feelings towards those she dislikes, or expose her cold feelings towards them in the way she behaves towards them and reacts to them. She should greet such women warmly, treat them gently and speak softly to them. This is the attitude adopted by the Prophet (ﷺ) and his Companions. Abu ad-Darda' (رضي الله عنه) said: "We smile at people even if in our hearts we are cursing them."[52]

'Urwah ibn az-Zubayr reported that 'Aa'ishah (رضي الله عنها) told him:

> "A man sought permission to see the Prophet, and he said, 'Let him in, what a bad son of his tribe (or bad brother of his tribe) he is!' When the man came in, the Prophet spoke to him kindly and gently. I said: 'O' Messenger of Allah, you said what you said, then you spoke to him kindly.' He said, 'O' 'Aa'ishah, the worst

[52] *Fatḥ al-Baari*, 10/527, *Kitaab al-Adab, baab al-madaarat ma'a an-naas.*

of the people in the sight of Allah is the one who is shunned by others or whom people treat nicely because they fear his sharp tongue.'"[53]

Being companionable, friendly and kind towards people are among the attributes of believing men and women. Being humble, speaking gently and avoiding harshness are approaches that make people like one another and draw closer to one another, as enjoined by Islam, which encourages Muslims to adopt these attitudes in their dealings with others.

The true Muslim woman is not swayed by her emotions when it comes to love and hate. She is moderate, objective, fair and realistic in her treatment and opinions of those women whom she does not like, and allows herself to be governed by her reason, religion, chivalry and good attitude. She does not bear witness except to the truth, and she does not judge except with justice, following the example of the Mothers of the Believers, who were the epitome of fairness, justice and *taqwa* (piety) in their opinions of one another.

'Aa'ishah (رضي الله عنها) was the closest of the Prophet's wives to his heart, and her main rival in this regard was Zaynab bint Jaḥsh (رضي الله عنها). It was natural for jealousy to be between them, but this jealousy did not prevent either of them from saying what was true about the other and acknowledging her qualities without undermining them.

In *Ṣaḥeeḥ* Muslim, 'Aa'ishah (رضي الله عنها) says of Zaynab (رضي الله عنها):

"She was the one who was somewhat equal in rank with me in the eyes of the Messenger of Allah. I have never seen a woman better in piety than Zaynab, or more fearing of Allah, or more true in speech, or more faithful in upholding the ties of kinship, or more generous in giving charity, or humble enough to work with her

---

[53] Ibid, 10/528.

> hands in order to earn money that she could spend for the sake of Allah. However, she was hot-tempered and quick to anger, but she would soon cool down and would take the matter no further."[54]

In *Ṣaḥeeḥ* Bukhari, in the context of her telling of the slander incident (*al-ifk*) concerning which Allah (ﷻ) Himself confirmed her total innocence, 'Aa'ishah referred to Zaynab's testimony concerning her:

> "The Messenger of Allah asked Zaynab bint Jaḥsh concerning me, saying: 'O' Zaynab, what did you see? What have you learnt?' She said, 'O' Messenger of Allah, I protect my hearing and my sight (by refraining from telling lies). I know nothing but good about her.' Then 'Aa'ishah said: 'She is the one who was my main rival, but Allah protected her (from telling lies) because of her piety.'"[55]

Anyone who reads the books of *Seerah* and the biographies of the *Ṣaḥaabah* will find many reports of the wives of the Prophets which describe fairness and mutual praise among co-wives.

Among these reports is Umm Salamah's comment about Zaynab:

> "Zaynab was very dear to the Prophet, and he liked to spend time with her. She was righteous, and frequently stood in prayer at night and fasted during the day. She was skilled (in handicrafts) and used to give everything that she earned in charity to the poor."

When Zaynab (رضي الله عنها) died, 'Aa'ishah (رضي الله عنها) said:

---

[54] Muslim, 15/206, *Kitaab Faḍaa'il aṣ-Ṣaḥaabah, baab faḍaa'il Umm al-Mu'mineen 'Aa'ishah.*

[55] *Fatḥ al-Baari*, 8/455, *Kitaab at-Tafseer, baab lao laa idh sami'timuhu ẓann al-mu'minoona wal-mu'minaat bi anfusihim khayran* (Qur'an 24: 12).

"She has departed praiseworthy and worshipping much, the refuge of the orphans and widows."[56]

When Maymoonah (رضي الله عنها) died, 'Aa'ishah (رضي الله عنها) said:

"By Allah, Maymoonah has gone... But by Allah she was one of the most pious of us and one of those who was most faithful in upholding the ties of kinship."[57]

The wives of the Prophet (ﷺ) displayed this attitude of fairness and justice towards co-wives in spite of the jealousy, competition and sensitivity that existed between them. We can only imagine how great and noble their attitude towards other women was. By their behaviour and attitude, they set the highest example for Muslim woman of human co-existence that absorbs all hatred by increasing the power of reason and controls the strength of jealousy — if it is present — by strengthening the feelings of fairness, good treatment and a sense of being above such negative attitudes. Thus the Muslim woman becomes fair towards those women whom she does not like, regardless of the degree of closeness between them, fair when judging them, and wise, rational and tactful in her treatment of them.

She does not rejoice in the misfortunes of others

The sincere Muslim woman who is truly infused with Islamic attitudes does not rejoice in the misfortunes of anyone, because schadenfreude (malicious enjoyment of others' misfortunes) is a vile, hurtful attitude that should not exist in the God-fearing woman who understands the teachings of her religion. The Prophet (ﷺ) forbade this attitude and warned against it:

"Do not express malicious joy at the misfortune of your

---

[56]   *As-Samṭ ath-Thameen*, 110; *Al-Istee'aab*, 4/1851; *Al-Iṣaabah*, 8/93.

[57]   *Al-Iṣaabah*, 8/192.

brother, for Allah will have mercy on him and inflict misfortune on you."[58]

There is no room for schadenfreude in the heart of the Muslim woman in whom Islam has instilled good manners. Instead, she feels sorry for those who are faced with trials and difficulties: she hastens to help them and is filled with compassion for their suffering. Schadenfreude belongs only in those sick hearts that are deprived of the guidance of Islam and that are accustomed to plotting revenge and seeking out means of harming others.

She avoids suspicion

Another attribute of the true Muslim woman is that she does not form unfounded suspicions about anybody. She avoids suspicion as much as possible, as Allah (ﷻ) has commanded in the Qur'an:

> "*O' you who believe! Avoid suspicion as much [as possible]: for suspicion in some cases is a sin...*"
>
> *(Qur'an 49: 12)*

She understands that by being suspicious of others she may fall into sin, especially if she allows her imagination free rein to dream up possibilities and illusions, and accuses them of shameful deeds of which they are innocent. This is the evil suspicion which is forbidden in Islam.

The Prophet (ﷺ) issued a stern warning against suspicion and speculation that has no foundation in reality. He said:

> "Beware of suspicion, for suspicion is the falsest of speech."[59]

---

[58] Tirmidhi, 4/662, *Kitaab Ṣifat al-Qiyaamah*, 54. He said it is a *ḥasan ṣaḥeeḥ* hadith.

[59] Bukhari and Muslim. See *Sharḥ as-Sunnah*, 13/109, *Kitaab al-Birr waṣ-Ṣilah, baab maa laa yajooz min aẓ-ẓann.*

The Prophet (ﷺ) counted suspicion as being the falsest of speech. The truly sincere Muslim woman who is keen to speak the truth always would never even allow words that carry the stench of untruth to cross her tongue, so how can she allow herself to fall into the trap of uttering the falsest of speech?

When the Prophet (ﷺ) warned against suspicion and called it the falsest of speech, he was directing the Muslims, men and women, to take people at face value, and to avoid speculating about them or doubting them. It is not the attitude of a Muslim, nor is it his business, to uncover people's secrets, to expose their private affairs, or to slander them. Only Allah (ﷻ) knows what is in people's hearts, and can reveal it or call them to account for it, for only He knows all that is secret and hidden. A man, in contrast, knows nothing of his brother except what he sees him do. This was the approach of the *Ṣaḥaabah* (the Companions of the Prophet ﷺ) and *Taabi'een* (followers of the Companions) who received the pure and unadulterated guidance of Islam.

'Abdur-Razzaq reported from 'Abdullah ibn 'Utbah ibn Mas'ood:

> "I heard 'Umar ibn al-Khaṭṭab (رضي الله عنه) say: 'People used to follow the *waḥy* (Revelation) at the time of the Prophet, but now the *waḥy* has ceased. So now we take people at face value. If someone appears good to us, we trust him and form a close relationship with him on the basis of what we see of his deeds. We have nothing to do with his inner thoughts, which are for Allah to judge. And if someone appears bad to us, we do not trust him or believe him, even if he tells us that his inner thoughts (intentions) are good.'"[60]

The true Muslim woman who is adhering to that which will help her to remember Allah (ﷻ) and do good deeds, will exercise the utmost

---

[60] *Ḥayaat aṣ-Ṣaḥaabah*, 2/151.

care in every word she utters concerning her Muslim sister, whether directly or indirectly. She tries to be sure about every judgement she makes about people, always remembering the words of Allah:

> "*And pursue not that of which you have no knowledge; for every act of hearing, or of seeing, or of [feeling in] the heart will be enquired into [on the Day of Reckoning].*" *(Qur'an 17: 36)*

So she does not transgress this wise and definitive prohibition: she does not speak except with knowledge, and she does not pass judgement except with certainty.

The true Muslim woman always reminds herself of the watching angel who is assigned to record every word she utters and every judgement she forms, and this increases her fear of falling into the sin of suspicion:

> "*Not a word does he utter, but there is a sentinel by him, ready [to note it].*" *(Qur'an 50: 18)*

The alert Muslim woman understands the responsibility she bears for every word she utters, because she knows that these words may raise her to a position where Allah is pleased with her, or they may earn her His wrath, as the Prophet (ﷺ) said:

> "A man could utter a word that pleases Allah, and not realize the consequences of it, for Allah may decree that He is pleased with him because of it until the Day he meets Him. Similarly, a man could utter a word that angers Allah, and not realize the consequences of it, for Allah may decree that He is angry with him because of it until the Day of Resurrection."[61]

---

[61] A *ṣaḥeeḥ* hadith narrated by Imam Maalik in *Al-Muwaṭṭa'*, 2/975, *Kitaab al-kalaam, baab maa yu'mar bihi min at-taḥaffuẓ fil-kalaam.*

How great is our responsibility for the words we utter! How serious are the consequences of the words that our garrulous tongues speak so carelessly!

The true Muslim woman who is God-fearing and intelligent does not listen to people's idle talk, or pay attention to the rumours and speculation that are rife in our communities nowadays, especially in the gatherings of foolish and careless women. Consequently, she never allows herself to pass on whatever she hears of such rumours without being sure that they are true. She believes that to do so would be the kind of *ḥaraam* lie that was clearly forbidden by the Prophet:

> "It is enough lying for a man to repeat everything that he hears."[62]

She refrains from backbiting and spreading malicious gossip

The Muslim woman who truly understands the teachings of Islam is conscious of Allah (ﷻ), fearing Him in secret and in the open. She carefully avoids uttering any word of slander or malicious gossip that could anger her Lord and include her among those spreaders of malicious gossip who are severely condemned in the Qur'an and Sunnah. When she reads the words of Allah:

> "*...Nor speak ill of each other behind their backs. Would any of you like to eat the flesh of his dead brother? Nay, you would abhor it... But fear Allah, for Allah is Oft-Returning, Most Merciful.*" *(Qur'an 49: 12)*

She is filled with revulsion for the hateful crime of gossip, which is likened to the eating of her dead sister's flesh. So she hastens to

---

62 Muslim, 1/73, Introduction, *baab an-nahy 'an al-ḥadeeth bi kulli maa sami'a.*

repent, as Allah (ﷻ) commands at the end of the *aayah* (verse), encouraging the one who has fallen into the error of backbiting to repent quickly of it.

She also heeds the words of the Prophet (ﷺ), who said:

> "The Muslim is the one from whose tongue and whose hand the Muslims are safe."[63]

So she feels that gossip is a sin which does not befit the Muslim woman who has uttered the words of the *Shahaadah*, and that the woman who is used to gossip in social gatherings is not among the righteous Muslim women. 'Aa'ishah (رضي الله عنها) said:

> "I said to the Prophet, 'It is enough for you that Ṣafiyah is such-and-such.' Some narrators said that she meant she was short of stature. The Prophet said: 'You have spoken a word that, if it were to be mixed with the waters of the sea, it would contaminate them.'"[64]

The Muslim woman pays attention to the description of the seven acts that may lead to a person's condemnation, which the Prophet (ﷺ) called on people to avoid. In this list, she finds something that is even worse and more dangerous than mere gossip, namely the slander of chaste, innocent believing women, which is a sin that some women fall into in their gatherings:

> "Avoid (the) seven things that could lead to perdition." It was asked, "O' Messenger of Allah, what are they?" He said: "*Shirk* (associating any partner with Allah); *siḥr* (witchcraft); killing anyone for whom Allah has forbidden killing, except in the course of justice;

---

[63] Muslim, 2/12, *Kitaab al-Eemaan, baab bayaan tafaaḍul al-Islam.*

[64] Abu Dawood, 4/371, *Kitaab al-Adab, baab fil-gheebah*; Tirmidhi, 4/660, *Kitaab Ṣifat al-Qiyaamah*, 51; he said it is a *ḥasan ṣaḥeeḥ* hadith.

> consuming the wealth of the orphan; consuming *riba* (usury); running away from the battlefield; and slandering chaste and innocent believing women."[65]

The Muslim woman who truly understands this teaching takes the issue of gossip very seriously, and does not indulge in any type of gossip or tolerate anyone to gossip in her company. She defends her sisters from hostile gossip and refutes whatever bad things are being said about them, in accordance with the words of the Prophet (ﷺ):

> "Whoever defends the flesh of his brother in his absence, Allah will save him from the Fire."[66]

The true Muslim woman also refrains from spreading malicious gossip, because she understands the dangerous role it plays in spreading evil and corruption in society and breaking the ties of love and friendship between its members, as the Prophet (ﷺ) explained:

> "The best of the servants of Allah are those who, when they are seen, Allah is remembered (i.e., they are very pious). The worst of the servants of Allah are those who spread malicious gossip, cause division between friends, and seek to cause trouble for innocent people."[67]

It is enough for the woman who spreads malicious gossip and causes trouble between friends and splits them up to know that if she persists in her evil ways, there awaits her humiliation in this life and a terrible destiny in the next, as the Prophet (ﷺ) declared that the blessings of Paradise will be denied to every person who spreads malicious gossip. This is stated clearly in the *ṣaḥeeḥ* hadith:

---

65 Bukhari and Muslim. See *Sharḥ as-Sunnah*, 1/86, *Kitaab al-Eemaan, baab al-kabaa'ir.*

66 Reported with a *ḥasan* isnad by Aḥmad, 6/461.

67 Reported with a *ṣaḥeeḥ* isnad by Aḥmad, 4/227.

> "The one who engages in malicious gossip will not enter Paradise."[68]

What fills the believing woman's heart with fear and horror of the consequences of spreading malicious gossip is the fact that Allah will pour His punishment upon the one who engaged in this sin from the moment he or she is laid in the grave. We find this in the hadith which Bukhari, Muslim and others narrated from Ibn 'Abbaas (رضي الله عنه):

> "The Messenger of Allah passed by two graves, and said: 'They are being punished, but they are not being punished for any major sin. One of them used to spread malicious gossip, and the other used not to clean himself properly after urinating.' He (Ibn 'Abbaas) said: 'He called for a green branch and split it in two, then planted a piece on each grave and said, 'May their punishment be reduced so long as these remain fresh.'''[69]

She avoids cursing and foul language

The Muslim woman who has absorbed the good manners taught by Islam never utters obscene language or foul words, or offends people with curses and insults, bacause she knows that the moral teachings of Islam completely forbid all such talk. Cursing is seen as a sin that damages the quality of a person's adherance to Islam, and the foul-mouthed person is intensely disliked by Allah.

Ibn Mas'ood (رضي الله عنه) related that the Prophet (صلى الله عليه وسلم) said:

---

[68] Bukhari and Muslim. See *Sharḥ as-Sunnah*, 13/147, *Kitaab al-Birr waṣ-Ṣilah, baab wa'eed an-nammaam.*

[69] Bukhari and Muslim. See *Sharḥ as-Sunnah*, 1/370, *Kitaab aṭ-Ṭahaarah, baab al-istitaar 'inda qaḍaa' al-ḥaajah.*

> "Cursing a Muslim is a sin and killing him is *kufr*."[70]

On another occasion the Prophet (ﷺ) said:

> "Allah does not love anyone who is foul-mouthed and obscene."[71]

> "Allah will hate the disgusting, foul-mouthed person."[72]

It is a quality that does not befit the Muslim woman who has been guided by the truth of Islam and whose heart has been filled with the sweetness of faith. So she keeps herself far away from disputes and arguments in which cheap insults and curses are traded. The alert Muslim woman is further encouraged to avoid such moral decadence whenever she remembers the beautiful example set by the Prophet (ﷺ) in all his words and deeds. It is known that he never uttered any words that could hurt a person's feelings, damage his reputation or insult his honour.

Anas ibn Maalik (رضي الله عنه), who accompanied the Prophet (ﷺ) closely for many years, said:

> "The Prophet never used foul language, or cursed, or swore. When he wanted to rebuke someone, he would say, 'What is wrong with him? May his forehead be covered with dust!'"[73]

He even refrained from cursing the *kaafireen* who had hardened their

---

[70] Bukhari and Muslim. See *Sharḥ as-Sunnah*, 1/76, *Kitaab al-Eemaan, baab 'alamaat an-nifaaq*.

[71] Aḥmad and Ṭabaraani; the men of its isnad are *thiqaat*. See *Majma' az-Zawaa'id*, 8/64.

[72] Ṭabaraani; the men of its isnad are *thiqaat*. See *Majma' az-Zawaa'id*, 8/64.

[73] *Fatḥ al-Baari*, 10/452, *Kitaab al-Adab, baab lam yakun an-Nabi faaḥishan wa laa mutafaḥḥishan.*

hearts to his message. He never spoke a harmful word to them, as the great *Ṣaḥaabi* Abu Hurayrah (ﷺ) said:

> "It was said: 'O' Messenger of Allah, pray against the *mushrikeen.*' He said, 'I am not sent as a curse, but I am sent as a mercy.'"[74]

The Prophet (ﷺ) excelled in removing the roots of evil, hatred and enmity in people's hearts when he explained to the Muslims that the one who gives his tongue free rein in slandering people and their wealth and honour is the one who is truly ruined in this world and the next. His aggressive attitude towards others will cancel out whatever good deeds he may have done in his life, and on the Day of Judgement he will be abandoned, with no protection from the Fire. The Prophet (ﷺ) said:

> "Do you know who is the one who is ruined?" They said, "It is the one who has no money or possessions." He said, "The one who is ruined among my ummah is the one who comes on the Day of Resurrection with prayer, fasting and zakah to his credit, but he insulted this one, slandered that one, devoured this one's wealth, shed that one's blood, and beat that one. So some of his *ḥasanaat* will be given to this one and some to that one... And if his *ḥasanaat* run out before all his victims have been compensated, then some of their sins will be taken and added to his, then he will be thrown into Hell.'"[75]

Not surprisingly, therefore, all of this nonsense is eliminated from the life of true Muslim women. Disputes and arguments which could

---

[74] Muslim, 16/150, *Kitaab al-Birr waṣ-Ṣilah wal-Adab, baab man la'anahu an-Nabi.*

[75] Muslim, 16/135, *Kitaab al-Birr aṣ-Ṣilah wal-Adab, baab taḥreem aẓ-ẓulm.*

lead to curses and insults are rare among true Muslim women whose community is based on the virtues of good manners, respect for the feelings of others, and a refined level of social interaction.

She does not make fun of anybody

The Muslim woman whose personality has been infused with a sense of humility and resistance to pride and arrogance cannot make fun of anybody. The Qur'anic guidance which has instilled those virtues in her also protects her from scorning or despising other women:

> "*O' you who believe! Let not some men among you laugh at others: it may be that the [latter] are better than the [former]: nor let some women laugh at others: it may be that the [latter] are better than the [former]: nor defame nor be sarcastic to each other, nor call each other by [offensive] nicknames: ill-seeming is a name connoting wickedness, [to be used of one] after he has believed: and those who do not desist are [indeed] doing wrong.*" *(Qur'an 49: 11)*

The Muslim woman also learns the attitude of modesty and gentleness from the example of the Prophet (ﷺ), so she avoids being arrogant and scorning or looking down on others when she reads the words of the Prophet as reported by Muslim, stating that despising her fellow Muslim women is pure evil:

> "It is sufficient evil for a man to despise his Muslim brother."[76]

---

[76] Muslim, 16/121, *Kitaab al-Birr, baab taḥreem ẓulm al-Muslim wa khadhlihi wa iḥtiqaarihi.*

She is gentle and kind towards people

It is in the nature of women to be gentle and kind, which is more befitting to them. This is why women are known as the "fairer sex."

The Muslim woman who has truly been guided by Islam is even more kind and gentle towards the women around her, because gentleness and kindness are characteristics which Allah, the Exalted, loves in His believing servants and which make the one who possesses them dear to others:

> "*Nor can Goodness and Evil be equal. Repel [Evil] with what is better: then will he between whom and you was hatred become as it were your friend and intimate! And no one will be granted such goodness except those who exercise patience and self-restraint — none but persons of the greatest good fortune.*" *(Qur'an 41: 34-35)*

Many *ayat* (verses) and *aḥaadeeth* (hadiths) reinforce the message that gentleness and kindness are to be encouraged and that they are noble virtues that should prevail in the Muslim community and characterize every Muslim member of that community who truly understands the guidance of Islam. It is sufficient for the Muslim woman to know that kindness is one of the attributes of Allah that He (ﷻ) has encouraged His servants to adopt in all their affairs.

> "Allah is Kind and loves kindness in all affairs."[77]

Kindness is a tremendous virtue which Allah (ﷻ) rewards in a way unlike any other:

> "Allah is kind and loves kindness, and He rewards it in a

---

[77] Bukhari and Muslim. See *Riyaaḍ aṣ-Ṣaaliḥeen*, 340, *baab al-ḥilm wal-anah war-rifq.*

> way that He does not reward harshness, and in a way unlike any other."[78]

The Prophet (ﷺ) praised kindness, regarding it as an adornment that beautifies and encourages others to adopt this trait:

> "There is no kindness in a thing but it makes it beautiful, and there is no absence of kindness in a thing but it makes it repugnant."[79]

The Prophet (ﷺ) taught the Muslims to be kind in their dealings with people, and to behave in an exemplary manner as befits the Muslim who is calling people to the religion of Allah, the Kind and Merciful, no matter how provocative the situation.

Abu Hurayrah (رضي الله عنه) said:

> "A Bedouin urinated in the mosque, and the people got up to sort him out. But the Prophet said, 'Leave him, and throw a bucket of water over his urine, for you have been raised to be easy on people, not hard on them.'"[80]

Kindness, gentleness and tolerance, not harshness, aggression and rebukes, are what open people's hearts to the message of truth. The Prophet (ﷺ) used to advise the Muslims:

> "Be cheerful, not threatening, and make things easy, not difficult."[81]

People are naturally put off by rudeness and harshness, but they are

---

[78] Muslim, 16/146, *Kitaab al-Birr waṣ-Ṣilah wal-Adab, baab faḍl ar-rifq.*

[79] Ibid.

[80] *Fatḥ al-Baari*, 1/323, *Kitaab al-wuḍoo', baab ṣabb al-maa' 'ala al-bole fil-masjid.*

[81] Bukhari and Muslim. See *Sharḥ as-Sunnah*, 10/67, *Kitaab al-Imaarah wal-qaḍaa', baab maa 'ala al-wulaat min at-tayseer.*

attracted by kindness and gentleness. Hence Allah said to His Prophet:

> "...*Were you severe or harsh-hearted, they would have broken away from about you.*" *(Qur'an 3: 159)*

This is an eternal declaration that applies to every woman who seeks to call other women to Islam. She has to find a good way to reach their hearts, for which purpose she utilizes every means of kindness, gentleness and tact at her disposal. If she encounters any hostility or resistance, then no doubt a kind word will reach their hearts and have the desired effect on the hearts of the women she addresses. This is what Allah told His Prophet Moosa (Moses) (ﷺ) and his brother Haroon (Aaron) (ﷺ) when He sent them to Pharaoh:

> "*Go, both of you, to Pharaoh, for he has indeed transgressed all bounds; but speak to him mildly; perchance he may take warning or fear [Allah].*"
> *(Qur'an 20: 43-44)*

Not surprisingly, kindness, according to Islam, is all goodness. Whoever attains it has been given all goodness, and whoever has been denied it has been denied all goodness. We see this in the hadith narrated by Jareer ibn 'Abdullah, who said: "I heard the Messenger of Allah (ﷺ) say:

> 'Whoever has been denied kindness has been denied all goodness.'"[82]

The Prophet (ﷺ) explained that this goodness will be bestowed upon individuals, households and peoples when kindness prevails in their lives and is one of their foremost characteristics. We find this in the hadith of 'Aa'ishah (رضي الله عنها) in which the Prophet (ﷺ) told her:

---

[82] Muslim, 16/145, *Kitaab al-Birr waṣ-Ṣilah wal-Aadaab, baab faḍl ar-rifq.*

> "O' 'Aa'ishah, be kind, for if Allah wills some good to a household, He guides them to kindness."[83]

According to another report, he (ﷺ) said:

> "If Allah wills some good to a household, He instills kindness in them."[84]

Jaabir (رضي الله عنه) said: "The Prophet (ﷺ) said:

> 'If Allah wills some good to a people, He instills kindness in them.'"[85]

What greater goodness can there be than a characteristic that will protect a man from Hell? As the Prophet (ﷺ) said in another hadith:

> "Shall I not tell you who shall be forbidden from the Fire, or from whom the Fire will be forbidden? It will be forbidden for every gentle, soft-hearted and kind person."[86]

The teachings of the Prophet (ﷺ) take man a step further, by instilling in him the attitude of kindness and requiring him to be kind even to the animals he slaughters. This is counted as one of the highest levels that the pious and righteous may reach:

> "Allah has prescribed proficiency[87] in all things. Thus if you kill, kill well, and if you slaughter, slaughter well.

---

[83] Aḥmad, 6/104; the men of its isnad are *rijaal aṣ-ṣaḥeeḥ.*

[84] Ibid.

[85] Al-Bazzaar; the men of its isnad are *rijaal aṣ-ṣaḥeeḥ*. See *Majma' az-Zawaa'id*, 8/18, *baab maa jaa' fir-rifq*.

[86] Tirmidhi, 4/654, *Kitaab Sifah al-qiyaamah*, 45; he said it is a *ḥasan* hadith.

[87] The word translated here as proficiency is *iḥsaan*, which also has connotations of doing well, decency, etc. (Translator)

> Let each one of you sharpen his blade and let him spare suffering to the animal he slaughters."[88]

Kindness to dumb animals that are to be slaughtered is indicative of the kindness of the man who slaughters them, and of his mercy towards all living creatures. The more a person understands this and treats all living creatures well, the more kind and gentle a person he is. This is the ultimate goal towards which Islam is guiding the Muslim, so that he is kind even to animals.

The true Muslim woman can imagine the comprehensiveness of the Islamic teachings enjoining kindness upon the sons of Adam, when even animals are included.

She is compassionate and merciful

The Muslim woman who truly understands the teachings of Islam is compassionate and merciful, for she understands that the compassion of people on earth will cause the mercy of heaven to be showered upon them. She knows that the one who does not show compassion towards others will not receive the mercy of Allah, and that the mercy of Allah is not withheld except from the one who is lost and doomed, as the Prophet (ﷺ) said:

> "Have compassion on those who are on earth so that the One Who is in the heaven will have mercy on you."[89]

> "Whoever shows not compassion to people, Allah will not show mercy to him."[90]

---

[88] Muslim, 13/106, *Kitaab aṣ-Ṣayd, baab al-'amr bi iḥsaan adh-dhabḥ.*

[89] Ṭabaraani; the men of its isnad are *rijaal aṣ-ṣaḥeeḥ*. See *Majma' az-Zawaa'id*, 8/187, *baab raḥmat an-naas.*

[90] Ibid.

> "Compassion is not taken away except from the one who is doomed."[91]

The true Muslim woman does not limit her compassion only to her family, children, relatives and friends, but she extends it to include all people. This is in accordance with the teachings of the Prophet (ﷺ), which include all people and make compassion a condition of faith:

> "You will not believe until you have compassion towards one another." They said, "O' Messenger of Allah, all of us are compassionate." He said, "It is not the compassion of any of you towards his friend, but it is compassion towards all people and compassion towards the common folk."[92]

This is a comprehensive, all-embracing compassion which Islam has awoken in the hearts of Muslim men and women, and made it one of their distinguishing characteristics, so that the Muslim community — men and women, rich and poor, all of its members — may become an integrated, caring community filled with compassion, brotherly love and true affection.

The Prophet (ﷺ) was a brilliant example of sincere compassion. If he heard a child crying when he was leading the people in prayer, he would shorten the prayer, out of consideration for the mother's feelings and concern for her child. Bukhari and Muslim report from Anas that the Prophet (ﷺ) said:

> "I commenced the prayer, and I intended to make it long, but I heard a child crying, so I cut my prayer short

---

[91] Bukhari: *Al-Adab al-Mufrad*, 1/466, *baab irḥam man fil-arḍ.*

[92] Ṭabaraani; the men of its isnad are *rijaal aṣ-ṣaḥeeḥ*. See *Majma' az-Zawaa'id*, 8/186, *baab raḥmat an-naas.*

> because of the distress I knew his mother would be feeling."[93]

A Bedouin came to the Prophet (ﷺ) and asked, "Do you kiss your sons? For we do not kiss them." He said,

> "What can I do for you when Allah has removed compassion from your heart?"[94]

The Prophet (ﷺ) kissed Al-Ḥasan ibn 'Ali when Al-Aqra' ibn Ḥaabis at-Tameemi was sitting with him. Al-Aqra' said: "I have ten children and I have never kissed any of them." The Prophet (ﷺ) looked at him and said,

> "The one who does not show compassion will not be shown mercy."[95]

'Umar (رضي الله عنه) wanted to appoint a man to some position of authority over the Muslims, then he heard him say something like Al-Aqra' ibn Ḥaabis had said, i.e., that he did not kiss his children. So 'Umar changed his mind about appointing him and said, "If your heart does not beat with compassion towards your own children, how will you be merciful towards the people? By Allah, I will never appoint you." Then he tore up the document he had prepared concerning the man's appointment.

The Prophet (ﷺ) extended the feeling of mercy in the hearts of Muslim men and women to cover animals as well as humans. This is reflected in a number of *ṣaḥeeḥ aḥaadeeth* (authentic hadiths), such as that reported by Bukhari and Muslim from Abu Hurayrah, in which the Prophet (ﷺ) said:

---

93 Bukhari and Muslim. See *Sharḥ as-Sunnah*, 3/410, *Kitaab aṣ-Ṣalaat, baab at-takhfeef li amr yaḥduth.*

94 Bukhari and Muslim. See *Sharḥ as-Sunnah*, 13/34, *Kitaab al-Birr waṣ-Ṣilah, baab raḥmat al-walad wa taqbeelihi.*

95 Ibid.

> "A man was walking along the road when he felt very thirsty. He saw a well, so he went down into it, drank his fill, then came out. He saw a dog panting and biting the dust with thirst, and said, 'This dog's thirst is as severe as mine was.' So he went back down into the well, filled his shoes with water, held them in his mouth (while he climbed out), and gave the dog water. Allah thanked him and forgave him. They asked, 'O' Messenger of Allah, will we be rewarded for kindness towards animals?' He said, 'In every living creature there is reward.'"[96]

Bukhari and Muslim also narrate from Ibn 'Umar that the Prophet (ﷺ) said:

> "A woman was punished because of a cat which she locked up until it died of starvation. She was thrown into Hell. It was said — and Allah knows best — 'You did not feed her or give her water when you locked her up, neither did you let her roam free so that she could eat of the vermin of the earth.'"[97]

The Prophet (ﷺ) reached such heights of mercy that once, "When he and his Companions stopped in some place, a bird appeared above his head, as if she were seeking his help and complaining to him of the wrongdoing of a man who had taken her egg. He said,

> 'Which of you has distressed her by taking her egg?' A man said, 'O' Messenger of Allah, I have taken it.' The Prophet said: 'Put it back, out of mercy to her.'"[98]

---

[96] Bukhari and Muslim. See *Sharḥ as-Sunnah*, 2/229, *Kitaab aṣ-Ṣalaah, baab faḍl ṣalaat al-'isha wal-fajr fil-jamaa'ah.*

[97] Bukhari and Muslim. See *Sharḥ as-Sunnah*, 6/171, *Kitaab az-Zakah, baab faḍl saqi al-maa'.*

[98] Bukhari: *Al-Adab al-Mufrad*, 1/472, *baab akhdh al-bayḍ min al-ḥammarah.*

The Prophet (ﷺ) wanted, in this instance, to instill a sense of all-encompassing mercy in the conscience of the Muslims, men and women alike, so that they would become compassionate by nature, even to animals, because whoever has the heart to be kind to animals will not be harsh towards his human brother.

The Prophet (ﷺ) was full of compassion towards humans and animals alike. He never stopped encouraging compassion among people, and sought to instill it deeply in the hearts of Muslim men and women, stating that it was the key to Allah's mercy, forgiveness and reward. Allah (ﷻ) would forgive those who were compassionate, even if they were sinners.

In *Ṣaḥeeḥ* Muslim, Abu Hurayrah (رضي الله عنه) said: "The Messenger of Allah (ﷺ) said:

> 'A dog was walking around a well, almost dying of thirst, when a Jewish prostitute saw him. She took off her shoe, brought water to him and gave him to drink. She was forgiven because of this deed.'"[99]

How great is the blessing of compassion and mercy for mankind! What beautiful attributes they are! It is sufficient honour and status to know that the Lord of Glory and Majesty derived His own name from *raḥmah* (mercy, compassion), and is called *Ar-Raḥeem, Ar-Raḥmaan.*

She strives for people's benefit and seeks to protect them from harm

The Muslim woman who has been truly guided by Islam is keen to be constructive and active in good and beneficial deeds, not only for

---

[99] Muslim, 14/242, *Kitaab Qatl al-Ḥayaat wa Naḥwahaa, baab faḍl saqi al-bahaa'im.*

herself, but for all people. So she always looks for opportunities to do good, and hastens to do as much as she can, in obedience to the words of the Qur'an:

> "*...And do good, that you may prosper.*" *(Qur'an 22: 77)*

She knows that doing good to others is an act of worship, so long as it is done purely for the sake of Allah. The door to good deeds is open to all Muslims, to enter whenever they wish and earn the mercy and pleasure of Allah. There are many aspects to goodness and piety, and they take many forms. Goodness includes all those who work for the sake of Allah, and any good deed that is done for the sake of Allah will be rewarded as an act of charity (*ṣadaqah*) in the record of their deeds:

> "Every good deed is a *ṣadaqah*."[100]

> "A good word is a *ṣadaqah*."[101]

The mercy of Allah encompasses every Muslim woman whose heart is pure and whose intention is sincerely to please Allah (ﷻ). It applies to her if she does good, and if she does not do good, so long as she refrains from doing evil.

Abu Moosa (رضي الله عنه) said: "The Prophet (ﷺ) said:

> 'Every Muslim must give charity.' Someone asked, 'What if he finds he has nothing with which to give charity?' He said, 'Let him work with his two hands and benefit himself and give charity (from his earnings).' Someone said, 'What if he does not do that?' He said, 'Let him help one who is in desperate need.' Someone

---

[100] Bukhari and Muslim. See *Sharḥ as-Sunnah*, 6/142, *Kitaab az-Zakah, baab kullu maa'roof ṣadaqah.*

[101] *Sharḥ as-Sunnah*, 6/145.

> said, 'What if he does not do that?' He said, 'Let him enjoin what is good.' Someone said, 'What if he does not do that?' He said, 'Let him refrain from doing evil, and that will be an act of charity.'"[102]

The Prophet (ﷺ) began this hadith with the words, "Every Muslim must give charity," then he went on to list various types of good deeds and acts of kindness by means of which a Muslim man or woman may earn reward for doing charity. Charity is a duty of the Muslim woman, that is, she must undertake deeds that are socially constructive in her community. If she is unable to do so, or does not do so for any reason, then at least she can restrain her tongue and refrain from doing evil; in this, too, there is reward. Thus both her positive and negative aspects (i.e., what she does and what she does not do) will be directed towards the service of the truth upon which the Muslim community is built. The Muslim is, "the one from whose tongue and hand the Muslims are safe."[103]

So the Muslim woman is always keen to do good, and hastens to do it, hoping that she will be the one to do it. She keeps away from evil, and is determined never to indulge in it. Thus, she is one of the best Muslims in the Muslim community, as the Prophet (ﷺ) said in the hadith narrated by Imam Aḥmad:

> "The Prophet stood up before some people who were seated and said: 'Shall I tell you who is the best of you and who is the worst of you?' The people were silent, so he repeated it three times, then one man said, 'Yes, O' Messenger of Allah.' He said: 'The best of you is the one from whom people expect good deeds, and from whose evil deeds people are safe; the worst of you is the

---

[102] *Sharḥ as-Sunnah*, 6/143, *Kitaab az-Zakah, baab kullu maa'roof ṣadaqah.*

[103] *Fatḥ al-Baari*, 1/53, *Kitaab al-Eemaan, baab al-Muslim man salima al-Muslimoon min lisanihi wa yadihi.*

> one from whom people expect good deeds but from whose evil deeds people are not safe.'"[104]

The Muslim woman who truly understands her Islam is one of those from whom good deeds are expected and from whose evil deeds people are safe. She is eager to do good deeds in this life, and she knows that her efforts will not be wasted, as she will be rewarded for it in this world and the next:

> "Whoever relieves a believer of some of the distress of this world, Allah will relieve him of some of the distress of the Day of Resurrection, and whoever comes to the aid of one who is going through hardship, Allah will come to his aid in this world and the next."[105]

The Muslim woman never spares any effort to do good deeds whenever she is able. How could she do otherwise, when she knows from the teachings of the Prophet (ﷺ) that failing to do good when one is able to do so carries the threat of losing the blessings of Allah, (ﷻ):

> "Never does Allah bless a servant with abundant bounty, then some needs of the people are brought to his attention and he feels annoyed and reluctant to help them, but that blessing will be exposed to the threat of loss."[106]

The Muslim woman does not think little of any good deed, no matter how small it may be, so long as it is accompanied by a sincere

---

[104] Aḥmad; the men of its isnad are *rijaal aṣ-ṣaḥeeḥ*. See *Majma' az-Zawaa'id*, 8/183, *baab feeman yurja khayrahu.*

[105] Muslim, 17/21, *Kitaab adh-Dhikr wad-Du'aa', baab faḍl al-ijtima' 'ala tilaawah al-Qur'an wa 'aladh-dhikr.*

[106] Reported with a *jayyid* isnad by Ṭabaraani in *Al-Awsaṭ*. See *Majma' az-Zawaa'id*, 8/192, *baab faḍl qaḍa' al-hawaa'ij.*

intention to please Allah (ﷻ). Doing good may consist of protecting the Muslims from harm, as is brilliantly described in a number of *aḥaadeeth*, for example:

> "I have seen a man who was enjoying the luxuries of Paradise because he removed a tree that used to harm the people from the side of the road."[107]

There are two aspects to doing good, and Muslims are obliged to do both of them and to compete with one another in earning the pleasure of Allah by doing them. They are: doing good deeds and seeking to benefit the people, and protecting the people from harm.

Seeking to protect the Muslims from harm is no less important than doing good and working for their benefit; both count as righteous deeds for which a person will be rewarded. All societies, no matter what their geographical location or historical era, need both of these deeds, operating in tandem. When both are present, goodness will spread in society, the ties of friendship will be established between its members, and their quality of life will be much improved. This is what Islam seeks to achieve when it constantly encourages Muslims to do good to people and to seek to protect them from harm.

Among the teachings which direct Muslims to protect others from harm is the hadith narrated by Abu Barzah, who said:

> "I said, 'O' Messenger of Allah, teach me something that I may benefit from.' He said, 'Remove anything harmful from the path of the Muslims.'"[108]

According to another report, Abu Barzah said:

---

[107] Muslim, 16/171, *Kitaab al-Birr waṣ-Ṣilah wal-Aadaab, baab faḍl izaalah al-adha 'an aṭ-ṭareeq.*

[108] Muslim, 16/171, *Kitaab al-Birr waṣ-Ṣilah wal-Aadaab, baab faḍl izaalah al-adha 'an aṭ-ṭareeq.*

> 'O' Messenger of Allah, tell me of a deed that will admit me to Paradise." The Prophet said: "Remove anything harmful from the road; this will be an act of charity on your part."[109]

What a highly-developed, civil community is the society that Islam has built and instilled in each of its members the idea that the good deeds which will bring one closer to Allah (ﷻ) and admit one to Paradise include removing anything harmful from the path of the people!

Humanity today is in the greatest need of this highly-developed, civil society that Islam builds, in which every member feels that his contribution to the good of society will bring him closer to Allah and grant him entrance to Paradise, even if his good deeds went no further than removing something harmful from the road. There is a huge difference between the society which forms sensitive souls such as these, who cannot bear to see carelessness and backwardness, and the society which pays no attention to the development of its members, so you see them not caring if the garbage and hazardous waste that they throw in the road harms people, and the authorities in those backward societies are obliged to issue laws and regulations to punish those who commit these offences.

How great is the difference between the society that is guided by Islam, whose members hasten to remove anything harmful from the road in obedience to Allah's command and in hope of reward from Him, and the society which has deviated from the guidance of Allah, whose members do not care on whom their garbage lands when they throw it from their balconies, windows and rooftops!

The civilized Western world has managed to excel in such matters of organization by making individuals become accustomed to

---

[109] A sound hadith from Aḥmad, 4/423.

respecting the system and following it strictly. But this high level of social organization in the West still falls far short of the true Islamic ideal, for one good reason: the Muslim who has received a sound Islamic education is even stricter and more sincere in adhering to the system, because he believes that stepping beyond the limits is an act of disobedience towards Allah, Who will punish him on the Day,

> "*whereon neither wealth nor sons will avail, but only he [will prosper] that brings to Allah a sound heart*"
> *(Qur'an 26: 88-89).*

Moreover, the Westerner does not see anything seriously wrong with transgressing the bounds of the system. His conscience may or may not trouble him, but there the matter ends, especially if the authorities are unaware of it.

She helps to alleviate the burden of the debtor

The true Muslim woman is distinguished by the nature of her moral and psychological make-up, and by her tolerant and easy-going personality. So if she is owed anything by her sister and her sister is in difficulty when the time comes to pay the debt, she postpones payment until another time, until the period of hardship is over, in obedience to the words of the Qur'an:

> "*If the debtor is in difficulty, grant him time till it is easy for him to repay...*" *(Qur'an 2: 280)*

Postponing debts is a generous attitude, one that is encouraged by Islam because it brings about humane standards in one's dealing with one's brother, even if he is indebted.

The Muslim woman who is infused with this humane attitude of postponing payment of her sister's debts is acting in obedience to the commands of Allah, storing up righteous deeds for her Hereafter that will save her from affliction on the Day of Judgement and shade her in the shade of Allah's Throne on the Day when there is no other shade.

Abu Qatadah (رضي الله عنه) said: "I heard the Messenger of Allah (ﷺ) say:

> 'Whoever would like Allah to save him from the hardship of the Day of Resurrection, let him alleviate the burden of a debtor,[110] or write off (part of the debt).'"[111]

Abu Hurayrah (رضي الله عنه) said: "The Messenger of Allah (ﷺ) said:

> 'Whoever allows a debtor to postpone payment, or writes off part of the debt, Allah will place him under the shade of His Throne on the Day of Resurrection, the Day when there will be no shade except His.'"[112]

The true Muslim woman is able to take the matter further and rise to a higher level, if she is well-off, by letting her sister off paying all or part of the debt. This will earn her a great reward, as Allah (سبحانه وتعالى) will compensate her for letting her sister off by letting her off even more, forgiving her for her errors and shortcomings, and saving her from the horror of the Day of Judgement.

Abu Hurayrah (رضي الله عنه) said: "The Messenger of Allah (ﷺ) said:

> 'There was a man who used to lend money to the people. He used to tell his employee: 'If you come across any debtor who is in difficulty, let him off. Perhaps Allah will let us off.' So when he met Allah, He let him off.'"[113]

---

[110] i.e., by postponing the payment, if he is the one to whom it is owed, or by paying off the debt for him. (Author)

[111] Muslim, 10/227, *Kitaab al-Musaaqah wal-Mazari'ah, baab faḍl inẓaar al-mu'sir.*

[112] Tirmidhi, 3/590, in *Kitaab al-Buyu', baab maa jaa' fi inẓaar al-mu'sir.*

[113] Bukhari and Muslim. See *Sharḥ as-Sunnah*, 8/196, *Kitaab al-Buyu', baab thawaab man anẓara mu'siran.*

Abu Mas'ood al-Badri (ﷺ) said: "The Messenger of Allah (ﷺ) said:

> 'A man from among those who were before you was called to account, and no good deeds were found in his record except that he used to have dealings with the people, and he was rich, so he used to tell his employees to let off those debtors who were in difficulty. Allah, may He be glorified, said: 'We should be more generous than he, so let him off.'"[114]

Hudhayfah (ﷺ) said:

> "Allah brought to account one of His servants to whom he had given wealth, and asked him, 'What did you do in the *dunya* (world)?' He said — and no-one can hide a single thing from Allah — 'O' my Lord, you gave me wealth, and I used to trade with people. It was my habit to be lenient; I would be easy-going with the one who could afford to pay his debt, and I would allow the one who was in difficulty to postpone payment.' Allah said, 'I should be more generous than you; let My servant off.' 'Uqbah ibn 'Aamir and Abu Mas'ood al-Anṣaari said, 'We heard something like this from the mouth of the Prophet (Blessings and Peace be upon him)."[115]

She is generous

One of the characteristics of the Muslim woman who adheres to the teachings of Islam is that she is generous and gives freely; her hands are always stretched forth to give to those who are in need. Whenever

[114] Muslim, 10/226, *Kitaab al-Musaaqah wal-Muzari'ah, baab faḍl inẓaar al-mu'sir.*

[115] Muslim, 10/225, *Kitaab al-Musaaqah wal-Muzari'ah, baab faḍl inẓaar al-mu'sir.*

she hears the call of one who is in difficulty, or it is appropriate to give generously, she responds to the need.

She is certain that whatever she gives will not go to waste, for it is recorded with One Who has full knowledge of all things:

> "*...And whatever of good you give, be assured that Allah knows it well.*" *(Qur'an 2: 273)*

She also believes, when she spends her money generously, that whatever she spends will come back to her manifold, and that Allah (ﷻ) will multiply its reward in this world and the next:

> "*The parable of those who spend their substance in the way of Allah is that of a grain of corn: it grows seven ears, and each ear has a hundred grains. Allah gives manifold increase to whom He pleases: and Allah cares for all and He knows all things.*" *(Qur'an 2: 261)*

> "*...And nothing do you spend in the least [in His Cause] but He replaces it...*" *(Qur'an 34: 39)*

> "*...Whatever of good you give benefits your own souls, and you shall only do so seeking the 'Face'* [116] *of Allah. Whatever good you give, shall be rendered back to you, and you shall not be dealt with unjustly.*" *(Qur'an 2: 272)*

She also knows that if she is not saved from the meanness of her own nature and her desire to hoard wealth and treasure, she will eventually lose her wealth and it will be wasted, as the Prophet (ﷺ) said:

> "Every morning that the servants of Allah get up, two angels come down. One of them says, 'O' Allah, give

[116] 'Face' here is the literal translation of the Arabic word '*wajh*', which in this context may also mean the sake, cause or presence of Allah. (Translator)

> compensation to the one who spends,' and the other says, 'O' Allah, cause loss to the one who is stingy.'"[117]

And in a hadith *qudsi*:

> "Spend, O' son of Adam, and I shall spend on you."[118]

The true Muslim woman believes that spending money for the sake of Allah will never decrease her wealth in the slightest; rather, it will bless, purify and increase it, as the Prophet (ﷺ) stated:

> "Charity does not decrease wealth..."[119]

She knows that whatever she spends for the sake of Allah is in fact that which is truly saved, because it is recorded in the book of her good deeds, whilst everything else will eventually disappear. The Prophet (ﷺ) drew the Muslims' attention to this higher understanding of generous giving when, "He asked 'Aa'ishah what was left of the sheep they had slaughtered. She told him, 'Nothing but the shoulder.' He said,

> 'Everything except the shoulder is saved.'"[120]

The true Muslim woman is highly motivated by all of this to give generously of whatever possessions and goods come to her.

An example of giving on the part of Muslim women is the well-

---

[117] Bukhari and Muslim, See *Sharḥ as-Sunnah*, 6/155, *Kitaab az-Zakah, baab maa yukrah min imsaak al-maal.*

[118] Bukhari and Muslim, See *Riyaaḍ aṣ-Ṣaliḥeen*, 301, *baab al-karam wal-jood wal-infaaq fi wujooh al-khayr.*

[119] Muslim, 16/141, *Kitaab al-Birr waṣ-Ṣilah wal-Aadaab, baab istiḥbaab al-'afu wat-tawaaḍu'.*

[120] Tirmidhi, 4/644, *Kitaab Ṣifat al-Qiyaamah*, 33. The reward for everything except the shoulder would be stored up for them in the Hereafter, as they had given it all away in charity. The part that they had kept for themselves, the shoulder, had in effect been "spent" as it carried no such reward. (Translator)

known report narrated by Bukhari from Ibn 'Abbaas (ﷺ), who said:

> "The Prophet went out on the day of 'Eid and prayed two *rak'ahs* (Units or cycles of prayer) with no prayer before or after them (i.e., he prayed only two *rak'ahs*). Then he came to the women, and commanded them to give in charity, so they started to give their earrings and necklaces in charity."[121]

According to another report also given by Bukhari:

> "He came to the women and commanded them to give in charity, so they began to throw their rings into Bilal's cloak."[122]

A third report by Bukhari, narrating from Ibn 'Abbaas, states that:

> "The Prophet (ﷺ) prayed two *rak'ahs* on the day of 'Eid with no prayer before or after them (i.e., he prayed only two *rak'ahs*), then he came to the women, and Bilal was accompanying him; he commanded them to give in charity, and the women began to throw down their earrings."[123]

The wives of the Prophet and the women of the *salaf* set the highest example of generous giving, and their deeds are recorded by history in letters of light.

In his biography of 'Aa'ishah given in *Siyar Aa'lam al-Nubala'*, Adh-Dhahabi states that:

> "She gave seventy thousand *dirhams* in charity, at the time when she was putting patches on her shield (dress).

---

121 *Fatḥ al-Baari*, 10/330, *Kitaab al-Libaas, baab al-qalaa'id wal-sikhaab lin-nisa'*.

122 *Fatḥ al-Baari*, 10/330, *Kitaab al-Libaas, baab al-khaatim lin-nisa'*.

123 *Fatḥ al-Baari*, 10/331, *Kitaab al-Libaas, baab al-qurṭ lin-nisa'*.

> Mu'aawiyah sent her a hundred thousand *dirhams*, and she gave it all away in charity before evening fell. Her servant said to her, 'Why did you not buy a *dirham's* worth of meat with it?' She said, 'Why did you not tell me to do so?' Mu'aawiyah also sent her bracelets worth a hundred thousand, which she shared out among the other wives of the Prophet. Ibn az-Zubayr sent her money in two containers, to the amount of a hundred thousand. She called for a large tray, and began to share the money among the people. When evening came, she said, 'O' young girl, bring me my *faṭoor* (food with which to break fast),' for she (ﷺ), used to fast all the time. The young girl — the maid servant — said to her, 'O' Mother of the Believers, could you not have bought us a *dirham's* worth of meat?' She said, 'Do not rebuke me; if you had reminded me I would have done so.'"

Her sister Asma' was no less generous. 'Abdullah ibn az-Zubayr (ﷺ) said:

> "I never saw two women more generous than 'Aa'ishah and Asma', but their ways of being generous were different. 'Aa'ishah would accumulate things and then share them out, whilst Asma' would never keep anything until the next day."

The Prophet's wife Zaynab bint Jaḥsh (ﷺ) used to work with her own hands and give in charity from her earnings. She was the most generous of the Prophet's wives in giving freely and doing good deeds. According to a hadith narrated by Imam Muslim from 'Aa'ishah (ﷺ), the Prophet (ﷺ) told his wives about Zaynab (ﷺ):

> "The first of you to join me (after death) will be the one who has the longest hand." 'Aa'ishah said: "They began to measure their hands against one another to see who had the longest hand, and the one who had the longest hands of all of us was Zaynab, because she used

to work with her hands and give charity from her earnings."[124]

'Umar ibn al-Khaṭṭab (رضي الله عنه) sent Zaynab her annual salary, and when it was brought to her, she said: "May Allah forgive 'Umar! Others of my sisters are more capable of sharing this out than I am." They told her, "This is all for you." She said, "*Subḥan Allah!* Pour it out (into the tray) and cover it with a cloth." Then she told Barzah bint Raafi', the narrator of this report: "Put your hand in and take a handful of it, and take it to Bani So-and-so and Bani So-and-so" — who were orphans or related to her. This was repeated until there was only a little left under the cloth. Barzah bint Raafi' said to Zaynab: "May Allah forgive you, O' Mother of the Believers! By Allah, it is our right to have some." Zaynab said: "What is left under the cloth is for you." (Barzah bint Raafi') said that they found eighty-five *dirhams* under the cloth. Zaynab said, "O' Allah, do not let me live to receive another payment like this from 'Umar," and she died before the time for the next payment came.[125]

Ibn Sa'd reported that when the money was brought to Zaynab, she started saying, "O' Allah, do not let me see this money again next year, for it is a *fitnah* (temptation)." Then she shared it out among her relatives and those who were in need, until it was all gone. 'Umar (رضي الله عنه) heard about this, and said, "This women is destined for good." He stood at her door and conveyed his *salaam* to her, then said: "I have heard about what you gave out to others." He then sent her a

---

Muslim, 16/8, *Kitaab Faḍaa'il aṣ-Ṣaḥaabah, baab faḍaa'il umm al-mu'mineen Zaynab.*

Ibn Sa'd, *Aṭ-Ṭabaqaat,* 8/109, 110; *Ṣifat aṣ-Ṣafwah,* 2/48,49; *Siyar Aa'laam an-Nubala',* 2/212.

thousand *dirhams* to keep for herself. But she did the same thing with that money, and did not keep even a single *dirham* or *dinaar* for herself.

Among the women to whose generosity history bears witness is Sakeenah bint al-Ḥusayn who would give generously of whatever she had. If she had no money, she would take off her own jewellery and give it to those who were destitute.

'Aatikah bint Yazeed ibn Mu'awiyah gave up all of her money to the poor members of Abu Sufyan's family.

Umm al-Banin, the sister of 'Umar ibn 'Abdul-'Aziz, was a marvellous example of generous giving. She said,

> "Everyone has a passion, and my passion is giving." She used to free slaves every week, and equip horsemen to fight for the sake of Allah. She would say, "Uff to stinginess! If it were a shirt I would not wear it, and if it were a road I would not follow it."[126]

Zubaydah, the wife of the *Khaleefah* Haroon ar-Rashid, had a channel dug to bring water from springs and rain-pools to Makkah, to provide fresh water for the inhabitants of the city and for the pilgrims. This was named *'Ayn* Zubaydah (the water-spring of Zubaydah), and was known as one of the wonders of the world at that time. When her treasurer objected to the high cost of this project, she told him: "Do it, even if every single blow of the axe costs a *dinaar*."

If we were to discuss all the women in our history who were pioneers of generous giving, we could fill entire volumes. It is enough for us to know that these kinds of generous, charitable, believing women have never disappeared from Muslim societies, from the dawn of Islam until the present day. In every era and region of the Islamic world,

---

126 Ibn al-Jawzi, *Aḥkaam an-Nisa'*, p. 446.

these women have held a noble and prominent position, and their generosity is enshrined in the many *awqaaf* (endowments), charitable institutions, schools, mosques, hospitals, etc., that exist throughout the Muslim lands. These women sought out areas of need, poverty, deprivation and misery, and showered their generosity on the less fortunate by establishing charitable institutions that would benefit the Muslims. They wiped away the tears of the orphan, relieved the suffering of the wretched, eased the hardship of the afflicted and clothed the body of the naked.

The Muslim woman who truly understands the teachings of her religion never looks down upon any charitable deed, no matter how small it may be; she strives to do as much as she is able, firm in her conviction that Allah (ﷻ) will reward her good deeds, no matter how small, as Allah says:

> "*On no soul does Allah place a burden greater than it can bear...*" *(Qur'an 2: 286)*

She also responds to the words of the Prophet (ﷺ):

> "Protect yourselves from the Fire even if it is with half a date."[127]

> "O' 'Aa'ishah, protect yourself from the Fire, even if it is only with half a date, for it can benefit a hungry person as much as one who has enough to eat."[128]

The Muslim woman may give charity with whatever she possesses of the food she has at home or her husband's money, so long as he is happy for her to do so. In this case, she will be rewarded for what she spends, her husband will be rewarded for what he has earned, and the

---

127 *Fatḥ al-Baari*, 3/283, *Kitaab az-Zakah, baab ittaqoo an-naar wa law bi shiqq tamarah.*

128 Reported with a *ṣaḥeeḥ* isnad by Aḥmad, 6/79.

treasurer will also be rewarded, as is stated in a number of hadith narrated by Bukhari, Muslim and others, for example:

> "If a women gives in charity of the food of her house (according to a report given by Muslim: of the house of her husband), without spending in such a way as could cause ruin to her husband, then she will be rewarded for what he earns, and the treasurer will be similarly rewarded, and the reward of any one of them will not detract from the reward of another."[129]

Islam wants the Muslims, men and women, to be constructive, beneficial members of their societies, always helping those who are deprived and destitute, to the best of their abilities. Every good deed is described as an act of charity (*ṣadaqah*), as the Prophet (ﷺ) said:

> "Every Muslim must give charity." They said, "O' Messenger of Allah, what if he cannot do that?" He said, "Then let him help one who is in desperate need." He said, "Then let him do good, and refrain from doing evil, and that will be an act of charity on his part."[130]

Islam has opened wide the doors of good deeds to men and women, rich and poor alike, so that anyone may have the opportunity to do good. Everyone who has uttered the words of the *Shahaadah* is required to do good deeds, which have been termed *ṣadaqah* (charity). The poor person needs not feel that he is deprived of the chance to take part in doing good in society just because he has little or no money. Every good deed or favour is described as *ṣadaqah*, and the poor man or woman will be rewarded for a good deed just as a

---

129 *Fatḥ al-Baari*, 3/293, *Kitaab az-Zakah, baab man amara khadimahu biṣ-ṣadaqah.*

130 Bukhari and Muslim, See *Sharḥ as-Sunnah*, 6/143, *Kitaab az-Zakah, baab kullu ma'roofin ṣadaqah.*

rich man or woman will be rewarded for money spent generously: "Every good deed is *ṣadaqah*."[131]

Thus Islam guarantees that all members of a society will participate in building, serving and improving it, and that all of them will feel the satisfaction of this participation which will give them back their pride and honour and will bring about their reward.

The generous Muslim woman gives to the poor and needy who are too proud to ask for any help, which makes people think that they are free from want. She tries to seek them out as much as she is able, for they are the first people who should be given help. These are the ones to whom the Prophet (ﷺ) referred when he said:

> "The poor man is not the one who takes a date or two, or a mouthful or two, then turns away. The poor man is the one who is too proud to ask for anything."[132]

The Muslim woman gives in charity to orphans as much as she is able. If she is well-off, she sponsors an orphan and helps to bring him up and educate him, spending on him and taking care of him, hoping for the high status that Allah (ﷻ) has prepared for the one who sponsors an orphan, which is the status of being in the vicinity of the Prophet (ﷺ) in Paradise:

> "I and the one who sponsors an orphan will be like this in Paradise," and he held up his index and middle fingers and held them apart.[133]

The Muslim woman also strives to help the widow and the poor, following the guidance of her religion, which has promised a great

---

[131] Op. cit, 6/142.

[132] Bukhari and Muslim, See *Riyaaḍ aṣ-Ṣaaliḥeen*, 167, *baab mulaṭafah al-yateem wal-masaakeen.*

[133] Bukhari and Muslim, See *Sharḥ as-Sunnah*, 13/43, *Kitaab al-Birr waṣ-Ṣilah, baab thawaab kafeel al-yateem.*

reward to the one who takes care of them, a reward that rivals that earned by the one who fasts during the day and stands in prayer at night, or the one who fights for the sake of Allah, as the Prophet (ﷺ) said:

> "The one who strives to help the widow and the poor is like the one who fights in jihad for the sake of Allah." And I (the narrator) believe he also said: "and like the one who stands at night in prayer without rest and fasts continually without breaking his fast."[134]

Taking care of widows and the poor, and sponsoring orphans, are among the most noble of humane deeds, and are most befitting to the Muslim woman, as they increase her in humanity, honour and gentility.

She does not remind the beneficiaries of her charity

If Allah (ﷻ) enables the Muslim woman to give generously, she should not fall into the sin of reminding people of her generosity or harming them; she should be keen to keep her giving pure and sincerely for the sake of Allah, so that she will be one of those whom Allah has described in the Qur'an:

> "*Those who spend their substance in the cause of Allah, and follow not up their gifts with reminders of their generosity or with injury — for them their reward is with their Lord; on them shall be no fear, nor shall they grieve.*" *(Qur'an 2: 262)*

The Muslim woman does not forget that there is nothing more likely to cancel out good deeds and destroy the reward of charity than

---

[134] Bukhari and Muslim, See *Sharḥ as-Sunnah*, 13/45, *Kitaab al-Birr waṣ-Ṣilah, baab as-saa'ee 'ala al-armalah.*

reminding others of it or harming them. Allah (ﷻ) warns the believers against these deeds in such a way that the believer is shaken and would not even think of reminding others of his charity or harming them:

> *"O' you who believe! Cancel not your charity by reminders of your generosity or by injury..."*
>
> *(Qur'an 2: 264)*

Reminding the poor man whom need has compelled to accept aid from others is humiliating and disrespectful. It is forbidden by Islam, which counts the one who gives and the one who takes as brothers, between whom there is no difference except in their *taqwa* and good deeds. A brother does not remind his brother of his charity; he does not humiliate him or cause him to lose face. In a hadith narrated by Muslim from Abu Dharr, the Prophet (ﷺ) issued a strong warning to those who remind others of their charity, and counted them among those doomed souls to whom Allah (ﷻ) will not even speak on the Day of Judgement:

> "There are three to whom Allah will not speak on the Day of Resurrection, nor look at, nor commend them, and theirs will be a severe punishment." The Messenger of Allah (Blessings and Peace be upon him) repeated this three times. Abu Dharr (may Allah be pleased with him) said, "They are truly lost and doomed. Who are they, O' Messenger of Allah?" He said, "The one who lets his garment trail below his ankles (out of pride), the one who reminds people of his charity, and the one who sells his goods by means of making false oaths."[135]

---

[135] Muslim, 2/114, *Kitaab al-Eemaan, baab taḥreem isbaal al-izaar wal-mann bil-'aṭiyah.*

She is patient

The Muslim woman who is truly guided by Islam and who is infused with its noble characteristics trains herself to be patient, to control her anger, to forgive and to respond to an evil deed with something better, in accordance with the words of the Qur'an:

> "*...Who restrain anger, and pardon [all] men — for Allah loves those who do good.*" (*Qur'an 3: 134*)
>
> "*Nor can Goodness and Evil be equal. Repel [Evil] with what is better: then will he between whom and you was hatred become as it were your friend and intimate! And no one will be granted such goodness except those who exercise patience and self-restraint — none but persons of the greatest good fortune.*" (*Qur'an 41: 34-35*)

Self-restraint at the time of anger, and adopting a calm and patient attitude, are among the most beautiful qualities of Muslim men and women that Allah loves to see in His believing servants. This is what was stated by the Prophet (ﷺ) in the hadith narrated by Ibn 'Abbaas:

> "The Prophet said to Ashajj 'Abdul-Qays: 'You have two qualities that Allah loves: patience and deliberation.'"[136]

Hence, the Prophet (ﷺ) told the man who came asking him for advice in just one word:

> "Do not become angry." The man repeated his request for advice several times, and each time the Prophet said: "Do not become angry."[137]

The Muslim woman may become angry sometimes, but her anger is

---

[136] Muslim, 1/189, *Kitaab al-Eemaan, baab mubayi'ah wafd 'Abdul-Qays.*

[137] *Fatḥ al-Baari*, 10/519, *Kitaab al-Adab, baab al-ḥadhr min al-ghaḍab.*

for the sake of Allah, not for her own sake. She may become angry when she sees carelessness, wilful neglect and downright insolence towards matters of religion among women. She has the right to be angry in such situations. This is how the Prophet (ﷺ) used to be, as Bukhari and Muslim narrated:

> "The Prophet never took revenge for his own sake, but if the laws of Allah were violated, he would take revenge for the sake of Allah."[138]

The Prophet (ﷺ) used to become furious, and his face would redden, if he heard some insult to the reputation of Islam, or if he discovered some error or negligence in applying its laws and carrying out its punishments.

He became furious the day a man came to him and said, "I always come late to *Ṣalaat aṣ-ṣubh* (*fajr* prayer) because of so-and-so, who always makes the prayer too lengthy." The Prophet (ﷺ) was never seen as angry in his rebuke as he was on that day. He said.

> "O' people, there are among you those who put others off from good deeds. When anyone leads the people in prayer, he should keep it short, for behind him are the old, the young, and the one who has a pressing need."[139]

He (ﷺ) also became angry the day he returned from a journey and found a thin curtain covered with pictures in 'Aa'ishah's house. When he saw it, he tore it down and his face reddened. He told her:

> "O' 'Aa'ishah, the people who will be most severely

---

[138] *Fatḥ al-Baari*, 10/519, *Kitaab al-Manaaqib, baab ṣifat an-Nabi*; Muslim, 15/83, *Kitaab al-Faḍaa'il, baab mubaa'idatahi lil-aathaam*.

[139] Bukhari and Muslim, See *Sharḥ as-Sunnah*, 3/409, *Kitaab aṣ-Ṣalaah baab al-Imam yukhaffif aṣ-ṣalaah*; this version is by Muslim

> punished by Allah on the Day of Resurrection will be those who imitate the creation of Allah."[140]

He also became angry when Usaamah ibn Zayd spoke to him concerning the Makhzoomi woman who had committed theft, and the Prophet (ﷺ) had decreed that the appropriate punishment be carried out on her. The people said, "Who will speak to the Prophet (ﷺ) about her?" Then they said, "Who dares to do this but Usaamah ibn Zayd, his beloved?" So Usaamah spoke to him, and the Prophet (ﷺ) said angrily,

> "Are you interceding to stop one of the punishments ordained by Allah?" Then he got up and addressed the people: "Those who came before you were destroyed because when one of their noblemen committed theft, they let him off, but when one of the weak among them committed theft, then they would carry out the punishment on him. By Allah, if Faṭimah the daughter of Muhammad were to commit theft, I would cut off her hand."[141]

Such was the anger of the Prophet (ﷺ), and these are the valid reasons for anger according to Islam. Anger should be for the sake of Allah, not for one's own ego.

The Muslim woman who understands the teachings of Islam and follows the example of the Prophet (ﷺ) always keeps his teachings, behaviour and deeds in mind, so she controls herself when she feels angry with people, and her anger is only for the sake of Allah, His religion and the sanctity of His laws.

---

[140] Bukhari and Muslim, See *Sharḥ as-Sunnah*, 12/128, *Kitaab al-Libaas, baab at-taṣaaweer*; this version is by Muslim.

[141] Bukhari and Muslim, See *Sharḥ as-Sunnah*, 10/328, *Kitaab al-Ḥudood, baab qaṭa' yad ash-shareef wal-mar'ah wash-shafaa'ah fil-ḥadd.*

She is easy-going and does not bear grudges

The Muslim woman does not bear grudges, and resentment has no room in her heart, because Islam has uprooted hatred from her heart, extinguished the flames of anger, cleansed her soul of enmity, and planted the seeds of sisterly love, tolerance and forgiveness.

Islam has uncompromisingly declared war on ignorance, tribalism, hostility, enmity and revenge, and has made forgiveness, tolerance, love and kindness dearer to the hearts of Muslim men and women. Allah (ﷻ) says:

> "*...Who restrain anger, and pardon all men — for Allah loves those who do good.*" *(Qur'an 3: 134)*

This praise is for those who restrain their anger and do not bear grudges, who have raised themselves to the level of forgiveness and tolerance, which is a high level indeed, and very difficult to attain. None can reach it except those who are pure of heart and have shed the inclination towards hostility, enmity and revenge and thus earned the right to reach the level of *iḥsaan*, and Allah (ﷻ) loves those who do good *(al-muḥsinoon)*.

Through this noble teaching, Islam was able to penetrate the hearts of the believers, and cleanse and purify them, so that hearts that had been dominated by anger and hatred became hearts that were filled with love and devotion.

One of the most striking examples of this miraculous change of heart is the story of Hind bint 'Utbah, whose heart before she embraced Islam was filled with the poison of hatred and enmity towards the Prophet (ﷺ) and his family and Companions. On the day of the Conquest of Makkah, the Prophet (ﷺ) even declared that her blood might be shed with impunity, as a punishment for her having mutilated the body of his uncle Hamzah (رضي الله عنه) on the day of Uḥud. When she embraced Islam and faith penetrated deep into her heart, she came to the Prophet (ﷺ) and said: "O' Messenger of Allah, there was no family on earth that I would have loved to see humiliated more than your family, but from this day on, there is no family on earth I would love to see honoured more than your family."[142]

For the sake of Allah and His Religion, blood feuds will be forgotten, hostility will vanish, those who previously hated one another will become friends, and the inclination towards enmity will be uprooted. In the most brilliant fashion, the Qur'an raises the human soul to this difficult, high level. It states that the one who has been treated unjustly has the right to defend himself and resist oppression (an eye for an eye), but it does not allow the one who has been wronged to be overtaken by the desire for revenge. Rather, it gently leads him or her towards the level of patience, tolerance and forgiveness, and states that this is something that takes a great deal of determination and willpower:

> "*And those who, when an oppressive wrong is inflicted on them, [are not cowed but] help and defend themselves. The recompense for an injury is an injury equal thereto [in degree]: but if a person forgives and makes reconciliation, his reward is due from Allah: for Allah loves not those who do wrong. But indeed if any do help and defend themselves after a wrong [done] to them, against such there is no cause of blame. The blame is only against those who oppress men with wrongdoing and insolently transgress beyond bounds through the land, defying right and justice: for such there will be a Penalty grievous. But indeed if any show patience and forgive, that would truly be an exercise of courageous will and resolution in the conduct of affairs.*" *(Qur'an 42: 39-43)*

---

142 *Fatḥ al-Baari*, 7/141, *Kitaab Manaaqib al-Anṣaar, baab dhikr Hind bint 'Utbah.*

When Abu Bakr (رضي الله عنه) was overwhelmed with sorrow because of the slander he heard uttered against his daughter 'Aa'ishah (رضي الله عنها), he vowed to himself to cut off his help to those ungrateful recipients of his bounty who had joined in the sinful gossip. But Allah, Who knew the purity of Abu Bakr's heart and his devotion to Allah and His Messenger, did not allow him to be taken over by the desire for revenge that crossed his mind, so He guided him back towards his essential good nature and purity of heart, and motivated him to strive for the higher level of tolerance and forgiveness:

> "*Let not those among you who are endued with grace and amplitude of means resolve by oath against helping their kinsmen, those in want, and those who have left their homes in Allah's cause: Let them forgive and overlook, do you not wish that Allah should forgive you? For Allah is Oft-Forgiving, Most Merciful.*"
>
> *(Qur'an 24: 22)*

Interactions between individuals in an Islamic society that is founded on the brotherhood of faith are not based on an attitude of watching for and counting mistakes, or the desire for revenge, or defensiveness; they are based on brotherhood, overlooking errors and tolerance. This is what Islam and the brotherhood of faith call for. Allah (سبحانه وتعالى) says:

> "*Nor can Goodness and Evil be equal. Repel [Evil] with what is better: then will he between whom and you was hatred become as it were your friend and intimate! And no one will be granted such goodness except those who exercise patience and self-restraint — none but persons of the greatest good fortune.*" *(Qur'an 41: 34-35)*

If evil is always repaid with evil, the result will be intense hatred and bitter grudges. But if evil is repaid with good, it will extinguish the fires of hatred, calm people down, and remove their grudges. The two women who were enemies will become true friends when one of them speaks a kind word or smiles compassionately at the other. This is a great victory for the one who repelled evil with something better, and turned enmity into friendship, hatred to love. No one attains this but persons of the greatest good fortune, as the Qur'an states. Such a person responds to the evil she faces with a measure of patience and self-control, and repels it with something good.

This is the attitude of true believing women in a Muslim community that is based on love, friendship and tolerance. Many *ayat* and hadith reinforce this message and seek to instill this attitude in believers' hearts, always training them to adopt that attitude of forgiveness that will leave no trace of hatred, resentment or malice:

> "*...So overlook [any human faults] with gracious forgiveness.*" *(Qur'an 15: 85)*

The Prophet (ﷺ), by his words and deeds, was a living example of this worthy human virtue of tolerance and forgiveness, and he urged others to adopt it also. 'Aa'ishah (رضي الله عنها) said:

> "The Prophet never struck any person, woman or servant with his hand, except when he was fighting in the way of Allah, and he never took offence at anything and sought revenge for it, except when one of the laws of Allah had been violated, and then he would take revenge for the sake of Allah."[143]

He (ﷺ) used to follow the commands of Allah:

> "*Hold to forgiveness; command what is right; but turn away from the ignorant.*" *(Qur'an 7: 199)*

By the following the command of Allah,

> "*...Repel Evil with what is better...*" *(Qur'an 41: 34)*

---

[143] Muslim, 15/84, *Kitaab al-Faḍaa'il, baab mubaa'idatihi lil-aathaam.*

— the Prophet (ﷺ) was a unique example of this sublime attitude, which encompassed and appealed to all people. He did not repay their evil with evil, rather he repelled it with an attitude of forgiveness and good manners, turning away from the ignorant and repelling evil with something better.

Anas (رضي الله عنه) said:

> "I was walking with the Messenger of Allah, and he was wearing a Najrani cloak with a stiff collar. A Bedouin came up to him and grabbed him roughly, and I looked at the Prophet's shoulder and saw the mark left by his collar because of this rough approach. Then the Bedouin said, 'O' Muhammad, order that I be given some of the wealth of Allah that you have!' The Prophet turned to him and smiled, then ordered that he be given something."[144]

The attitude of forgiveness was so deeply entrenched in his noble heart that he even forgave the Jewish woman who sent him poisoned mutton, as Bukhari, Muslim and others narrate.

> "This Jewish woman sent a gift of poisoned mutton to the Prophet, and he and a group of his Companions began to eat it, then he said, 'Stop! It is poisoned!' The woman was brought to the Prophet and he asked her, 'What made you do that?' She said: 'I wanted to know if you were really a Prophet, in which case Allah would warn you and the poison would not harm you. If you were not a Prophet, then we would have been rid of

---

[144] Bukhari and Muslim, See *Riyaaḍ aṣ-Ṣaaliḥeen*, 344, *baab al-'afu wal-i'raaḍ 'an al-jaahileen.*

> you.' The Companions asked, 'Shall we kill her?' He said, 'No,' and forgave her."[145]

When the tribe of Daws rebelled and refused to follow the commands of Allah and His Messenger, Aṭ-Ṭufayl ibn 'Amr ad-Dawsi came to the Prophet (ﷺ) and said, "Daws have rebelled, so pray to Allah against them." The Prophet faced the *qiblah* and raised his hands, and the people said, "They are finished!" But the Prophet (ﷺ), who was merciful and tolerant, and did not want to see the punishment of Allah befall people, prayed for Daws, saying,

> "O' Allah, guide Daws and bring them here; O' Allah, guide Daws and bring them here; O' Allah, guide Daws and bring them here."[146]

The Prophet (ﷺ) instilled in people's hearts the attitude of always forgiving and being tolerant, even when faced with harshness and being boycotted. With the deep insight with which Allah (ﷻ) had endowed him, he understood that people respond better to tolerance than to harshness. Therefore when 'Uqbah ibn 'Aamir asked him,

> "O' Messenger of Allah, tell me the best of deeds," he told him, "O' 'Uqbah, maintain ties with the one who cuts you off, give to the one who deprives you, and do not seek revenge on the one who wrongs you." According to another report, he said, "Forgive the one who wrongs you."[147]

---

[145] Bukhari and Muslim. See *Fatḥ al-Baari*, 7/497, *Kitaab al-Maghaazi, baab ash-shaat al-masmoomah* and 5/230, *Kitaab al-Hibbah, baab qabool al-hadiyah min al-mushrikeen*; Muslim, 14/178, *Kitaab as-Salaam, baab as-summ.*

[146] Bukhari and Muslim, See *Sharḥ as-Sunnah*, 5/150, *Kitaab ad-Da'waat, baab ad-du'aa' lil-kuffaar bil-hidaayah.*

[147] Aḥmad and Ṭabaraani; the men of Aḥmad's isnad are *thiqaat*. See *Majma' az-Zawaa'id*, 8/188, *baab makaarim al-akhlaaq.*

The Mothers of the Believers, (may Allah be pleased with them all) also adopted this sublime attitude. An example of this is the attitude of Ṣafiyah (رضي الله عنها) towards her female slave who went to the *Khaleefah* 'Umar ibn al-Khaṭṭab (رضي الله عنه) and said,

> "O' *Ameer al-Mu'mineen*, Ṣafiyah loves the *Sabbath* (Saturday) and maintains ties with the Jews." 'Umar sent for Ṣafiyah and questioned her about that. She replied: "As far as the *Sabbath* is concerned, I have no love for it since Allah replaced it with *Jumu'ah* (Friday) for me. As for the jews, I have relatives among them with whom I uphold the ties of kinship." Then she turned to her slave and asked her what had made her tell such a lie. The slave woman answered, "*Shayṭaan*." Ṣafiyah distinguished herself by responding to evil with something better. She told the slave woman: "Go, you are free."[148]

No doubt Ṣafiyah (رضي الله عنها) was one of those to whom the words of the Qur'an applied:

> "*Nor can Goodness and Evil be equal. Repel [Evil] with what is better: then will he between whom and you was hatred become as it were your friend and intimate! And no one will be granted such goodness except those who exercise patience and self-restraint — none but persons of the greatest good fortune.*" *(Qur'an 41: 34-35)*

She was most certainly a person of the greatest good fortune.

She is easy on people, not hard

The Muslim woman who truly understands the teachings of Islam is easy on people, not hard, because making things easy for others is the

---

148 Ibn 'Abdul-Barr, *Al-Isti'aab*, 4/1872; Ibn Ḥajar, *Al-Iṣaabah*, 8/127.

best attitude that Allah (ﷻ) likes to see in His believing servants:

> "*...Allah intends every facility for you; He does not want to put you to difficulties...*" *(Qur'an 2: 185)*

Therefore the Prophet (ﷺ) encouraged the Muslims to be easy on people, and forbade them to make things difficult:

> "Teach and make things easy, do not make them difficult. If any of you becomes angry, let him keep silent."[149]

The woman who resorts to making things difficult and complicating matters when the teachings of Islam are so clear is a woman who is neither pious nor sound; nobody does such a thing except the one whose nature is twisted and mean-spirited and whose education is lacking. The Muslim woman who is straightforward and is obedient to Allah and the teachings of Islam does not like to cause difficulties or complicate matters. In this way she is following the example of the Prophet (ﷺ) whom 'Aa'ishah (رضي الله عنها) described as follows:

> "The Messenger of Allah was never faced with the choice between two things but he took the easier of the two, so long as it was not a sin. If it was a sin, he would be the furthest of the people from it. And the Messenger of Allah never took revenge for himself, but if the bounds of Allah were transgressed, then he would take revenge for the sake of Allah."[150]

The true Muslim woman adheres to the teachings of the Prophet (ﷺ); she does not go beyond the limits set by him, or disobey his commands.

---

[149] Bukhari: *Al-Adab al-Mufrad*, 1/342, *baab al-'afu waṣ-ṣafḥ 'an an-naas.*

[150] Bukhari and Muslim, See *Sharḥ as-Sunnah*, 13/260, *Kitaab al-Faḍaa'il, baab ikhtiyarihi aysar al-amrayn.*

She is not envious

How often does the ordinary women fall into the sin of envy, when she sees many of those who are inferior to her in beauty, knowledge and intelligence wallowing in riches and luxury when she does not have even the smallest part of what they enjoy? The alert, truly-guided Muslim woman, however, is saved from stumbling into such error because she has learnt, from the teachings of Islam, that everything that happens in life happens according to the will and decree of Allah. The pleasures of this life, no matter how great, are as nothing in comparison to the reward that Allah (ﷻ) has prepared for those believing women who are content with what Allah has given them. The true value of a woman rests in her level of *taqwa* and good deeds, not in her transient worldly earnings. The more these values are reinforced in the woman's soul, the purer and more tranquil her soul becomes, and she will become one of the people of Paradise who have earned the pleasure of Allah, even if her acts of worship are few. Imam Aḥmad reported, with a *ṣaḥeeḥ* isnad from Anas ibn Maalik:

> "We were sitting with the Prophet and he said, 'One of the people of Paradise will now come to you,' and a man of the Anṣaar came along, his beard dripping from his *wuḍoo'*, and carrying his sandals in his left hand. The next day, the Prophet said the same thing, and the same man appeared, looking the same as he had on the previous day. On the third day, the Prophet again said the same thing, and the same man appeared again. When the Prophet left, 'Abdullah ibn 'Amr ibn al-'Aaṣ followed the man and said, 'I have fallen out with my father and sworn that I will not enter his house for three (days), and I thought that I could stay with you until the time is up.' He said, 'That's fine.' Anas said: 'Abdullah used to tell how he stayed with him for those three

> nights and never saw the man get up to pray at night, but when he awoke and turned over in his sleep, he would mention Allah and say *Allahu Akbar*, until he got up for *Ṣalaat al-fajr.* 'Abdullah said: 'But I never heard him say anything but good. When the three days were over and I had begun to think that his deeds were nothing remarkable, I said, 'O' servant of Allah! There was no quarrel between me and my father, but I heard the Prophet say three times, 'One of the people of Paradise will come to you,' and you appeared each time, so I wanted to come and stay with you to see what you did, so that I could follow your example, but I did not see you do anything out of the ordinary. What is it that has raised you to such a great status as the Prophet said? The man said, 'It is only what you have seen.' When I turned away, he called me back and said, 'It is only what you have seen, but I do not hold anything against any Muslim in my heart, and I do not envy anyone for the blessings that Allah has bestowed on him.' 'Abdullah said: 'This is what raised you to that great status, and this is what we could not achieve.'''[151]

This hadith indicates the effects of having a heart that is free of hatred, envy, malice and treachery, and its impact on deciding a person's fate in the Hereafter, raising his status in the sight of Allah and making his deeds acceptable, even if they are few. These effects can be clearly seen in the example of this man whose acts of worship were few, but he would enter Paradise because of the purity of his heart and the fact that people were safe from harm on his part. These effects are in direct contrast with the woman about whom the Prophet (ﷺ) was asked; although she spent her nights in prayer and her days

---

151 *Musnad Aḥmad*, 3/166.

in fasting, she used to insult and mistreat her neighbours, so the Prophet (ﷺ) said:

> "She will be in Hell."[152]

The person who weighs heavily in the balance of Islam (i.e., is successful) is the one whose heart is always pure and free from hatred, malice, envy and resentment, even if his acts of worship are few. A person who performs many acts of worship when his or her heart is filled with feelings of resentment, envy and hatred, is merely performing an outward, mechanical action that clearly has no solid foundation of faith. Hence it has no effect in purifying his soul of envy which the Prophet (ﷺ) stated does not belong in the heart of the one who has true faith:

> "Faith and envy do not go together in the heart of the believer."[153]

Ḍamurah ibn Tha'labah (رضي الله عنه) said: "The Messenger of Allah (ﷺ) said:

> 'The people will do fine so long as they do not envy one another.'"[154]

The true Muslim woman is the one who combines proper worship with purity of heart, uncontaminated by envy, malice and hatred. In this way she may scale the heights of true *taqwa* and attain a high status in the sight of Allah, and also earn the love and respect of other people in this world. Thus she will become a solid brick in the structure of a pure, cohesive Muslim community that deserves to carry the message of Allah to mankind.

---

152 Bukhari: *Al-Adab al-Mufrad*, 1/210, *baab la yu dhi jaarahu*

153 Ibn Ḥibban in his *Ṣaḥeeḥ*, 10/466, *Kitaab as-Siyar, baab faḍl al-jihaad.*

154 Ṭabaraani; the men of its isnad are *thiqaat*. See *Majma' az-Zawaa'id*, 8/78, *baab maa jaa' fil-ḥasad waẓ-ẓann.*

She avoids boasting and seeking fame

Among the attributes of the Muslim woman who understands and follows the teachings of Islam are her humility, truthfulness and realistic approach. She does not have an attitude of superiority, self-admiration and telling lies, and she does not claim to have more than she actually has in order to show off to her friends and peers under false pretences.

She tries to avoid such unpleasant habits, because they do not befit the nature of a woman whose personality has been moulded by the principles of Islam. A woman came to the Prophet (ﷺ) asking whether she would be permitted to say that her husband had given her something which he had not given her, in order to boast and show off. The Prophet (ﷺ) replied:

> "The one who creates a false impression of having been given something which he was not given is like the one who wears the garment of falsehood."[155]

Islam is a religion that is based on sincerity, purity, humility and realism; it abhors deception, haughtiness, arrogance, conceit and false claims. So it hates to see its followers boasting under false pretences, looking down on others, or hoarding wealth for love of fame. It sharply criticizes those who adopt such attitudes, just as it rebukes the one who wears the garment of falsehood.

Her speech is not exaggerated or affected

The true Muslim is natural in her behaviour and conduct; she does not exaggerate or affect her speech in order to attract attention, because these are sickening, hateful attributes that do not exist in

[155] Muslim, 14/110, *Kitaab al-Libaas waz-Zeenah, baab an-nahy 'an at-tazweer fil-libaas wa ghayrihi.*

people of sound nature. Only those who are twisted or whose sound nature is lacking speak in an exaggerated or affected (artificial) manner. For this reason the Prophet (ﷺ) was very harsh on those men and women who exaggerate in their speech, and after his death, Abu Bakr and 'Umar were similarly harsh on them, to the extent that 'Abdullah ibn Mas'ood said:

> "By Him besides Whom there is no other god, I never saw anyone who was harsher on those who exaggerate in their speech than the Messenger of Allah, and I never saw anyone who was harsher on them after his death than Abu Bakr, and I think that 'Umar feared the most for them of all people on earth."[156]

She has a likeable personality

The Muslim woman is keen to be liked by others, through her good deeds and through the positive effect she has on them, as well as by having a good reputation in society.

People's love for her is a sign that Allah (ﷻ) loves her too, because in this case He opens people's hearts to her and makes her accepted and well-liked by everyone who meets her or hears about her. Concerning this, the Prophet (ﷺ) said:

> "When Allah loves a person, He calls Jibreel (Gabriel) and says: 'I love so-and-so, so love him.' So Jibreel will love him, and will call out in the heavens: 'Allah loves so-and-so, so love him.' Then the people of heaven will love him, and he will be well-accepted on earth. If Allah hates a person, He calls Jibreel and says: 'I hate so-and-so, so hate him., so Jibreel will hate him, and will call

---

[156] Abu Ya'la and Ṭabaraani; the men of its isnad are *thiqaat*. See *Majma' az-Zawaa'id*, 10/251, *baab maa jaa' fil-mutana' 'ameen wal-mutanaṭṭa'een.*

> out in the heavens: 'Allah hates so-and-so, so hate him.' Then the people of heaven will hate him, and he will be despised on earth."[157]

This is the unseen, divine reason why some Muslim men and women enjoy the love of others towards them. It is the love of Allah which He has spread among the people of heaven and earth, and makes those fortunate people well-accepted on earth, or else His hatred causes them to be despised on earth.

No-one can earn the love of Allah except the one who turns to Him seeking His pleasure, and no-one earns His hatred except the one who turns away from His guidance and disobeys Him.

The good news of Allah's love and pleasure is given only to believing men and women, those who believe and do good works, which are commended by other people. Allah (ﷻ) will hasten to bring them glad tidings in their own lifetimes, so He causes people to praise them and love them, as is seen in the *ṣaḥeeḥ* hadith narrated by Muslim from Abu Dharr, who said:

> "The Prophet was asked, 'What do you think of a man who does a good deed, and people praise him for it?' He said, 'That is glad tidings for the believer that he has received in this world.' According to another report also narrated by Muslim: 'and the people love him for it.'"[158]

The Muslim woman who has the best characteristics and is adhering to the limits set by Allah (ﷻ), doing what He commands and avoiding what He forbids, is the woman who deserves to receive these glad tidings in this world. She deserves to be loved by everyone

---

157 Muslim, 16/184, *Kitaab al-Birr waṣ-Ṣilah wal-Aadaab, baab idha aḥabba Allah 'abdan.*

158 Muslim, 16/189, *Kitaab al-Birr waṣ-Ṣilah wal-Aadaab, baab uthnia 'ala aṣ-Ṣaaleḥ fa hia bushra.*

who knows her or hears of her good deeds, such as tolerance, turning away from ignorant women, responding to evil with good, helping the poor and destitute, wanting the best for others, denying herself, speaking the truth, refraining from talking unnecessarily, being fair in her judgement and treatment of others, avoiding malicious gossip and hurting others, and other righteous attitudes and virtues that Islam encourages and describes as an adornment for the Muslim woman. Such a woman has truly understood the teachings of her religion; she has earned the love of people in this world and the pleasure of Allah and Paradise in the Hereafter.

She is friendly and likeable

The sensitive Muslim woman is friendly and likeable. She makes friends with other women and mixes with them, and they in turn like to meet her and make friends with her, because of her gentle, refined, attractive character and good treatment of them. These are the best characteristics that a woman may attain, as they entitle her to mix with other women, earn their trust and have an influence on them. Women will only listen to the one whom they like and trust and feel comfortable with, and they will only be persuaded by a woman who brings with her an attitude of trust, friendship and respect.

Hence there are many hadiths which commend the type of person who is friendly and liked by others. Such a person, whether man or woman, is one of those chosen ones who are beloved to the Prophet (ﷺ) and will be closest to him on the Day of Judgement:

> "Shall I not tell you who among you is most beloved to me and will be closest to me on the Day of Resurrection?" He repeated it three or two times, and they said, "Yes, O' Messenger of Allah." He said, "Those of you who are the best in attitude and character."[159] Some reports add: "Those who are down

---

[159] Reported with a *jayyid* isnad by Aḥmad, 2/185.

> to earth and humble, who get along with others and with whom others feel comfortable."

One of the most important attributes of the Muslim woman is that she gets along with others and others feel comfortable with her. She likes people and they like her. If she is not like this, then she will not be able to convey the message or achieve anything of significance. Whoever is like that has no goodness in him, as in the hadith:

> "The believer gets along with people and they feel comfortable with him. There is no goodness in the one who does not get along with people and with whom they do not feel comfortable."[160]

The Prophet (ﷺ) set the highest example of good behaviour towards people. He was skillful in softening their hearts and called them to follow him in word and deed. He demonstrated how to reach people's hearts and win their love and admiration. He was always cheerful and easy-going, never harsh. When he came to any gathering, he would sit wherever there was a free space, and he told others to do likewise. He treated everyone equally, so that no-one who was present in a gathering would feel that anyone else was receiving preferential treatment. If anyone came to him and asked for something, he would give it to him, or at least respond with kind words. His good attitude extended to everyone and he was like a father to them. The people gathered around him were truly equal, distinguished only by their level of *taqwa*. They were humble, respecting their elders, showing compassion to young ones, giving priority to those in need, and taking care of strangers.

The Prophet (ﷺ) never disappointed anyone who came to ask from him. There are three characteristics that he did not possess: he was

---

160 Aḥmad and Al-Bazzar; the men of Aḥmad's isnad are *rijaal aṣ-ṣaḥeeḥ*. See *Majma' az-Zawaa'id*, 8/87, *baab al-mu'min ya'laf wa yu'lif.*

not argumentative, he did not talk too much, and he did not concern himself with matters that were not his business. There are three things that he never did to people: he never criticized anyone, he never said "Shame on you!" to anyone, and he never looked for anyone's faults. He never said anything but that for which he hoped to earn reward. When he spoke, the people around him would listen earnestly, sitting still as if there were birds on their heads. When he was silent, then they would speak. They never argued with one another in his presence. They would smile at whatever he smiled at, and would be impressed by whatever impressed him. He would be patient with a stranger who might be harsh in his requests or questions, and his Companions would ask the stranger to speak gently. He said, "If you see someone in need, then help him." He never accepted praise except from someone who was thanking him for a favour, and he never cut short anyone who was speaking; he would wait until the person indicated that he had finished, or stood up.[161]

'Aa'ishah (ﷺ) tells us that he (the Prophet) (ﷺ) used to be cautious of the worst type of people, and he would speak gently to them and treat them well. A man sought permission to see him and he said,

> "Let him in, what a bad brother of his tribe he is!" When the man came in, he spoke gently to him. 'Aa'ishah said, "O' Messenger of Allah, you said what you said, then you spoke gently to him." He said, "O' 'Aa'ishah, the worst of people is the one whom people avoid (or are gentle towards) because they fear his slander."[162]

No doubt the mature Muslim woman who is receptive to the

---

[161] *Ḥayaat aṣ-Ṣaḥaabah*, 1/22, 23.

[162] *Fatḥ al-Baari*, 10/471, *Kitaab al-Adab, baab maa yajooz min ightiyab ahl al-fasaad war-riyab*; Muslim, 16/144, *Kitaab al-Birr waṣ-Ṣilah wal-Aadaab, baab madaarah man yutqi fuḥshihi.*

guidance of Islam follows the footsteps of her Prophet in her dealings with all people, whether they (the people) are good or bad, so that she will be liked, well accepted and respected among all the women who know her or hear of her.

She keeps secrets

It is obvious to the mature, wise Muslim woman that keeping secrets is one of the best characteristics that a person, man or woman, can have. Keeping secrets is a sign of a person's maturity, moral strength, wisdom and balanced personality. Therefore, the true Muslim woman keeps those secrets that Islam urges her to keep. This was the attitude of the best personalities of Islam, and was one of their most beautiful characteristics.

One of the best examples of this virtue and the determination to adhere to it among the most prominent *Ṣaḥaabah* was the attitude of Abu Bakr and 'Uthman (may Allah be pleased with them) towards 'Umar when he offered them his daughter Ḥafṣah's hand in marriage after she was widowed, and their concealing the secret of the Prophet (ﷺ) from him.

Imam Bukhari reported from 'Abdullah ibn 'Umar that 'Umar said, concerning events after his daughter Ḥafṣah was widowed: "I met 'Uthmaan ibn 'Affan and offered him Ḥafṣah's hand in marriage. I said, 'If you wish, I will marry Ḥafṣah to you.' He said: 'I will think about it.' A few days passed, then he met me and said, 'I think that I do not wish to get married just now.' Then I met Abu Bakr aṣ-Ṣiddiq, and said, 'If you wish, I will marry Ḥafṣah bint 'Umar to you.' Abu Bakr remained silent and made no reply to me, and I was more upset with him than with 'Uthmaan. A few days passed, then the Prophet (ﷺ) asked for her hand, and I gave her to him in marriage. Abu Bakr met me and said, 'Perhaps you were angry with me for when you offered me Ḥafṣah's hand and I did not reply?' I said, 'Yes.' He said, 'Nothing kept me from answering you except the fact that I knew the

Prophet (ﷺ) had mentioned her, and I could not disclose the secret of the Messenger of Allah (ﷺ). If he had decided not to marry her, then I would have married her.'"[163]

The virtue of keeping secrets was not confined only to the men of the *salaf*, it also included women and children whose hearts were filled with the guidance of Islam. We see this in the report given by Imam Muslim from Anas (رضي الله عنه), who said:

> "The Messenger of Allah (ﷺ) came to me while I was playing with some other boys. He greeted me, then sent me on an errand. I was late coming home to my mother, and when I came, she asked, 'What kept you so long?' I said, 'The Messenger of Allah sent me on an errand.' She asked me, 'What errand?' I said, 'It is a secret.' She said, 'Do not tell anyone the secret of the Messenger of Allah.' Anas said: 'By Allah, if I had told anyone about it, I would have told you, O' Thaabit.'"[164]

Umm Anas saw that her son was keen to keep the secret entrusted to him by the Prophet (ﷺ), so she reinforced this keen attitude by telling him not to disclose this secret to anyone. So Anas did not speak of it to anyone, not even to the great *Taabi'i* Thaabit al-Bunani. She did not allow her curiosity to make her quiz her young son about the secret he was keeping from her. This is the true Islamic *tarbiyah* (education, upbringing), and this is the sublime level to which it raised men, women and children alike.

Telling secrets is one of the worst habits a person could have, and the worst form of this habit is disclosing secrets that relate to the intimacies of married life. A person who is afflicted with this

---

163 *Fatḥ al-Baari*, 9/175, *Kitaab an-Nikaaḥ* and 7/317, *Kitaab al-Maghaazi, baab 'arḍ al-insaan ibnatahu 'ala ahl al-khayr*

164 Muslim, 16/41, *Kitaab Faḍaa'il aṣ-Ṣaḥabah, baab faḍaa'il Anas*. Thaabit is the name of the *Taabi'i* (follower - the one who narrates from a *Ṣaḥaabi*) who narrated this hadith from Anas.

abhorrent habit will be among the worst people on the Day of Judgement, as the Prophet (ﷺ) explained:

> "The most evil of people in the sight of Allah on the Day of Resurrection will be a man who was intimate with his wife, then went and told others about her secrets."[165]

Private matters should remain utterly secret, known only to those concerned. No-one broadcasts his private matters except the person who is somewhat crazy, stupid and unsound, and whose attitude is dirty, cheap and shameless. Muslim men and women are protected from such folly by the noble characteristics that they have learned from their religion.

She is of cheerful countenance

It is clear to the Muslim woman that one of the most important factors in her success both in her private life with her husband and in her social life in general, is that she should be of cheerful countenance, smiling often and overflowing with warmth. All of this will endear her to people and open their hearts to her. It is also the good attitude, positive personality and physical attractiveness encouraged by Islam. Muslim reported that the Prophet (ﷺ) said:

> "Do not think little of any good deed, even if it is just meeting your brother with a cheerful countenance."[166]

The Prophet (ﷺ) taught that the Muslim should smile at his brother, and he never met any of his *Ṣaḥaabah* without smiling at them, as is reported in the hadith of the great *Ṣaḥaabi* Jareer ibn 'Abdullah, who said:

---

[165] Muslim, 10/8, *Kitaab an-Nikaaḥ, baab taḥreem ifsha' sirr al-mar'ah.*

[166] Muslim, 16/177, *Kitaab al-Birr waṣ-Ṣilah wal-Aadaab, baab istiḥbaab ṭalaaqat al-wajh.*

> "The Prophet never refused to see me, after I embraced Islam, and he never saw me without smiling at me."[167]

The Muslim woman who is cheerful and smiles a lot brings joy to her husband's heart, which increases his love and respect for her. This is also the attitude which she brings to the social circle of women with whom she mixes: nothing spreads love and affection in a community like a smiling face and a happy and content soul. These are the characteristics which are most befitting to the gentle, polite Muslim woman who seeks to call others to Islam, because it is through these attitudes that she will be able to reach people's hearts.

She is lighthearted and has a sense of humour

The true Muslim woman is lighthearted and has a sense of humour. She is kind in her treatment of others and gentle in her speech. She does not disdain to joke with her sisters and friends on appropriate occasions. But the Muslim woman's jokes are distinguished by their legitimate Islamic nature, and never sink to the level of being cheap, dirty or stupid.

The Prophet (ﷺ) used to joke with his Companions, but his jokes never went beyond the bounds of truth. It was narrated that the *Ṣaḥaabah* said to the Prophet (ﷺ): "You joke with us." He said,

> "But I never say anything except the truth."[168]

The *Ṣaḥaabah* took the same approach to humour. There are many delightful and entertaining reports about the jokes exchanged between the Prophet (ﷺ) and his Companions.

---

[167] *Fatḥ al-Baari*, 10/504, *Kitaab al-Adab, baab at-tabassum waḍ-ḍaḥk*; Muslim, 16/35, *Kitaab Faḍaa'il aṣ-Ṣaḥaabah, baab faḍaa'il Jareer ibn 'Abdullah.*

[168] Bukhari in *Al-Adab al-Mufrad*, 1/365, *baab al-mazaaḥ.*

Among the reports related in the books of hadith and *seerah* is that which tells of how the Prophet (ﷺ) used to joke with the small child of one of his *Ṣaḥaabah*, a boy called Abu 'Umayr, who had a little bird he used to play with. One day he saw the child looking sad, so he asked,

> "Why do I see Abu 'Umayr looking sad?" The *Ṣaḥaabah* told him, "The nughar[169] which he used to play with has died, O' Messenger of Allah." The Prophet (ﷺ) began to gently joke with the child, saying, "O' Abu 'Umayr, what happened to the nughayr?"[170]

A man came to the Prophet (ﷺ) to ask him to give him a beast to ride. The Prophet (ﷺ) jokingly told him:

> "I will give you the offspring of a she-camel to ride." He said, "O' Messenger of Allah, what shall I do with the offspring of a she-camel? The Prophet (ﷺ) said: "Are riding-camels born except from she-camels?"[171]

Imam Aḥmad reported from Anas (رضي الله عنه) that there was a man from the desert people whose name was Zaahir. He used to bring gifts from the desert to the Prophet (ﷺ), and in return the Prophet (ﷺ) would provide him with whatever he needed when he went out to fight. The Prophet (ﷺ) said:

> "Zaahir is our man of the desert, and we are his town-dwellers." The Prophet loved him very much, and he (Zaahir) was an ugly man. One day the Prophet came to him whilst he was selling some goods. He embraced

---

[169] Nughar: a small bird, like a sparrow. (Author)

[170] Nughayr: diminutive of nughar (Author). In Arabic, this is play on words because of the rhyme between the boy's name and that of the bird. (Translator) This story was narrated in *Ḥayaat aṣ-Ṣaḥaabah*, 3/149.

[171] Bukhari in *Al-Adab al-Mufrad*, 1/366, *baab al-mazaaḥ*.

> him from behind. The man could not see him, so he said, "Let me go! Who is this?" Then he turned around and recognised the Prophet, so he tried to move closer to him once he knew who it was. The Prophet started saying, "Who will buy this slave?" Zaahir said, "O' Messenger of Allah, you will find me unsellable." The Prophet said, "But in the sight of Allah you are not unsellable," or he said, "But in the sight of Allah you are valuable."[172]

An old woman came to the Prophet (ﷺ) and said, "O' Messenger of Allah, pray to Allah that I will enter Paradise." He said jokingly,

> 'O' Mother of So-and-so, no old women will enter Paradise.' The old woman went away crying, so the Prophet said: 'Tell her that she will not enter Paradise as an old woman, for Allah says:
> '*We have created [their companions] of special creation, and made them virgin-pure [and undefiled].*'
> *(Qur'an 56: 35-36).*'"[173]

One of the hadith that reflect the Prophet's sense of humour and enjoyment of fun is the report narrated by Imam Aḥmad from 'Aa'ishah (رضي الله عنها), who said: "I went out with the Prophet (ﷺ) on a journey. At that time I was still young and was quite slender. The Prophet (ﷺ) told the people, 'Go on ahead,' and they went on ahead, then he said to me, 'Come, let us have a race.' So I raced with him, and I won. He let the matter rest until I had gained weight. Later, I accompanied him on another journey. He told the people, 'Go on ahead,' and they went on ahead. He said to me, 'Come, let us have a

---

172 Aḥmad; the men of its isnad are *rijaal aṣ-ṣaḥeeḥ*. See *Majma' az-Zawaa'id*, 9/368, *baab maa jaa' fi Zaahir ibn Ḥizaam.*

173 Tirmidhi in *Ash-Shama'il*, 111; it is *ḥasan* because of the existence of corroborating reports.

race.' So I raced with him, and he won. He began to laugh, and said, 'This is for that.'"[174]

The Prophet (ﷺ), the Imam, the leader and teacher of the Muslims, liked to joke and have fun sometimes, no matter how busy he was with the burdens of leadership and the effort to establish the Islamic state, direct the forces of jihad, and so on. All of this did not keep him from engaging in entertaining jokes and lighthearted fun that would make his Companions — or his wives, on other occasions — feel happy.

Another example is the report narrated by 'Aa'ishah (رضي الله عنها), who said: "I came to the Prophet (ﷺ) with some *ḥareerah* (a dish made with flour and milk) that I had cooked for him, and told Sawdah (رضي الله عنها), as the Prophet (ﷺ) was sitting between me and her — 'Eat.' She refused, so I said, 'Either you eat, or I will fill your face!' She still refused, so I put my hand in the *ḥareerah* and daubed her face with it. The Prophet (ﷺ) laughed, put some *ḥareerah* in her hand, and said,

'Do the same to her!'"

According to another report: "He lowered his knee (moved out of the way) so that she could get her own back on me, then she took some from the plate and wiped my face with it, and the Prophet (ﷺ) laughed."[175]

These reports are a clear indication of the tolerance of Islam and its followers, and of the kind of lightheartedness and humour that it wants to see in the Muslims. It is a quality that is liked in the serious Muslim woman, for it adds beauty, attraction and influence to her character.

---

174 Aḥmad, 6/264 and Abu Dawood, 3/41, *Kitaab al-Jihad, baab fi as-sabaq 'ala ar-rajul.*

175 Abu Ya'la; the men of its isnad are *rijaal aṣ-ṣaḥeeḥ*, except for Muhammad ibn 'Amr ibn 'Alqamah, whose hadith is *ḥasan*. See *Majma' az-Zawaa'id*, 4/316.

She tries to make people happy

The Muslim woman is keen, in her conversations with other women, to bring happiness to them and make them feel cheerful and lively by means of the good news and pleasant jokes that she tells them. Making people happy, within the framework of that which is permitted, is an Islamic duty that is strongly encouraged, so that the environment of the believers, men and women, may be filled with friendliness, happiness and joy, ready to undertake serious work and the sacrifices and difficulties that it entails.

For this reason Islam tells us that the reward of one who makes Muslims happy will be the greater happiness that Allah (ﷻ) will bestow upon him on the Day of Resurrection:

> "Whoever meets his Muslim brother and makes him happy with something that Allah likes, Allah will make him happy on the Day of Resurrection."[176]

The clever Muslim woman will find different ways to make her sisters happy in ways that are permitted — a warm greeting, a kind word, a clever comment, a pleasant joke, good news, a friendly smile, a sincere visit, a charming gift, always keeping in touch, sincere help, comforting consolation — which will open their hearts, sow the seeds of love and strengthen the ties of friendship and sisterhood.

She is not over-strict

Another of the qualities of the true Muslim woman is that she is not over-strict, and does not go to extremes with regard to matters that Islam has permitted on certain occasions, such as the singing that is permitted on *'Eid* and at weddings, or watching some entertaining

---

[176] Reported with a *ḥasan* isnad by Ṭabaraani in *Aṣ-Ṣagheer*. See *Majma' az-Zawaa'id*, 8/193, *baab faḍl qaḍa' al-ḥawa'ij*.

games or sports, so long as they are not accompanied by any form of corruption that may lead to *fitnah*.

Although she may accept to watch or join in entertainment on certain occasions, she does not make this her main concern in life. She follows the teachings of Islam which permit fun and entertainment on occasion, as is reported in a number of *ṣaḥeeḥ* hadith.

In *Ṣaḥeeḥ* Bukhari, 'Aa'ishah (رضي الله عنها) is reported to have arranged a marriage for a woman who was an orphan under her care, to a man of the Anṣaar. The Prophet (ﷺ) asked her:

> "O' 'Aa'ishah, what sort of fun and entertainment do you have? For the Anṣaar love fun and entertainment."[177]

Imam Bukhari also narrates from 'Aa'ishah: "The Prophet (ﷺ) came to me when there were two young girls singing the songs of Bu'ath[178]. He lay down on his bed and turned his face away. Then Abu Bakr entered, and told me off, saying: 'Musical instruments of *Shayṭaan* in the house of the Prophet!' The Messenger of Allah (ﷺ) turned to him and said: 'Let them be.' When he was no longer paying attention, I signalled to them, and they left."[179]

According to another report, also narrated by Bukhari, the Prophet (ﷺ) said:

> "O' Abu Bakr, every nation has a day of festival celebration, and this is our day of celebration."[180]

---

177 *Fatḥ al-Baari*, 9/225, *Kitaab an-Nikaaḥ, baab an-niswah allaati yahdeena al-mar'ah ila zawjiha.*

178 Bu'ath: A place in the environs of Madeenah where war took place between the Aws and Khazraj before Islam. It was known as the battle of Bu'ath, and poets composed many verses about it. (Author)

179 *Fatḥ al-Baari*, 2/440, *Kitaab al-'Eidayn, baab al-ḥiraab wad-daraq yawm al-'eid.*

180 *Fatḥ al-Baari*, 2/445, *Kitaab al-'Eidayn, baab sunnah al-'eidayn li ahl al-Islam.*

Another report narrated by Bukhari from 'Aa'ishah says:

> "It was the day of *'Eid*, and the black people were playing with shields and spears. Either I asked the Prophet (ﷺ), or he said to me: 'Would you like to watch?' I said, 'Yes.' So he let me stand behind him, his cheek against my cheek, and he was saying, 'Carry on, O' Banu Arfidah[181]!' When I got tired, he asked me, 'Have you had enough?' I said, 'Yes.' He said, 'Then go.'"[182]

Ibn Ḥajar reported a number of versions of this hadith from 'Aa'ishah, such as that recorded by Az-Zuhri:

> "...Until I ('Aa'ishah) was the one who had had enough."[183]

Muslim also narrates from Az-Zuhri:

> "Then he stayed standing there for my sake until I was the one who decided to leave."[184]

Nasaa'i reports from Yazeed ibn Rooman:

> "The Prophet (ﷺ) said: 'Have you had enough? Have you had enough?' She said, 'I decided to say No, just to see how where I stood with him (i.e. how much he loved me).'"[185]

Nasaa'i reports from Abu Salamah from 'Aa'ishah: "I said, 'O' Messenger of Allah, do not rush.' So he remained standing for my

---

181 Banu Arfidah: A nickname given to Abyssinians. (Author)

182 *Fatḥ al-Baari*, 2/440, *Kitaab al-'Eidayn, baab al-ḥiraab wad-daraq yawm al-'eid.*

183 Ibid, 2/444.

184 Opt. cit.

185 Ibid.

sake, then said, 'Have you had enough?' I said, 'Do not rush.' ...It was not that I wanted to watch them, but I wanted all the women to know how I stood with him."

In the chapter on marriage, there is a report narrated by Az-Zuhri which adds:

> "You should understand that young girls like to have fun."[186]

In *Fatḥ al-Baari*[187] As-Siraaj reports via Abu az-Zinaad from 'Urwah from 'Aa'ishah that the Prophet (ﷺ) said on that day:

> "Let the Jews know that in our religion there is room for entertainment, and I have been sent with a tolerant, pure religion."

Tirmidhi reports in his *Sunan* that 'Aa'ishah (رضي الله عنها) said:

> "The Prophet was sitting, and we heard some noise and children's voices outside. The Prophet stood up, and saw an Abyssinian woman dancing, with children around her. He said, 'O' 'Aa'ishah, come and see!' So I came, and put my chin on his shoulder, looking through the gap between his head and his shoulder. He asked me, 'Have you had enough?' and I decided to say 'No,' just to see where I stood with him. Suddenly 'Umar appeared, and the people scattered. The Prophet said: 'I can see that the devils among jinn and mankind flee from 'Umar!' 'Aa'ishah said: 'Then I went back.'"[188]

---

[186] See the reports given in *Fatḥ al-Baari*, 2/444.

[187] *Fatḥ al-Baari*, 2/444, *Kitaab al-'Eidayn, baab al-ḥiraab wad-daraq yawm al-'eid.*

[188] Tirmidhi: *Manaaqib 'Umar*. He said: it is a *ḥasan ṣaḥeeḥ ghareeb* hadith; this version is *ghareeb*. See 5/621, *Kitaab al-Manaaqib*, 18.

These and similar texts, as understood in the books of hadith, are clear evidence of the Prophet's kind and gentle treatment to his wife, and his eagerness to make her happy. They are also proof of the tolerance and ease of Islam, and its concern that women should be allowed to enjoy the kinds of fun and entertainment that it has permitted, unlike some of those overstrict people nowadays who regard such fun as a serious crime for which women should be severely punished by being imprisoned (in the home).

The Muslim woman who understands the teachings of Islam should be very serious in her attitude, concentrating on noble aims and shunning frivolities. But this should not stop her from having fun occasionally, in ways that are permitted by Islam, which leaves room for such entertainment. The wise Lawgiver understands the nature of people and their inclination to relax and have fun from time to time, so that they can then return refreshed to their serious pursuits, with renewed vigour, stronger determination, and more prepared to shoulder the burdens of their responsibilities. This is the balanced, integrated, wise approach that Islam brings.

She is not arrogant or proud

The true Muslim woman is not arrogant or proud; she does not look down her nose at other women who may be inferior to her in terms of beauty, wealth, lineage or status, because the Muslim woman who understands the teachings of Islam knows that arrogance and pride in this world will deny a woman the blessings of the Hereafter, which Allah (ﷻ) will deny to men and women who are arrogant. These blessings are only for those who shun arrogance and pride in this world:

> "*That House of the Hereafter We shall give to those who intend not high-handedness or mischief on earth: and the End is [best] for the righteous.*" *(Qur'an 28: 83)*

She also knows that Allah (ﷻ) does not love those who arrogantly boast:

> "*And swell not your cheek [for pride] at men, nor walk in insolence through the earth: for Allah loves not any arrogant boaster.*" *(Qur'an 31: 18)*

Whoever examines the hadith texts will be astonished at the attention given by the Prophet (ﷺ) to eradicating arrogance from people's hearts by forbidding it, deterring it and warning those men and women who were afflicted with it that they stand to lose everything in the Hereafter for the sake of an atom's-weight (a speck of ash's-weight) of pride that the *Shayṭaan* has placed in their hearts. Such people are among the arrogant ones to whom Allah (ﷻ) has denied entry to Paradise, as is stated in the hadith narrated by Muslim:

> "No one will enter Paradise who has an atom's-weight of pride in his heart." A man asked, "What if a man likes his clothes and his shoes to look good?" He said, "Allah is Beautiful and loves beauty (i.e. wanting to look good is not pride or arrogance). Pride is denying the truth and despising people."[189]

Ḥarithah ibn Wahb (رضي الله عنه) said: "I heard the Messenger of Allah (ﷺ) say:

> 'Shall I not tell you about the people of Hell? Everyone who is harsh, proud, disdainful and arrogant.'"[190]

It is enough for those arrogant, proud women who boast to their friends to know of the moral humiliation that Allah, the Almighty, All-Powerful, has prepared for them in the Hereafter: Allah (ﷻ) will

---

[189] Muslim, 2/89, *Kitaab al-Eemaan, baab taḥreem al-kibr.*

[190] (Bukhari and Muslim), See *Riyaḍ aṣ-Ṣaliheen*, 334, *baab taḥreem al-kibr wal-i'jaab.*

not even look at them or speak to them or praise them, and this will be the ultimate humiliation.

The Prophet (ﷺ) said:

> "On the Day of Resurrection, Allah will not look at those who let their garments trail on the ground out of arrogance."[191]

> "There are three whom Allah will not speak to, or praise, or look at on the Day of Judgement, and they will have a severe punishment: an old man who commits adultery, a king who tells lies, and a poor man who is arrogant."[192]

Pride is one of the divine attributes and weak human creatures have no right to it. Those who are arrogant and proud transgress into the realm of the divine, vying with the Almighty Creator for one of His sublime attributes, so they deserve the severe punishment to which the Prophet (ﷺ) referred:

> "Allah says: 'Might is My cloak and pride is My garment. Whoever vies with Me for either of them, I will punish him.'"[193]

Many hadiths warn the believers against being tempted by pride at moments of human weakness. The Prophet (ﷺ) used various methods to warn them so that the pious believers would be protected from the awful disease of arrogance. For example:

---

[191] (Bukhari and Muslim), See *Sharḥ as-Sunnah*, 12/9, *Kitaab al-Libaas, baab taqṣeer al-thiyaab.*

[192] Muslim, 2/115, *Kitaab al-Eemaan, baab bayaan al-thalatha alladhina la yukallimuhum Allah yawm al-qiyaamah.*

[193] Muslim, 16/173, *Kitaab al-Birr waṣ-Ṣilah wal-Aadaab, baab taḥreem al-kibr*; also narrated by Bukhari: *Al-Adab al-Mufrad*, 2/9, *baab al-kibr.*

> "Whoever thinks highly of himself, or walks with an arrogant attitude, will meet Allah when He is angry with him."[194]

She is humble and modest

It comes as no surprise that the Muslim woman who understands anything of the teachings of Islam should be humble and modest, gentle, tolerant and kind in her dealings with others. She finds hadiths which compliment those that warn men and women against arrogance, texts that encourage modesty and humility, promising everyone who humbles himself for the sake of Allah that he or she will be raised in status, as the Prophet (ﷺ) said in the hadith narrated by Muslim:

> "No one is humble for the sake of Allah, but Allah will raise him in status."[195]
>
> "Allah told me that you should be so humble towards one another that no one should boast to anyone else and no one should oppress anyone."[196]

The Muslim woman who studies the life of the Prophet (ﷺ) will find in his sublime character a unique, living example of modesty, humility, gentleness, genuineness, noble attitudes and tolerance. Whenever he passed a group of boys playing, he would stop and greet them, joking naturally with them. His high status as Prophet and leader of the ummah did not prevent him from being spontaneous and natural with others.

---

194 Bukhari: *Al-Adab al-Mufrad*, 2/7, *baab al-kibr.*

195 Muslim, 16/141, *Kitaab al-Birr waṣ-Ṣilah wal-Adab, baab istiḥbaab al-'afu wat-tawaaḍu'.*

196 Muslim, 18/200, *Kitaab al-Jannah waṣ Ṣifat na'imiha wa ahliha, baab aṣ-ṣifaat allati yu'raf biha fid-dunya ahl al-jannah.*

Anas (اللَّه) said that he passed by a group of children and greeted them. He added, "The Prophet (ﷺ) used to do that."[197]

Anas gave another account of the Prophet's humility: he reported that one of the slave-women of Madeenah used to take the Prophet's hand and lead him about wherever she wanted, until he had sorted out her needs.[198]

Tameem ibn Usayd came to Madeenah to ask about the rules of Islam. He was a stranger, but he did not find any barrier or guard between him and the Prophet (ﷺ), the first man in the Islamic state, who was on the *minbar* addressing the people. Tameem came forward to ask some questions, and the Prophet (ﷺ) welcomed him with all warmth, humility and compassion. Tameem tells the story, as was related by Imam Muslim:

> "I came to the Prophet whilst he was giving a speech. I said, 'O' Messenger of Allah, a stranger has come to ask about his religion; he does not know what his religion is.' The Prophet welcomed me, interrupted his speech, and came to me. A chair was brought for him, so he sat down and began to teach me from what Allah had taught him. Then he resumed his speech and finished what he had been saying."[199]

The Prophet (ﷺ) used to instill the attitude of humility, based on tolerance, gentleness and a good nature, in the hearts of his Companions. He (ﷺ) said:

> "If I were to be invited to a simple meal of a sheep's foot or leg, or if I were to be offered this food as a gift, I would accept."[200]

---

[197] (Bukhari and Muslim), See *Riyaḍ aṣ-Ṣaliḥeen*, 331, *baab at-tawaḍu'*.

[198] *Fatḥ al-Baari*, 10/489, *Kitaab al-Adab, baab al-kibr.*

[199] Muslim, 6/165, *Kitaab al-Jumu'ah, baab at-ta'leem fil-khuṭbah.*

[200] *Fatḥ al-Baari*, 5/199, *Kitaab al-Hibbah, baab al-qaleel min al-hibbah.*

This is modesty in its purest form and human greatness of the highest degree.

She is moderate with regard to her clothing and appearance

The Muslim woman who understands the teachings of Islam adheres to the principle of modesty in all things, and especially in the way she dresses and looks. She is keen to look good, but without any extravagance, excess or conceit. She does not blindly follow those who throw aside new clothes after wearing them only once and exhaust themselves trying to keep up with the latest fashion, which is forever changing, as is the habit of some foolish, ignorant women who have nothing better to do. On the other hand, she does not neglect her clothes or appearance, and she tries to look good in moderation.

She abides by the limits of moderation set out in the Qur'an, which describes moderation as one of the qualities of the believing servants of Allah, men and women alike:

> "*Those who, when they spend, are not extravagant and not niggardly, but hold a just [balance] between those [extremes].*" *(Qur'an 25: 67)*

The Muslim woman is careful not to fall victim to the enslavement of fashion and those behind it, the people who have no fear of Allah and do not have the best interests of women — especially Muslim women — at heart. She is careful to avoid this enslavement which the Prophet (ﷺ) warned against and told us that it is a source of great misery:

> "Wretched is the slave of the *dinaar, dirham* and fancy clothes of velvet and silk! If he is given, he is pleased, and if he is not given, he is displeased."[201]

---

[201] *Fatḥ al-Baari*, 6/81, *Kitaab al-Jihad, baab al-ḥirasah fil-ghazu fi sabeel-Allah.*

The Muslim woman is protected by the teachings of Islam from falling into the error of arrogance or conceit regarding her appearance, and other deeds which may lead to a person's downfall, as the Prophet (ﷺ) said:

> "There was a man who walked with pride because of his fine cloak and because he was pleased with himself. Allah caused him to sink in the earth, and he will go on sinking into it until the Day of Resurrection."[202]

The Muslim woman uses means of adornment that are within the limits of what is permitted by Islam. She wears elegant, expensive clothes, which are among the good things permitted by Allah (سبحانه وتعالى), without going to extremes of excess. This is the moderation advocated and encouraged by Islam, and there is a huge difference between the wise, moderate woman, and the foolish, empty-headed woman who goes to extremes.

The Muslim woman avoids both extremes with regard to her dress and appearance. She does not exaggerate or go to extreme limits of excess, neither does she neglect her clothes and appearance to the point of appearing to be miserly or ascetic, thinking that this asceticism is a form of worship that will earn her the pleasure of Allah.

The woman who wears beautiful clothes to show off in front of her friends is a sinner, because Allah does not love every arrogant boaster. But the one who wears beautiful clothes to display the bounty of Allah and seeking His help, is an obedient servant who will be rewarded.

The one who neglects her appearance out of stinginess enjoys no position of respect among people, and will have no reward from

---

[202] Muslim, 14/64, *Kitaab al-Libaas waz-Zeenah, baab taḥreem at-tabakhtur fil-mashee.*

Allah (ﷻ). The one who neglects her appearance out of an attitude of other-worldliness, thinking that she is worshipping Allah by denying herself what is permitted, is also a sinner, as *Shaykh al-Islam* Ibn Taymiyah, may Allah have mercy on him, said.[203] The essence of a woman's happiness in this world and the next is purposefulness, moderation and balance. This is the attitude of the Muslim woman who understands and adheres to the teachings of Islam. So her clothes are clean, beautiful, neat and suited to the Muslim woman, demonstrating Allah's blessings to her without going to the extreme of showing off.

She loves noble things and always aims high

The Muslim woman who understands the teachings of Islam is concerned only with noble matters, and shuns those trivial, cheap matters that do not deserve the attention of the serious, refined person. She builds her relationships with other women on this basis of high concerns and noble aims. She has no room in her life for making friends with foolish, empty-headed prattlers or for keeping busy with trivial matters. She has no time to spend on idle talk and foolish issues. This is what Allah (ﷻ) loves to see in His believing servants, men and women, as the Prophet (ﷺ) said:

> "Allah is noble (*Kareem*) and loves noble people. He loves noble things and hates foolishness."[204]

She is concerned about the affairs of the Muslims

The Muslim woman who truly understands the teachings of Islam is not concerned only with her own household, husband and children;

---

[203] *Fataawa Ibn Taymiyah*, 22/138, 139.

[204] Ṭabaraani: *Al-Kabeer*; the men of its isnad are *thiqaat*. See *Majma' az-Zawaa'id*, 8/188, *baab makaarim al-akhlaaq*.

she takes an interest in the affairs of the Muslims in general. By doing so she is following the guidance of Islam which counts all Muslims as a single brotherhood, and compares them, because of their mutual love, affection and compassion, to a single body: if one part of it suffers, the rest of the body will stay awake in pain.[205] Islam also likens the believers to a solid structure, in which some bricks support others.[206]

The modern Muslim woman's concern for Muslim individuals, families, societies and the ummah as a whole, stems from her Islamic character, her adherence to the teachings of Islam, her Islamic world-view, and her sense of the responsibilities that Islam has given to every Muslim man and woman to convey and expound its teachings.

Islamic history is filled with many examples of virtuous women who were renowned for their concern about the Muslims, men and women. One example is the report given by Imam Muslim from Saalim, the freed slave of Shaddaad, who said:

> "I went to the house of 'Aa'ishah, the wife of the Prophet on the day that Sa'd ibn Abi Waqqaas died. 'Abdur-Raḥmaan ibn Abi Bakr also came in, and performed *wuḍoo'* in 'Aa'ishah's presence. She said, 'O' 'Abdur-Raḥmaan! Perform your *wuḍoo'* properly, as I heard the Messenger of Allah say: 'Woe to the heels because of Hell-fire.'""[207]

'Aa'ishah noticed that her brother 'Abdur-Raḥmaan had not washed his heels properly in *wuḍoo'*, and she did not keep silent about what she had seen. She reminded him that it was essential to perform

---

[205] Muslim, 16/140, *Kitaab al-Birr waṣ-Ṣilah wal-Aadaab, baab taraaḥum al-mu'mineen wa ta'aṭufihim.*

[206] Ibid, 16/139.

[207] Muslim, 3/128, *Kitaab aṭ-Ṭaharah, baab wujoob ghusl ar-rijlayn.*

wuḍoo' properly, as she had heard from the Prophet (ﷺ). This is an example of the kind of commendable concern that is the duty of every Muslim man and woman whenever there is a need to enjoin what is good or forbid what is evil.

When 'Umar ibn al-Khaṭṭab (رضي الله عنه), the second *khaleefah* (Caliph) of the Muslims, was stabbed, and he felt that death was near, he told his son 'Abdullah: "Go to 'Aa'ishah, say *salaam* to her, and ask her permission for me to be buried in her house alongside the Messenger of Allah (ﷺ) and Abu Bakr. So 'Abdullah came to her and conveyed this message. She said, 'Certainly, he is most welcome.' Then she said: 'O' my son, convey my *salaam* to 'Umar, and tell him: 'Do not leave the ummah of Muhammad without a protector. Appoint a successor to take care of them. Do not leave them untended after your death, for I fear *fitnah* for them.''''"[208]

This was a far-sighted, common-sense attitude of concern for the ummah, that they should not be left without a leader to govern their affairs and maintain their unity and security.

In these words of 'Aa'ishah (رضي الله عنها), the modern Muslim woman has a prime example which will help her to understand the essence of Islam, her responsibilities towards her religion and her ummah, and the importance of being concerned about the affairs of the Muslims. This will give her insight and understanding that will enable her to undertake her duties of contributing to the revival of Islam and calling Muslim men and women to return to the position of being the Best of Peoples evolved for mankind, as Allah (سبحانه وتعالى) wants them to be.

She honours her guest

The true Muslim woman is happy to welcome guests, and hastens to honour them, in response to the call of faith in Allah (سبحانه وتعالى) and the Last

---

208 *Ṭabaqaat Ibn Ṣa'd,* 3/363.

Day, as the Prophet (ﷺ) said:

> "Whoever believes in Allah and the Last Day, let him honour his guest."[209]

The Muslim woman who honours her guest thus confirms that she is a believer in Allah and the Last Day. Therefore this honouring of the guest is called a reward that is given to the guest as if thanking him for the opportunity he has given to his host to do a good deed, put his faith into practice, and please Allah (ﷻ):

> "Whoever believes in Allah and the Last Day, let him honour his guest by giving him his reward.' They asked, 'What is his reward, O' Messenger of Allah?' He said: 'One day and one night. The right of hospitality is three days, and anything beyond that is an act of charity.'"[210]

Honouring guests is regarded in Islam as a great deed which is encouraged, and for which the sincere Muslim woman will be rewarded. But Islam regulated it and set limits for it. The "reward" of the guest is one day and one night, then comes the duty of hospitality, which is three days. Anything beyond that is an act of charity which will be recorded among the good deeds of the hospitable, generous woman.

In Islam, honouring the guest is not a matter of choice to be followed or not according to one's mood or personal feelings. It is a duty on the Muslim, man or woman, who must hasten to fulfil this duty as soon as a guest knocks at the door or enters one's yard:

---

[209] (Bukhari and Muslim), See *Sharḥ as-Sunnah*, 14/312, *Kitaab ar-Riqaaq, baab ḥifẓ al-lisaan.*

[210] (Bukhari and Muslim), See *Riyaḍ aṣ-Ṣaliḥeen*, 379, *Kitaab al-Adab, baab ikraam al-ḍayf.*

> "Accommodating a guest for one night is an absolute duty on every Muslim. Whoever gets up in the morning and finds a guest waiting in his yard has a duty to fulfil, and it is up to him what he will do about it."[211]

Those who do not like to receive a guest and close their doors to him are not good people, as is stated in the hadith reported by Imam Aḥmad, in which the Prophet (ﷺ) said:

> "There is no goodness in the one who is not hospitable."[212]

Islam has made hospitality the duty of every Muslim man and woman, and considers it to be the guest's right. No Muslim should fall short in carrying out this duty. If a spirit of miserliness has overtaken a people to the extent that they deny their guest his right, then Islam permits the guest to take his right from them. This is seen in the hadith narrated by Bukhari, Muslim and others from 'Uqbah ibn 'Aamir, who said:

> "I said, 'O' Messenger of Allah, you are sending us to people who do not feed us. What do you think about this?' He said, 'If you go to a people and they order that something appropriate be brought (i.e., food and drink), then accept it, and if they do not do that, then take the things you, as a guest, are entitled to, that they should have provided.'"[213]

Hospitality is a basic Islamic attitude, so you will never find a Muslim woman whose Islam is genuine being stingy to her guest, no matter what her or her husband's circumstances. Islam has taught her

---

211 Bukhari: *Al-Adab al-Mufrad*, 2/207, *baab ja'izah aḍ-ḍayf.*

212 Imam Aḥmad, 4/155; its men are *rijaal aṣ-ṣaḥeeḥ.*

213 Bukhari, Muslim and others. See *Al-Adab al-Mufrad*, 2/210, *baab idha aṣbaha aḍ-ḍayf maḥrooman.*

that the food of two people will feed three, and that the food of three will feed four. So she need never worry about an unexpected guest knocking suddenly at her door. Abu Hurayrah (ﷺ) said: "The Messenger of Allah (ﷺ) said:

> 'The food of two people is enough for three, and the food of three is enough for four.'"[214]

Jaabir (ﷺ) said: "I heard the Messenger of Allah (ﷺ) say:

> 'The food of one is enough for two, the food of two is enough for four, and the food of four is enough for eight.'"[215]

The Muslim woman whose personality has been cleansed and moulded by Islam does not worry about there being too many people at the table, unlike the Western woman who does not receive a guest for whom she has not prepared food in advance. The Muslim woman welcomes her guests even if the visit is unannounced, and invites them to share her family's food, no matter that her own share may be reduced by a few mouthfuls. The true Muslim woman prefers hunger to ignoring the rights of this guest, whom Allah (ﷻ) and His Messenger have commanded her to honour. Indeed, Allah will bless the food of one so that it will become enough for two, and He will bless the food of two so that it will become enough for four, and so on. There is no need for that dryness and inhospitability from which Western-influenced materialistic people are suffering in both East and West.

The righteous *salaf* set the highest example of honouring one's guest, so much so that Allah Himself commended the way in which some of

---

[214] (Bukhari and Muslim), See *Sharḥ as-Sunnah*, 11/320, *Kitaab al-Aṭ'imah, baab ṭa'am al-ithnayn yakfi ath-thalaathah.*

[215] Muslim, 14/22, *Kitaab al-Ashribah, baab faḍeelah al-mawaasat fit-ṭa'am al-qaleel.*

them honoured their guests. An example of this is the hadith narrated by Bukhari and Muslim from Abu Hurayrah. A man came to the Prophet (ﷺ) and he sent word to his wives (to prepare food). They said, "We have nothing but water." So the Prophet (ﷺ) said,

> "Who will play host to this man?" One of the Anṣaar said: "I will." So he took the man to his wife and told her: "Honour the guest of the Messenger of Allah." She said, "We do not have anything but the boys' food." He said, "Prepare the food, light the lamp, and put the boys to sleep if they want some supper." So she prepared the food, lit the lamp, and put the boys to sleep. Then she got up as if to adjust the lamp, but she extinguished it. The couple pretended to eat (with their guest), but in fact they went to bed hungry. The next morning, the Anṣaari went to the Prophet, who told him: "Allah has commended what you two did last night." Allah revealed:
>
> "*But [they] give them preference over themselves, even though poverty was their [own lot]. And those saved from the covetousness of their own souls — they are the ones that achieve prosperity.*" *(Qur'an 59: 9)*[216]

The Muslim woman is generous and hospitable, she welcomes guests no matter when they arrive, and never worries about the sudden arrival of guests. In this way she provides the best help to enable her husband to be generous and hospitable like her, welcoming guests and hastening to honour them with a cheerful, smiling face, as the poet[217] said:

> "I smile at my guest and make him smile before he brings in his luggage,

---

[216] *Fatḥ al-Baari*, 8/631, *Kitaab at-Tafseer, baab wa yu'thiroon 'ala anfusihim*; Muslim, 4/12, *Kitaab al-Ashribah, baab ikraam aḍ-ḍayf.*

[217] Ḥaatim aṭ-Ṭaa'iyy, as in *Al-'Aqad al-Fareed*, 1/236.

As if I had plenty to offer him at the time when I am suffering hardship.
Hospitality does not consist of piling up food in front of him;
The face of the generous man is the essence of hospitality."

She prefers others over herself

The true Muslim woman prefers others over herself, even if she is poor and does not have much, because Islam teaches its followers to do so. This selflessness is a basic characteristic of the true Muslim, which distinguishes him or her from other people.

The Anṣaar, (may Allah be pleased with them), were the first pioneers in selflessness after the Prophet (ﷺ) himself. A verse of the Qur'an was revealed commending their unique selflessness, which would remain for all time a shining example to humanity of how generosity and selflessness should be. They welcomed their *Muhaajireen* brothers, who had nothing, and gave them everything:

> "*But those who before them, had homes [in Madeenah] and had adopted the Faith — show their affection to such as came to them for refuge, and entertain no desire in their hearts for things given to the [latter], but give them preference over themselves, even though poverty was their [own lot]. And those saved from the covetousness of their own souls — they are the ones that achieve prosperity.*" *(Qur'an 59: 9)*

The life of the Prophet (ﷺ) abounded with selflessness, and he also instilled this attitude in the hearts of the first Muslims. Sahl ibn Sa'd (رضي الله عنه) reported:

> "A woman brought a woven garment (*burdah*) and said, 'I wove it with my own hands for you to wear.' The Prophet took it, as he needed it. He came out to us,

wearing it wrapped around his waist. So-and-so said, 'Give it to me, how nice it is!' The Prophet said, 'Of course.' The Prophet was sitting in a gathering, and when he came back, he folded up the *burdah* and sent it to that man. The people told the man: 'You should not have done that. The Prophet wore it because he needed it, then you asked for it and you knew that he does not refuse requests.' He said, 'I did not ask for it so that I could wear it. I asked for it so that it could be my shroud.'" Sahl said: "And (later on) it was his shroud."[218]

The Prophet (ﷺ) used to feel happy whenever he saw his teaching of selflessness bearing fruits in the Muslims' lives when there was some crisis such as drought or famine. This is seen in his words:

"When a number of their men are killed in battle, or they do not have enough food for their children, the Ash'aris (a tribe) gather whatever they have in one cloth and share it out equally. They belong to me and I belong to them."[219]

How beautiful is the attitude of selflessness that we learn about from the Anṣaar, the Ash'aris and others like them! How great is the virtue of the Prophet (ﷺ) who implanted this attitude in the hearts of the first generation of Muslim men and women, from whom successive generations of Muslims inherited it until it became a basic characteristic of the Islamic society.

---

[218] *Fatḥ al-Baari*, 3/143, *Kitaab al-Janaa'iz, baab man ista'adda al-kafn* and 4/318, *Kitaab al-Buyu', baab an-nissaj.*

[219] (Bukhari and Muslim), See *Riyaḍ aṣ-Ṣaliḥeen*, 310, *baab al-ithaar wal-mawaasaat.*

She checks her customs and habits against Islamic standards

The Muslim woman who has insight into the rulings of Islam does not accept every tradition and custom that is widely accepted by others, for there may be customs that are derived from ancient or modern *jaahiliyah* (pre-Islamic) traditions which go against Islam. These are unacceptable to the Muslim woman, even if everybody else accepts them unanimously.

The Muslim woman does not decorate her house with statues or pictures (of animate objects), neither does she keep a dog at home, unless it is a guard dog, because the Prophet (ﷺ) has forbidden all of that. The *ṣaḥeeḥ* hadiths on this matter are very emphatic in their prohibition, and there is no room for prevarication or excuses.

Ibn 'Umar reported that the Prophet (ﷺ) said:

> "Those who make these images will be punished on the Day of Resurrection and will be told: 'Give life to that which you have created.'"[220]

'Aa'ishah (رضي الله عنها) said:

> "The Messenger of Allah returned from a journey, and I had covered a small window with a curtain that had images on it. When the Messenger of Allah saw it, his face changed colour (with anger) and he said, 'O' 'Aa'ishah! Those who will be the most severely punished by Allah on the Day of Resurrection will be those who imitated the creation of Allah.' She said: 'So we cut it up and made one or two pillows from it.'"[221]

---

220 (Bukhari and Muslim), See *Riyaḍ aṣ-Ṣaliḥeen*, 741, *Kitaab al-Umoor al-Munhi 'anha, baab taḥreem aṣ-ṣuwar.*

221 Ibid, 742.

Ibn 'Abbaas (ﷺ) said: "I heard the Messenger of Allah (ﷺ) say:

> 'Every maker of images will be in the Fire; every image that he made will be brought to life and will punish him in Hell.' Ibn 'Abbaas said: 'So if you must do that, make pictures of trees and inanimate objects.'"[222]

Abu Ṭalḥah (ﷺ) said that the Messenger of Allah (ﷺ) said:

> "The angels do not enter a house in which there is a dog or an image."[223]

'Aa'ishah (ﷺ) said:

> "Jibreel (Gabriel) promised to come to the Prophet at a certain time. That time came and went, and he did not come. The Prophet was holding a stick in his hand, which he threw aside, saying, 'Allah does not break His promise and neither do His Messengers.' Then he turned around and saw a puppy underneath his bed. He said, 'When did this dog get in?' I said, 'By Allah, I did not even notice it.' He gave orders that it should be taken out, and it was removed. Then Jibreel came to him, and the Messenger of Allah said, 'You promised to come and I was waiting for you, but you did not come.' He said, 'The dog that was in your house prevented me. We do not enter a house where there is a dog or an image.'"[224]

There are many hadiths which prohibit pictures and statues, and the wisdom behind this prohibition is apparent especially nowadays

---

[222] Ibid.

[223] Ibid, 743.

[224] Muslim, 14/81, *Kitaab al-Libaas waz-Zeenah, baab taḥreem ṭasweer al-ḥayawaan.*

when hypocrites, sycophants and those possessed by greed and ambition encourage tyrants in their oppression. One of their favoured methods is to erect statues to them, both during their lifetimes and after their deaths, thus turning them into gods and demigods seated on thrones of glory, whipping the backs of the oppressed.

Islam brought the doctrine of *Tawḥeed* (Islamic monotheism), and destroyed the statues of *shirk* (polytheism) and *jaahiliyah* (pre-Islamic period — time of ignorance) fifteen hundred years ago. It will not permit these graven images to come back into the lives of Muslim men and women, whether it be in the name of commemorating a leader, honouring an artist or glorifying a scientist, poet or writer. The Islamic society is a monotheistic society where glorification, sanctification and veneration are only for Allah (سُبْحَانَهُ وَتَعَالَى). So there is no room in the Islamic society for these statues and images.

As for keeping a dog is concerned, there is nothing wrong with that if the dog is kept for hunting or farming purposes, as in the hadith of Ibn 'Umar (رَضِيَ ٱللَّهُ عَنْهُ), who said: "I heard the Messenger of Allah (ﷺ) say:

> 'Whoever keeps a dog, unless it is a dog for hunting or herding livestock, his reward will decrease by two *qiraats* every day.'"[225]

Keeping dogs in the house after the Western fashion, spoiling them, manufacturing special food and shampoo for them, setting up "beauty parlours" for them and all the other things on which people in the West and the U.S. spend millions upon millions of dollars annually has nothing whatsoever to do with Islam and its tolerant customs. The psychological state of Westerners, and the dry, materialistic life they lead, had driven them to these extremes in caring for their dogs, to compensate for the lack of human love in

---

[225] (Bukhari and Muslim), See *Riyaḍ aṣ-Ṣaliḥeen*, 744, *Kitaab al-Umoor al-Munhi 'anha, baab taḥreem ittikhaadh al-kalb illa li ṣayd aw maashiyah.*

their social lives. But the social life of Islam is filled with human emotion, so Muslims have no need to go to such absurd extremes.[226]

The Muslim woman who understands the teachings of Islam does not eat or drink from vessels of gold or silver, no matter how rich she may be or how luxurious a life she may enjoy, because to do so is *ḥaraam* according to Islam. We find this prohibition in a number of definitive, *ṣaḥeeḥ* hadiths.

Umm Salamah (ﷺ) reported that the Prophet (ﷺ) said:

> "Whoever drinks from a vessel of silver, is as if he is throwing Hell-fire into his stomach."[227]

According to a report given by Muslim, the Prophet (ﷺ) said:

> "Whoever eats or drinks from vessels of gold or silver" — (in another report: whoever drinks from a vessel of gold or silver) — is as if he is throwing fire from Hell into his stomach."[228]

The alert Muslim woman, no matter where she lives, examines every custom that is followed in her society and measures it against the rulings, values and principles of Islam. Whatever is compatible with Islam, she accepts, but whatever contradicts Islam, she rejects outright, whether it is a custom relating to betrothal and marriage, or in family or social life. What matters is whether the custom is compatible with Islam, not how widely it is spread among people.

---

[226] See discussion of this deviation on chapter 9.

[227] (Bukhari and Muslim), See *Riyaḍ aṣ-Ṣaliḥeen*, 788, *Kitaab al-'Umoor al-Munhi 'anha, baab taḥreem isti'maal inaa' adh-dhahab wal-fiḍḍah.*

[228] Muslim, 14/29-30, *Kitaab al-Libaas waz-Zeenah, baab taḥreem isti'maal awani adh-dhahab wal-fiḍḍah.*

She follows Islamic manners in the way she eats and drinks

The alert Muslim woman is distinguished by her keenness to follow Islamic etiquette in the way she eats and drinks. If you were to see her at the table eating food, or if you saw the way she sets the table, you would know her by the Islamic manners that she has adopted in the way she eats, drinks and sets the table.

She does not begin to eat until she has mentioned the name of Allah (ﷻ), and she eats with her right hand from the food directly in front of her,[229] according to the teaching of the Prophet (ﷺ):

> "Mention the name of Allah, eat with your right hand, and eat from what is directly in front of you."[230]

If she forgets to mention the name of Allah (ﷻ) at the beginning of her meal, she will rectify that by saying: "*Bismillahi awwalahu wa akhirahu* (in the name of Allah at its beginning and at its end)," as is taught in the hadith narrated by 'Aa'ishah (رضي الله عنها): "The Messenger of Allah (ﷺ) said:

> 'Whenever any of you eats, let him mention the name of Allah, may He be glorified. If he forgets to mention the name of Allah at the beginning, let him say '*Bismillahi awwalahu wa akhirahu.*'''"[231]

The second issue is eating with the right hand. The Muslim woman who is acting according to Islamic manners eats and drinks with her

---

[229] The custom at the time of the Prophet (ﷺ) was for all present to eat from one dish or platter; this is still the custom in some Muslim countries. (Translator)

[230] (Bukhari and Muslim), See *Riyaḍ aṣ-Ṣaliḥeen*, 394, *Kitaab Aadaab aṭ-Ṭa'am, baab at-tasmiyah fi awwalihi wal-ḥamd fi aakhirihi.*

[231] Abu Dawood, 3/475, *Kitaab al-Aṭ'imah, baab at-tasmiyah*; Tirmidhi, 4/288, *Kitaab al-Aṭ'imah, baab maa jaa' fit-tasmiyah 'ala aṭ-ṭa'am.*

right hand. The commandment to eat with the right hand, and the prohibition of eating with the left hand, are clearly reported in numerous hadiths, for example:

> "When any one of you eats, let him eat with his right hand, and if he drinks, let him drink with his right hand, for the *Shayṭaan* eats with his left hand and drinks with his left hand."[232]

> "None of you should eat with his left hand or drink with his left hand, for the *Shayṭaan* eats with his left hand and drinks with his left hand." Naafi' added that the Prophet said: "Do not give or take with it (the left hand)."[233]

If the Prophet (ﷺ) saw anyone eating with his left hand, he would tell him to stop, and would teach him the proper manners. If the person arrogantly persisted, he would rebuke him more sternly and pray against him. Salamah ibn al-Akwa' (رضي الله عنه) said that a man ate with his left hand in the presence of the Prophet (ﷺ). He said,

> "Eat with your right hand." The man said, "I cannot." He said, "May you never be able to use it!" The only thing that stopped him was arrogance, and he never raised his right hand to his mouth after that.[234]

The Prophet (ﷺ) always liked to start things from the right, and he encouraged others to do likewise. Bukhari, Muslim and Maalik reported from Anas that the Prophet (ﷺ) was given some milk that had been mixed with water from the well. There was a Bedouin sitting on his right, and Abu Bakr aṣ-Ṣiddiq was sitting on his left. He

---

232 Muslim, 13/191, *Kitaab al-Ashribah, baab aadaab aṭ-ṭa'am wash-sharaab.*

233 Ibid, 13/192.

234 Opt. cit.

drank some of the milk, then he passed it to the Bedouin and said: "Start on the right and pass to the right."[235]

On one occasion, he asked a young boy [236] seated on his right to give up his turn for some elders, but the boy insisted on taking his turn and obtaining *barakah* (blessing) from the left-over of the Prophet (ﷺ), and the Prophet (ﷺ) did not criticize or rebuke him for doing so. Suhayl ibn Ṣa'd (رضي الله عنه) described the incident:

> "The Messenger of Allah was given something to drink, and he drank some of it. There was a young boy on his right, and some old men on his left. He asked the boy, 'Will you let me give some to these men?' The boy said, 'No, by Allah, I will not give up my share from you to anyone.' So the Messenger of Allah put it in his hand."[237]

There are many such reports and texts that definitively show that using the right hand is an important aspect of Islamic manners, which the true Muslim adopts readily and does not try to find excuses. This is what the *Saḥaabah* and *Taabi'een* used to do, without exception. When 'Umar ibn al-Khaṭṭab (رضي الله عنه) was the *Khaleefah* (Caliph), he used to patrol the city himself and check up on the people. Once, he saw a man eating with his left hand, so he told him, "O' servant of Allah, eat with your right hand." He saw him a second time eating with his left hand, so he hit him with his whip and said, "O' servant of Allah, eat with your right hand." He saw him a third time eating with his left hand, so he hit him with his whip and said angrily, "O' servant of Allah, your right hand!" The man replied, "O' *Ameer al-*

---

235 (Bukhari and Muslim), See *Sharḥ as-Sunnah*, 11/385, *Kitaab al-Ashribah, baab al-bidaa'h bil-ayman.*

236 This was Ibn 'Abbaas (Author).

237 (Bukhari and Muslim), See *Sharḥ as-Sunnah*, 11/386, *Kitaab al-Ashribah, baab al-bidaa'h bil-ayman.*

Mu'mineen, it is busy." 'Umar said, "What is keeping it busy?" He said, "The day of Mu'tah."[238] 'Umar began to weep, and came to the man apologizing and consoling him. He asked him, "Who helps you make *wuḍoo'*? Who helps you with what you need?" Then he ordered that the man should be treated fairly and taken care of.

'Umar's concern for this aspect of the conduct of one of the people demonstrates the importance of this apparently minor issue. It is indicative of the Muslim's personality and unique identity. 'Umar was very keen to apply this rule to the Muslims, so he did not allow them to take it lightly or ignore it.

I would like to address this to those Muslim ladies who have adopted Western table manners which dictate that the fork should be held in the left hand, and the knife in the right, so that the food is cut with the right hand and placed in the mouth with the left. These people follow this practice without adjusting it, so that they are eating with their left hands, contradictory to the teachings of their religion. They do not bother to move the fork to the right hand and the knife to the left, so that they may eat with their right hand, because they do not want to change this Western "etiquette." This is just one example of the moral defeat from which our ummah is suffering at the hands of modernism, which we are following slavishly without adjusting or adapting foreign customs to suit our own identity, religion and values. The true Muslim should be the furthest removed from such blind, ignorant imitation.

The true Muslim woman who is proud of her religion and its noble guidance in all aspects of life insists on eating with her right hand and calls on others to do likewise. She is not ashamed to announce it in gatherings where people still adhere slavishly to practices that have come from the West, so that she may explain it to those men and women who are ignorant and careless, and bring them back to their

---

238 i.e., he lost his hand in the battle of Mu'tah. (Author)

senses. Then they will follow the sunnah and eat and drink with their right hands.

With regard to the third issue, eating from what is nearest to one, this is in accordance with the Islamic manners of eating. The Prophet (ﷺ) clearly commanded this, along with mentioning the name of Allah (ﷻ) and eating with the right hand. It is recorded in numerous hadith, such as the report of ‘Umar ibn Abi Salamah (رضي الله عنه), who said: “I was a young boy under the care of the Messenger of Allah (ﷺ). My hand used to wander all over the plate, so the Prophet (ﷺ) told me,

> ‘O’ young boy, mention the name of Allah, eat with your right hand, and eat from what is directly in front of you.’”[239]

When the Muslim woman eats with her hand, she does so in a nice, good-mannered fashion, as the Prophet (ﷺ) used to do. He used to eat with just three fingers; he did not plunge his whole hand into the food in a way that would put others off. This was reported by Ka‘b ibn Maalik:

> “I saw the Messenger of Allah eating with three fingers, and when he had finished he would lick them.”[240]

The Prophet (ﷺ) commanded people to lick their fingers and clean their plates, as Jaabir (رضي الله عنه) reported that he (ﷺ) said:

> “You do not know where in the food is the blessing.”[241]

Anas (رضي الله عنه) said:

> “When the Messenger of Allah ate, he would lick his three fingers. He said: ‘If any of you drops a mouthful,

---

[239] (Bukhari and Muslim), See *Riyaḍ aṣ-Ṣaliḥeen*, 399, *Kitaab Aadaab aṭ-ṭa‘am, baab al-akl mimma yalih.*

[240] Muslim, 13/204, *Kitaab al-Ashribah, baab istiḥbab la‘q al-aṣaabi‘.*

[241] Ibid, 13/207.

> let him pick it up, remove the dirt, and eat it, and not leave it for the *Shayṭaan*.' He commanded us to clean our plates and said: 'You do not know in which part of your food is the blessing.'"[242]

Besides seeking the blessing in the food, this Prophetic teaching also encourages Muslims to clean their hands and their plates. Cleaning them of whatever food is left befits the person who is clean and well mannered, and is indicative of his or her sensitivity and good taste. The West has now adopted this good practice which was commanded by the Prophet (ﷺ) fifteen hundred years ago: nowadays the Europeans clear their plates and do not leave anything.

Of course, the sensitive, well-mannered Muslim woman does not eat noisily, making disgusting sounds, nor does she take large mouthfuls such as would cause her to make a revolting spectacle of herself.

When she has finished eating, she praises Allah (ﷻ) as the Prophet (ﷺ) taught us to do, thanking Allah for His blessing and seeking the reward of those who give praise and thanks.

Abu Umamah (رضي الله عنه) said that when the Prophet (ﷺ) finished his meal, he would say:

> "*Al-ḥamdu lillahi katheeran ṭayyiban mubarakan fihi, ghayra makfiyyin wa laa muwadda'in wa laa mustaghnan 'anhu, rabbana* (Praise be to Allah, much good and blessed praise. O' our Lord, we cannot compensate Your favour, nor leave it nor dispense with it)."[243]

Another Companion Mu'aadh ibn Anas (رضي الله عنه) said: "The Messenger of Allah (ﷺ) said:

---

[242] Ibid.

[243] *Fatḥ al-Baari*, 9/580, *Kitaab al-Aṭ'imah, baab maa yaqool idha faragha min ṭa'amihi.*

> 'Whoever eats a meal then says *Al-ḥamdu lillahi alladhi aṭ'amani hadha wa razaqanihi min ghayri hawlin minni wa laa quwwatin* (Praise be to Allah Who fed me and bestowed this provision upon me with no power or ability on my part)', will be forgiven for the sins committed prior to it."[244]

The well-mannered Muslim woman does not criticize food, no matter what it is, following the teaching and example of the Prophet (ﷺ).

Abu Hurayrah (رضي الله عنه) said:

> "The Messenger of Allah never criticized food. If he liked it, he ate it, and if he did not like it, he left it."[245]

The Muslim woman's manners with regard to drinking are also derived from the teachings of Islam, which impart good manners to man in every aspect of life.

After mentioning the name of Allah (سبحانه وتعالى), she drinks in two or three draughts. She does not breathe into the cup, nor does she drink from the mouth of the jug or bottle if she can help it. She should not breathe into her drink, and she should drink sitting down if she can.

Drinking in two or three draughts is what the Prophet (ﷺ) used to do, as Anas (رضي الله عنه) reported:

> "The Messenger of Allah used to breathe three times[246] when drinking."[247]

---

[244] Abu Dawood, 4/63, *Kitaab al-Libaas*, chapter - 1; and Tirmidhi, 5/508, *Kitaab ad-Da'waat*, 56. He said it is a *ḥasan* hadith.

[245] (Bukhari and Muslim), See *Sharḥ as-Sunnah*, 11/290, *Kitaab al-Aṭ'imah, baab laa yu'eeb aṭ-ṭa'am.*

[246] i.e., he would pause and take a breath outside the cup. (Author)

[247] (Bukhari and Muslim), See *Riyaḍ aṣ-Ṣaliḥeen*, 406, *Kitaab Aadaab aṭ-Ṭa'am, baab fi adab ash-sharaab.*

The Prophet (ﷺ) discouraged drinking in one draught:

> "Do not drink in one draught like camels do; drink in two or three. Mention the name of Allah when you drink, and give praise to Him when you finish drinking."[248]

The Prophet (ﷺ) forbade blowing into one's drink, as is mentioned in the hadith of Abu Sa'eed al-Khudri:

> "A man said, 'I see some dirt in it.' The Prophet said, 'Then pour it out.' He said, 'One draught is not enough for me.' The Prophet said, 'Take the cup away from your mouth, then take a breath.'"[249]

The hadith on the manners of drinking makes it clear that it is better for the well-mannered Muslim woman to avoid drinking from the mouth of the bottle or jug if she can, and to drink sitting down if possible. This is preferable, but drinking from the mouth of the jug or while standing are permitted, because the Prophet (ﷺ) did so on occasion.

Spreading the greeting of Islam

One of the distinctive aspects of the Muslim woman's social conduct is her insistence on the greeting of Islam, which she gives to every Muslim man and woman she meets, in accordance with the rules of giving *salaam* outlined by Islam, which command us to spread *salaam* in a number of *ayat* (verses) and hadiths.

In Islam, greeting with *salaam* is a clearly defined etiquette which has been commanded by Almighty Allah (ﷻ) in His Book, and rules

---

[248] Tirmidhi, 4/302, *Kitaab al-Ashribah*, 13. He said it is a *ḥasan* hadith.

[249] Tirmidhi, 4/304, *Kitaab al-Ashribah*, 15. He said it is a *ḥasan ṣaḥeeḥ* hadith.

and regulations concerning this greeting have been set out in numerous hadiths to which the scholars of hadith devoted entire chapters called *Kitaab as-Salaam* or *Baab as-Salaam.*

Allah (ﷻ) commanded the Muslims to greet one another with *salaam* in clear, definitive terms in the Qur'an:

> "*O' you who believe! Enter not houses other than your own, until you have asked permission and saluted those in them...*" *(Qur'an 24: 27)*

Allah commanded the Muslims to return the greeting with something similar or something better, hence it is an obligation on the one who hears a greeting to return it, and not to ignore it:

> "*When a [courteous] greeting is offered to you, meet it with a greeting still more courteous, or [at least] of equal courtesy...*" *(Qur'an 4: 86)*

The Prophet (ﷺ) strongly encouraged the Muslims to spread *salaam* and to greet those they know and those they do not know. 'Abdullah ibn 'Amr ibn al-'Aaṣ (رضي الله عنه) said:

> "A man asked the Prophet, 'Which type of Islam is the best?' He said, 'To feed people, and to say *salaam* to those you know and those you do not know.'"[250]

Greeting with *salaam* is one of the seven things which the Prophet (ﷺ) commanded his Companions, and the Muslim ummah after them, to adhere to. They were listed by Al-Barra' ibn 'Aazib (رضي الله عنه):

> "The Messenger of Allah commanded us to do seven things: to visit the sick, to attend funerals, to bless someone when he sneezes, to support the weak, to help

---

[250] (Bukhari and Muslim), See *Sharḥ as-Sunnah*, 12/260, *Kitaab al-Isti'dhaan, baab faḍl as-salaam.*

> the one who is oppressed, to spread *salaam*, and to help people fulfil their oaths."[251]

The Prophet (ﷺ) placed great emphasis on *salaam* (greeting) and encouraged Muslims to use this greeting in many hadith, because he understood its effects in spreading brotherly love and strengthening the ties of love, closeness and friendship between individuals and groups. He described it as something which would lead to love, and love would lead to faith, and faith would lead to Paradise. Jareer narrated on the authority of Aa'mash that the Messenger of Allah (ﷺ) observed:

> "By the One in Whose hand is my soul, you will not enter Paradise until you believe, and you will not believe until you love one another. Shall I not tell you of something which, if you do it, you will love one another? Spread *salaam* amongst yourselves."[252]

He (ﷺ) also said that the one who initiated the greeting would be closer to Allah (ﷻ) and more deserving of His pleasure, favour and blessing:

> "The closest of the people to Allah is the one who starts the greeting of *salaam*."[253]

'Abdullah ibn 'Umar (رضي الله عنه) used to go to the market in the morning, and he did not pass by anybody without saying *salaam* to him. One day he was asked, "What do you do in the market, when you do not sell anything, or ask about prices, or haggle, or join any gatherings?" He said,

---

251 (Bukhari and Muslim), See *Riyaḍ aṣ-Ṣaliḥeen*, 437, *Kitaab as-Salaam, baab faḍl as-salaam*; this wording is taken from a report narrated by Bukhari.

252 Muslim, 2/35, *Kitaab al-Eemaan, baab bayaan annahu la yadkhul al-jannah illa al-mu'minoon.*

253 Reported with a *jayyid* isnad by Abu Dawood, 5/380, *Kitaab al-Adab, baab fi faḍl man bada'a as-salaam.*

"We go there in the morning for the purpose of saying *salaam* to whoever we meet."[254]

In Islam, greeting with *salaam* is not considered to be the matter of a social custom defined by men, that may be changed and adapted according to time and circumstances. Greeting with *salaam* is a clearly-defined etiquette which has been commanded by Almighty Allah in His Book, and rules and regulations concerning this greeting have been set out, as described above.

There is only one form of the greeting, to which Muslim men and women who are aware of Islamic manners and are keen to apply Islamic teachings adhere to. It is: "*As-Salaamu 'alaykum wa raḥmatul lahi wa barakatuhu* (peace be upon you, and the mercy and blessings of Allah)." The man or woman who is initiating the greeting says it like this — in the plural form — even if he or she is greeting only one person. The man or woman thus addressed responds: "*Wa'alaykum as-salaam wa raḥmatullahi wa barakatuhu.*"[255]

The Muslim woman who is keen to be distinguished by her Islamic identity adheres to this blessed form of greeting, which is the original greeting of Islam, and does not substitute any other kind of greeting.

This correct Islamic greeting should not be replaced by other greetings, such as the old-fashioned Arabic greeting "*'Im ṣabaḥan,*" or modern greetings such as "*Ṣabah al-khayr,*" "Good morning," or "*Bonjour*" (in Arabic, English and French, respectively), and other usages which arc spreading in the Muslim societies that have deviated from the guidance of Islam.

---

254 Bukhari: *Al-Adab al-Mufrad*, 2/465, *baab man kharaja yusallim wa yusallam 'alayhi.*

255 The greeting should always be spoken in Arabic, regardless of whatever one's native tongue is or whatever language is being spoken at any given time. (Translator)

This Islamic greeting is the greeting which Allah (ﷻ) chose for His creation from the time of Adam, to whom He taught it and commanded him to greet the angels with it. He wanted Adam's descendants in all times and places to use this greeting, because of its meaning of peace which is something most beloved by man regardless of where or when he lives. This divinely-ordained greeting is preserved nowhere except in the ummah of Islam who has adhered to the true way and has not changed it or deviated from it.

The Prophet (ﷺ) said:

> "When Allah created Adam, He told him, 'Go and greet those' — a group of angels who were sitting — 'and listen to how they greet you, for it will be your greeting and that of your descendants.' So he said: '*As-Salaamu 'alaykum*,' and they responded, '*Wa 'alayka as-Salaamu wa raḥmatullah*.' They added '*Wa raḥmatullah*.'"[256]

No wonder this form is such a blessed greeting, for it comes from Allah (ﷻ), Who commanded us to adopt it as our greeting and never to replace it with anything else:

> "*...But if you enter houses, salute each other — a greeting or blessing and purity as from Allah...*"
>
> *(Qur'an 24: 61)*

Therefore Jibreel (Gabriel) (عليه السلام) used this form of the greeting when he greeted 'Aa'ishah. She used the same form in returning the greeting. This is reported in the hadith from 'Aa'ishah (رضي الله عنها):

> "The Messenger of Allah told me: 'This is Jibreel who is saying *salaam* to you.' She said, I said: '*Wa 'alayhi*

[256] (Bukhari and Muslim), See *Riyaḍ aṣ-Ṣaliḥeen*, 437, *Kitaab as-Salaam, baab fi faḍl as-salaam.*

as-salaamu wa raḥmatullahi wa barakatuhu (and upon him be peace and the mercy and blessings of Allah).'"[257]

There are also rules concerning the greeting of *salaam*, which the true Muslim tries to adhere to and apply properly in his or her own social life. These rules are summed up in the hadith reported by Bukhari and others from Abu Hurayrah (رضي الله عنه): "The Messenger of Allah said:

'The one who is riding should say *salaam* to the one who is walking, the one who is walking to the one who is sitting, and the smaller group to the larger group.'"[258]

A report narrated by Bukhari adds the words, "And the young to the old."[259]

The greeting is given to men and women alike, as Asma' bint Yazeed (رضي الله عنها) reported that the Prophet (ﷺ) passed by the mosque one day when a group of women were sitting there and he waved his hand to them in greeting.[260]

The greeting is also to be given to children, to acquaint them with the manners of greeting and giving *salaam* (peace). It is reported that Anas (رضي الله عنه) passed by some children and greeted them with *salaam*, then said, "The Messenger of Allah (ﷺ) used to do that."[261]

When the greeting is given at night, it should be spoken softly and in a quiet voice, so that those who are awake might hear it without

---

[257] (Bukhari and Muslim), See *Riyaḍ aṣ-Ṣaliheen*, 439, *Kitaab as-Salaam, baab kayfiyyat as-salaam.*

[258] (Bukhari and Muslim), See *Riyaḍ aṣ-Ṣaliheen*, 440, *Kitaab as-Salaam, baab fi aadaab as-salaam.*

[259] Ibid.

[260] Tirmidhi, 5/58, in *Kitaab al-Isti'dhaan, baab maa jaa' fit-tasleem 'alan-nisa'.* He said it is a *ḥasan* hadith.

[261] (Bukhari and Muslim), See *Riyaḍ aṣ-Ṣaliheen*, 442, *Kitaab as-Salaam, baab as-salaam 'ala aṣ-ṣubyaan.*

disturbing those who are asleep. This is what the Prophet (ﷺ) used to do, according to the lengthy hadith of Al-Miqdaad (رضي الله عنه) in which he says:

> "We used to put aside the Prophet's share of the milk and he would come at night and greet us in such a way as not to wake those who were asleep, but those who were awake would hear it. So the Prophet came and greeted us as he usually did..."[262]

Salaam should be given when joining a gathering and when leaving it. The Prophet (ﷺ) said:

> "When any one of you comes to a gathering, let him say *salaam*, and when he wants to leave, let him say *salaam*. The former is not more important than the latter."[263]

The Muslim woman who is distinguished by her true Islamic manners understands the sublime teachings of the Prophet (ﷺ) concerning the greeting of *salaam* and its etiquette. She follows this etiquette precisely in her private and social life, and encourages others to do likewise.

She does not enter a house other than her own without permission

The Muslim woman who is truly guided by Islam does not enter a house other than her own without seeking permission and saying *salaam* to the people who live there. This seeking permission is a divine commandment which is not to be evaded or ignored:

---

262 Muslim, 14/14, *Kitaab al-Ashribah, baab ikraam aḍ-ḍayf*. See also *Riyaḍ aṣ-Ṣaliḥeen*, 439.

263 Abu Dawood, 5/386, *Kitaab al-Adab, baab fis-salaam*; Tirmidhi, 5/62, *Kitaab al-Isti'dhaan*, 15. Tirmidhi said it is a *ḥasan* hadith.

> "*O' you who believe! Enter not houses other than your own, until you have asked permission and saluted those in them: that is best for you, in order that you may heed [what is seemly]. If you find no one in the house, enter not until permission is given to you: if you are asked to go back, go back: that makes for greater purity for yourselves: and Allah knows well all that you do. — But when the children among you come of age, let them [also] ask for permission, as do those senior to them [in age]...*" *(Qur'an 24: 27-28 and 59)*

The Muslim woman should never even think of seeking permission to enter a house that she is not permitted to enter, such as a house where there are only non-*maḥram* men present. When she seeks permission to enter, it is to go to where there are other women or men who are permitted to see her (i.e. *maḥram*), and no one else — in accordance with the commands of Allah and His Messenger.

There are certain manners in seeking permission which Islam urges Muslim men and women to follow whenever they want to visit somebody:

1. The woman who is seeking permission to enter should not stand squarely in front of the door, but to the right or left of it. This is what the Messenger of Allah (ﷺ) used to do. 'Abdullah ibn Busr (رضي الله عنه), the Companion of the Prophet said:

> "Whenever the Prophet came to a door seeking permission to enter, he did not stand facing it; he would stand to the right or the left. If he was given permission, he would enter, otherwise he would leave."[264]

The rule of seeking permission has been given to protect privacy, as Sahl ibn Ṣa'd (رضي الله عنه) reported that the Prophet (ﷺ) said:

[264] Bukhari: *Al-Adab al-Mufrad*, 2/513, *baab kayfa yaqooma 'ind al-baab...*

> "Seeking permission has been made a rule for the sake of not seeing[265]."[266]

Therefore the man or woman who is seeking permission is not allowed to stand facing the door, as this would allow him or her to see inside when the door is opened.

2. She should say *salaam* and then ask for permission. Seeking permission before saying *salaam* is incorrect. This is the teaching of the Prophet (ﷺ) as given in the hadith of Rib'ee ibn Ḥiraash who said:

> "A man of Bani 'Aamir told us that he had sought permission to see (meet) the Prophet, who was in a house. He said, 'Shall I get in?' The Messenger of Allah told his servant, 'Go out to this person and teach him how to seek permission to enter. Tell him to say '*As-Salaamu 'alaykum*, may I enter?" The man heard, so he said '*As-Salaamu 'alaykum*, may I enter?' Then the Prophet gave him permission and he entered."[267]

3. She should identify herself clearly when asked "Who are you?" by giving her name or *kunyah*. She should not reply in vague terms, such as "It is me." The Prophet (ﷺ) disliked such an answer from a person knocking at the door, as such words do not give a clear idea of the person's identity. He said that a person should state his or her name clearly when asking to come in.

Jaabir (رضي الله عنه) said: "I came to the Prophet (ﷺ) and knocked at the door.

---

[265] i.e., so that the one seeking permission will not see anything that the people whose house it is do not want him/her to see. (Translator)

[266] (Bukhari and Muslim), See *Riyaḍ as-Ṣaliḥeen*, 445, *Kitaab as-Salaam, baab al-isti'dhaan wa aadaabihi.*

[267] Bukhari: *Al-Adab al-Mufrad*, 2/518, *baab idha qaala: udkhul? wa lam yusallim*; see also *Riyaḍ aṣ-Ṣaliḥeen*, 445.

He said, 'Who is this?' I answered, 'Me,' and he said, 'Me? Me?' as if he disliked this answer."[268]

The Prophet (ﷺ) thus taught us that the sunnah, when seeking permission to enter is to state one's name clearly. This is what he and his noble Companions used to do. Abu Dharr (رضي الله عنه) said:

> "I went out one night and saw the Messenger of Allah walking on his own. I began to walk in the shadows cast by the moonlight. He turned around and saw me, so he said, 'Who is this?' and I said, 'Abu Dharr.'"[269]

Umm Hani' (رضي الله عنها) said:

> "I came to the Prophet's house while he was having *ghusl*. Faṭimah was screening him and he said, 'Who is this?' I said, 'I am Umm Hani' '"[270]

4. She should go back if she is asked to do so, without getting upset or angry. This is the commandment of Allah (سبحانه وتعالى) in the Qur'an:

> "*...If you are asked to go back, go back: that makes for greater purity for yourselves: and Allah knows well all that you do.*" *(Qur'an 24: 28)*

The Prophet (ﷺ) taught that permission to enter should only be sought three times, then if permission is given one may enter, otherwise one should go back. Abu Moosa al-Ash'ari (رضي الله عنه) said: "The Messenger of Allah (ﷺ) said:

> 'Seek permission to enter three times, then if permission is given to you, enter, otherwise go back.'"[271]

---

268 (Bukhari and Muslim), See *Riyaḍ aṣ-Ṣaliḥeen*, 447, *Kitaab as-Salaam, baab fi bayaan an as-sunnah an yusammi al-musta'dhin nafsahu.*

269 Ibid.

270 Op. cit.

271 (Bukhari and Muslim), See *Riyaḍ aṣ-Ṣaliḥeen*, 445, *Kitaab as-Salaam, baab fil-isti'dhaan wa aadaabihi.*

Abu Moosa once asked 'Umar (رضي الله عنه) for permission to enter, and it was not given, so he went away. 'Umar called him to come back, and they had a lengthy conversation about seeking permission and going away. It is useful to quote this conversation, to demonstrate how meticulous the *Ṣaḥaabah* were in finding out the teachings of the Prophet (ﷺ) and in applying them. Abu Moosa said:

"I sought permission to see 'Umar three times, and permission was not given, so I went away. 'Umar called me back and said: 'O' servant of Allah, did you find it hard to be kept waiting at my door? You should know that people find it just as hard to be kept waiting at your door.' I said, 'No, I asked permission from you three times and it was not given, so I went away (and we were commanded to do this).' He said, 'From whom did you hear this?' I said, 'I heard it from the Prophet (ﷺ).' He said, 'Have you heard something from the Prophet (ﷺ) that we have not heard? If you do not bring some evidence for this I will make an example of you.' So I went out until I came to a group of the Anṣaar who were sitting in the mosque. I asked them about it and they said, 'Does anyone doubt you concerning this?' So I told them what 'Umar had said. They said, 'No one but the youngest of us will come with you.' So Abu Sa'eed al-Khudri — or Abu Mas'ood — came with me to 'Umar, and told him, 'We went out with the Prophet (ﷺ) to visit Ṣa'd ibn 'Ubadah. When we got there, (the Prophet) said *salaam*, but no permission to enter was given. He said *salaam* a second and a third time, but no permission was given. He said, 'We have done what we had to,' then he went away. Ṣa'd came after him and said, 'O' Messenger of Allah, by the One Who sent you with the truth, you did not say *salaam* but I heard you and returned the greeting, but I wanted to increase the number of times you said *salaam* to me and my household.'" Abu Moosa said: "By Allah, I was being honest in what I reported of the words of the Messenger of Allah. He ('Umar) said: 'I agree, but I wanted to be sure.'"[272]

---

[272] *Fatḥ al-Baari*, 11/26, *Kitaab al-Isti'dhaan, baab at-tasleem wal-isti'dhaan*; Muslim, 14/130, *Kitaab al-Aadaab, baab al-isti'dhaan.*

In another report narrated by Muslim, it is stated that when this hadith was proven, 'Umar rebuked himself, as it were, by saying, "Was any teaching of the Messenger of Allah hidden from me? My business in the market kept me busy."[273]

These are the Islamic rules and manners pertaining to seeking permission to enter a house. No doubt the true Muslim woman who is keen to follow Islamic etiquette will apply these rules in her everyday life, each time she knocks on a door to seek permission to enter, and she will also teach these manners to her sons and daughters.

She sits wherever she finds room in a gathering

Another aspect of the manners of the true Muslim woman is that she sits wherever she finds room when she joins a gathering where other women have arrived before her and found a place to sit. This is a refined social etiquette that is derived from the example, in word and deed, of the Prophet (ﷺ), and is a sign of good taste, sensitivity and politeness in the person who adopts it.

Such a refined Muslim woman does not force her way through the group of women who are sitting, or push them aside in order to force them to make space for her. This is in accordance with the teachings of the Prophet (ﷺ) which he taught his Companions to adopt when they joined his gathering.

Jaabir ibn Samurah (رضي الله عنه) said:

> "When we came to the Prophet, we would sit wherever we found room."[274]

The well-mannered Muslim woman avoids pushing between two people, and comes between them only with their permission, if it is

---

[273] Muslim, 14/134, *Kitaab al-Aadaab, baab al-isti'dhaan.*

[274] Abu Dawood, 5/164, in *Kitaab al-Isti'dhaan*, 16, and Tirmidhi, 5/73, *Kitaab al-Isti'dhaan*, 29. Tirmidhi said it is a *ḥasan ṣaḥeeḥ gharib* hadith.

necessary to do so. Pushing between two people without their permission is something which the Prophet (ﷺ) forbade and warned against:

> "It is not permitted for a man to come between two people except with their permission."[275]

Pushing between two people, whether in a gathering or in other circumstances, is odd behaviour which Islam has made clear is disliked. Muslims are to avoid such behaviour. There are many hadiths and *athaar* (reports) to that effect; these reports are narrated in the masculine form, as they were spoken to the men who were usually around the Prophet (ﷺ), to remind them of correct Islamic manners, but these rules apply equally to women. The laws and commandments of Islam are addressed to all Muslims, and both men and women are responsible for obeying Islam's commands and following their guidance.

One of these reports is that of Sa'eed al-Maqbari who said:

> "I passed by Ibn 'Umar and there was a man with him talking to him. I stood by them, and Ibn 'Umar slapped my chest and said: 'If you find two people talking, do not stand by them and do not sit with them, until you have asked their permission.' I said, 'May Allah guide you, O' Abu 'Abdur-Raḥmaan! I only hoped to hear something good from you both.'"[276]

If someone gets up to let her sit in her place, she should not accept. This is better and more noble, and it is closer to the practice of the *Ṣaḥaabah*, may Allah be pleased with them all. Ibn 'Umar (رضي الله عنه) said: "The Messenger of Allah (ﷺ) said:

---

[275] Abu Dawood, 5/175, *Kitaab al-Adab*, 24, and Tirmidhi, 5/44, *Kitaab al-Adab*, 11. Tirmidhi said it is a *ḥasan* hadith.

[276] Bukhari: *Al-Adab al-Mufrad*, 2/580, *baab idha raa'a qawman yatanaajuna fa laa yadkhul ma'ahum.*

> 'None of you should make another get up then sit in his place. All of you should move up and make space (for a latecomer).'"[277]

If anyone stood up to give his place to him, Ibn 'Umar would never accept it.[278]

On such occasions, the Muslim woman always abides by the guidance of Islam and the conduct of the *Ṣaḥaabah*, may Allah be pleased with them all. So she attains the social manners that are encouraged by Islam, and earns the reward of Allah for following the Sunnah of His Prophet (ﷺ).

She does not converse privately with another woman when a third is present

Islam came to form human beings who are sensitive and civil, with an awareness and understanding of the feelings of others. Therefore, Islam has set out social and moral guidelines that are at the heart of this religion, and we are commanded to follow these guidelines and apply them in our own lives.

One of the guidelines laid down by the Prophet (ﷺ) is that two people should not talk privately between themselves when a third person is present:

> "If you are three, two should not converse privately to the exclusion of the other, until more people join you, because that will make him sad."[279]

---

[277] (Bukhari and Muslim), See *Sharḥ as-Sunnah*, 12/296, 297, *Kitaab al-Isti'dhaan, baab laa yuqeem ar-rajul min majlisihi idhaa haḍara.*

[278] Muslim, 14/161, *Kitaab as-Salaam, baab taḥreem iqaamah al-insaan min mawḍa'ihi.*

[279] (Bukhari and Muslim), See *Sharḥ as-Sunnah*, 13/90, *Kitaab al-Birr was-Ṣilah, baab laa yunaaja ithnaan doona ath-thaalith.*

The Muslim woman whose solid grounding in Islamic teaching has given her intelligence, sensitivity and good manners, avoids whispering and conversing privately when she is in a group of no more than three women. She is careful not to hurt the feelings of the third woman, lest she should feel excluded and offended. If there is an urgent need for two of them to converse privately, then they must ask the permission of the third woman, speak briefly, then apologize to her.

This is the attitude of the Muslim woman who is truly guided by Islam, and this is the civil way in which she deals with other women. She learns all this from the teachings of Islam and the stories of the *Ṣaḥaabah*, whose lives and manners were so completely permeated with the teachings and morals of Islam, that they never ignored these sensitive issues in their dealings with people. This is reflected in many reports which describe their careful respect for human feelings. An example is the report given by Imam Maalik in *Al-Muwaṭṭa'*, from 'Abdullah ibn Dinaar who said:

> "Ibn 'Umar and I were at the house of Khalid ibn 'Uqbah, which was in the market, when a man came in, wanting to speak to Ibn 'Umar in private. I was the only other person present, so Ibn 'Umar called another man to make our number up to four. Then he told me and the newcomer, 'Move a little way off together, for I heard the Messenger of Allah (ﷺ) say,
>
> 'Two should not converse privately to the exclusion of another.'''"[280]

The Muslim woman who is truly guided by the teachings of Islam and the way in which the best of generations (i.e. the *Ṣaḥaabah*) applied them, follows the example of Ibn 'Umar, who did not want to listen to a man who had come in, off the street suddenly, to converse

[280] *Al-Muwaṭṭa'*, 2/988, *Kitaab al-Kalaam* (6).

with him in private, because he knew that there was a third person present whose feelings could be hurt if he asked him to move away on his own. He waited to listen to the man who wanted to converse in private, until he had called a fourth man, then he explained to all of them that this was the sunnah of the Prophet (ﷺ), and repeated the hadith to them, reminding the Muslims that this is the approach they should take when they find themselves in such situations, respecting people's feelings and following the sunnah of the Prophet.

How fine are the social manners encouraged by Islam! How great is the honour which Islam bestows upon human beings and the respect and consideration it shows towards their feelings!

She respects elders and distinguished people

Islam brought a host of fine social rules which instill an attitude of chivalry, nobility, good manners and politeness in the heart of the Muslim. One of the most prominent of these teachings is to give due respect to elders and those deserving respect (such as scholars, etc.).

The Muslim woman who is truly guided by Islam does not neglect to follow this most essential, basic Islamic ruling, which gives the Muslim woman her genuine identity in the Islamic society. Whoever lacks this quality forfeits his or her membership in this community and no longer has the honour of belonging to the ummah of Islam, as the Prophet (ﷺ) stated:

> "He does not belong to my ummah who does not honour our elders, show compassion to our young ones, and pay due respect to our scholars."[281]

Respect for elders and giving them priority over those who are younger, are indications of a community's or society's level of

---

[281] Aḥmad and Ṭabaraani. See *Majma' az-Zawaa'id*, 8/14, *baab tawqeer al-kabeer wa raḥmat aṣ-ṣagheer.*

civility, of its members' understanding of the rules of human morality, and of their high level of good manners. This is just as true of women as it is of men. Hence the Prophet (ﷺ) was keen to reinforce this understanding in the hearts of the Muslims, whilst he was raising the structure of the Islamic society. Among the evidence of his concern to achieve this are his words to 'Abdur-Raḥmaan ibn Sahl, who was speaking although he was the youngest member of the delegation that had come to the Prophet (ﷺ). The Prophet told him,

> "Let someone who is older than you speak, let someone who is older than you speak."

So Abdur-Raḥmaan fell silent, and someone who was older than him spoke.[282]

When the modern Muslim woman shows respect to a lady who is older than her, or honours a woman who is deserving of respect, she is doing a worthwhile moral duty that in fact is a part of worship, because honouring one's elders and those who are distinguished is part of glorifying Allah (سبحانه وتعالى), as the Prophet (ﷺ) said:

> "Part of glorifying Allah is honouring the grey-haired (i.e., older) Muslim, the one who has learnt the Qur'an by heart without exaggerating about it or ignoring its teachings, and honouring the just ruler."[283]

By behaving in this way, the Muslim woman follows the command of the Prophet (ﷺ) to give people their rightful positions in the Islamic society. Imam Muslim mentions this at the beginning of his *Ṣaḥeeḥ*, where he says: "It was reported that 'Aa'ishah (رضي الله عنها) said, 'The Messenger of Allah (ﷺ) ordered us to put people in their rightful positions.'"[284]

---

282 (Bukhari and Muslim), See *Riyaḍ aṣ-Ṣaliḥeen*, 207, *baab tawqeer al-'ulama' wa al-kibaar wa ahl al-faḍl.*

283 A *ḥasan* hadith narrated by Abu Dawood, 5/174, *Kitaab al-Adab*, 23.

284 Muslim, 1/55.

The Muslim woman should not forget that giving people their rightful position means recognizing their positions and giving priority to elders, scholars, those who have memorised the Qur'an, those who are wise and those who are distinguished, whether they are men or women.

She does not look into other people's houses

Another one of the qualities of the well-mannered Muslim woman is that she does not look around the home of her host or seek to inspect its contents. This is not the behaviour that befits the wise, decent Muslim woman; it is a hateful, undesirable attitude. The Prophet (ﷺ) warned those who let their gaze wander in gatherings and try to see things that are none of their business, and he even said that it was permissible to put their eyes out:

> "Whoever looks into someone's home without their permission, then it is permissible for the people of the house to put their eyes out."[285]

She avoids yawning in a gathering as much as she can

The Muslim woman who is sensitive and well-mannered does not yawn in a gathering if she can help it. If the urge to yawn overtakes her, then she tries to resist it as much as possible. This is what the Prophet (ﷺ) advised:

> "If any of you wants to yawn, then let him suppress it as much as possible."[286]

---

[285] Muslim, 14/138, *Kitaab al-Aadaab, baab taḥreem an-naẓr fi bayt ghayrihi.*

[286] *Fatḥ al-Baari*, 10/611, *Kitaab al-Adab, baab idha tatha'ab fa layaḍa' yadahu 'ala fayhi*; Muslim, 18/123, *Kitaab az-Zuhd, baab kiraahah at-tathaa'ub.*

If the urge to yawn cannot be resisted, then she should cover her mouth with her hand, as the Prophet (ﷺ) commanded:

> "If any of you yawns, let him cover his mouth with his hand so that the *Shayṭaan* does not enter."[287]

Yawning in front of others is unpleasant and off-putting. It does not befit the decent person. Therefore he or she must resist the urge to yawn, or at least cover his or her open mouth with his or her hand, so that the others present need not see it. The Prophet (ﷺ) taught the Muslims, men and women, how to behave properly in a social setting so that they will not put people off or make them feel that they are bored with them and want to leave them or want them to leave. This is the way in which the polite Muslim woman who follows Islamic etiquette conducts herself.

She follows Islamic etiquette when she sneezes

It is no secret to the Muslim woman that just as Islam has defined the manners governing the act of yawning in gatherings, it has also defined the etiquette to be observed when one sneezes. Islam teaches the Muslims, men and women, how they should behave when they sneeze, what they should say to the one who sneezes, and how they should pray for him or her.

Abu Hurayrah (رضي الله عنه) said: "The Prophet (ﷺ) said:

> 'Allah likes the act of sneezing and dislikes the act of yawning. When any one of you sneezes and says '*Al-ḥamdu-lillah*,' then he has the right to hear every Muslim say '*Yarḥamuk Allah*.' But yawning is from the *Shayṭaan* (Satan) , so if any of you feels the urge to

---

[287] Muslim, 18/122, *Kitaab az-Zuhd, baab kiraahah at-tathaa'ub.*

> yawn, he should resist it as much as he can, for when any of you yawns, the *Shayṭaan* laughs at him.'"[288]

This simple reflex action does not occur in the Muslim's life without being regulated by certain manners which make the Muslims feel, in the depths of their heart, that this religion came to reform all issues in this life, great and small alike, and to give them certain words to say which would constantly connect humanity to Allah (ﷻ), the Lord of the Worlds.

When a Muslim woman sneezes, she should say "*Al-ḥamdu lillah* (all praise be to Allah)," and the one who hears her should say, "*Yarḥamuk Allah.*" Then she must respond to her sister's *du'aa'* by saying "*Yahdeekum Allah wa yuṣliḥ baalakum* (may Allah guide you and correct your thinking)". This is the teaching of the Prophet (ﷺ) according to the hadith narrated by Bukhari:

> "When any one of you sneezes, let him say '*Al-ḥamdu lillah*,' and let his brother or companions say '*Yarḥamuk Allah* (may Allah have mercy on you).' And if he says '*Yarḥamuk Allah*,' let the first one say, '*Yahdeekum Allah wa yuṣliḥ baalakum.*'"[289]

This *du'aa'* (supplication), *Yarḥamuk Allah*, is said to the one who sneezes in response to his or her saying '*Al-ḥamdu lillah.*' If he or she does not say '*Al-ḥamdu lillah*,' then there is no obligation to respond in this way. The Companion Abu Moosa Ash'ari narrated that he heard the Prophet (ﷺ) say:

> "When any of you sneezes and praises Allah, then respond to him (by saying *Yarḥamuk Allah*), but if he does not praise Allah, then do not respond to him."[290]

---

[288] *Fatḥ al-Baari*, 10/611, *Kitaab al-Adab, baab idha tatha'ab fa layaḍa' yadahu 'ala fayhi.*

[289] *Fatḥ al-Baari*, 10/608, *Kitaab al-Adab, baab idha 'aṭasa kayfa yashammut.*

[290] Muslim, 18/121, *Kitaab az-Zuhd, baab tashmiyat al-'aaṭis.*

Anas (رضي الله عنه) said:

> "Two men sneezed in the presence of the Prophet, and he responded to one of them and not the other. The one to whom he did not respond said, 'So-and-so sneezed and you responded. I sneezed and you did not respond.' He said, 'He praised Allah, but you did not.'"[291]

Discussing these words which the Prophet (ﷺ) encouraged the Muslims to say when someone sneezes highlights their ultimate aim, which is to mention and praise Allah (تعالى), and to strengthen the ties of brotherhood and friendship among all Muslims, men and women. The one who sneezes praises Allah for relief from some sensitivity or irritation which he had in his nose, and the one who hears him praising Allah, prays for mercy for him, because the one who praises Allah deserves mercy. The one who sneezes then responds with a longer and more comprehensive *du'aa'* which is full of meanings of goodness, love and friendship; also deserves mercy

Thus Islam takes these involuntary actions of Muslims and makes them opportunities for remembering and praising Allah and reinforcing the feelings of brotherhood (and sisterhood), love and compassion in their hearts.

Another one of the good manners to be observed when sneezing is to place one's hand over one's mouth and to make as little noise as possible. This is what the Prophet (ﷺ) used to do. Abu Hurayrah (رضي الله عنه) said,

> "When the Messenger of Allah sneezed, he used to place his hand or part of his garment over his mouth and thus reduced the noise he made."[292]

---

[291] (Bukhari and Muslim), See *Riyaḍ aṣ-Ṣaliḥeen*, 448, *Kitaab as-Salaam, baab istiḥbaab tashmiyat al-'aaṭis.*

[292] Abu Dawood, 5/288, *Kitaaab al-Adab*, 98; Tirmidhi, 5/86, *Kitaab al-Adab*, 6. Tirmidhi said it is a *ḥasan ṣaḥeeḥ* hadith.

The well-mannered Muslim woman who is aware of Islamic etiquette does not forget, in such situations where a person may be taken by surprise, to conduct herself in the manner prescribed by the Prophet (ﷺ) and to use the same words that he is reported to have used when he sneezed. This is the etiquette to be observed, in obedience to the words of the Prophet (ﷺ), whenever she or another person sneezes, or in response to a sister who "blesses" her (says, '*Yarḥamuk Allah*') when she sneezes.

She does not seek the divorce of another woman so that she may take her place

The true Muslim woman feels that she is living in a Muslim community, whose members are her brothers and sisters. In such a divinely-guided community, cheating, deceit, treachery and all the other vile attitudes that are rampant in societies that have deviated from the guidance of Allah, the Almighty, All-Glorious, are forbidden.

One of the worst of these attitudes is that of the woman who looks at a married man with the intention of snatching him from his wife once they are divorced so that he will be all hers. The true Muslim woman is the furthest removed from this vile attitude, which the Prophet (ﷺ) forbade, when he forbade a number of other, similar evil attitudes and practices. We see this in the hadith narrated by Bukhari and Muslim from Abu Hurayrah (رضي الله عنه), who said: "The Messenger of Allah (ﷺ) said:

> 'Do not outbid one another (in order to raise prices artificially)[293]; do not undercut one another[294]; a town-

[293] i.e., a person should not raise the price of something he has no intention of buying, in order to mislead another. (Author)

[294] i.e., do not ask a person to return something he has bought so that you may sell him something similar for a lower price. (Author)

> dweller should not sell something on behalf of a Bedouin[295]; a man should not propose to a woman to whom his brother has already proposed; a woman should not ask for the divorce of another so that she might deprive her of everything that belongs to her[296]."[297]

According to a report narrated by Bukhari, also from Abu Hurayrah, the Prophet (ﷺ) said:

> "It is not permitted for a woman to ask for her sister's divorce so that she may take everything she has, for she will have what has been decreed for her."[298]

The Muslim woman is the sister of another, and believes that what Allah (ﷻ) has decreed for her must surely happen. She cannot be a true believer unless she likes for her sister what she likes for herself, as the Prophet (ﷺ) said:

> "None of you truly believes until he likes for his brother what he likes for himself."[299]

The Muslim woman is protected by her knowledge and faith from falling into the trap of this sin. She is saved from such appalling error

---

[295] i.e., he should not act as an agent for him, controlling prices in a way that harms the community. (Author)

[296] i.e., she should not ask a man to divorce his wife and marry her instead, so that she will enjoy all the comforts and good treatment that were previously enjoyed by the one who is divorced. (Author)

[297] *Fatḥ al-Baari*, 4/352, 353, *Kitaab al-Buyu', baab laa yabee' 'ala bay' akheehi*; Muslim, 9/198, *Kitaab an-Nikaaḥ, baab taḥreem khuṭbat ar-rajul 'ala khuṭbatu akheehi*. This version is that narrated by Muslim.

[298] *Fatḥ al-Baari*, 9/219, *Kitaab an-Nikaaḥ, baab ash-shurooṭ allati laa tuḥall fin-Nikaaḥ*.

[299] (Bukhari and Muslim), See *Sharḥ as-Sunnah*, 13/60, *Kitaab al-Birr waṣ-Ṣilah, baab yuḥibb li-akheehi maa yuḥibb linafsihi.*

by her obedience to Allah (ﷻ) and His Messenger, and by her acceptance of the high human values that Islam has made part of her nature. She does not avoid this sin only to be protected from the scandal that surrounds a woman who commits such a vile deed; a woman could conceal her evil schemes and thus be spared social blame, but she can never escape the punishment of Allah,

> "*...Who knows what is secret and what is yet more hidden.*" *(Qur'an 20: 7).*

She chooses the work that suits her feminine nature

Islam has spared women the burden of having to work to earn a living, and has made it obligatory on her father, brother, husband or other male relative to support her. So the Muslim woman does not seek work outside the home unless there is pressing financial need due to the lack of a relative or spouse to maintain her honourably, or her community needs her to work in a specialised area such as befits her feminine nature and will not compromise her honour or religion.

Islam has made it obligatory for a man to spend on his family, and has given him the responsibility of earning the costs of living, so that his wife may devote herself to being a wife and mother, creating a joyful and pleasant atmosphere in the home and organising and running its affairs.

This is the Islamic view of woman and the family, and this is the Islamic philosophy of marriage and family life.

The Western philosophy of women's role, the home, the family and children is based on the opposite of this. When a girl reaches a certain age — usually seventeen years old — neither her father, her brother nor any of her male relatives are obliged to support her. She has to look for work to support herself, and to save whatever she can to offer to her future husband. If she gets married, she has to help her husband with the expenses of the home and children. When she gets old, if she is still able to earn, she must continue to work to earn a living, even if her children are rich.

No doubt the wise Muslim woman understands the huge difference between the position of the Muslim woman and the position of women in the West. The Muslim woman is honoured, protected, and guaranteed a decent living; the Western woman works hard and is subjected to exhaustion and humiliation, especially when she reaches old age.

Since the end of the last century, Western thinkers have continually complained about the plight of Western women. They have warned their people about the impending collapse of Western civilization, due to women's going out to work, the disintegration of the family and the neglect of the children.

The great Islamic *da'ee* Dr. Muṣṭafa as-Sibaa'ee, may Allah have mercy on him, collected a number of comments by Western thinkers in his book *Al-Mar'ah bayna al-fiqh wal-Qanoon* (Woman between *Fiqh* and Law). These comments reflect the severe anger and deep anguish felt by those thinkers when they see how low the position of women in the West has become. We will look here at a few of these comments that give a vivid impression of the state of women in the West.

The French economic philosopher Jules Simon said:

> "Women have started to work in textile factories and printing presses, etc.... The government is employing them in factories, where they may earn a few francs. But on the other hand, this has utterly destroyed the bases of family life. Yes, the husband may benefit from his wife's earnings, but apart from that, his earnings have decreased because now she is competing with him for work."

He also commented:

> "There are other, higher-class women, who work as book-keepers or store-keepers, or who are employed by the government in the field of education. Many of them work for the telegraph service, the post office, the railways or the Bank of France, but these positions are taking them away from their families completely."[300]

> "A woman must remain a woman, because with this quality she can find happiness or bring it to others. Let us reform the position of women, but let us not change them. Let us beware of turning them into men, because that would make them lose much, and we would lose everything. Nature[301] has done everything perfectly, so let us study it and try to improve it, and let us beware of anything that could take us away from its laws."[302]

The famous English writer Anna Ward said:

> "It is better for our daughters to work as servants in houses or like servants at home. This is better, and less disastrous than letting them work in factories, where a girl becomes dirty and her life is destroyed. I wish that our country was like the lands of the Muslims, where modesty, chastity and purity are like a garment. Servants and slaves there live the best life, where they are treated like the children of the house and no-one harms their honour. Yes, it is a source of shame for England that we make our daughters examples of promiscuity by mixing so much with men. Why do we not try to pursue that

---

[300] *Al-Mar'ah bayna al-Fiqh wa al-Qanoon*, 176.

[301] This is an atheistic Western expression, which refers to "nature" instead of Allah the Creator, after the West turned its back on religion. (Author)

[302] *Al-Mar'ah bayna al-Fiqh wa al-Qanoon*, 178.

> which makes a girl do work that agrees with her natural temperament, by staying at home, and leaving men's work for the men, to keep her honour safe."[303]

The Western woman envies the Muslim woman, and wishes that she could have some of the rights, honour, protection and stability that the Muslim woman enjoys. There are many proofs of this, some of which have been quoted above (see p 86 of orig.). Another example is the comment of an Italian student of law at Oxford University, after she had heard something of the rights of women in Islam and how Islam gave women all kinds of respect by sparing her the obligation to earn a living so that she may devote herself to caring for her husband and family. This Italian girl said:

> "I envy the Muslim woman, and wish that I had been born in your country."[304]

This reality sunk into the minds of the leaders of the women's movement in the Arab world, especially those who were reasonable and fair. Salma al-Haffaar al-Kazbari, who visited Europe and America more than once, commented in the Damascus newspaper *Al-Ayyaam* (September 3, 1962), in response to Professor Shafeeq Jabri's remarks on the misery of the American woman in his book *Arḍ as-Siḥr* (The Land of Magic):

> "The well-travelled scholar noted, for example, that the Americans teach their children from a very early age to love machines and heroism in their games. He also remarked that the women have started to do men's work, in car factories and street-cleaning, and he felt sorry for the misery of the woman who spends her youth and her life doing something that does not suit her feminine nature and attitude. What Professor Jabri

---

[303] Ibid, 179.

[304] Opt. cit., 181.

> has to say made me feel happy, because I came back from my own trip to the United States five years ago, feeling sorry for the plight of women to which they have been drawn by the currents of blind equality. I felt sorry for their struggle to earn a living, for they have lost even their freedom, that absolute freedom for which they strived for so long. Now they have become prisoners of machines and of time. It is too difficult to go back now, and unfortunately it is true that women have lost the dearest and best things granted to them by nature, by which I mean their femininity, and their happiness. Continuous, exhausting work has caused them to lose the small paradise which is the natural refuge of men and women alike. Children cannot grow and flourish without the presence of a woman who stays at home with them. It is in the home and in the bosom of the family that the happiness of society and individuals rests; the family is the source of inspiration, goodness and genius."

Throwing women into the battlefield of work, where they must compete with men to take their place or share their positions, when there is no need to do so and the interests of society as a whole do not require it, is indeed a grave mistake. It is a great loss that nations and peoples suffer from at times of decline, tribulation and error. The Muslim woman who is guided by the Qur'an and Sunnah does not accept to be thrown into that battlefield, and refuses to become some cheap commodity that is fought over by the greedy capitalists, or some gaudy doll whose company is enjoyed by immoral so-called men. She rejects, with fierce pride, that false "progress" that calls for women to come out uncovered, almost naked and adorned with make up, to work alongside men in offices. With this wise, balanced, honourable attitude, she is in fact doing a great service to her society and nation, by calling for an end to this ridiculous competition of women with men in the workplace, and the resulting corruption, neglect of the family, and waste of money. This is the best good deed a woman can do, as was reflected by the comments of the ruler of North Korea to the Women's Union conference held in his country in 1971:

> "We make women enter society, but the reason for that is definitely not a lack of workers. Frankly speaking, the burden borne now by the state because of women's going out is greater than any benefits that may result from women's going out to work... So why do we want women to go out and be active in society? Because the main aim is to make women become revolutionary, so that they will become part of the working class through their social activity. Our party encourages women to go out and be active in revolutionising women and making them part of the working class, no matter how great a burden this places on the state."

No doubt the truly-guided Muslim woman knows exactly where she stands when she realises the great difference between the laws of Islam and the laws of *jaahiliyah*. So she chooses the laws of Allah, and does not pay any attention to the nonsense calls of *jaahiliyah* that come from here and there every so often:

> "*Do they then seek a judgement of [the Days of] Ignorance? But who, for a people whose faith is assured, can give better judgement than Allah?*"
>
> *(Qur'an 5: 50)*

She does not imitate men

The Muslim woman who is proud of her Islamic identity does not imitate men at all, because she knows that for a woman to imitate men, or a man to imitate women, is forbidden by Islam. The wisdom and eternal law of Allah dictate that men have a character distinct from that of women, and vice versa. This distinction is essential for both sexes, because each of them has its own unique role to play in life. The distinction between the basic functions and roles of each sex is based on the differences in character between them; in other words, men and women have different characters and personalities.

Islam put things in order when it defined the role in life of both men and women, and directed each to do that for which they were created. Going against this divinely-ordained definition is a rebellion against the laws of nature according to which Allah (سبحانه وتعالى) created man, and is a distortion of the sound, original nature of man. This is surely abhorrent to both sexes, and nothing is more indicative of this than the fact that women despise those effeminate men who imitate women, and men despise those coarse, rough women who act like men. The universe cannot be cultivated and populated properly, and humanity cannot achieve true happiness, unless the sexes are clearly differentiated, so that each may appreciate and enjoy the unique character of the other, and both may work together to achieve those aims.

For all these reasons, Islamic teachings issue a severe and clear warning to men who imitate women and women who imitate men.

Ibn 'Abbaas (رضي الله عنه) said:

> "The Messenger of Allah cursed the men who act like women and the women who act like men."[305]

In another report, Ibn 'Abbaas said:

> "The Prophet cursed men who act effeminate and women who act like men, and said, 'Expel them from

---

[305] *Fatḥ al-Baari*, 10/332, *Kitaab al-Libaas, baab al-mutashabbiheen bin-nisa' wal-mutashabbihaat bir-rijaal.*

> your houses.' The Prophet expelled So-and-so (a man), and Abu Bakr expelled So-and-so (a woman)."[306]

Abu Hurayrah (رضي الله عنه) said:

> "The Messenger of Allah cursed the man who dresses like a woman and the woman who dresses like a man."[307]

When the Muslims were in good shape, governed by the shari'ah of Allah and guided by the light of Islam, there was no trace of this problem of men and women resembling one another. But nowadays, when the light of Islam has dimmed in our societies, we find many young girls wearing tight, body-hugging trousers and unisex shirts, with uncovered heads and arms, who look like young men; and we find effeminate men, wearing chains of gold around their necks that dangle on their bare chests, and with long flowing hair that makes them look like young women. It is very difficult to tell the difference between them — between the sexes.

These shameful scenes, that may be seen in some Islamic countries, that have been overcome by *Al-Ghazw al-Fikri* (intellectual colonialism), whose youth are spiritually defeated, are alien to the Islamic ummah and its values and customs. They have come to us from both the corrupt West and faithless East, which have been overwhelmed by waves of hippies, existentialism, frivolity and nihilism, and other deviant ideas that have misguided humanity and caused great suffering, as they have led people far away from their true, sound nature (*fiṭrah*) and distorted them, bringing the worst problems and diseases to those people as a result.

---

306 *Fatḥ al-Baari*, 10/333, *Kitaab al-Libaas, baab ikhraaj al-mutashabbiheen bin-nisa' min al-buyoot.*

307 Abu Dawood, 4/86, *Kitaab al-Libaas*, 31; Ibn Ḥibbaan (13) 63, *Kitaab al-Hiẓr wa al-Ibaaḥah, baab al-la'n.*

We have also suffered from the fall-out of all this, which overtook the lives of men and women who deviated from the guidance of Allah in some Muslim countries after the collapse of the *khilaafah* (Caliphate) and the disintegration of the ummah. Many Islamic values were lost, and these deviant men and women became alienated from the ummah, rebelling against its true, original values and distinct character.

She calls people to the truth

The true Muslim woman understands that mankind was not created in vain, but was created to fulfil a purpose, which is, to worship Allah, the Creator, the Lord of the Universe:

> "*I have only created Jinns and men, that they should may worship Me, Alone.*" *(Qur'an 51: 56)*

Worshipping Allah may be done through any positive, constructive action undertaken to cultivate and populate the world, to make the word of Allah supreme on earth, and to apply His laws in life. All of these constitute part of that truth to which Muslim men and women are required to call people.

Hence the true Muslim woman is aware of her duty to call as many other women as possible to the truth in which she believes, seeking thereby the great reward which Allah (سبحانه وتعالى) has promised those who sincerely call others to the truth, as the Prophet (صلى الله عليه وسلم) said to his cousin 'Ali (رضي الله عنه):

> "By Allah, if Allah were to guide just one man through you it would be better for you than red camels."[308]

A good word which the Muslim woman says to other women who are careless about matters of religion, or to a woman who has deviated

---

[308] *Fatḥ al-Baari*, 7/476, *Kitaab al-Maghaazi, baab ghazwah Khaybar.*

from the guidance of Allah, will have an effect on them, and will come back to the sister who calls others to Allah with a great reward that is worth more than red camels, which were the most precious and sought-after wealth among the Arabs at that time. In addition, a reward like that of the ones who are guided at her hands will also be given to her, as the Prophet (ﷺ) said:

> "Whoever calls people to the truth will have a reward like that of those who follow him, without it detracting in the least from their rewards."[309]

The Muslim woman does not think little of whatever knowledge she has if she is calling other women to Allah. It is sufficient for her to convey whatever knowledge she has learned, or heard from other peoples' preaching, even if it is just one *aayah* (verse) from the Book of Allah. This is what the Prophet (ﷺ) used to tell his Companions to do:

> "Convey (knowledge) from me even if it is just one *aayah*..."[310]

This is because whether or not a person is guided may depend on just one word of this *aayah* which may touch her heart and ignite the spark of faith, so that her heart and her life will be illuminated with the light of guidance.

The Muslim woman who is calling others to Allah does not spare any effort in calling other women to the truth — and how great is the need for this call in these times — seeking the pleasure of Allah and spreading awareness among those women who were not fortunate enough to receive this teaching and guidance previously, and thus proving that she likes for her sister what she likes for herself. These

---

[309] Muslim, 16/227, *Kitaab al-'Ilm, baab man sanna sunnah ḥasanah.*

[310] *Fatḥ al-Baari*, 6/496, *Kitaab Aḥaadeeth al-Anbiya', baab maa dhukira 'an Bani Isra'eel.*

are the characteristics of the woman who calls others to Allah, that distinguish her from ordinary women. They are noble, worthy characteristics that were highly praised and encouraged by the Prophet (ﷺ). Tirmidhi reported that the Prophet (ﷺ) said:

> "May Allah make his face shine, the one who hears something from us and conveys it as he hears it, for perhaps the one to whom it is conveyed will understand it better than the one who conveyed it."[311]

The Muslim woman who is truly guided by the Qur'an and Sunnah is like a lighted lamp that shows travellers the way during the darkest night. She cannot conceal her light from her sisters who are stumbling in the darkness when she has seen the great reward that Allah (ﷻ) has prepared for true, sincere callers to the truth.

She enjoins what is good and forbids what is evil

The duty of enjoining what is good and forbidding what is evil (*Al-Amr bil-Ma'roof wan-Nahyi 'an al-Munkar*) is not confined only to men; it applies equally to men and women, as is stated in the Glorious Qur'an:

> "*The Believers, men and women, are protectors, one of another: they enjoin what is just, and forbid what is evil: they observe regular prayers, practice regular charity, and obey Allah and His Messenger. On them will Allah pour His Mercy: for Allah is Exalted in Power, Wise.*" *(Qur'an 9: 71)*

Islam gave women a high social standing when it gave her this great social responsibility of enjoining what is good and forbidding what is evil. For the first time in history, women were to be the ones issuing

---

311 Tirmidhi, 5/34, in *Kitaab al-'Ilm*, 7; he said it is a *ḥasan ṣaḥeeḥ* hadith.

instructions, whereas everywhere else except in Islam they had been the ones to receive instructions.

In response to this responsibility, which in fact is a great honour, the Muslim woman rises up to carry out the duty of enjoining what is good and forbidding what is evil, within the limits of what suits her feminine nature. Within the limits of her own specialised field, she confronts evil — which is no small matter in the world of women — whenever she sees it, and she opposes it with reason, deliberation, wisdom and a clever, good approach. She tries to remove it with her hand, if she is able to and if doing so will not lead to worse consequences. If she cannot remove it by her actions, then she speaks out to explain what is right, and if she is not able to do so, then she opposes it in her heart, and starts to think of ways and means of opposing and eradicating it. These are the means of opposing evil that were set out by the Prophet (ﷺ):

> "Whoever of you sees an evil action, let him change it with his hand, and if he is not able to do so, then with his tongue, and if he is not able to do so, then with his heart — and that is the weakest of faith."[312]

When the alert Muslim woman undertakes this duty of enjoining what is good and forbidding what is evil, she is in effect being sincere towards her wayward or negligent Muslim sisters, for religion is sincerity (or sincere advice), as the Prophet (ﷺ) explained most eloquently when he summed up Islam in one word: *naṣeeḥah*. If that is indeed the case, then the Muslim woman has no option but to enjoin what is good and forbid what is wrong, in order to fulfil the definition of sincerity as stated by the Prophet (ﷺ):

> "Religion is sincerity (*naṣeeḥah*)." We asked, "To whom?" He said, "To Allah, to His Book, to His

[312] Muslim, 2/22, *Kitaab al-Eemaan, baab bayaan kawn an-nahy 'an al-munkar min al-eemaan.*

> Messenger, and to the leaders of the Muslims and their common folk."[313]

The Muslim woman's speaking out to offer *naṣeeḥah* and to enjoin what is good and forbid what is evil in women's circles will lead to the correction of many unIslamic customs, traditions and habits that are prevalent among some women. How many such practices there are among women who neglect or deviate from Islam; the Muslim woman who confronts these customs and explains the correct Islamic point of view is doing the best thing she can for her society and ummah, and she is one of the best of people:

> "A man stood up whilst the Prophet was on the *minbar* and asked: 'O' Messenger of Allah, which of the people is the best?' He said, 'The best of the people are those who are most well-versed in the Qur'an, those who are most pious, those who enjoin most of what is good and forbid what is evil, and those who are most respectful towards their relatives.'"[314]

The alert Muslim woman is a woman with a mission. She never remains silent about falsehood or fails to uphold the truth or accepts any deviation. She always strives to benefit her sisters in the Muslim community, and save them from their own shortcomings, backwardness, ignorance and deviations. She undertakes her duty of enjoining what is good and forbidding what is evil, in obedience to the command of Allah and His Messenger, and to protect herself from the punishment of Allah which befalls those societies where no voice is raised to enjoin what is good and forbid what is evil.

When Abu Bakr (ﷺ) became the *khaleefah* (Caliph), he ascended

---

313 Muslim, 2/37, *Kitaab al-Eemaan, baab bayaan un ad-deen naṣeeḥah.*

314 Aḥmad and Ṭabaraani; the men of their isnads are *thiqat*. See *Majma' az-Zawaa'id*, 7/263, *baab fi ahl al-ma'roof wa ahl al-munkar.*

the *minbar* (pulpit), praised Allah, then said,
"O' people, you recite the *aayah,*

> *'O' you who believe! Guard your own souls: if you follow [right] guidance no hurt can come to you from those who stray...'* *(Qur'an 5: 105)*

— and you are misinterpreting it. Verily I heard the Prophet (ﷺ) say:

> 'Those people who see some evil and do not oppose it or seek change will shortly all be punished by Allah.'"[315]

The Muslim woman who is sincere in her Islam, whose faith is strong and whose mind is open to the guidance of Islam, is always active in the cause of goodness, enjoining what is good and forbidding what is evil, offering sincere advice and reforming corrupt situations. She does not accept negativity, passiveness, negligence or vacillation in herself, and never accepts any compromise or deviance in matters of Islam and its rituals. Religion and *'Aqeedah* are serious matters; it is no joke, and it is not permitted to remain silent about any deviance or error in religious matters, otherwise we will end up like the Jews, who earned Allah's wrath when they vacillated and became careless with regard to their religion:

> "Among the people who came before you, the children of Israel, if any one of them did wrong, one of them would denounce him so that he could say that he had done his duty, but the next day he would sit and eat with him as if he had never seen him do anything wrong the day before. When Allah saw this attitude of theirs, he turned the hearts of some of them against others and cursed them by the tongue of Prophet Dawood and

---

[315] *Ḥayaat aṣ-Ṣaḥabah*, 3/233.

> Prophet 'Eesa ibn Maryam, because they disobeyed and persisted in excesses (cf. Qur'an 5: 78). By the One in Whose hand is my soul, you must enjoin what is good and forbid what is evil, and you must restrain the hand of the wrongdoer and give him a stern warning to adhere to the truth, otherwise Allah will surely turn the hearts of some of you against others, and curse you as He has cursed them."[316]

She is wise and eloquent in her da'wah (preaching)

The Muslim woman who seeks to call others to Allah is eloquent and clever in her *da'wah*, speaking wisely and without being pushy to those whom she calls, and taking into account their intellectual levels and social positions. With this wise and good preaching, she is able to reach their hearts and minds, just as the Qur'an advises:

> "*Invite [all] to the Way of your Lord with wisdom and fair preaching...*" *(Qur'an 16: 125)*

The sister who is calling others is careful not to be long-winded or boring, and she avoids over-burdening her audience. She does not speak for too long, or discuss matters that are difficult to understand. She introduces the idea that she wants to convey in a brief and clear fashion, using attractive and interesting methods, and presenting the information in stages, so that her audience will understand it easily and will be eager to put their new knowledge into practice. This is what the Prophet (ﷺ) used to do in his own preaching, as the great *Ṣaḥaabi* 'Abdullah ibn Mas'ood (رضي الله عنه) tells us. He (Ibn Mas'ood) used to preach a little at a time to the people, every Thursday. A man said to him, "I wish that you would teach us every day." He said, "What prevents me from doing so is the fact that I would hate to bore

---

316 Ṭabaraani, 10/146; the men of its isnad are *rijaal aṣ-ṣaḥeeḥ*.

you. I show consideration towards you by choosing a suitable time to teach you, just as the Prophet (ﷺ) used to do with us, for fear of making us bored."[317]

One of the most important qualities of the wise and eloquent *daa'iyah* is that she is gentle with the women she is calling. She is patient with the slowness or inability to understand on the part of some of them, their ignorance of many matters of religion, their repeated mistakes and their many tedious questions, following the example of the master of all those men and women who call others to the way of Allah (ﷻ) — the Prophet (ﷺ) — who was the supreme example of patience, kindness and open-heartedness. He responded to questioners like a tolerant, caring guide and gently-correcting teacher, never frustrated by their slowness to understand, or irritated by their many questions and the need to repeat the same answers many times until they understood and left him, content with the lesson they had learned.

An example of this gentle approach is the account of the *Ṣaḥaabi* Mu'awiyah ibn al-Ḥakam as-Sulami (رضي الله عنه), who said: "Whilst I was praying with the Prophet (ﷺ), one of the men in the congregation sneezed, so I said, '*Yarḥamuk Allah* (may Allah have mercy on you).' The people glared at me, so I said, 'May my mother be bereft of me! What are you staring at me like that for?' They began to strike their thighs with their hands, and when I realised that they were telling me to be quiet, I fell silent. The Prophet (ﷺ), may my father and mother be sacrificed for him, finished the prayer, and I have never seen a better teacher than he, before or since. By Allah, he did not rebuke me or strike me or insult me. He merely said,

---

317 Bukhari and Muslim. See *Riyaḍ aṣ-Ṣaliḥeen*, 374, *Kitaab al-Adab, baab fil-wa'z wal-iqtiṣaad feehi.*

> 'This prayer should contain nothing of the everyday speech of men; it is just *tasbeeḥ, takbeer* and recitation of the Qur'an,' or words to that effect. I said, 'O' Messenger of Allah, I am still very close to the time of *jaahiliyah* (i.e., I am very new in Islam). Allah has brought us Islam, yet there are some among us who still go to soothsayers.' He said, 'Never go to them.' I said, 'And there are some who are superstitious.' He said, 'That is just something that they imagine; it should not stop them from going ahead with their plans.'"[318]

Another characteristic of the successful *daa'iyah*, and one of the most attractive and influential methods she can use, is that she does not directly confront wrongdoers with their deeds, or those who are failing with their shortcomings. Rather she is gentle in her approach when she addresses them, hinting at their wrongdoing or shortcomings indirectly rather than stating them bluntly, and asking them, gently and wisely, to rid themselves of whatever bad deeds or failings they have. She is careful not to hurt their feelings or put them off her *da'wah*. This wise, gentle approach is more effective in treating social ills and moral and psychological complaints, and it is the method followed by the Prophet (ﷺ), as 'Aa'ishah (رضي الله عنها) said:

> "When the Prophet heard that someone had done something wrong, he did not say 'What is wrong with so-and-so that he says (such-and-such)?' Rather, he would say, 'What is wrong with some people that they say such-and-such?...'"[319]

Another important feature of the *daa'iyah*, that will guarantee her success, is that she speaks clearly to her audience and repeats her words without boring them until she is certain that they have

---

[318] Muslim, 5/20, *Kitaab al-Masaajid, baab taḥreem al-kalaam fiṣ-ṣalaah.*

[319] *Ḥayaat aṣ-Ṣaḥabah*, 3/129.

understood and that her words have reached their hearts. This is what the Prophet (ﷺ) used to do, as Anas (رضي الله عنه) said:

> "The Prophet used to repeat things three times when he spoke, so that they would be understood. When he came to a people, he would greet them with *salaam* three times."[320]

'Aa'ishah (رضي الله عنها) said: "The speech of the Prophet was very clear. Everyone who heard it understood it."[321]

She mixes with righteous women

In her social life, the Muslim woman seeks to make friends with righteous women, so that they will be close friends and sisters to her, and she will be able to co-operate with them in righteousness, *taqwa* and good deeds, and in guiding and teaching other women who may have little awareness of Islam. Mixing with righteous women always brings goodness, benefits and a great reward, and deepens women's sound understanding of Islam. For this reason it was encouraged in the Qur'an:

> "*And keep your soul content with those who call on their Lord morning and evening, seeking His Face, and let not your eyes pass beyond them, seeking the pomp and glitter of this Life; nor obey any whose heart We have permitted to neglect the remembrance of Us, one who follows his own desires, whose case has gone beyond all bounds.*" *(Qur'an 18: 28)*

The true Muslim woman makes friends only with noble, virtuous, righteous, pious women, as the poet said:

---

320 *Fatḥ al-Baari*, 1/188, *Kitaab al-'Ilm, baab man a'aada al-ḥadeeth thalaathan li yufham 'anhu.*

321 Abu Dawood, 4/360, *Kitaab al-Adab*, 21; its isnad is *ṣaḥeeḥ*.

"Mixing with people of noble character, you will be counted as one of them,
So do not take anyone else for a friend."

The true Muslim woman does not find it difficult to mix with righteous women, even if they are apparently below her own socio-economic level. What really counts is a woman's essential personality, not her physical appearance or wealth. Moosa (Moses) (ﷺ), the Prophet of Allah, followed the righteous slave so that he might learn from him, saying with all good manners and respect:

> "*May I follow you on the footing that you teach me something of the [Higher] Truth which you have been taught?*" *(Qur'an 18: 66)*

When the righteous slave of Allah answered:

> "*Verily, you will not be able to have patience with me!*" *(Qur'an 18: 67)*

Moosa said, with all politeness and respect:

> "*You will find me, if Allah so will, [truly] patient: nor shall I disobey you in aught.*" *(Qur'an 18: 69)*

When choosing friends from among the righteous women, the Muslim woman does not forget that people are like metals, some of which are precious while others are base, as the Prophet (ﷺ) explained when describing different types of people:

> "People are metals like gold and silver. The best of them at the time of *Jaahiliyah* will be the best of them in Islam, if they truly understand. Souls are like conscripted soldiers: if they recognise one another, they will become friends, and if they dislike one another, they will go their separate ways."[322]

---

[322] Muslim, 16/185, *Kitaab al-Birr waṣ-Ṣilah wal-Aadaab, baab al-arwaaḥ junood mujannadah.*

The Muslim woman also knows from the teachings of her religion that friends are of two types: the righteous friend and the bad friend. The good friend is like the bearer of musk: when she sits with her, there is an atmosphere of relaxation, generosity, perfume and happiness. The bad friend is like the one who operates the bellows: when one sits with her, there is the heat of flames, smoke, stench and an atmosphere of gloom. The Prophet (ﷺ) gave the best analogy of this:

> "The good companion and the bad companion are like the bearer of musk and the one who pumps the bellows. With the bearer of musk, either he will give you a share, or you will buy from him, or you will smell a pleasant scent from him; but with the one who pumps the bellows, either he will burn your clothes or you will smell a foul stench from him."[323]

Therefore the *Ṣaḥaabah* used to encourage one another to visit good people who would remind them of Allah (ﷻ) and fill their hearts with fear of Allah, religious teaching and respect. Anas (رضي الله عنه) reported the following incident:

"Abu Bakr (رضي الله عنه) said to 'Umar (رضي الله عنه), after the Prophet (ﷺ) had died, 'Let us go and visit Umm Ayman[324] as the Messenger of Allah used to do.' When they reached her, she wept, so they asked her, 'Why do you weep? What is with Allah is better for the Prophet (than this world).' She said, 'I am not weeping because I do not know that what is with Allah is better for the Prophet. I am weeping because the

323 (Bukhari and Muslim), See *Riyaḍ aṣ-Ṣaliḥeen*, 211, *baab ziyarat ahl al-khayr wa majaalisatihim.*

324 Umm Ayman was the Prophet's nursemaid during his childhood. When he grew up, he gave her her freedom and married her to Zayd ibn Ḥarithah. He used to honour her and treat her with kindness and respect, and say, "Umm Ayman is my mother." (Author)

Revelation from Heaven has ceased.' She moved them deeply with these words, and they began to weep with her."[325]

The gatherings of righteous women, where Allah (ﷻ) is remembered and the conversation is serious and beneficial, are surrounded by the angels and shaded by Allah (ﷻ) with His mercy. In such gatherings, souls and minds are purified and refreshed. It befits righteous, believing women to increase their attendance at such gatherings and benefit from them, as this will do them good in this world and bring them a high status in the Hereafter.

She strives to reconcile between Muslim women

The Muslim community is distinguished by the fact that it is a community in which brotherhood prevails, a society that is filled with love, communication, understanding, tolerance and purity. However, it is still a human society, and as such it cannot be entirely free of occasional disputes and conflicts which may arise among its members from time to time and lead to division and a breaking of ties.

But these disputes, which emerge sometimes in the Muslim community, soon disappear, because of the divine guidance that the members of this community have received, which reinforces the feelings of brotherhood, love and closeness among them, and destroys the roots of hatred and enmity, and because of the good efforts for reconciliation that Islam urges its followers to make whenever there is a dispute between close friends, where the *Shayṭaan* has caused conflict and division between them. We have seen above how Islam forbids two disputing Muslims to forsake one another for more than three days:

> "It is not permitted for a believer to forsake another for more than three days. If three days have passed, let him

---

325 Muslim, 16/9, *Kitaab Faḍaa'il aṣ-Ṣaḥaabah, baab faḍaa'il Umm Ayman.*

meet him and greet him with *salaam*. If he returns the greeting, then they will both share in the reward, and if he does not return the greeting, then the one who initiated the greeting will be free of blame."[326]

Islam also commands the Muslims, men and women, to reconcile between two conflicting parties:

"*If two parties among the Believers fall into a quarrel, make peace between them: but if one of them transgresses beyond bounds against the other, then fight [all of you] against the one that transgresses until it complies, then make peace between them with justice, and be fair: for Allah loves those who are fair [and just].*" *(Qur'an 49: 9)*

The society of believing men and women should be governed by justice, love and brotherhood:

"*The Believers are but a single Brotherhood: so make peace and reconciliation between your two [contending] brothers; and fear Allah, that you may receive Mercy.*" *(Qur'an 49: 10)*

Therefore the Muslim woman is required to reconcile between her disputing sisters, following the guidance of Islam. Islam has permitted women to add words for the purpose of bringing disputing parties together and softening stony hearts. Such comments are not considered to be the kinds of lies that are *ḥaraam*, and the one who says them is not regarded as a liar or a sinner.

We find evidence of this in the hadith of Umm Kalthum bint 'Uqbah ibn Abi Mu'ayṭ (رضي الله عنها), who said: "I heard the Messenger of Allah

---

[326] Bukhari: *Al-Adab al-Mufrad*, 1/505, *baab innas-salaam yujzi' min aṣ-ṣaum.*

(Blessings and Peace be upon him) say:

> "He is not a liar who reconciles between people by telling them good news or saying something good.'"[327]

According to a report narrated by Muslim, she added:

> "I did not hear him permit anything of what people might say except in three cases." She meant: war, reconciling between people, and the speech of a man to his wife or a wife to her husband.[328]

She mixes with other women and puts up with their insults

The active Muslim woman is a woman with a mission who has a message to deliver. Whoever undertakes this important mission should prepare herself to be patient and steadfast, and to make sacrifices along the way.

The active Muslim woman has no other choice but to put up with the bad attitude and rude reactions of some women, their misinterpretation of her aims, their mocking of her call to adhere to the morals and manners of Islam, their shallow and confused thinking, their slow response to the truth, their focus on themselves and their own interests, their concern with foolish, trivial matters, their devotion to this world and its pleasures, their failure to take the Hereafter into account or to follow the commandments of Islam, and other foolish things that may annoy the *daa'iyahs* and make them, in moments of irritation and frustration, think of isolating themselves and keeping away from people, and abandoning their work for the

---

[327] (Bukhari and Muslim), See *Riyaḍ uṣ-Ṣaliḥeen*, 687, *Kitaab al-Umoor al-munhi 'anha, baab bayaan maa yajooz min al-kadhib.*

[328] Muslim, 16/157, *Kitaab al-Birr waṣ-Ṣilah wal-Aadaab, baab taḥreem al-kadhib wa bayaan maa yubaaḥ minhu.*

sake of Allah. This is what all those men and women who seek to call others to Allah (ﷻ) face in every place and time.

For this reason the Prophet (ﷺ) sought to strengthen the resolve of the believers and reassure them, by announcing that those who have patience in treading the long and difficult path of *da'wah* are better, according to the scale of *taqwa* and righteous deeds, than those who have no patience:

> "The believer who mixes with people and bears their insults with patience is better than the one who does not mix with people or bear their insults with patience."[329]

The Prophet (ﷺ), and the other Prophets before him, represent the supreme example of patience in the face of people's misbehaviour, suspicions and foolishness. The *daa'i* needs to hold fast to this example every time he feels his patience running out, or that he is under stress and overwhelmed by the insults and hostility of people.

One example of the Prophet's supreme patience comes in a report given by Bukhari and Muslim. The Prophet (ﷺ) divided some goods as he usually did, but one of the Anṣaar said, "By Allah, this division was not done for the sake of Allah." The Prophet (ﷺ) heard these unjust words and was deeply offended by them. His expression changed and he became angry, but then he said,

> "Prophet Moosa suffered worse insults than these, and he bore them with patience."

With these few words, the Prophet's anger was dispelled and his noble, forgiving heart was soothed.

This is the attitude of the Prophets and the sincere *daa'is* in every time and place: patience in the face of people's insults, suspicions and

---

329 Bukhari: *Al-Adab al-Mufrad*, 1/478, *baab alladhi yuṣbir 'ala adha an-naas.*

rumours. Without this patience, the *da'wah* could not continue and the *daa'is* could not persevere.

The clever Muslim woman who calls other to Allah is not lacking in intelligence; she is able to understand the psychology, intellectual level and social position of her audience, and she addresses each type of woman in the way that will be most appropriate and effective.

She repays favours and is grateful for them

One of the characteristics of the true Muslim woman is that she is faithful and loyal: she appreciates favours and thanks the one who does them, following the command of the Prophet (ﷺ):

> "Whoever has a good turn done to him should return the favour."[330]

> "Whoever seeks refuge with Allah, then grant him protection... and whoever does you a good turn, then return the favour."[331]

For the alert Muslim woman, gratitude for favours is a religious matter encouraged by the teachings of the Prophet (ﷺ). It is not merely the matter of social courtesy dictated by mood or whatever interests may be at stake. The one who does a favour deserves to be thanked, even if no particular interest is served by her deed. It is sufficient that she has done a favour, and for this she deserves to be sincerely thanked. This is what Islam expects of Muslim men and women. One thanks the other person for her good intentions and chivalrous motives, and for hastening to do good, regardless of the actual or potential outcome in terms of one's interests and desires.

---

330 Tirmidhi, 4/380, *Kitaab al-Birr waṣ-Ṣilah*, 87, a *ḥasan jayyid ghareeb* hadith.

331 Abu Dawood, 2/172, *Kitaab az-Zakah*; Aḥmad, 2/68. Its isnad is *ṣaheeḥ*.

The concern of Islam to establish this attitude in the heart of the Muslim reached the extent that gratitude towards Allah (ﷻ) is deemed to be incomplete and imperfect without gratitude towards people for their favours and good deeds. The one who does not thank people for their acts of kindness or find a word to say that will make them feel chivalrous, is an ungrateful wretch who does not appreciate blessings or give thanks for them. Such a one is not qualified to give thanks to Allah, the Giver of all blessings and favours. Concerning this the Prophet (ﷺ) said:

> "He does not give thanks to Allah who does not give thanks to people."[332]

The wise Muslim woman does not forget that thanking the one who has done a favour encourages good deeds and makes people become accustomed to acknowledging and appreciating good deeds. All of this will strengthen the ties of friendship between the members of a community, open their hearts to love, and motivate them to do good deeds. This is what Islam aims at to instill and reinforce in the Islamic society.

She visits the sick

Visiting the sick is one of the Islamic social customs that was established and encouraged by the Prophet (ﷺ), who made it a duty on every Muslim, man and woman, and made it a right that one Muslim may expect from another:

> "The rights of a Muslim over his brother are five: he should return his *salaam*, visit the sick, attend funerals, accept invitations, and 'bless' a person (by saying '*Yarḥamuk Allah*') when he sneezes."[333]

---

[332] Bukhari: *Al-Adab al-Mufrad*, 1/310, *baab man lam yashkur an-naas.*

[333] (Bukhari and Muslim), See *Riyaḍ aṣ-Ṣaliḥeen*, 452, *baab 'iyaadah al-mareeḍ.*

According to another report, the Prophet (ﷺ) said:

> "The rights of the Muslim over his brother are six." It was asked, "What are they?" The Prophet said: "When you meet him, greet him with *salaam*; when he invites you, accept his invitation; when he seeks your advice, advise him; when he sneezes and says '*Al-ḥamdu-lillah*', 'bless' him (by saying '*Yarḥamuk Allah*'); when he is ill, visit him; and when he dies, follow the bier — attend his funeral — to his grave."[334]

When the Muslim woman visits the sick, she does not feel that she is merely doing a favour or trying to be nice; she feels that she is doing an Islamic duty that the Prophet (ﷺ) urged Muslims to do:

> "Feed the hungry, visit the sick, and ransom the prisoners of war."[335]

Al-Bara' ibn 'Aazib (رضي الله عنه) said:

> "The Messenger of Allah commanded us to visit the sick, to attend funerals, to 'bless' someone when he sneezes, to fulfil all oaths, to come to the aid of the oppressed, to accept invitations, and to greet everyone with *salaam*."[336]

When the Muslim woman visits the sick, she does not feel that this is a burdensome duty that could depress her because of the atmosphere of gloom and despair that may surround the sick person. On the contrary, she senses a feeling of spiritual joy and satisfaction which

---

334 Muslim, 14/143, *Kitaab as-Salaam, baab min ḥaqq al-Muslim lil-Muslim radd as-salaam.*

335 *Fatḥ al-Baari*, 9/517, *Kitaab al-Aṭ'imah, baab kuloo min ṭayibaat maa razaqnaakum.*

336 (Bukhari and Muslim) See *Riyaḍ aṣ-Ṣaliḥeen*, 451, *Kitaab 'Iyaadah al-Mareeḍ, baab 'iyaadah al-mareeḍ.*

none can feel except those who truly understand the hadith which describes the goodness, reward and blessing contained in such visits. The Prophet (ﷺ) said:

> "Allah will say on the Day of Resurrection: 'O' son of Adam, I fell ill and you did not visit Me.' He will say, 'O' Lord, how could I visit You when You are the Lord of the Worlds?' He will say, 'Did you not know that My servant so-and-so had fallen ill, and you did not visit him? Did you not know that had you visited him, you would have found Me with him? O' son of Adam, I asked you for food and you did not feed Me.' He will say, 'O' Lord, how could I feed you when You are the Lord of the Worlds?' He will say, 'Did you not know that My servant so-and-so asked you for food, and you did not feed him? Did you not know that had you fed him you would surely have found that (i.e., the reward for doing so) with Me? O' son of Adam, I asked you to give Me to drink and you did not give Me to drink.' He will say, 'O' Lord, how could I give You to drink when You are the Lord of the Worlds?' He will say, 'My servant so-and-so asked you to give him to drink and you did not give him to drink. Had you given him to drink you would surely have found that with Me.'"[337]

How blessed is such a visit, and how great a good deed, which a man undertakes to do for his sick brother, when by doing so he is in the presence of the Almighty Lord who witnesses his noble deed and rewards him generously for it. Is there any greater and more blessed visit which is honoured and blessed and encouraged by the Lord of Heavens and Earth? How great is the misery and loss that will befall

[337] Muslim, 16/125, *Kitaab al-Birr waṣ-Ṣilah wal-Aadaab, baab faḍl 'iyaadah al-mareeḍ.*

the one who failed in this duty! How great will be his humiliation when the Almighty Lord declares, before all present: "O' son of Adam, I fell ill and you did not visit Me... Did you not know that My servant so-and-so had fallen ill, and you did not visit him? Did you not know that had you visited him, you would have found Me with him?" We will leave to our imagination the sense of regret, humiliation and shame that will overwhelm the man who neglected to visit his sick brother, at the time when such regret will be of no avail.

The sick person in an Islamic community feels that he is not alone at his hour of need; the empathy and prayers of the people around him envelop him and alleviate his suffering. This is the pinnacle of human civility and emotion. No other nation in history has ever known such a level of emotional and social responsibility as exists in the ummah of Islam.

The sick person in the West may find a hospital to admit him and a doctor to give him medicine, but rarely will he find a healing touch, compassionate word, kindly smile, sincere prayers, or true sympathy. The materialistic philosophy that has taken over Westerners' lives has extinguished the light of human emotion, destroyed brotherly feelings towards one's fellow-man, and removed any motives but materialistic ones for doing good deeds.

The Westerner does not have any motive to visit the sick, unless he feels that he may gain some material benefit from this visit sooner or later. In contrast, we find that the Muslim is motivated to visit the sick in the hope of earning the reward which Allah (ﷻ) has prepared for the one who gets his feet dusty (i.e., goes out and about) for His sake.

There are many hadith texts on this topic, which awaken feelings of brotherhood in the Muslim's heart and strongly motivate him to visit his sick brother. For example:

> "When the Muslim visits his (sick) Muslim brother, he remains in the fruits, garden of Paradise[338] until he returns."[339]

> "No Muslim visits a (sick) Muslim in the morning but seventy thousand angels will bless (and pray for) him until the evening, and if he visits him in the evening, seventy thousand angels will bless (and pray for) him until the morning, and fruits from Paradise will be his."[340]

With his deep insight into human psychology, the Prophet (ﷺ) understood the positive impact of such visits on the sick person and his family, so he never neglected to visit the sick and speak to them the kindest words of prayer and consolation. He was the epitome of such kindness, which led him to visit a young Jewish boy who used to serve him, as Anas (رضي الله عنه) narrated:

> "A young Jewish boy used to serve the Prophet. He fell ill, so the Prophet went to visit him. He sat by his head and told him, 'Enter Islam.' The boy looked to his father, who was present with him. His father said, 'Obey Abu'l-Qaasim.' So the boy entered Islam. The Prophet left, saying, 'Praise be to Allah, Who has saved him from the Fire.'"[341]

When visiting this sick Jewish boy, the Prophet (ﷺ) did not neglect to call him to Islam, because he knew the effects his visit would have

---

338 A metaphor for the reward earned. (Translator)

339 Muslim, 16/125, *Kitaab al-Birr waṣ-Ṣilah wal-Aadaab, baab faḍl 'iyaadah al-mareeḍ.*

340 Tirmidhi, 3/292, *Kitaab al-Janaa'iz*, 2. He said it is a *ḥasan* hadith.

341 *Fatḥ al-Baari*, 3/219, *Kitaab al-Janaa'iz, baab hal yu'raḍ 'ala aṣ-ṣabi al-Islam?*

on the boy and his father, who were overwhelmed by his generosity, kindness and gentle approach. So they responded to him. This visit bore fruits of guidance, and the Prophet (ﷺ) left praising Allah (ﷻ) that a soul had been saved from the Fire. What a great man, and what a wise and eloquent *daa'i* the Prophet (ﷺ) was!

The Prophet (ﷺ) was so concerned about visiting the sick that he set out principles and guidelines for so doing, which were followed by the *Ṣaḥaabah* and recorded in the books of Sunnah.

One of these practices is to sit at the head of the sick person, as we have seen in the story of the Jewish boy, and as Ibn 'Abbaas said:

> "When the Prophet visited a sick person, he would sit by his head then say seven times: 'I ask Almighty Allah, the Lord of the Mighty Throne, to heal you.'"[342]

Another of these practices is to wipe the body of the sick person with the right hand and pray for him, as 'Aa'ishah (رضي الله عنها) reported:

> "The Prophet used to visit some of his relatives and wipe them with his right hand, saying 'O' Allah, Lord of mankind, remove the suffering. Heal for You are the Healer. There is no healing except for Your healing, the healing which leaves no trace of sickness.'"[343]

Ibn 'Abbaas (رضي الله عنه) said:

> "The Prophet went to visit a Bedouin who was sick, and whenever he visited a sick person, he would say, 'No worry, (it is) purification[344], *insha Allah.*'"[345]

---

[342] Bukhari: *Al-Adab al-Mufrad*,1/633, *baab ayna yaq'ud al-'aa'id.*

[343] (Bukhari and Muslim), See *Riyaḍ aṣ-Ṣaliḥeen*, 454, *Kitaab 'Iyaadah al-Mareeḍ, baab fi ma yud'aa bihi lil-mareeḍ.*

[344] i.e., may your sickness be an expiation and cleanse you of your sins. (Author)

[345] *Fatḥ al-Baari*, 10/118, *Kitaab al-Marḍa, baab 'iyaadah al-a'araab.*

The Muslim woman whom Islam has filled with a sense of great humanity hastens to visit the sick whenever she hears news of someone's illness. She does not try to postpone or avoid such visits, because she feels the importance of them in the depths of her heart, as the Prophet (ﷺ) described it and as the virtuous early Muslim women put it into practice in the most praiseworthy fashion. They did not only visit women who were sick; they also visited men, within the framework of modesty and avoiding *fitnah.*

Ṣaḥeeḥ Bukhari states that Umm ad-Darda' visited an Anṣaari man who lived in the mosque (when he was sick).

The same source also gives the following account: "Qutaybah told us, from Maalik, from Hisham ibn 'Urwah, from his father, from 'Aa'ishah who said: 'When the Messenger of Allah (ﷺ) came to Madeenah, Abu Bakr and Bilal, may Allah be pleased with them, fell ill. I visited them and said, 'O' my father, how are you feeling? O' Bilal, how are you feeling?''''[346]

The Muslim women of the early generation understood the meaning of visiting the sick and the role it plays in maintaining the ties of friendship, compassion and affection. So they hastened to perform this noble duty, lifting the spirits of the sick person, wiping away the tears of the grief-stricken, alleviating the burden of distress, strengthening the ties of brotherhood, and consoling the distressed. The modern Muslim woman could do well to follow the example of the early Muslim women and revive this praiseworthy sunnah.

She does not wail over the dead

The Muslim woman who knows the teachings of her religion has insight and is balanced and self-controlled. When she is stricken by the death of one of those whom she loves, she does not let grief make

---

346 *Fatḥ al-Baari*, 10/117, *Kitaab al-Marḍa, baab 'iyaadah an-nisa' ar-rijaal.*

her lose her senses, as is the case with shallow, ignorant women who fall apart with grief. She bears it with patience, hoping for reward from Allah (ﷻ), and follows the guidance of Islam in her behaviour at this difficult time.

She never wails over the deceased, because wailing is not an Islamic deed; it is the practice of the *kuffaar*, and one of the customs of *jaahiliyah*. The Prophet (ﷺ) was very explicit in his emphatic prohibition of wailing, to the extent that it was regarded as *kufr*:

> "There are two qualities in people that are indicative of *kufr*: casting doubts on a person's lineage, and wailing over the dead."[347]

The Prophet (ﷺ) effectively excluded from the Muslim community those men and women who wail and eulogise the dead when he said:

> "He is not one of us who strikes his cheeks, or tears his garment, or speaks the words of *jaahiliyah*."[348]

The Muslim woman who understands the teachings of Islam knows that death is real, that everyone on this earth is mortal and that this life is merely a corridor to the Hereafter, where eternity will be in the presence of Allah. So there is no need for this uncontrollable grief which makes a person become unbalanced and lose his reason so that he starts to strike his own face and tear his clothes, screaming with grief and loss.

The *Ṣaḥaabah* understood this ruling of Islam, even though they had only very recently left the *jaahiliyah* behind. They used to forbid themselves to eulogise the dead or raise their voices or scream or tear

---

[347] Muslim, 2/57, *Kitaab al-Eemaan, baab iṭlaaq al-kufr 'ala aṭ-ṭa'an fin-nasab wan-niyaaḥah.*

[348] (Bukhari and Muslim), See *Sharḥ as-Sunnah*, 5/436, *Kitaab al-Janaa'iz, baab an-nahy 'an an-niyaaḥah wan-nadab.*

their clothes, which were the actions done by the women at the time of *jaahiliyah*. They knew that Islam does not accept the deeds of *jaahiliyah* and does not permit them to return to from time to time. They used to condemn such actions just as the Prophet (ﷺ) did.

Abu Burdah ibn Abi Moosa said:

"Abu Moosa suffered from some pain, and fell into a coma. His head was in the lap of a woman from his family. She shouted at him, but he was not able to respond. When he regained his strength he said: 'I shun whatever the Messenger of Allah (ﷺ) shunned, for he shunned every women who raises her voice, cuts her hair and tears her clothes (at the time of disaster).'"[349]

Although Islam has forbidden senseless *jaahili* actions like sticking one's cheeks, tearing one's garment, wailing and eulogising, it recognises the grief that overwhelms the heart and the tears that softly flow at the departure of a loved one. All of this is part of the legitimate human emotion and gentle compassion that Allah (ﷻ) has instilled in people's hearts, as was demonstrated by the Prophet (ﷺ) in his words and deeds.

Usaamah ibn Zayd said:

> "We were with the Prophet when one of his daughters sent for him, calling him to come and telling him that her boy — or son — was dying. The Prophet said: 'Go back to her and tell her that whatever Allah gives and takes belongs to Him, and everything has its appointed time with Him. Tell her to have patience and to seek reward from Allah.' The one who conveyed this message came back and said: 'She swore that you should come to her.' The Prophet got up, as did Ṣa'd ibn

---

[349] Muslim, 2/110, *Kitaab al-Eemaan, baab taḥreem ḍarb al-khudood wa shiqq al-juyoob.*

'Ubadah and Mu'aadh ibn Jabal, and I went with them. The boy was lifted up to him, and his soul was making a sound like water being poured into an empty container (i.e., the death-rattle). The Prophet's eye's filled with tears, and Ṣa'd said to him, 'What is this, O' Messenger of Allah?' He said, 'This is the compassion that Allah has placed in the hearts of His servants, and Allah will show compassion to those of His slaves who have compassion.'"[350]

'Abdullah ibn 'Umar (ﷺ) said:

"Ṣa'd ibn 'Ubadah fell ill with some complaint that he suffered from, and the Prophet came to visit him, accompanied by 'Abdur-Raḥmaan ibn 'Awf, Ṣa'd ibn Abi Waqqas and 'Abdullah ibn Mas'ood (may Allah be pleased with them all). When he entered and found him in a coma, he asked, 'Has he passed away?' They said, 'No, O' Messenger of Allah.' The Messenger of Allah wept, and when the people saw him weeping, they wept too. He said, 'Are you not listening? Allah will not punish a man for the tears that fall from his eyes or for the grief that he feels in his heart, but He will either punish or have mercy on a man because of this,' and he pointed to his tongue."[351]

Anas (ﷺ) said:

"The Messenger of Allah went to his son Ibraheem as he was surrendering his soul (i.e., dying). Tears began to well up in the Prophet's eyes. 'Abdur-Raḥmaan ibn

---

[350] Muslim, 6/224, 225, *Kitaab al-Janaa'iz, baab al-buka' 'ala al-mayyit.*

[351] (Bukhari and Muslim), See *Sharḥ as-Sunnah*, 5/429, *Kitaab al-Janaa'iz, baab al-buka' 'ala al-mayyit.*

> 'Awf said to him, 'Even you, O' Messenger of Allah?' He said, 'O' Ibn 'Awf, this is compassion.' Then he wept some more and said, 'The eyes shed tears, and the heart feels grief, but we say only that which will please our Lord. And truly we are deeply grieved by your departure, O' Ibraheem.'"[352]

The Prophet (ﷺ) approved of expressing grief by letting tears flow, because people have no power to restrain tears at times of grief, but he forbade every deed that can inflame and exacerbate grief. Shedding tears, in moderation, can help to soothe the pain of grief, but wailing, eulogising, screaming and other *jaahili* actions only increase the anguish and make a person more prone to collapse. These actions are what the Arabs used to do at the time of *jaahiliyah*, when a person would even request it before his death, so that others would come and wail over the dead, enumerating his good qualities and exaggerating about the impact of this bereavement. An example of this is to be seen in the poetry of Ṭarafah ibn al-'Abd:

> "When I die, mention my qualities as befits me,
> And rend your garments for me, O' daughter of Ma'bad.
> Do not make me like a man whose aspirations are not
> Like my aspirations, who could not do what I could do, or play the role I played."

All of this is forbidden by Islam most emphatically, because it is a waste of energy and contradicts the acceptance of Allah's will and decree; it also opens the way for the *Shayṭaan* to lead people astray and cause *fitnah*. The Prophet (ﷺ) referred to this, in the hadith narrated by Umm Salamah (رضي الله عنها), who said:

> "When Abu Salaamah died, I said, 'He is a stranger in a strange land. I shall certainly cry over him in such a way

---

[352] Bukhari and Muslim. See *Riyaḍ aṣ-Ṣaliḥeen*, 463, *Kitaab 'Iyaadah al-Mareeḍ, baab jawaaz al-bukaa' 'ala al-mayyit bi ghayri nadab wa laa niyaḥah.*

> that people will talk about it.' I prepared myself to cry over him, but a woman who was coming from the high places of Madeenah to help me (in crying and wailing) was met by the Messenger of Allah. He asked, 'Do you want to let the *Shayṭaan* (Satan) enter a house from which Allah has expelled him twice?'[353] So I stopped crying, and I did not cry."[354]

The Prophet's concern to forbid wailing, especially among women, reached such a level that when he accepted the oath of allegiance (*bay'ah*) from women, he asked them to pledge to keep away from wailing. This is seen in the hadith narrated by Bukhari and Muslim from Umm 'Atiyah who said:

> "The Prophet accepted the pledge of allegiance from us on the basis that we would not wail."[355]

According to a report narrated by Muslim also from Umm 'Atiyah, she said:

> "When the *aayah* (verse),
>
> '*When believing women come to you to take the oath of fealty to you, that they will not associate in worship any other thing except Allah... And that they will not disobey you in any just matter...*' *(Qur'an 60: 12)*,

---

353 The first time was when Abu Salamah surrendered his soul (died), and some of his family were grief-stricken. The Prophet (ﷺ) told them, "Do not pray for anything but good for yourselves, for the angels are saying '*Ameen*' to whatever you say," then he prayed for Abu Salamah. The second time was when Umm Salamah started telling herself that she would exaggerate in her crying for him, then she changed her mind. (Author)

354 Muslim, 6/224, *Kitaab al-Janaa'iz, baab al-bukaa' 'ala al-mayyit.*

355 *Fatḥ al-Baari*, 3/176, *Kitaab al-Janaa'iz, baab maa yunha min an-nawḥ wal-buka'*; Muslim, 6/237, *Kitab al-Janaa'iz, baab taḥreem an-niyaḥah.*

— was revealed, she said, part of that was wailing."[356]

The Prophet (ﷺ) warned the woman who wails over the dead that if she does not repent before her own death, she will be raised on the Day of Resurrection in a most fearful state:

> "The woman who wails, and does not repent before she dies, will be raised on the Day of Resurrection wearing a shirt of tar and a garment of scabs."[357]

He also warned that the angels of mercy would be kept away from her, and she would be deprived of their *du'aa'* for her, as long as she insisted on wailing and making grief worse. This is seen in the hadith narrated by Aḥmad:

> "The angels will not pray for the one who wails and laments."[358]

Because of this clear, definitive prohibition of wailing, screaming, eulogising, tearing one's garments and other *jaahili* actions, the Muslim woman can do nothing but submit to the commands of Allah and His Messenger, and keep away from everything that could compromise the purity of her faith in the will and decree of Allah. She does not just stop there, however, she also calls women who may be unaware of this to obey the laws of Allah and to keep away from wailing, once they have understood the commandments of Allah and His Messenger.

She does not attend funerals (follow bier)

The Muslim woman who truly understands the teachings of Islam does not attend funerals, in obedience to the command of the Prophet

---

[356] Muslim, 6/238, *Kitaab l-Janaa'iz, baab taḥreem an-niyaḥah.*

[357] Ibid, 6/235.

[358] Imam Aḥmad, *Al-Musnad*, 2/362; the men of its isnad are *thiqaat.*

(ﷺ), as reported by Umm 'Atiyah (رضي الله عنها):

> "We were forbidden to attend funerals, but not strictly."[359]

In this case, women's position is the opposite of men's position. Islam encourages men to attend funerals and to accompany the body until it is buried, but it dislikes women to do so, because their presence could result in inappropriate situations that would compromise the dignity of death and the funeral rites. Accompanying the deceased until the burial offers a great lesson to those who do it, and seeking forgiveness for the deceased, and thinking of the meaning of death that touches every living thing:

> "*Wherever you are, death will find you out, even if you are in towers built up strong and high!...*"
>
> *(Qur'an 4: 78)*

The Prophet (ﷺ) discouraged women from attending funeral procession (made it *makrooh*), but did not forbid it outright, because his discouraging it should be enough to make the obedient Muslim woman refrain from doing it. This is a sign of the strength of her Islam, her sincere obedience to Allah and His Messenger, and her willingness to adopt the attitude, which is better and more befitting.

---

359 *Fatḥ al-Baari*, 3/144, *Kitaab al-Janaa'iz, baab ittiba' an-nisa' al-janaa'iz*; Muslim, 7/2, *Kitaab al-Janaa'iz, baab nahy an-nisa' 'an ittiba' al-janaa'iz.*

Conclusion

In the preceding pages, I have explained the character of the Muslim woman as Islam wants her to be, according to the wise guidance it gives her in all aspects of life and in the forming of her mind, soul, psyche, morals and behaviour. This is referred to quite clearly in many *ayat* and *ṣaḥeeḥ* hadiths, which strike a precise balance in her character, in such a way that no one aspect dominates at the expense of another, and vividly describe the ideal way of dealing with one's parents, relatives, husband, children, neighbours, friends and sisters in Islam, and others whom one meets in the society in which one lives.

The previous chapters explained that the Muslim woman's role is not merely to stay at home, nursing children and taking care of the home. In addition to all that, the Muslim woman is in fact raising a heroic new generation, playing an important role in *da'wah* and making an important, constructive contribution in all areas of life, working side-by-side with men to populate and cultivate the earth, enrich life and make people happy.

It is abundantly clear that the Muslim woman who is guided by Islam is pure, constructive, productive, alert, aware, educated and refined. She fully understands her duties towards Allah (ﷻ), and towards herself, her parents, her husband and children, her relatives, her neighbours, her friends and sisters in Islam, and her society as a whole, with all the different types of people, events and transactions it includes.

She believes in Allah and the Last Day; she is alert to the trials of this life and the traps of the *Shayṭaan*; she worships Allah, obeys His commands, heeds His prohibitions, accepts His will and decree, returns to His protection and seeks His forgiveness when she stumbles or becomes negligent; she is aware of her responsibility before Allah towards the members of her family; she is keen to please Him by whatever she does; she understands the true meaning of being a servant of Allah and supports His true religion; she enjoins what is good and forbids what is evil as much as she is able.

She is aware of her obligations towards herself, understanding that she is a human being composed of a body, mind and soul, each of which has its own needs and requirements. Hence she is careful to strike the right balance between her body, mind and spirit; she does not devote attention to one at the expense of the others, rather, she devotes to each of them the attention that is needed to form a balanced personality, always guided by the wise teachings of Islam as seen in the Qur'an, the Sunnah and example of the righteous *salaf* (predecessors) who followed in the footsteps of the Prophet (ﷺ) with all sincerity.

She takes care of her outward appearance without going to extremes of excess or showing off, and she takes care of her inner nature in a manner that befits the human being whom Allah has honoured by making the angels prostrate to him and subjugating all that is in heaven and earth for his benefit. In this way, she develops a balanced, likeable character, one that is attractive both in appearance and in her thinking, reasoning, behaviour and reactions.

She does not allow her care of her body and mind to distract her from spiritual matters; she devotes just as much attention to her spiritual development, and polishes her soul through worship, *dhikr* and reading the Qur'an. Her guideline in all of this is to maintain a precise balance between all aspects of her personality.

She treats her parents with kindness and respect. She knows their status, and her duties towards them, and she is very cautious not to disobey them. She never spares any effort to find the best way to treat them properly, and she surrounds them with every type of care, honour and respect.

With her husband, she is an ideal wife, intelligent, respectful, obedient, tolerant and loving, eager to please him and to respect and honour his family. She conceals his secrets, and helps him to be righteous, to fear Allah and to do good deeds. She fills his heart with happiness, peace and tranquillity.

With her children, she is a loving, compassionate mother who wisely understands the great importance of her motherly role in bringing them up. She makes them aware of her love and care for them, and never withholds right guidance from them or fails to correct them if they need it, so that they will grow up with an ideal Islamic upbringing that will cultivate in them the best morals and attitudes and a love for the highest things.

With her daughters- and sons-in-law, she is kind, fair and wise, and offers them sincere advice. She does not interfere in their private matters. She treats them well and strives to strengthen the bonds of love and to ward off the evils of disputes.

With her relatives, she upholds the ties of love, and does not neglect to keep in touch and treat them well. She is keen to maintain the relationship even if they do not uphold the ties, acting in obedience to the teachings of Islam, which urge the upholding of the ties of kinship with love and affection.

She treats her neighbours well and is concerned about them. She knows the great rights they have, which Jibreel (Gabriel) emphasised to the Prophet (ﷺ) so strongly that the Prophet thought he was going to make them his heirs. So she likes for them what she likes for herself. She treats them well, respects their feelings, puts up with their insults, turns a blind eye to their faults and mistakes, and is careful not to mistreat them or to fall short in her treatment of them.

With her friends and sisters in Islam, she is distinguished from other women by way in which she builds her relationship with them on a basis of love for the sake of Allah, which is the highest and purest love that exists among human beings, as it is free from any impurity or ulterior motive and its purity is derived from the light of the Revelation and Prophetic guidance. Therefore, the Muslim woman is sincere and tolerant in her feelings of love and sisterhood towards her sisters, and she is keen to maintain the ties of sisterhood and love between her and them. She does not: cut them off, forsake them, gossip about them, hurt their feelings with hostile arguments and disputes, bear grudges, or withhold any favour she could do for them, and she always greets them with a cheerful, smiling face.

In her relationship with her society, she is a social being of the highest class, because of what she has learned of the wise teachings of Islam concerning social dealings and high morals. From the rich spring of Islam she derives her customs, habits and behaviour and the ethics and values which purify her soul and form her distinct social character.

She is of good character (has a good attitude towards others) and is sincere and straightforward with all people. She does not cheat, deceive or stab in the back. She is not a hypocrite. She does not speak falsely (or bear false witness). She offers sincere advice and guides others to good deeds. She keeps her promises. She has the characteristic of modesty and self-respect. She does not interfere in that which does not concern her. She avoids slandering the honour of others and seeking out their faults. She does not show off. She is fair in her judgements of others. She does not oppress others. She is fair even to those whom she does not like. She does not rejoice in the misfortunes of others. She avoids suspicion. She restrains her tongue from malicious gossip. She avoids cursing and obscene speech. She does not make fun of anybody. She is gentle with people. She is compassionate. She strives to benefit others and protect them from harm. She eases the hardship of one who is suffering. She is generous. She does not remind the beneficiaries of her charity. She is patient. She is tolerant. She does not bear grudges or harbour resentment. She is easy-going, not harsh. She is not envious. She avoids boasting and showing off. She does not speak in an affected or exaggerated manner. She has a likeable personality. She is friendly and likeable. She keeps secrets. She is of cheerful countenance. She has a sense of humour. She tries to make people happy. She is not over-strict. She is not arrogant. She is humble. She is modest in her dress and appearance. She pursues noble things. She is concerned about the affairs of the Muslims. She honours guests. She prefers others to herself. She measures her habits and customs against the standards of Islam. She uses the greeting of Islam. She does not enter any house other than her own without permission. She sits wherever she finds room in a gathering. She does not converse privately with another woman when a third is present. She respects her elders and distinguished people. She does not look into any house other than her own. She chooses work that suits her feminine nature. She does not imitate men. She calls others to the truth. She enjoins what is good and forbids what is evil. She is wise and eloquent in her *da'wah*. She mixes with righteous women. She hastens to reconcile between Muslim women. She mixes with women and puts up with their insults. She appreciates favours and is grateful for them. She visits the sick. She does not attend funeral procession (i.e., follow bier).

This is the personality of the Muslim woman as defined by the teachings of Islam.

No doubt the Muslim woman is the most refined example of womanhood ever known in any human society. Along with all the fine qualities listed above, the Muslim woman also possesses wisdom, purity of soul, a high level of spirituality, a sound concept of life, the universe and humanity, and a deep awareness of her important role in life.

Surely a woman's reaching such a high level of intellectual, psychological, spiritual and moral development is a great human blessing, which is unequalled by any of the many other blessings that human beings enjoy. It is a cultural achievement greater than any other reached by humanity in its long history. The fact that women have reached this high level of development means that they are mature and are fully qualified to play their important role in life.

What we see today in many parts of the Muslim world of Muslim women's backwardness and failure to reach that high level that Islam wants for them, is a result of the fact that the Muslims in general have wandered far away from the pure sources of Islam and have become lost in various kinds of *jaahiliyah* or intellectual and psychological dependency on others. None of this would have happened to the Muslims in general, and Muslim women in particular, if the Muslims had preserved their spiritual and intellectual sources properly, and men and women had drunk from these pure sources which would have given them immunity, originality and distinction.

Whilst the attack on the Muslim world was aimed at the identity of the Muslims in general, men and women alike, to disrupt it and to contaminate its original intellectual sources, no doubt many prongs of this attack were aimed at the Muslim woman in particular, with the aim of stripping her of the dress of virtue by which she had been known throughout history, and making her wear the alien, tight-fitting, borrowed dress that makes her look like a copy of foreign women in her appearance, thinking and behaviour.

Tremendous efforts were devoted to the call for the Westernization of Muslim women by various societies, organizations and movements. *Al-ḥamdu lillah*, all of it ended in failure in the face of the reawakening of educated Muslim women who understood the teachings of Islam. Many of the men and women who supported Westernization have now retreated, admitting the depth of the Muslim woman's belief, and the originality of Islam in her thinking, psychology and feelings.

The great hopes that are pinned on the Muslim woman, who is aware of her role, require her to be even stronger in proving her Islamic identity, wherever she may live and whatever her circumstances may be. By reinforcing her Islamic identity, she clearly demonstrates her awareness, high aims, sincerity and devotion to Islam and its distinctive culture. This is also indicative of her ability to contribute to the revival of the ummah to which she belongs and the development of the country she lives in.

Directory of Symbols

(سبحانه وتعالى) : *Subhaanahu wa Ta'aala* — "The Exalted."

(ﷺ) : *Ṣalla-Allahu 'Alayhi wa Sallam* —
"Blessings and Peace be upon him."

(عليه السلام) : *'Alayhis-Salaam* — "May Peace be upon him."

(رضي الله عنه) : *Raḍi-Allahu 'Anhu* — "May Allah be pleased with him."

(رضي الله عنها) : *Raḍi-Allahu 'Anha* — "May Allah be pleased with her."

Glossary

Adhaan	آذان	:	Call to Prayer.
Adhkaar	أذكار	:	Sing. *Dhikr*; Remembrance of Allah.
Al-Ḥamdu lillah	الحمدُ لِلّهِ	:	Praise be to Allah, All praise and thanks belong to Allah Alone.
Allahu Akbar	اللّهُ أكبر	:	Allah is All-Great.
Anṣaar	أنصار	:	Sing. *Naaṣir*; Lit. "helpers." The Muslims of Madeenah who welcomed and helped the Prophet Muhammad and those who migrated from Makkah for the sake of the religion (Islam).
'Aqeedah	عقيدة	:	Belief, Doctrine, Creed.
'Aashoora	عاشوراء	:	The tenth day of the month of Muharram. It is a sunnah to fast on the ninth and tenth or tenth and eleventh of Muharram.
Astaghfirullah	أستغفِرُ اللّه	:	I seek forgiveness from Allah.
Awqaaf	أوقاف	:	Sing. *Waqf*; Endowment. A charitable trust for the sake of Allah, usually set up in perpetuity for the purpose of teaching, feeding the poor or treating the sick, etc.
Aayah	آية	:	Pl. *Aayaat*; Lit. "Sign." A verse of the Qur'an.

Bani (objective case of Banu)	بني	:	Tribe.
Bay'ah	بيعة	:	Oath of allegiance to the Prophet sworn in by those who embraced Islam during his lifetime.
Bid'ah	بِدعة	:	(Reprehensible) innovation, heresy, introduction of rites or beliefs into Islam which have no basis in the Qur'an and the Sunnah.
Birr	بِرّ	:	Righteousness, kindness, good treatment. *Birr al-Waalidayn* — Filial piety.
Daa'i	داعي	:	Lit. "caller." One who calls people to Islam, a missionary.
Dajjal	دجّال	:	Lit. "Liar." Pseudo-Christ. Calling people to believe in him as (the promised) messiah.
Da'wah	دَعوة	:	Lit. "Invitation or call." Calling people to Islam.
Dhikr	ذِكر	:	Lit. "Rememberance." Remembering Allah should be a constant feature of the Muslim's life. The Prophet also taught some phrases that help us to remember Allah.
Ḍuḥa	ضحىٰ	:	Lit. "Forenoon." An optional prayer performed after the bright morning and before meridian, name of the 93rd chapter of the Qur'an.

Dunya	دُنيا	:	This world, as opposed to the Hereafter, the transient physical world.
Du'aa'	دُعاء	:	Supplication, prayer which may be in Arabic or in one's own language.
Fajr	فجر	:	Dawn, Morning (sunrise) prayer, name of the 89th chapter of the Qur'an.
Fiqh	فِقه	:	Islamic Jurisprudence, the understanding and application of Shari'ah.
Fitnah	فِتنة	:	Trial, temptation, tribulation, tumult.
Fiṭrah	فِطرة	:	The Nature, the natural state of man.
Ghusl	غُسل	:	Full ablution, complete ritual bath.
Ḥadith	حديث	:	Pl. *Aḥaadeeth* (hadiths); The sayings, tradition and deeds of approval by the last Prophet Muhammad.
Ḥadith Qudsi	حديث قُدسي	:	Lit. "Sacred ḥadith." A ḥadith containing message of Allah narrated by the Prophet in his own words. These do not form part of the Qur'an.
Ḥajj	حجّ	:	Pilgrimage to Makkah from the 8th to the 13th day in the 12th month of the Muslim calender,

			Dhul-Hijjah; this is one of the pillars of Islam, obligatory to be performed once in lifetime by every Muslim who can afford to do that.
Ḥalaal	حلال	:	Things permitted by the Shari'ah.
Ḥaraam	حرام	:	Things forbidden by the Shari'ah.
Ḥaya'	حياء	:	Bashfulness, shyness.
Ḥijaab	حِجاب	:	Lit. Covering, veil; It refers specifically to Muslim woman. She is obliged to cover herself before a male save her husband, father, brother, sons and others who are barred to marry her; An Islamic dress-code.
Hijrah	هِجرة	:	Lit. "to leave"; In Islamic terminology it is migration for the sake of Allah. The *Hijrah* is the historic migration of the Prophet and his Companions from Makkah to Yathrib later named as Madeenah. The *Hijrah* of the Prophet also marks the beginning of the Islamic calender termed as Hijri calender.
'Iddah	عِدّة	:	Waiting period, usually three menstrual cycles, which a divorced woman in Islam must observe before she is free to

			remarry. For the pregnant, the *'iddah* lasts until the baby is born.
Imam	إمام	:	Lit. "Leader." May refer to the person who leads others in prayers, or to the ruler or leader of an Islamic state. The word is also used as a title of respect for eminent scholars.
Iqaamah	إقامة	:	Call to prayer, similar to the *adhaan*, called immediately before the prayer to begin it.
'Ishaa'	عِشاء	:	Night prayer, after *Maghrib*.
Isnad	إسناد	:	Authentication by reliable chain of narrators.
I'tikaaf	إعتكاف	:	Seclusion or spiritual retreat. It was the custom of the Prophet to spend the last ten days of Ramaḍaan in seclusion in the mosque, concentrating on prayer and worship. It is a community obligation. If some members (even one) do it, would suffice.
Jaahili	جاهِلي	:	Of or pertaining to *jaahiliyah* period and customs preceding the prophet-hood of Muhammad; non-Islamic.
Jaahiliyah	جاهِلية	:	Ignorance. The time preceding the revelation of Islam is known as the "Time of ignorance."
Jama'ah	جماعة	:	Group or congregation.

Jibreel	جِبرِيل	:	Gabriel. The archangel who conveyed the revelation of the Qur'an to the Prophet Muhammad.
Jihad	جِهاد	:	Lit. "Struggle or striving." Although this word is often translated as holy war, it has a broader meaning than warfare on the battlefield. Any act of striving to please Allah may be described as jihad.
Jilbaab	جِلباب	:	Woman's long, loose outer-garment.
Jinn	جِنّ	:	The Genie; a created being made from smokeless fire. The Satan belongs to this specie.
Jumu'ah	جُمعة	:	Friday, the Muslim day of gathering when men have to go to the mosque to hear the *khuṭbah* and pray the congregational prayer. (Attendence is optional for women)
Kaafir	كافِر	:	Pl. *Kuffaar*; Disbeliever, one who rejects the truth.
Khaleefah	خليفة	:	Caliph, successor, vicegerent, viceroy. It refers specifically to the Muslim ruler till the abolition of the institute of caliphate in 1924 by Kamal Ataturk of Turkey.

Al-Khulafa' ar-Rashideen	الخُلفاء الراشدين	:	The four Caliphs right after Prophet Muhammad (bpuh).
Khuṭbah	خُطبة	:	Sermon, speech or address, especially the one delievered before the Friday and after the *'Eid* prayers and also at the time of marraiage after the *nikaaḥ*.
Kufr	كُفر	:	Disbelief, rejection of the truth.
Kunyah	كُنْية	:	Agnomen, beginning with Abu or Umm (father of or mother of) and the name of the eldest child or more frequently, the name of the eldest son. This is an ancient Arabic custom, continued also in Islam and adopted by other people who became Muslims. The *kunyah* of the Prophet was Abu al-Qaasim.
Laa ilaaha illa Allah	لا إِلٰه إلّا الله	:	There is no god but Allah. The fundamental declaration of *Tawḥeed*, the central tenet of Islam.
Laylat al-Qadar	ليلةُ القَدر	:	The "Night of Decree", (The night the Qur'an was revealed), one of the odd-numbered nights of the last ten days of Ramaḍaan.
Maghrib	مغرِب	:	The prayer offered after sunset.
Maḥram	مَحرم	:	The husband; A man whom a woman may never marry because of the degree of closeness of the blood-relationship, i.e., father,

brother, son, uncle, etc. A woman is not required to observe *ḥijaab* in front of her *maḥram*.

Minbar مِنبر : Pulpit, the steps on which the Imam stands to deliver *khuṭbah*.

Mufassir مُفسِّر : The Qur'anic exegete, a scholar who comments on and explains the meanings of the Qur'an. Many scholars have written such works, known as *Tafseer*. Famous books of *Tafseer* include those by Ibn Katheer, Syed Quṭb and Maulana Mawdudi, also available in English translation.

Muhaajir مُهاجِر : Migrant, one who migrates for the sake of Allah. The original *muhaajireen* were the Muslims who migrated from Makkah to Madeenah at the time of the Prophet.

Muḥarram مُحرّم : The first month of the Islamic calender.

Mujahideen مجاهدين : Fighters in the cause of Allah.

Munaafiq مُنافِق : Hypocrite, one who pretends to believe in Islam, but does not.

Mushrik مُشرِك : Polytheist, one who associates others in worship with Allah.

Nafl نَفْل : Supererogatory or optional prayers, fastings or charity.

Nifaas نِفاس : A period of woman's impurity

upon delivery, during which no intercourse with husband is allowed (usually 40 days).

Qaaḍi	قاضي	:	Judge in Shari'ah court.
Qawwaam	قَوّام	:	Protector, maintainer.
Qiblah	قِبلة	:	The direction faced when praying, i.e., the direction of the Ka'bah in Makkah.
Qiwaamah	قِوامة	:	Position or role of being a *qawwaam.*
Qiyaam al-layl	قِيام الليل	:	Standing in prayer during the night.
Rak'ah	ركعة	:	A unit or cycle of prayer. Prayer consists of two, three or four *rak'ahs.*
Ṣadaqah	صدقة	:	Charity, also used for zakah.
Ṣaḥaabah	صحابة	:	Sing. *Ṣaḥaabi*; the Companions of the Prophet Muhammad.
Ṣaḥeeḥ	صَحيح	:	Lit. "Correct, sound, authentic." In Islamic terminology a hadith fulfilling the conditions and criteria set by hadith scholars is termed as *ṣaḥeeḥ*, that is sound and most reliable.
Salaf	سلف	:	The early generations of Muslims, the pious predecessors i.e., the Companions of the Prophet and the generations immediately following them termed as *Tabi'oon* — the Followers.

Ṣalaah	صلاة / صلٰوة	:	The "formal" prayer obligatory and/or optional.
sanad		:	Chain of authority, the chain of people who conveyed a hadith from the Prophet.
Shari'ah	شريعَة	:	Islamic law.
Shawwaal	شوّال	:	The tenth month of the Islamic calendar, immediately following Ramaḍaan.
Shirk	شِرك	:	Polytheism, associating anyone or anything in worship with Allah. This is the only sin for which there will be no forgiveness. If a person dies as a *mushrik*, he is truly doomed.
Seerah	سيرة	:	Biography, specially that of the Prophet Muhammad.
Siwaak	سِواك	:	A small stick which comes from a specific tree that is known to grow only in Hijaz, and is used as a tooth brush. In the West, *siwaak* may be purchased at any Islamic bookstore and *ḥalaal* grocery store.
Ṣubḥ	صُبح	:	Another name of *fajr* (early morning) prayer.
Suḥoor	سُحور	:	The pre-dawn meal taken for fasting the following day. It is taken before the *adhaan* for the *Fajr* prayer.

Tabarruj تبرُّج : Wanton display, flaunting oneself in contradiction to the Islamic rulings on dress and modest behaviour.

Tabi'ee تابِعي : Lit. "Follower." A member of the generation of Muslims following the *Ṣaḥaabah*. A Muslim who met or saw a *ṣaḥaabi* is described as a *tabi'ee (singular)*.

Tabi'een تابعين : Plural of Tabi'ee.

Tahajjud تهجُّد : Voluntary prayer that is performed at night between the times of *'isha* and *fajr*.

Tajweed تَجويد : Correct recitation of the Qur'an, following precise rules of pronunciation and articulation.

Takbeer تكبير : Saying, "*Allahu Akbar.*" Allah is All-Great.

Taqwa تقوى : Piety, "God-consciousness." *Taqwa* involves constant awareness and remembrance of Allah, and conscious efforts to adhere to His commandments and abstaining from whatever He has forbidden.

Taraaweeḥ تراويح : Extra/additional prayers that are performed after *'isha* during Ramaḍaan. They are usually performed in congregation and as much of the Qur'an as possible is recited during these prayers.

Tasbeeḥ تَسبيح : Saying, "*Subḥan-Allah*", Glory be to Allah.

'Ulama' عُلَماء : Sing. *'Aalim*. Scholars, people of knowledge.

Ummah أُمّة : Community or nation, the body of Muslims as a distinct entity. The ummah of Islam is not based on language, race or ethnicity, but encompasses everyone who believes in Allah alone and in the Prophethood of Muhammad.

'Umrah عُمرة : The "lesser pilgrimage," consisting of fewer rites than Ḥajj. 'Umrah may be performed at any time of the year.

Waḥy وحي : Revelation, inspiration.

Waajib واجب : Obligatory, compulsory.

Witr وِتر : A prayer which has an odd number of *rak'ahs*. It is offered last thing at night before sleeping, or following *tahajjud.*

Wuḍoo' وضُوء : Partial ritual ablution which is required before prayer if one has passed wind, urine or stool or taken camel's meat.

Yawm 'Arafah يومُ عَرفة : The ninth day of the 12th Islamic month, *Dhu'l-Hijjah*. It is the most essential part of Ḥajj, the pilgrims spend this day standing and praying at 'Arafah, a mountain and plain outside

			Makkah. Muslims who are not on Ḥajj may observe this sacred day by fasting (this fast is optional but highly encouraged).
Ẓaalimoon	ظالِمُون	:	Sing. *Ẓaalim*; Wrongdoers and polytheists.
Zakah	زَكاة / زَكوة	:	Poor due or obligatory charity tax. Muslims whose wealth is above a certain limit must pay a percentage of it (in most cases 2.5%) to the poor and needy. Zakah is one of the pillars of Islam.
'Aṣr	عصر	:	Afternoon prayer.
Dhuhr	ظُهر	:	Noon (mid-day) prayer.

Transliteration Chart

أ	a
آ . ى	aa
ب	b
ت	t
ة	h or t (when followed by another Arabic word)
ث	th
ج	j
ح	ḥ
خ	kh
د	d
ذ	dh
ر	r
ز	z
س	s
ش	sh
ص	ṣ
ض	ḍ
ط	ṭ

ظ	ẓ
ع	‘
غ	gh
ف	f
ق	q
ك	k
ل	l
م	m
ن	n
ـه – ه – هـ	h
و	w
و (as vowel)	oo
ي	y
ي (as vowel)	ee
ء	’ (Omitted in initial position)

َ	Fatḥah	a
ِ	Kasra	i
ُ	Ḍammah	u
ّ	Shaddah	Double letter
ْ	Sukoon	Absence of vowel

References

Ibn Ḥibban: *Al-Iḥsaan fi Taqreeb Ṣaḥeeḥ ibn Ḥibban*, Ar-Risaalah Est., Beirut, 1412 AH.

Ibn al-Jawzi: *Aḥkaam an-Nisa'*, Al-Maktaba al-'Arabiyah, Ṣaida, Beirut, 1405 AH.

Bukhari: *Al-Adab al-Mufrad, Faḍlullah aṣ-Ṣamad fi Tawḍeeḥ al-Adab al-Mufrad.*

An-Nawawi: *Al-Adhkaar an-Nawawi*, Daar al-Qiblah, Jeddah, 1413 AH.

Ibn Abd al-Barr: *Al-Istee'aab fi Ma'arifat al Aṣḥaab*, Daar Nahḍah, Cairo.

Ibn al-Atheer al-Jazari: *Usud ul-Ghaabah fi Ma'arifat aṣ-Ṣaḥaabah*, Egypt.

Al-Iṣaabah fi Tamyeez aṣ-Ṣaḥaabah, Daar Nahḍah, Egypt.

Al-Faraj al-Asbahaani: *Kitaab al-Aghaani*, Daar al-Kutub, Egypt.

Baladhuri: *Ansaab al-Ashraaf*, Daar al-Ma'arif, Egypt.

Ibn Katheer: *Al-Bidayah wan-Nihaayah*, Daar al-Kutub al-'Ilmiyah, Beirut, 1409 AH.

Adh-Dhahabi: *Tareekh al-Islam*, Daar al-Kitaab al-'Arabi, Beirut, 1407 AH.

Aṭ-Ṭabari: *Taareekh aṭ-Ṭabari*, Daar al-Kutub al-'Ilmiyah, Beirut, 1407 AH.

'Alaauddin as-Samarqandi: *Tuḥfat al-Fuqaha*, Idaarat Iḥiyā' at-Turaath al-Islami, Qatar.

Bint ash-Shaṭi': *Taraajim Sayidaat Bayt an-Nuboowah*, Daar al-Kitaab al-'Arabi, Beirut.

Al-Mundhiri: *At-Targheeb wa at-Tarheeb*, Qatar.

Aḥmad Zaki Ṣafwat: *Jamharat Khuṭub al-'Arab*, Al-Maktabah al-'Ilmiyah, Beirut.

Abi Tamaam: *Al-Ḥamaasa*, Imam Muhammad Islamic University, Riyadh, 1401 AH.

Kaandhlawi: *Ḥayaat aṣ-Ṣaḥaabah*, Daar al-Qalam, 1403 AH.

Al-Bayhaqi: *Dalaai'l an-Nubuwaah*, Daar al-Kutub al-'Ilmiyah, Beirut, 1405 AH.

An-Nawawi: *Riyaḍ aṣ-Ṣaaliḥeen min Kalaam Sayid al-Mursaleen*, Beirut.

Ibn al-Qayyim: *Zaad al-Ma'ad fi Hady Khayr al-'Ibaad*, Ar-Risaalah Est. and Maktabat al-Manar al-Islamiyah, 1401 AH.

Abu Dawood: *Sunan Abi Dawood*, Maṭba'at as-Sa'adah, Egypt, 1369 AH, Daar al-Hadeeth, Syria, 1388 AH.

Ibn Maajah: *Sunan Ibn Maajah*, Daar Iḥiyā' al-Kutub al-'Arabiah, Egypt.

Tirmidhi: *Sunan at-Tirmidhi (Jamey' aṣ-Ṣaḥeeḥ)*, Daar al-Fikr, Beirut.

An-Nasaai': *As-Sunan al-Kubra*, Daar al-Kutub al-'Ilmiyah, Beirut, 1411 AH.

An-Nasaai': *Sunan an-Nasaai'*, Daar al-Bashaaer al-Islamiyah, Beirut, 1406 AH and Al-Baabi al-Ḥalabi, Egypt, 1398 AH.

Adh-Dhahabi: Siar A'alaam an-Nubalaa, Ar-Risaalah Est., Beirut, 1401 AH.

Ibn Hishaam: *As-Seerat an-Nabawiyah*, Daar al-Qalam, Beirut.

Baghawi: *Sharḥ as-Sunnah*, Al-Maktab al-Islami, 1390 AH.

Tirmidhi: *Ash-Shamaai'l al-Muḥammadiya*, Daar al-Ḥadeeth, Beirut,

1405 AH.

Muslim: *Ṣaḥeeḥ Muslim bi Sharḥ an-Nawawi*, Daar al-Fikr, Beirut, 1401 AH.

Ibn al-Jawzi: *Ṣifat aṣ-Ṣafwah*, Daar al-Wa'ee, Aleppo, 1389 AH.

Ibn Sa'ad: *Aṭ-Ṭabaqaat al-Kubra*, Daar Beirut, 1398 AH.

Al-Hashimi: *Ṭurfah ibn al-'Abd — His life and His Poetry*, Daar al-Bashaaer al-Islamiyah, 1400 AH.

Nasaai': *'Ashrah an-Nisaa'i*, Maktabah as-Sunnah, Egypt, 1408 AH.

Ibn Abd Rabbahu: *Al-'Iqd al-Fareed*, Daar al-Kitaab al-'Arabi, Beirut, 1384 AH.

Ibn Ḥajar: *Fatḥ al-Baari Sharḥ Ṣaḥeeḥ al-Bukhari*, Daar al-Ma'arifah.

Faḍlullah al-Jeelani: *Faḍlullah aṣ-Ṣamad fi Tawḍeeḥ al-Adab al-Mufrad lil Bukhari*, Al-Maktaba as-Salafiyah, 1407 AH.

Haithami: *Kashf al-Astaar*, Ar-Risaalah Est., 1404 AH.

Hussamuddin al-Hindi: *Kanz al-'Ummaal fi Sunan al-Aqwaal wal Af'aal*, Ar-Risaalah Est., 1399 AH.

Haithami: *Majma' az-Zawaa'id wa Manba' al-Fawaa'id*, Daar al-Kitaab al-'Arabi, Beirut, 1967 CE.

Ibn Katheer: *Mukhtaṣar Tafseer Ibn Katheer*, Daar al-Qur'an al-Kareem, 1402 AH.

Muṣṭafa as-Sibaa'ee: *Al-Mara'h Bayn al-Fiqh wal Qaanoon*, Al-Maktab al-Islami, 1404 AH.

Ma'aroof ad-Dawaalibi: *Al-Mara'h fil Islam*, Daar al-Nafaa'is, 1409 AH.

Al-Haakim: *Al-Mustadrak*, Maktabat an-Naṣr al-Ḥadeethah, Riyadh.

Aḥmad ibn Ḥanbal: *Musnad al-Imam Aḥmad ibn Ḥanbal*, Daar Saadir, Beirut.

At-Tabraani: *Al-Mu'jam al-Kabeer*, Maṭba'at az-Zahraa', Mowṣal, 1406 AH.

Waqidi: *Al-Mughaazi*, 'Aalam al-Kutub, Beirut.

Ibn Quḍamah: *Al-Mughni*, Maktabat ar-Riyaḍ al-Ḥadeethah, 1401 AH.

Sakhaawi: *Al-Maqaaṣid al-Ḥasanah*, Maktabat al-Khanji, Egypt, 1375 AH.

Sameha al-Wardi: *Min ar Riq ila as-Siyaadah*, DAMLA.

Imam Maalik: *Muaṭṭa*, Daar Iḥiya' al-Kutub al-'Arabia, Egypt.

Adh-Dhahabi: *Meezaan al-I'itidaal*, Daar Iḥiya' al-Kutub al-'Arabia, Egypt, 1382 AH.

Notes

Notes

Notes

Notes

Notes

Notes

Notes

Notes

Notes

Notes